The What, Where, When, How & Why
Of Gardening In North Carolina

North Carolina GARDENER'S GUIDE

TOBY BOST

COOL
SPRINGS
PRESS

Toby Bost.
    North Carolina Gardener's Guide by Toby Bost.

    p.   cm.
    Includes bibliographical references and index.
    ISBN 1-888608-09-9
    1. Gardening--North Carolina
    2. Plants; Ornamental--North Carolina
    I. Title.
635.9--dc20
Bos

Cool Springs Press, Inc.
118 Fourth Avenue South
Franklin, Tennessee 37064

First printing 1997
Printed in the United States of America
10 9 8 7 6 5

Visit the Cool Springs Press website at: www.coolspringspress.com.

On the cover (clockwise from top left):
Pansy, Rhododendron, Dogwood,
Daylily

DEDICATION

*T*O THE MASTER GARDENER VOLUNTEERS OF THE NORTH CAROLINA Cooperative Extension Service, who have enriched my life with their friendships and their zeal for gardening.

To my fan club, my loving wife Becky, who did a major part of the typing, and my wonderful children, Terri and Brandon, who were reasonably understanding of my late-night schedule when it came time for bedtime "goodnights."

To my father, Ben R. Bost, who allowed me to experiment in the garden as a child and taught me a good work ethic. To my mother, Peggy E. Bost, for her unconditional love and for buying me my first bulbs, seeds, and the tree peony. To the memory of my "Grandma Betty," Elizabeth F. Anderson, for her love of flowers and compost ("woods dirt").

To God, for the strength to garden, a fascination with plants, and everlasting life.

ACKNOWLEDGEMENTS

*A*S SURELY AS THE SAP RISES IN THE SPRING, every gardening book is a collection of experiences and personal encounters. The joy of writing a book is in sharing your knowledge with others and acknowledging the help you've gotten along the way from seasoned gardeners and friends.

I owe a debt of gratitude to numerous North Carolina friends in horticulture for their contributions to this book.

First, my co-workers at the North Carolina Cooperative Extension Service, recognized horticulturists in their respective counties, who assist home gardeners on a daily basis:
Linda Blue (Buncombe County), Karen Neill and Garry Bradley (Guilford County), Willie Earl Wilson (Union County), Milton Parker (Bladen County), Gwyn Riddick (Guilford County), Roger Galloway (Montgomery County), Darrell Blackwelder (Rowan County), Lewis Howe (Wayne County), Bill Lord (Franklin County), and David Barkley, Dr. Bruce Williams (New Hanover County) and John Vining (Polk County).

I would also like to express my appreciation to the Extension Specialists in the North Carolina State University Horticulture Department for the use of their publications. And a special thanks to Richard E. Bir.

There are many friends in the nursery industry who have shared their plant knowledge and nursery catalogs freely for the book:
David Pike, Witherspoon Nursery in Durham, N.C.; Morris Newland, New Garden Nursery, Greensboro, N.C.; John Heitman, The Heitman Place in Winston-Salem, N.C.; Kim Hawks, Niche Gardens, Chapel Hill, N.C.; Tony Avent, Plant Delights, Juniper Level, N.C.; John Edwards, Avalon Garden Center, Winston-Salem, N.C.; Ken Long and staff, L.A. Reynolds Garden Showcase, Winston-Salem, N.C.; Nancy Goodwin, Montrose in Hillsborough, N.C.; Mary Nell Jones, Jones Nursery, Advance, N.C.; Mike Garner and staff, Sedge Garden Nursery, Kernersville, N.C.; Frank Sink, Designer Groundcovers, Winston-Salem, N.C.; Joe Marion, Joe's Nursery, Lewisville, N.C. and John Hoffman, Hoffman Nursery.

Acknowledgements

A host of talented plantsmen answered questions and shared personal experiences while I was preparing the book:

Dr. Robert Means, Winston-Salem; Ed Steffek, Duke Gardens; Preston Stockton and Camilla Wilcox, Reynolda Gardens, WFU; Martha Vaughn, Mount Airy; A.C. McGraw, Garden Writer, *Winston-Salem Journal*; Jane Welshmer and Derek Morris of Winston-Salem; Peter Loewer, Asheville; David Massee, North Carolina Department of Agriculture Marketing Specialist; and Bill Wilder, N.C. Association of Nurserymen.

Many thanks to some special Master Gardener Volunteers who gathered cultural information on various plants: Joyce Adams, President, Winston-Salem Garden Council; Dr. Ken Bridle; Gary Dean; and Mary Elliott.

Many thanks to my bosses for endorsing this project: Maurene Rickards, County Director; Dr. Clyde Chesney, District Extension Director; and Ron Graham, Assistant Forsyth County Manager. Three special people helped me resolve numerous computer glitches: Lisa Byrd, Linda Dunn, and Alan Anderson.

And last, to Hank McBride at Cool Springs Press in Franklin, TN, I say "thank you" for the opportunity to write this book. You have the patience of the patriarch, Job!

The publisher wishes to acknowledge Andrew Bunting, Scott Arboretum, for his horticultural edit.

IN MEMORIAM

Dr. J.C. Raulston

*I*N THE FINAL STAGES OF COMPLETING THIS BOOK, I received a telephone call from a nurseryman. It was hard to comprehend: J.C. Raulston had been killed in a tragic automobile accident the night before on his way home to Raleigh. The horrible news sent shock waves across the country from universities and arboretums to the homes of his former students and "Raulston groupies." Death seemed so far removed from J.C. Raulston, a man who seemed to stay one pace ahead of the times.

I remember when Dr. J.C. Raulston came to North Carolina State University. His first slide presentation, a panoramic show of marvelous pictures of landscapes from exotic gardens across the world, was a eye-opener for an aspiring horticulturist. As a sophomore in the Horticulture Department, I was impressed, to say the least. His classroom lectures and whirlwind field trips were a harbinger of things to come for the world of ornamental horticulture in this state.

Over the last twenty years, Dr. Raulston created the North Carolina State University Arboretum, working tirelessly with an evangelistic fervor. He brought the Arboretum to national attention by collecting and propagating plants, raising money through speaking engagements, and recruiting volunteers, while working as a full-time professor of horticulture. He introduced hundreds of plants to the nursery trade, adding diversity to the product line at every garden center in this state and perhaps the country. A whole generation of landscape professionals, architects, and plantsmen hung on to his every word of wisdom regarding the future of this industry. He was a walking encyclopedia to many, sharing his knowledge unselfishly on every occasion no matter how rushed he was at the moment.

Dr. J.C. Raulston will be sorely missed. He was a mentor who was adored by both students and colleagues.

The references in this book to Dr. Raulston are a personal memorial to his significant contributions to the career of this author. Part of

In Memoriam

the proceeds from the sale of the *North Carolina Gardener's Guide* will be donated to the arboretum he loved, now named in his honor, the J.C. Raulston Arboretum at North Carolina State University.

One of Raulston's "Laws of the Universe" states: "The closer something is to you , the less likely it is that you will ever see it." *(About visiting well-known gardens in your community.)*

Raulston's "Law of Landscape Plant Diversity" states: "In any given region of the United States, forty shrubs and trees make up over ninety percent of the landscape plantings." *(About the fact that high-quality landscape plants are frequently overlooked and not utilized in our gardens.)*

PREFACE

*T*HE *NORTH CAROLINA GARDENER'S GUIDE* WAS
WRITTEN for the thousands of newcomers to the Tar Heel
State each year. Most move to the Sunbelt for its favorable climate
and promising high-tech career opportunities in industry and
medicine.

Many, like Carol Meredith, came to North Carolina from much
colder regions of the country where many wonderful landscape
plants were only marginally hardy in their gardens. Carol said it
eloquently in a note she attached to the application form for the
Forsyth County Master Gardener Program. "Although I have gardened in California, Florida, and Ohio, many of the plants in North
Carolina and certainly the soil and climate are unfamiliar to me. I
have been gardening for enough years so that when I embark upon
a new gardening experience, I know many of the right questions,
but often not the answers. Although my philosophy of gardening is
still developing, I try to limit myself to plants which will thrive
without extensive soil modification or use of pesticides."

As an Extension Horticulturist, I consult with countless newcomers on a regular basis; like Carol, they want to "cut to the chase"
and find the best plants for their gardens.

This book will help them do just that. It provides more than
170 choice plants and the cultural information needed to establish
great lawns and gardens in North Carolina. The plant descriptions
offer tips on how to use these terrific plant materials effectively. The
cultivars have been evaluated across this state by gardeners themselves. The anecdotes are the author's way of making light-hearted
recommendations about the plants he grows. The *North Carolina
Gardener's Guide* offers unique ways to use dependable plants for
creating great lawns and gardens.

CONTENTS

North Carolina Gardening
10

Annuals
20

Bulbs
46

Deciduous Trees
74

Evergreens
114

Fruits
136

Groundcovers and Ornamental Grasses
158

Herbs and Perennials
192

Lawns
268

Roses
282

Shrubs
298

Vines
376

Resources
394

Index
397

INTRODUCTION

North Carolina Gardening

*I*N MANY WAYS, WE LIVE IN A PLANT PARADISE here in North Carolina. From the Outer Banks to the Great Smokies, our diverse climate and topography afford us tremendous opportunities for growing plants that are indigenous to many continents.

The challenge for us as gardeners is to select the proper location for our choice plants and provide the best cultural practices to keep our lawns and gardens growing. Before you put the first seed in the ground, or plant that potted perennial, spend some time learning about your soil, nutrients, potential pests, and plant diseases.

SOIL

Most of the soils in North Carolina are suitable for gardening. Seasoned gardeners know that a sandy loam is best, but I have gardened in clay soils most of my life and have done so quite successfully. The key to success is good soil management.

The first principle of good soil management is to add organic matter, because humus is the life of the soil. Second, don't work in our soils, particularly clay soils, when they are wet. (If you can make a mudball out of a handful of earth, don't spade or rototill it for several days or longer.) Third, have the soil tested periodically to monitor the pH, and correct acidity or alkalinity conditions as needed for the plant selected.

All soils are comprised of varying amounts of sand, silt, and clay particles. (A soil that is predominantly sand particles is classified as a loam.) Roots prefer a loose soil that has half of its pore space reserved for oxygen and moisture. Roots will grow in the direction of least resistance. In fact, it has been said that roots don't grow in soil at all, they grow in air spaces. That is why it is so important to spade up a wide planting hole when planting trees. Most roots will ultimately spread to a diameter equal to two times or greater than the height of the particular plant.

ORGANIC MATTER

Organic matter is a component that increases a soil's water-holding capability while giving it a dark, earthy appearance. It is found in manure, compost, aged leaves, sawdust, and decomposing mulches. Peat moss is readily available to gardeners and is suitable for amending sandy soils. In most North Carolina soils, ground pine bark is a marvelous soil amendment. (Its general particle size should be 3/8 inch or smaller.) Tight clay soils can be improved if thirty to fifty percent (by volume) of pine-bark soil conditioner is tilled into the garden. (Spread a three-inch layer over the bed and spade or till six inches in depth.) Hardwood mulch should not be used as a soil conditioner.

COMPOST

No gardener should be without a compost bin. Compost is biologically active organic matter that is made at home by nature (humus or "woods dirt"). Stir a little compost into the top few inches of soil and your plants will flourish. (Compost does for plants what steroids do for athletes—but safely, of course!) Gardeners gloat over their compost. Some even call it "Black Gold." The billions of living creatures found in compost help plant roots absorb water and nutrients.

Making compost is simple. Just layer "green and brown" organic yard wastes, and in six months or so you will have a high-quality organic material that can be used as a soil amendment. I make a quick compost using two trash bags of shredded hardwood leaves combined with one bag of grass clippings. There are numerous recipes and instructions for composting available at any county Extension Center or public library. You will need two cubic feet of compost for every eight square feet of garden bed you plan to amend.

BED PREPARATION

Poorly drained clay soils are the norm throughout much of the state. When preparing a new bed for planting, there are several tricks that will help you avoid "wet feet" and subsequent root rot. The simplest method is to borrow topsoil from one area and add it to the new bed. Rototill the bed and rake it smooth. Adding a few inches of topsoil can have a profound influence on whether a plant lives or flounders.

Landscape timbers or ties, rock retaining walls, and steel edging materials are frequently used to facilitate bed preparation. Or you can create berms for planting using another technique that involves incorporating large volumes of organic matter into the native soil. Finally, where soil drainage is questionable, "French Drain" installation can be employed. This is a project best assisted with a backhoe. Slotted-drain tile is laid in the bottom of a two-foot-deep trench that has a two-percent slope to daylight. The pipe is surrounded by a bed of crushed stone and then backfilled with a loose soil mix. This is the method often used for preparing beds for roses and rhododendrons.

After all is said and done about bed preparation, many gardeners will continue to dig a planting hole and throw a few inches of gravel into the bottom. Though they may feel good about this effort, it is a total waste of time and will more than likely worsen soil drainage. And digging a hole in a poorly drained site is something like constructing a pool or creating an in-ground aquarium—only riparian plants thrive under such conditions.

When in doubt, check soil drainage before planting. You can do this with a post hole digger or shovel and a bucket of water. Dig a hole one foot deep and fill it with water. Let it drain cleanly, then refill it with water. If the water is still there the next day, don't plant until you install drain tiles or create berms. Haphazardly installed irrigation systems often compound drainage problems in garden beds.

Nutrients and Fertilization

Although there are seventeen essential nutrients for plant growth and development, there are only three that are important to remember when gardening in North Carolina. A healthy plant will consume the largest amounts of three basic nutrients, nitrogen (N), phosphorus (P), and potassium (K). These elements are the main ingredients in a bag of fertilizer, and are expressed in terms of a percentage weight. For example, a general garden fertilizer is labeled 10-10-10. The numbers tell that the bag contains 10 percent nitrogen, 10 percent phosphorus, and 10 percent potassium. The other 70 percent is filler or clay.

Each nutrient serves a function in the overall good health of a plant. Nitrogen promotes vegetative or foliar growth. Higher nitrogen percentages in a bag are beneficial for lawns or evergreen plants. Phosphorus enhances root and flower development. "Starter" fertilizers and "bloom boosters" are rich in this nutrient. Potassium is important for the overall health of a plant. "Winterizer"

fertilizers have a high percentage of potassium and may help a plant tolerate drought, cold, or disease stress. (A general rule of thumb when applying garden fertilizers is to use 2 to 3 pounds of product per 100 square feet. That's equivalent to one gallon of 10-10-10 for every 1000 square feet of garden area.)

The soil's pH determines the availability of the plant nutrients. Limestone helps fertilizers work. Acidic soils can waste more than half of the fertilizer applied. Wasted fertilizers are an environmental hazard. Monitor the soil pH by soil testing.

Though selecting the right fertilizer can be a bit frustrating, it's really just a numbers game. Compare the costs of fertilizer products by the amount you are paying for each pound of nitrogen or other dominant nutrient in the package. Slow-release fertilizers generally cost more, but they have some distinct advantages over common garden fertilizers. They release nutrients slowly to plants, making them less likely to burn roots with high salt concentrates. For best results, apply a fertilizer with at least thirty to forty percent of its nitrogen in the ammoniac or urea form. Slow-release fertilizers are an ecologically sound way to supply nutrients, since excess nutrients will not leave the garden after a heavy rain. Last, but not least, these fertilizers need not be applied more often than once or twice each season, freeing the gardener for more important tasks.

SOIL TEST

When it comes to soil testing kits, you get what you pay for. The inexpensive chemical kits and probes are acceptable for a "ball park" analysis. If you test this way, I still recommend the services of a professional laboratory every few years and for major garden installations. In North Carolina, the Department of Agriculture's Agronomic Services will analyze your soil without charge. Contact a county Extension Center for the soil test kits. Many large farm-supply stores offer their customers a similar service; take them up on it.

No amount of fertilizer will compensate for a soil pH that is out of kilter. More than half of the problems identified by our Plant Disease Clinic at North Carolina State University were caused by fertilizers—too much, in most cases. The optimum pH for most lawns and gardens is 5.5 to 6.5. (Remember that a pH from 1 to 6.9

is acidic, and above pH 7 is considered alkaline.) The addition of limestone reduces the acidity of soil and raises the soil pH. How much limestone you need depends on the type of soil, amount of organic matter, residual nutrients, and other factors.

PESTS AND DISEASES

The conditions that make our gardens flourish in North Carolina are the same conditions that make our state a happy homeland for insect and disease pests. Mild winters and wet, humid summers ensure healthy populations of bugs and blights each growing season. There are quarantines for gypsy moths and fire ants currently in place in this state. We are holding our breaths in hopes that these most recent garden pests will not become widespread throughout all of North Carolina.

A prudent axiom to garden by is "the best defense against pests is a healthy plant." Most gardening plants can tolerate moderate amounts of leaf injury before a pest control strategy should be implemented. Natural predators often lurk on the garden fringes, waiting to help when problems arise. Second only to a vigorously growing plant is variety selection. The strength of this book is in its plant variety recommendations. The industry has made great strides over the last three decades in the selection and breeding of genetically superior plant varieties. Choose these plants and you will have an ally in the fight against pests.

INTEGRATED PEST MANAGEMENT

Pest control is something like a puzzle. There are numerous "management" pieces in the puzzle including cultural practices, pesticides, and bio-rational products. My approach to pest control in the lawn and garden utilizes the principles of Integrated Pest Management (IPM). Proper identification of the pest and of the host plant is of paramount importance in the IPM system.

Information can be gathered about a pest's life cycle, and the pieces of the puzzle are examined closely for each occurrence. This may appear to be a slow, painstaking course of action, but it does make more sense than the "Spray and Pray" philosophy of some gardeners today. In one situation, pruning a diseased twig may solve the problem. In another case, a fungicide application may be justified. Removal of a certain plant variety may be required in another situation.

The IPM philosophy and germane practices are certainly an important part of pest control. IPM is here to stay—learn more about it.

Weed Control

Ask any gardener what he or she dislikes most about gardening, and nine out of ten times the response will be "weeding." Gardeners and professionals alike go to great lengths to keep weeds under control. In fact, the lion's share of the pesticide market is in herbicide sales.

The most ecologically sound approach to weed control is mulching landscape beds and gardens. Organic materials such as bark, compost, and pine needles are good choices for mulch. On steep banks and slopes, use shredded hardwood bark or pine needles; on flat surfaces, use bark nuggets, which won't float off in a rainstorm. The rule for mulches is to apply to a depth of one to three inches. Don't heap the mulch up against the trunks of trees.

Plastic films have no place in gardening, except possibly when placed under gravel or brick chips. Landscape fabrics can be useful in areas where irrigation is not an option.

There are a few excellent pre-emergent herbicides that will keep crabgrass out of beds; apply these in late February or March. To get the grassy weeds out of shrub and perennial borders, hand weed or apply a grass killer, such as Vantage™ or Poast™. Finale and Roundup™ (or another glyphosate product) are excellent for clearing a new bed prior to planting. If you spot-spray with any of these, be sure that they don't contact the green tissues of any garden plant.

Irrigation

Unless you design your garden using plants that are drought tolerant (a practice called xeriscaping), irrigation will be necessary. There is *no* substitute for water in gardening! Plants cannot produce their own food via photosynthesis without sufficient water.

Although lawns consume more water than ornamentals, herbs and groundcovers prefer drier conditions by virtue of their native habitats. Most regions of North Carolina have 35 inches of rainfall each year and some have twice this amount. The wet periods are interspersed with dry seasons, and supplemental irrigation can play a vital role in garden survival.

Most plants in our gardens need 1 inch of water a week, whether measured with a rain gauge or a tunafish can. That's the equivalent of 600 gallons of water a week for a 20- by 50-foot garden. It would take several hours to apply this amount with a handheld garden hose, so it is best to buy a sprinkler of some type.

Supplemental watering is a must during the first season. With the use of sprinklers, hand watering, or more elaborate permanent systems that have time clocks, the garden can be kept in good health. In clay soils where soils absorb water slowly, drip irrigation in combination with mulch is the preferred method for watering woody ornamentals. An inexpensive water timer and a few soaker hoses can be the gardener's best friends. Hand watering is terribly inefficient except during the initial planting stages.

Many gardeners prefer to water "on demand," especially in established gardens. Given time and experience, even the novice can take this approach. You must learn to recognize the symptoms of water stress before irreparable harm is done to the garden because of negligence or oversight.

HARDINESS ZONES

When Adam and Eve left the Garden of Eden, one might imagine they took along some seeds and plants and started the first plant nursery. The success or failure of their first horticultural venture would have provided the information necessary to develop a plant hardiness zone map.

Zone maps rate how much cold a plant can take, giving an idea of its survivability at low winter temperatures. The most common map in current use is the United States Department of Agriculture (USDA) Plant Hardiness Zone Map. Each ten-degree drop in temperature places a region in the next lower-numbered hardiness zone. In North Carolina, gardeners in the Mountain regions are in Zone 6, while gardeners near Fort Fisher and south to Bald Head Island live in Zone 9.

Introduction

Remember that these are averages and seasonal extremes of cold will limit what grows in your garden. Other maps are now available, the newest being from Rutgers University. This map accounts for rainfall and sunshine, two other important climatological factors that determine a plant's hardiness in the garden. Work is underway at the National Arboretum for a new map for soon release, according to a recent conversation I had with Dr. Marc Cathey, the arboretum's director.

PLANT NAMES

Computers have changed the way we live and work forever (an understatement, you'll probably agree!). While searching the Internet recently, I learned a lesson many amateur gardeners can learn. With just a few clicks of a mouse, you now have the plant world at your fingertips. In seconds, you can retrieve plant lists (databases) from foreign countries that can be of tremendous help in gardening. (In one search I found American nurseries that I never knew existed listed on a Finnish website!)

The key to using the computer and other references is to learn the scientific names of plants. Although common names are easier to remember and pronounce, a scientific or botanical name allows you to communicate with a gardener in China or a horticulturist in Argentina. The new world opening up to us via the Internet makes knowledge of plant nomenclature even more essential.

Both the common and botanical names are used throughout this book. A plant's botanical name consists of a genus and an epithet, both italicized. For example, all hollies belong to the genus *Ilex*. The epithet identifies a specific kind of holly: *Ilex cornuta* is a Chinese holly. To identify a plant even further, we add a cultivar name that describes a special feature or tells the name of the person who selected the plant. The cultivar name is set off by single quotation marks. For example, the needlepoint holly's botanical name is *Ilex cornuta* 'Needlepoint.' Some plants that occur naturally in the wild are collected for sale. They may be denoted with the abbreviation "var." and another word following the epithet.

Knowing these straightforward rules of taxonomy will be of use as you search catalogs and websites for new and interesting garden varieties.

SUNLIGHT REQUIREMENTS

For best growing results plants need to be placed where they will receive the proper amount of sunlight. I have indicated the amount of sunlight suitable for each plant's growing requirements. The following symbols indicate full sun, partial sun, and shade.

Full Sun   Partial   Shade
Sun

CONCLUSION

Weeks before the first words of this text were set on paper, I mailed a survey to more than 300 Master Gardeners. These volunteers were asked to name "their favorite plants." More specifically, they were asked to respond to the question: If a hurricane destroyed your garden, which plants would you most likely replant in your landscape?

After tallying the results of the survey, a plant list was developed which has served as the basis for the *North Carolina Gardener's Guide*. The turfgrasses and garden plants described in this book are time-tested and durable in our Tar Heel gardens.

The plant list is by no means a complete list, and it was necessary to exclude some fine ornamentals. But the plants on these pages are readily available at the major wholesale/retail nurseries in our state. Certainly the list is a good starting point for creating a new garden or revitalizing an existing one in the Old North State.

In a recent national survey, 68 percent of the respondents stated that they wanted gardening simplified. This book makes an attempt to meet the wishes of this majority. Gardening is America's Number One "Leisure" activity—it should not be a drudgery! Gardening books should be enjoyable to read.

I hope the *North Carolina Gardener's Guide* will accomplish its goal of taking the mystery out of gardening in our state. This book offers a wealth of information gathered through networking with home gardeners and professionals alike. It contains the latest research findings on plant varieties, practical gardening techniques, and "how-to" suggestions set in an easy-to-read format.

U.S.D.A. PLANT
HARDINESS MAP

North Carolina

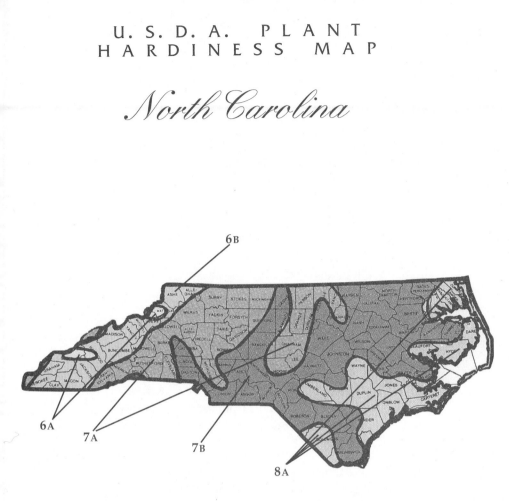

AVERAGE ANNUAL MINIMUM TEMPERATURES

6A	-5° F TO -10° F
6B	0° F TO -5° F
7A	5° F TO 0° F
7B	10° F TO 5° F
8A	15° F TO 10° F

CHAPTER ONE

Annuals

*A*N ANNUAL IS A GARDEN PLANT THAT COMPLETES ITS LIFE CYCLE IN ONE YEAR. A hard frost in autumn will blacken the foliage of annuals and terminate the bedding plant season. Most of us buy the expensive seedlings in cell packs from the local garden center for planting out after danger of frost has passed. Many of the annuals, however, lend themselves to direct-seeding into garden. New gardeners may feel uncomfortable with seed germination at first, so it may be better for them to stick with the greenhouse-grown plants. For the more experienced, starting the newest annual introductions from seed in February on a sunny windowsill can give us a diversion from the winter doldrums.

Annuals are the backbone of the summer garden and are important for supplying early color in perennial beds. Weeks before perennials begin to flower, petunias, salvias, and ageratum are dazzling with color. Annuals are easy to grow in otherwise-barren gardens that are just waking up from a winter rest. They can be massed in huge beds for great color accent. Some gardeners find monochromatic plantings of annuals to be effective, such as a "white garden" that consists of vinca, white petunias, and white marigolds or salvia. Being a Southerner, I find it difficult to stay with a single color scheme. I *have* managed to avoid planting petunias in old tire planters (though I have bought a few half-whisky barrels in days gone by).

North Carolina has a dynamic plant evaluation network in place. Every year residents and tourists alike can enjoy the wildflower beds along our highways courtesy of the fine work of the North

Chapter One

Carolina Department of Transportation. The staff of the North Carolina Botanical Garden in Chapel Hill is always hard at work at the business of learning to propagate and preserve our native flora, both annuals and perennials. The most ambitious program for evaluating annuals goes on at North Carolina State University under the leadership of Dr. Doug Bailey, Extension Floriculture Specialist. More than 500 entries are maintained at the Horticulture Field Laboratory and rated as to suitability for planting in our gardens in the Tar Heel State. This program is beneficial to flower growers who must select the best varieties to purchase for the upcoming season. A summary of the best varieties from these trials are available from county Extension Centers.

For the amount of color you will get for the effort, annuals are hard to beat. Keep in mind that there are two groups of annuals. First, the ones with tiny seeds should be sown indoors many weeks before the planting season in order to have sufficient time to flower. This is especially important where there are shorter growing seasons such as in the Mountain regions. Then there are the annuals that "self-sow." These varieties can be a blessing or a curse. Such was the case with 'Flamingo Feather' celosia, which I planted four years ago, and now provides seedlings every spring in every crack in my asphalt driveway. I do look forward to the impatiens and vinca seedlings every year to use as filler in borders.

There are hundreds of varieties available, and there should be no shortage of possibilities for creating stunning beds of annuals in our North Carolina gardens. Peruse the seed catalogs for the newest flower selections for sowing at home, or buy healthy, compact seedlings at the garden shop each spring. The seedlings can be planted out in the garden in late April or May after the chance of late frost is behind us.

Salvia farinacea

Blue Sage

OTHER COMMON NAME: Mealy-cup Sage

*L*ike most Tar Heel gardeners, I have grown salvias all my life. For years, the red-flowering variety called scarlet sage could be found near the back of all my flower gardens. The tall, stately flower spikes added vertical interest to the garden and were attractive to hummingbirds as well. It wasn't until the mid-1980s that I discovered the marvelous blue sage 'Victoria' through my friend Edith Eddleman, curator of the perennial border at the North Carolina State University Arboretum. Little did I know that this annual would eventually perennialize in flowerbeds as far west as Winston-Salem. Blue sages have become very popular with gardeners. The proverbial blue flowers have a calming effect in the garden. The 'Victoria' salvia reaches a height of 18 to 24 inches with a spread of 9 to 12 inches. The leaves are narrow and gray-green with prominent veins. The whorled flower spikes stand tall on the upper part of the plant, allowing the use of smaller edging annuals in front of the bed. One good example of this use can be seen next to the guardhouses at Arlington National Cemetery in Washington, D.C., in an impressive border of pink geraniums flanked with blue sage. Blue sage blooms make good cut flowers and are terrific when dried for decorations.

WHEN TO PLANT

Container-grown blue salvias can be planted from spring to fall. I have divided and transplanted established clumps of 'Victoria' salvia in November after frost burned back the plants. Seeds can be planted indoors during the winter under fluorescent lights. Some sow the seeds directly into the garden in spring, but I have not tried this.

WHERE TO PLANT

Salvias will rot if planted where the soil is poorly drained. Flowering is much improved when these annuals get full sun. They grow well in a half-day of shade, though their blooms will be sparse. When planted in masses, blue salvias will be a main feature or accent in the garden. The blue flowers offer a cool color that is best viewed close-up. Plant them in the cutting garden or with companions like marigolds and snapdragons.

How to Plant

In soils that contain a lot of clay, spade in 3 inches of pine-bark soil conditioner. A raised bed insures perfect drainage for the annual salvias. If you do not perform a soil test, scatter 5 pounds of lime-stone and 2 pounds of 0-45-0 fertilizer over a 100-square-foot bed. Till amendments into the soil and rake the bed for a smooth surface. The blue salvias should be planted 15 inches apart. Keep in mind that these plants are perennials in USDA Zones 7 and 8. Set the transplants in the bed after scoring the rootballs and shaking some of the soil mix free. The plants should be planted at grade in pre-pared beds. When planted individually, dig wide, shallow holes in which the roots will be higher than grade. Firm the soil and water.

Care and Maintenance

Water the newly set plants twice each week until established. Blue sage is a care-free beauty that will tolerate dry conditions, so don't overwater in the early weeks. This plant will produce most of its flowers in summer and early fall, so be patient. If you buy leggy transplants, prune them back halfway to get dense plants. Fertilize twice during the growing season for the health of the plants. It takes a hard freeze to kill blue sage, but if it does become wilted, cut it to the ground. When sage is used as a perennial, weak plants should be replaced.

Additional Information

In the western region of North Carolina, plant blue sage in the spring and maintain as annuals. Applying a thick mulch may allow the plants to survive for another season if the winter is mild. In gen-eral, avoid using deep mulch layers around blue sage. Pine-bark mulch is preferred over moisture-holding hardwood mulches. Remove diseased plants promptly.

Additional Species, Cultivars, or Varieties

The bright-blue 'Blue Bedder' grows to 24 inches and may need staking. 'Rhea,' a free-flowing dwarf variety that grows to 14 inches, is good for small spaces. 'Victoria' grows to 20 inches. Tender, fall-flowering *S. leucantha* (Mexican bush sage) grows 4 to 5 feet tall and has velvety violet-blue and white bean-like blooms. Another nice cultivar is *S.* 'Lady In Red.' *S. × superba* is best for gardens in western North Carolina.

Cosmos

*W*ant a fast-growing annual for the butterfly or cutting garden? Try sowing the seed of cosmos. Though it is a delicate-looking, willowy plant with feathery foliage, cosmos is a real garden work-horse. It offers 2- to 3-inch brightly colored single and double flowers in a wide variety of pleasing colors. Most North Carolinians know only the orange flowers that are planted by the state in our highway wildflower beds. But you can also enjoy colorful cosmos flowers that are crimson-and-rose to yellow-and-white. The neophyte gardener can take heart in the dependability of this annual. The seeds can be sown at any time in spring, and you will get a 100% return on your invest-ment! Cosmos can reach a height of 5 feet, so give this plant plenty of space to grow. When grown from seed, it offers daisy-faced blooms in 2 months or less. The clear-orange sulfur-cosmos adds color in summer and fall to our highways. For this we can be grateful to the administrators and horticulturists who maintain the North Carolina Department of Transportation Wildflower Program.

WHEN TO PLANT

Many of the species cosmos will self-sow from year to year, but it is best not to depend on this. Seed of the improved varieties are best sown in late spring, after the last frost. As seen by the North Carolina Department of Transportation plantings each year, fall-seeding cosmos gives fair results.

WHERE TO PLANT

Plant cosmos in sunny beds as a backdrop for dwarf annual plant-ings. Cosmos grows in a wide range of soils as long as the soil drains quickly. The North Carolina Department of Transportation has had no trouble growing wonderful beds of cosmos in dry clay soil.

I suggest watering cosmos during the hotter summer months to prevent the plants from wilting. Cosmos is excellent for a cutting garden.

ZONE
6,7,8

HOW TO PLANT

Cosmos plants grow quickly from seeds—an advantage if you have a child who likes gardening. Germination is best when the seeds are sown on well-tilled soil to which lime and organic matter has been added. Sow the seeds as you would those of turnip greens, in wide beds or in rows where they can be thinned properly. When planted as a wildflower in the fall, eliminate broadleaf weeds and sow the seeds in beds that have been raked or mechanically aerified. After the seeds are broadcast over the bed, use a rake to cover them with 1/3 inch of topsoil or sand. Keep the planting evenly moist until the seedlings emerge in a week or so.

CARE AND MAINTENANCE

Cosmos will get too leggy if overfertilized or planted in shade. Afternoon sun is best for this flower; otherwise, it will need staking. A seed-starter fertilizer can be applied to the bed 2 weeks after the seedlings emerge. Fish emulsion sprays and other liquid organic concoctions applied as soil drenches are sufficient for plant health. Remember that cosmos is a wildflower and does not need huge amounts of fertilizer. I recommend a flower fertilizer high in phosphorus. Watering may be necessary in the early weeks of growth and in dry periods. Cosmos are quite tolerant of drought.

ADDITIONAL INFORMATION

Plant beds of cosmos rather than rows of single plants, or the tall plants will flop over in the wind. Staking may be useful in small plantings. Scan the seed catalogs for dwarf varieties of cosmos. Many gardeners have discovered that cosmos is a staple at farmers' markets and is good for fresh cut flower arrangements.

ADDITIONAL SPECIES, CULTIVARS, OR VARIETIES

The range of available colors is incredible. *C. sulphureus* 'Sunny Red' is a dwarf bearing single red-orange flowers. 'Bright Lights,' which grows to 30 inches, is perfect for a tall border. 'Sonata Dwarf' is a Fleuroselect Winner that has huge blooms. 'Candy Stripe' is a unique picotee-type that offers blooms edged in red. 'Sea Shells' is a long bloomer.

Geranium

"*If* a window or a garden could have but one plant, that plant would likely be a geranium," wrote the great American horticulturist Liberty Hyde Bailey in 1935. Few plants have seen as many changes over the decades as have geraniums. Once planting geraniums was quite simple: they were propagated by nursery owners and sold to the public as potted plants for bedding in the flower garden. In the summer, gardeners took cuttings for the next year's garden. Nowadays, gardeners can plant coated seed of the F1 hybrids in the winter and grow dazzling new seedlings in a myriad of colors and leaf variations. Most of the 250 species of pelargoniums are succulents that grow in dry habitats in South Africa and Australia. The plant matures to a rounded 20-inch-high bush with a similar spread. In temperate regions like North Carolina, it is a herbaceous annual unless removed from the garden and carried inside before frost. Many Tar Heel gardeners delight in the challenge of holding the plant indoors in order to begin the spring with large mother plants. The bright geranium flowers are arranged in terminal clusters above the foliage. The round leaves have wavy edges and when bruised emit a characteristic odor.

WHEN TO PLANT

Geraniums should be planted outside in the garden after the last frost or as soon as the soil has warmed sufficiently. There's no hurry to plant them in spring since they can be planted throughout the growing season. Seeds of the zonal geraniums can be sown indoors by a sunny window in late winter. These usually begin blooming in 90 days or less.

WHERE TO PLANT

Geraniums are popular bedding plants. They grow best in full sun, but they tolerate a few hours of shade as long as they have a minimum of 6 hours of direct sunlight. Beds of geraniums in light shade produce good foliage, but few flowers. Geraniums are a good addition to a butterfly garden and make stunning container or patio plants. Plant them where there is good air circulation.

How to Plant

A well-prepared loamy garden soil is best for geranium root growth.
Mix a generous amount of organic matter (such as bark soil conditioner) into sandy or poor soils. This will help retain the moisture
which is beneficial to geraniums when dry weather arrives. If you
do not have a soil test, spade under 4 pounds of dolomitic limestone
and 2 pounds of 5-10-10 fertilizer for each 100 square feet of bed. Do
not use fresh manure! Remove the plants from their pots or break up
the peat pots, and shake off most of the potting soil from the roots.
Straighten out the circling roots and carefully firm the soil around
them. Water the newly set plants every 2 to 3 days for the first week,
then water weekly as needed.

Care and Maintenance

Geraniums will establish quickly with very little care. In fact,
too much water in the spring planting season will rot the roots.
Geraniums respond well to fertilization; they will be stunted if
grown in soils that lack a ready source of nitrogen. Small yellow
leaves are an indication that additional fertilizer is needed. A soluble
fertilizer (the "blue stuff") is suitable for bimonthly applications. Try
to keep the foliage dry during watering. Drip irrigation works well
for avoiding the leaves while wetting the soil. Don't be afraid to
prune leggy geraniums; they will respond with more flowers.

Additional Information

In recent years, our wet summers have led to geranium leaf diseases
that have diminished the geranium's popularity as a bedding plant.
To ensure good soil drainage, consider planting in slightly raised
beds that are well amended with soil conditioner. Always remove
blighted foliage by hand.

Additional Species, Cultivars, or Varieties

Seed-grown varieties include the early-flowering 'Orbit' series in 17
colors; the 'Pinto' series, a great garden cultivar in 11 colors with
deeply zonal leaves; the 'Pulsar' series F-1 hybrids, very floriferous
and excellent in the garden; and the earliest-blooming 'Ringo 2000'
series, in 9 colors. The ivy-leaved geraniums include 'Breakaway'
and 'Summer Showers.'

Globe Amaranth

*T*his resilient annual bedding plant is drought tolerant and free flowering. Globe amaranth's 1-inch-round flowers resemble fluffy clover heads in white, mauve, lavender, and salmon. The sparse gray-green foliage grows to 18 inches tall and a bit wider by summer's end. Globe amaranth tolerates wind and searing sun and keeps right on blooming when many annuals take a reprieve from the heat. Exciting new cultivars are extra-compact and hold their color longer, flowering in containers until frost. One variety, 'Lavender Fields,' bears huge 1–2 inch lilac blooms which provide wonderful cut flowers for both fresh and dried arrangements. Globe amaranth joins strawflower as one of the most popular everlastings. Its dependability when grown from seed and its durability in North Carolina gardens put it at the top of the list of plants to be used in low-maintenance flower gardens.

WHEN TO PLANT

Selected varieties of globe amaranth are always available in spring at the large garden centers. Most are sold in plastic cell packs in multiples of two. Try your hand at sowing seed of the new cultivars after the soil warms.

WHERE TO PLANT

Globe amaranth needs a sunny location with well-drained soil; even a dry spot in the garden will do. Plant in large beds as an accent or grow a few in container gardens. The medium texture of globe amaranth will be most enjoyed in front of a hedge or wooden fence.

HOW TO PLANT

Seeds can be sown in the garden, but they must be covered with soil or newspaper to keep out light. Small potted seedlings are a better bet for most gardeners. Plant globe amaranth in the flowerbed after danger of frost has past. It can then be planted any time right on through the summer months. Prepare the soil by rototilling or hand-working the beds. Add 2 pounds of 5-10-10 fertilizer per 100 square feet; add bark soil conditioner to heavy soils. Plant with the roots barely covered. It is important that the soil pH be close to 6.0.

CARE AND MAINTENANCE

Water newly sown beds daily until the seeds germinate. Seedling transplants should be watered 3 times every week until vigorous growth begins. Globe amaranth can fend for itself after its roots get established. Apply general garden fertilizer every 4 to 6 weeks. A 1- to 2-inch layer of mulch will suffice for routine irrigation.

ADDITIONAL INFORMATION

Don't overwater this annual. Globe amaranth thrives on neglect. Prune the plants if they get leggy.

ADDITIONAL SPECIES, CULTIVARS, OR VARIETIES

The 'Gnome' series offers 6-inch dwarf plants in various colors. 'Strawberry Fields' is an orange-red color and has large blooms. The 8-inch 'Dwarf Cissy' is creamy white. 'Tall Mixed' offers 36-inch plants in mixed colors that are suitable for cutting and drying. 'Lavender Fields' displays 1- to 2-inch blooms in a lilac-lavender color.

Impatiens

OTHER COMMON NAME: Busy Lizzy

*F*or decades, Tar Heel gardeners have found impatiens to be incredibly versatile in the landscape. When established in a moist bed, they will frequently self-sow, returning the next summer for a floral display that is even better than the year before. It is not surprising that this plant is the top seller in garden centers across this state. Find an area where there is filtered light or some shade. Your goal is to bring that area to life! Impatiens come in a wide variety of colors and can be mixed effectively. Be sure to plant some white with your selection. White makes a good background for the colorful varieties and shows up very well at night. Impatiens are the most shade-tolerant of annual flowers, and they come in an incredible range of colors. The color they provide to the garden does not stop until the first killing frost. If you don't have shade, try planting New Guinea impatiens, whose lustrous dark-green leaves and 2-inch flowers thrive in the sun.

WHEN TO PLANT

Set out transplants in spring after the danger of frost has passed. It is best to buy seedlings in cell packs from a garden center or nursery. Some varieties will voluntarily reseed from pods; when touched, the pods pop open "impatiently" and spill seeds on the ground. Six-inch potted impatiens can be planted any time during the warm months.

WHERE TO PLANT

Most impatiens varieties prefer partial- to full-shade areas. (The New Guinea hybrids will grow in areas of full sun to partial shade.) Plant impatiens in slightly acidic, moist, well-draining soil. They make a fine edging when used with foundation shrubs planted on the north or east side of a house. Plant them in mass groupings by color or in mixed borders. Tuck them into corners by entranceways, or in windowboxes and hanging baskets.

How to Plant

Impatiens love humus-laden soils, so unload your compost bin into the annual bed before planting. Incorporate a flower fertilizer or a garden fertilizer (1-2-2 analysis) into the soil. I have discovered that a lightweight tiller is great for reworking the beds each spring. After setting out the transplants, water them with a liquid starter solution such as fish emulsion or Peter's products to insure quick establishment. Then lightly mulch to conserve moisture and control weeds. In large beds, put the mulch down before planting and consider using a weed-preventer chemical.

Care and Maintenance

Newly planted impatiens are quite succulent and will wilt readily if the soil dries out. Keep the bed moist for the first month. For bushier plants, cut back new seedlings one-third at planting time. A midsummer supplemental feeding with a dry granular flower food should be considered for extra growth and color. Maintain moist conditions throughout the growing season. When frost threatens, cover your bed with a polyester sheet and you will be able to keep impatiens for several weeks longer.

Additional Information

Slugs may be a problem in the damp, shady environment which suits impatiens. You will reduce the chance of slug infestation if you avoid watering at night. To make "slug hotels," punch thumb-sized holes in the sides of plastic containers, put slug baits inside the containers, seal the containers, and place them in the flowerbeds—or set out stale beer in saucers to drown the slugs!

Additional Species, Cultivars, or Varieties

Numerous impatiens series are available to growers, including 'Starbright Mix' and plants in the 'Deco Hybrid' series and 'Sunbelt' series. The 'Swirl' series includes 'Super Elfin Swirl,' with big flowers in colors that range from peach to violet. 'Accent' series offers compact plants. The 'Blitz 2000' series is best for heat and drought tolerance. 'Blitz Orange' is an AAS winner. 'Showstopper' is a cascading type.

Marigold

he marigold is one of the most popular annuals in North Carolina. All marigolds are native to Mexico, even though some are called French or African. Marigolds grow quickly from seed to flowering and are usually in bloom when found at garden centers. Most Tar Heel gardeners are familiar with 2 marigold colors: yellow and orange. Some new marigold cultivars produce vibrant blossoms in maroon, white, and bicolors. Marigolds are easy to grow and they provide color from spring through fall. Marigolds come in an abundance of heights and various flower forms. African (and American) marigolds are large, growing from 14 to 36 inches tall and 20 inches wide. Their carnation-like blooms that grow up to 4 inches in diameter make fine cut flowers and can be planted at the back of a border. Try some of the new varieties such as 'Pineapple Crush' or 'Inca Orange.' French marigolds grow 8 to 12 inches tall and have smaller, 2-inch blooms. These plants are excellent for growing in poor soil in the hot summer months.

WHEN TO PLANT

Sow seeds outdoors or set out transplants in the spring after all danger of frost has passed. Successive plantings can lengthen the season of color. To produce autumn color that will complement beds of chrysanthemums, some gardeners sow a late crop in summer.

WHERE TO PLANT

Plant marigolds in full sun in ordinary garden soil. Be careful not to plant in rich, high-nitrogen soil; this will produce foliage at the expense of flowers. Marigolds are awe-inspiring when grouped in large mass plantings. Plant in mixed patio containers or in raised beds for contrasting colors and textures. To make a welcoming sign for friends, plant bright yellow marigolds in an entrance bed or by a mailbox.

HOW TO PLANT

Marigold seeds are quite large and thin, easy for both children and adults to handle. Before planting the seeds, prepare the soil by tilling to a depth of 4 inches. Mix in a little organic matter if you like,

though this may not be necessary for soils that don't crust over. The seeds should be planted at a depth of 1/3 inch. They will germinate in 7 to 10 days in temperatures of 75 degrees Fahrenheit and higher. For early flowers, use transplants or start seeds indoors 5 to 6 weeks before the planting date. Space African and American varieties 18 to 24 inches apart; space French varieties 9 to14 inches apart; dwarf varieties may be spaced closer. Keep seedbeds moist until the seedlings mature.

CARE AND MAINTENANCE

Avoid the overstimulation provided by nitrogen fertilizers. Use a specialty flower fertilizer (bloom-starter type) or a 1-2-2 analysis garden fertilizer that is high in phosphorous. After planting, apply the fertilizer at least once near the plants (this is called "sidedressing"). Never put fertilizer closer than 3 inches away from the stem (to avoid injury). Fertilizer is taken up by feeder roots that are found near the tips of the stems. Always water well after feeding. When using marigolds as cut flowers, remove the foliage before cutting. Remove spent blooms to promote continuous flowering. Stake taller varieties for support. Water weekly, more often during dry spells.

ADDITIONAL INFORMATION

No serious diseases occur except in plantings where the soil drains poorly. Insect pests are problematic, especially leafhoppers and, in dry weather, spider mites. Miticides or Horticultural Oil will take care of these pests. French marigolds are used as a control tactic (trap crop) for nematodes in vegetable gardens.

ADDITIONAL SPECIES, CULTIVARS, OR VARIETIES

There are several marigold species. *T. tenuifolia* (Signets) has single, small-sized blooms. Triploid marigolds ('Zenith Mix') are double-crested. Look for French marigolds *T. patula*: 'Auroras,' 'Boy,' 'Bonanza,' and 'Hero' series. African or American marigolds are *T. erecta*: 'Inca,' 'Excel,' 'Discovery,' 'Antiqua,' 'Jubilee,' and 'Galore' series. 'Harlequin' and 'Tiger Eyes' are unusual cultivars.

Melampodium

*G*ot a friend whose green thumb is a little pale? Share some melampodium and see if your friend's luck doesn't change. Melampodium is a rugged annual, a compact, self-branching plant that flowers freely all summer with no need for deadheading. It is durable in dry soils, and the coarse plants stubbornly succumb only to the first hard freeze in autumn. The dime-size, butter-colored flowers resemble dense little dandelion blooms. Its large 2- to 3-inch-long arrow-shaped leaves are light green. If planted after the soil warms thoroughly in spring, melampodium is a rapid grower and an early bloomer. It is a good substitute for French marigolds, since it is pest-free and has no ugly seedheads to remove. Consider using the dwarf cultivars as edging plants. In good locations, the species plant grows to 2 feet tall and 3 feet wide. Mail-order seed is expensive, costing up to $40.00 for 3 ounces.

WHEN TO PLANT

Sow melampodium in well-prepared flowerbeds in mid-spring. Greenhouse-grown plants generally look pitiful when available in spring, partially because of melampodium's dislike of humid environments.

WHERE TO PLANT

Use melampodium as bedding plants or for container gardens. This annual prefers full sun and well-drained soil. In dry sites, be prepared to do a little watering periodically. Raised bed gardens are ideal for this fast-growing annual.

HOW TO PLANT

The seeds are quite large and should be planted at a depth of one-eighth inch. They will germinate in 7 to 10 days if the temperatures are 75 degrees Fahrenheit or higher. To get early flowers, use transplants or start seeds indoors 5 to 6 weeks before the planting date. Space tall varieties 12 to 24 inches apart. Dwarf varieties need to be placed 12 inches apart.

Care and Maintenance

Melampodium will frequently reseed the second year. Transplant these seedlings into a flower border when they are at least 2 inches tall. Water them weekly using a soluble fertilizer. Melampodium requires very little watering once the plants are established. In fact, it is ideal for large flowerbeds in parks and commercial landscaping projects. Fertilize every 6 weeks with a bloom-booster specialty fertilizer made for flower gardens. After the first hard freeze, pull up the frozen plants, roots and all. This is a good time to take a soil test and prepare the flowerbed for next year's annuals, or you may want to plant pansies for fall color.

Additional Information

I have seen no pests on melampodium in the 3 years I've grown this plant. A good practice is to rotate flowers from bed to bed to prevent a buildup of diseases or weeds—in other words, do not use mono-cultures of the same plant variety in the same bed in successive years. You can collect seed immediately after the fall freeze and save it for the following season.

Additional Species, Cultivars, or Varieties

'Derby,' the first dwarf melampodium introduced, must be spaced on 1-foot centers. 'Showstar' is a compact cultivar offered by most North Carolina garden centers. *Note:* The species *Melampodium* is certainly an acceptable variety.

Pansy

What would we plant for color in a winter landscape if we didn't have pansies? Pansies grow more popular every year in North Carolina. The new hybrids are quite heat tolerant and often last from their fall plantings right on through June. I've seen pansies linger even longer in wet summer weather. Pansies are my favorite cool-season annual. This flower is loved for its bright velvety faces that are available in numerous color combinations. The beautiful new rose and blue shades have given garden designers a new palette, but I am a little nostalgic. I think I will always prefer the old-fashioned pansies with their rich yellow blooms and black "clown faces" that I marveled at as a child. The clear-faced 'Crystal Bowl' varieties are exceptional. Classifying pansies as annuals may be confusing, since they reappear in spring from earlier plantings like biennials. But pansies can only survive for 6 to 8 months before they need to be replaced. When choosing your pansies, consider the 'Majestic Giants' and 'Bingo' hybrids; they are great bloomers. Pansies provide 2 wonderful seasons of color from one planting. They may soon surpass impatiens as America's favorite bedding plant.

WHEN TO PLANT

You can begin planting greenhouse-grown pansies in late August and continue planting through late fall. Plant pansies in large containers on the patio in late winter and spring. Seeds of the viola may self-sow in moist beds. I generally prefer to let the flower growers start the expensive, finicky hybrid seed in climate-controlled germination facilities.

WHERE TO PLANT

Place pansies in a full-sun to partial-shade location. For maximum flowering, make sure there is some direct sunlight and fertile soil. Use pansies in rock gardens, hanging baskets, containers, and mass groupings. Many public gardens interplant pansies with Darwin tulips so that the pansies serve as a groundcover. It is hard to beat the sight of red tulips poking out of a bed of blue 'Crystal Bowl' pansies—wow!

How to Plant

When I am selecting pansies for planting, I look for large transplants grown in 4-inch pots or in large peat cups. (Overgrown pansies bought in six-packs are often leggy; they must be cut back halfway to look good.) Plant transplants in moist, fertile soil. In poor soil, mix in several inches of compost, cow manure, or bark soil conditioner. (A dusting of lime and superphoshate is usually beneficial in the absence of a soil test.) Loosen the roots of the pansies using a handtool. Plant at the depth at which they grew in their containers. Where soil drainage is suspect, berm up the soil 4 inches or so to get better results. Mulch to keep the soil cool and to retain moisture. Water the bed twice each week for 2 to 3 weeks.

Care and Maintenance

Pansies respond to supplemental feeding. Use a granular slow-release fertilizer made for flowers or a general fertilizer that is high in phosphorous. Make the spring fertilizer application when daffodils are in full bloom—your pansies will remain healthy and bloom more profusely if fertilized at this time. Deadhead and cut back leggy plants in mid-spring to prolong the flowering period. Water as needed in dry periods during the fall. In western North Carolina, mulch pansies as the ground begins to freeze.

Additional Information

Leaf spot and stem rot diseases can occur in poorly drained or crowded beds. Give your pansies sufficient space! Pansyworms are generally not a major concern for home gardeners. You may want to sprinkle pine straw over the pansies for protection if temperatures fall into the teens.

Additional Species, Cultivars, or Varieties

There are many pansy cultivars. The most adaptable series for our gardens include: 'Crystal Bowl' hybrids, 'Majestic Giants,' 'Super Swiss Giants,' 'Melody,' 'Rally' (best for overwintering), and 'Regal Hybrids' (free-flowering and bred for the heat). My personal favorites are 'Jokers,' 'Yellow Giants,' and 'Burgundy Lace.'

Petunia

T actually gave up on growing petunias once long ago, and I know other gardeners who did the same. Though petunias were dependable for early spring color, they did terribly in our hot, wet North Carolina summers. But with the arrival of the new introductions in the early '90s, my enthusiasm for petunias was rekindled. These workhorses are now terrific plants for many purposes. The new cultivar 'Purple Wave' is one versatile example—it can be planted in a windowbox or can serve as a groundcover on a hot, steep bank. Petunias are sturdy annuals that come in a myriad of colors. They produce masses of trumpet-shaped blooms on drooping branches. They may cascade to 2 to 3 feet, or they may form compact bushes that reach no more than 15 inches in height. The new millifloras, with their quarter-size flowers, are especially dense. When I needed an edging by my foundation in 1996, I grew 'Fantasy Pink Morn,' and was delighted that this pale pink millifora needed no pruning to stay low and compact. One garden center in western Forsyth County was the talk of the town when 'Purple Wave' petunias were planted in masses around the perimeter of the center. What a beautiful sight!

WHEN TO PLANT

Petunias are the most cold-sensitive of all the annuals. Plant petunias when the soil is warm and the chance of frost has passed. In Piedmont, North Carolina, the last frost date usually falls between April 12 and May 1, but I have seen our oaks lose their leaves to frost later than May 1!

WHERE TO PLANT

Petunias need lots of sunshine to thrive and show off their brilliantly colored flowers. Good soil drainage is a must, as is air circulation to thwart leaf diseases during summer rains. Use petunias in mass groupings for a color accent, and interplant them with perennials to provide flowers during lapses in the flowering season. The cascading habit of petunias makes them ideal for container gardening.

How to Plant

Prepare beds well by amending with compost or bark soil conditioner. Add limestone to soil whose pH is below 6.0. Slow-release flower fertilizer or organic products are available for supplying nutrients. Space seedlings or cuttings 10 to 24 inches apart, depending on the cultivar. Remove the transplants from cell packs, loosen the roots with a handtool, then plant. *Note:* The seeds of petunias are produced through hand-pollination and are quite expensive. There are only limited numbers of seed packets for sale. Leave the seed propagation to the greenhouse growers and purchase their seedlings in cell packs at garden shops.

Care and Maintenance

Newly planted petunias need to be thoroughly watered after planting. I use a transplant solution of fish emulsion or Peter's 20-20-20 to water the plants on the first day. Water every third day for 2 weeks, then weekly and as needed to prevent wilting. Once they begin to grow, petunias are drought tolerant and need only occasional irrigation. (Water in the morning to prevent leaf diseases.) Fertilize every 4 to 6 weeks, using a soluble fertilizer or a 1-2-2 analysis garden product. Mulch the bed early in the season for weed control and to prevent muddy foliage. A 1- to 2-inch layer will do. Pinch or shear back petunias any time they appear leggy.

Additional Information

Petunias are great plants to follow pansies; plant the petunias when the pansies fade out in late May. You will discover that petunias look dog-eared by autumn, and the cycle with pansies can be repeated. In my experience, the double-flowering multiflora petunias, though spectacular in form, require too much pinching and care.

Additional Species, Cultivars, or Varieties

Single and double grandifloras, for cool climates, have red to yellow early blooms. Single floribunda 'Total Madness' blooms "like mad." Single multiflora 'Joy' thrives in heat. Double multifloras have fragrance. New classes of petunias include millifloras.

Spreading Zinnia

OTHER COMMON NAME: Narrow-Leaf Zinnia

This zinnia species was bred for gardeners who enjoy plants that flower all season but who detest the labor-intensive care required by many annuals. Spreading zinnias are heat and drought resistant, and they have a long blooming season. They grow well in beds and are adaptable to container gardening. Zinnia 'Crystal White' is the newest All-America Selections introduction. It is a compact plant that grows to 10 inches in height and has an equal spread. Its single pure-white flowers are over an inch in size and they are punctuated with golden-yellow centers that are reminiscent of field daisies. The small medium-green leaves of this spreading zinnia are narrow and resistant to disease. Unlike the standard garden zinnias (Z. *elegans*) that are plagued by powdery mildew disease, spreading zinnias are highly tolerant of North Carolina's climate conditions. 'Crystal White' can be grown from seed. Zinnias are popular annuals because their flowers are long-lasting in the garden. They also make wonderful bouquets. The garden zinnias have been improved over the years and now come in a myriad of vibrant colors. The compact cultivars make great annual beds, growing quickly in average soil.

WHEN TO PLANT

Both seeds and plants of zinnia should be planted outside well after the danger of frost has passed. In the Piedmont, May and June are good months for sowing seed. In warm soil, the seed will germinate in a week's time. Small transplants are available from most garden centers in the spring; it is best to select stocky plants that have few blooms.

WHERE TO PLANT

Spreading zinnias prefer full sun in ordinary soil that is well drained. They perform equally well in a garden or a container. Use zinnias near steps or other garden features that need accenting. For highest visibility at dusk, plant the white-blooming zinnias that reflect the diminishing sunlight. Spreading zinnias can be used in mass groupings, as flower borders, and for edging the perennial garden.

How to Plant

These zinnias have a low-growing habit. Transplants must be allowed adequate spacing in order to fully mature—place the plants 10 inches apart. Sow seed in soil that has been tilled to a depth of 4 to 6 inches. Limestone should be added to new beds, along with a complete garden fertilizer. Rake the soil surface smooth before sowing. Cover the seed lightly with 1/3 inch of soil and firm the seed by hand or with a rake. Water the bed thoroughly, using a watering wand or a nozzle that is designed for misting seedbeds. Keep the bed or row moist until the seeds germinate. Thin the seedlings to 10 inches apart. Irrigate regularly with the equivalent of an inch of water a week. Seedlings can be started indoors in March.

Care and Maintenance

Spreading zinnias usually do not require major pruning. In late summer, they can be sheared to rejuvenate the planting. Fertilize the plants monthly with a 1-2-2 or similar analysis fertilizer (for example, a 5-10-10) to keep the plants healthy and blooming. If the seedlings were not thinned properly, some plants may become crowded. This may contribute to mildew susceptibility during wet summers.

Additional Information

Spreading zinnias are durable little plants. Give them plenty of room and lots of sunshine and they will be content. These zinnias make dainty cut flowers that last for a long time in arrangements. I grow a row of garden zinnias (Z. elegans) in the vegetable garden to produce the large dahlia-like flowers for cutting.

Additional Species, Cultivars, or Varieties

Z. angustifolia and Z. linearis (Mexican zinnia) are synonymous. The cultivars 'Crystal White,' 'Star Gold,' and 'Golden Orange' are all compact plants with 1- to 2-inch blooms. 'Pinwheel' is a new cross that has 3-inch flowers in colors ranging from rose and salmon to white or mixed.

Sunflower

Sunflowers are hot! The sunflower was declared the 1996 Flower of the Year by the National Gardening Bureau. Visit a farmers' market in midsummer to see prominent displays of sunflowers at the peak of their bloom. Gigantic flowerheads steal the show at the State Fair. Available in either single- or double-head varieties, most come in shades of yellow and have the sunflower's signature dark eyes. New cultivars include a white one, 'Italian White,' and an unusual variety that has 6-inch burgundy-red flowers. I never tire of sunflowers in my garden. Their large heads can reach a foot across and their seeds ripen in early fall. Birds, bees, and butterflies visit the blooms to feast on the sunflower's nectar. One of my fondest memories of my agricultural career is finding myself standing in an endless field of sunflowers in North Dakota in the 1980s. It was a spiritual experience for this floriculturist! I have since experimented with many sunflower varieties, and have been delighted with the performance of most. They are reliable when directly seeded into the garden or when potted for a patio. Remember to select the dwarf sunflower varieties—the gigantic plants will overpower your garden.

WHEN TO PLANT

Plant sunflowers when the soil is sufficiently warm—that is, about 2 weeks after the last frost date in your planting zone. In the Piedmont, mid-May is a good time to put seeds in the ground. Don't miss the opportunity to get kids involved in planting sunflowers! The seeds are large and easily handled by children.

WHERE TO PLANT

In order to produce stocky plants that stay upright, sunflowers need full sun. If their heads grow heavy with rain, spindly plants will fall down. Because this annual can reach 6 to10 feet high very fast, it makes a quick screen for the garden or along a fence row. A bed of the dwarf cultivar 'Sunspot' is a real eye-catcher. Use 'Sunspot' to accent a feature in the landscape, or grow it in a container.

ANNUALS

How to Plant

One good sunflower quality is its tolerance of poor soils. Ordinary garden soil is perfect for growing this annual, provided the soil is well drained. Seeds can be started indoors in late March for larger transplants. They are quick to germinate and can get leggy if not given supplemental lighting. Cover the seeds with 1/2 inch of soil and keep them moist. When planting directly in the garden, till a row or bed, and amend the soil by adding a 1-2-2 analysis fertilizer and some limestone, as you would for tomatoes. Rake the soil up to form a 4-inch-high raised row to insure adequate drainage and warm the soil. Keep the soil moist.

Care and Maintenance

In the garden, thin seedlings to 18 inches apart. Space the larger varieties 2 to 3 feet apart. Water new seedlings and transplant weekly until they begin strong growth. Sunflowers tolerate heat and drought well. Once established, they should be watered only during extended dry spells. A general garden fertilizer can be used as a sidedress application once during the growing season. No pruning is required. Control worm and beetle pests. The dwarf varieties will "play out" after the main flowerheads develop. These sunflowers should be replanted, or another annual such as pansy can be used in the bed after the sunflowers are removed.

Additional Information

The large-headed varieties that are grown for birdseed or for showing at the Fair should be staked for support. Use an 8-foot, 2-inch by 2-inch wooden stake with canvas straps to stake the sunflower. When the neck of the flowerhead forms a shepherd's crook and the back of the head turns from green to yellow, you will know the seeds are mature.

Additional Species, Cultivars, or Varieties

Dwarf cultivars include 'Music Box,' a mix of multicolored 28-inch sunflowers; 'Sunspot,' which has 10-inch blooms on 30-inch plants; and 'Teddy Bear,' a compact double-flowered cultivar. Tall cultivars include 'Floristan,' 5 feet tall and red-banded; 'Italian White,' 6 feet tall and white; 'Valentine,' a 5-foot bushy plant with long-lasting 6-inch blooms; and 'Sonja,' a 42-inch plant that is ideal for cut flowers.

Wax Leaf Begonia

*P*erhaps because of its great tolerance of summer droughts and scorching temperatures, wax leaf begonia has been overused in mass plantings and subdivision entrances. But if you are looking for a colorful annual to dress up an entrance bed, it may be the right choice for you. Do not confuse this begonia with the tuberous types used in states north of North Carolina, or with the fine pink perennial *Begonia grandis* that is often used in shade gardens. The wax leaf is an annual variety grown from seed each year by greenhouse growers. Its waxy leaves come in several shades of green, red, and even bronze. Bloom colors can be pink, coral, white, red, or bicolored. The blooms are now available in gorgeous singles and in doubles that look like little rosebuds. The plants will grow from 6 to 12 inches high, depending on the variety selected, and may spread to one foot in width. The wax leaf begonia is wonderfully tolerant of extreme neglect, heat, and drought. Planting can take place any time during spring or summer for an instant show of flowers and foliage.

WHEN TO PLANT

You may plant begonias safely after the last killing frost of the year. Planting is always safe by mid-May. If you are planting from seed, start them indoors in February for later planting in the garden. Begonia seeds are like dust and can be a challenge to handle. Use sterile potting soil and cover the pots or seed flats with a clear plastic cover.

WHERE TO PLANT

If the soil is well drained, wax leaf begonias can thrive in full sun to partial shade. They are very effective in mass plantings, at front entrances, in commercial beds, or near mailboxes. "Difficult-to-water" spots are ideal for begonias. The red- or bronze-leaved varieties appear to be more sun tolerant than the green-leaved ones.

HOW TO PLANT

Spade or till the soil and add a little organic matter into the bed In the eastern regions of North Carolina where the soil types are sand to sandy loams, some gardeners prefer to use peat moss. In the clay

soils of the Piedmont and westward, pine-bark soil conditioner spread 3 inches deep over the bed prior to tilling will loosen the soil significantly. Generally, most soils need limestone; spade some in at the rate of 1 cup per square yard of bed area. Dig a hole a little larger than the rootball of the plant. Loosen the roots gently and place the plant into the hole. Cover the roots with soil and mulch lightly. Be sure to water well with a liquid starter fertilizer.

CARE AND MAINTENANCE

Be sure to water at least twice a week for 3 to 4 weeks after planting. Though fertilizing is not essential, begonias will perform better if watered every 10 to 14 days with a water-soluble flower fertilizer. A granular fertilizer that is high in phosphorous can be used at planting time and later scratched in around the plants once or twice during the growing season. Be sure to water well after each application. Space your wax leaf begonias on 12- to 15-inch centers to allow them to fill out properly. Crowded beds may lead to diseases. No pruning is necessary. Once the first frost has arrived, the "melted" plants can be added to your compost pile.

ADDITIONAL INFORMATION

Be aware that the wax leaf begonia is extremely sensitive to any light frost and must be covered with a polyester cloth (floating cover) or a bedsheet for protection. If your begonias get leggy in midsummer, you can prune them back halfway. Fertilize after pruning, and you will have nice fall color!

ADDITIONAL SPECIES, CULTIVARS, OR VARIETIES

Popular series include 'Cocktail,' standard bronze plants which grow to 8 inches; 'Vodka'; 'Whisky'; 'Senator,' a new series (improved sunbelt begonias); the green-leaved 'Olympia' series; 'Viva'; 'Scarlanda'; and the 'Ambassador' series.

CHAPTER TWO

Bulbs

A PASSION FOR FLOWERS OFTEN BEGINS WITH A HANDFUL OF BULBS. Many a beginning gardener has gotten a start in the field of horticulture with a plump amaryllis bulb or a few paperwhite narcissus. Bulb culture opens up a whole new realm of gardening for skilled gardeners as well.

When we gardeners think of bulbs, what usually comes to mind is Holland, not North Carolina! There is no doubt that Holland is world renowned for its tulip tradition and its famous Keukenhof Gardens that have ten million flowering bulbs on display. In the Netherlands, bulbs have been grown as an economic staple since the 16th century. With some planning you can create a Dutch delight, but you can get the greatest enjoyment from bulbs by planting varieties other than tulips.

Bulb flowers are not just spring flowers. On the contrary, bulbs can bloom ten months of the year, from January to October. While the familiar crocus and daffodils are valuable garden bulbs and require little care, they finish their showy performance before spring is even over.

Indulge yourself with the wonderful woodland varieties like magic lilies and cyclamen. For vertical accent, scatter a few gladiolus bulbs in the perennial border. The Oriental lilies produce large, exquisite, picture-perfect blooms. If you want a heavenly fragrance to permeate your home, place a few tuberose stems in a vase and you will be delighted for days!

Chapter Two

I believe the summer-flowering bulbs are much better landscape plants than their spring counterparts. Their foliage as well as their flowers can make a statement in the garden. The bold variegated foliage of the cannas and caladiums provides an exclamation point in a border or in the shadow of a majestic shade tree. If big leaves suit your fancy, the monstrous elephant ear bulbs can be used judiciously.

There are many bulb choices available for gardening year-round. There is a bulb for every sunny garden or shady nook. Some may be left in the ground for years, producing many flowers for your enjoyment. Others will need to be lifted following the first frosts of autumn. You won't be disappointed with your bulb choices when you find the perfect places for them in your garden.

Hippeastrum spp.

Amaryllis

*M*ost gardeners think of amaryllis as the pear-shaped bulbs in pretty boxes that show up at the discount store just in time for holiday gift-giving. Most amaryllis are indeed sold for forcing indoors during the winter months. But from Raleigh eastward, this hardy bulb can be added to the perennial border or used en masse for a striking display when the rest of the spring garden has passed its peak. As its leaves emerge from the ground, this bulbous plant blooms with a cluster of 4 to 6 extraordinary trumpet-shaped flowers. The 6-inch outward-facing flowers can be white, pink, red, salmon, orange, or striped. Strap-like leaves appear later in the summer. The bulbs perennialize in the warmer regions of the Carolinas, growing larger each year, until as many as 3 stalks of blooms rear up from each plant in a season. Amaryllis are not difficult to grow in well-drained sites of any soil type. Once they establish their permanent root systems, they provide the brilliant color and bold forms that are sorely needed until perennials reach their peak. If for no other reason, grow a few amaryllis for superb cut flowers.

WHEN TO PLANT

West of the Triangle Region of North Carolina, plant amaryllis in the spring, and handle them as you would dahlias. In the milder parts of the state and the Coastal region, plant in the fall. Fall is also a good time to divide established and crowded beds. Though amaryllis can be planted from seed, divisions, or bulb cuttings, it is best to stick with the bulbs!

WHERE TO PLANT

Amaryllis prefer rich, well-drained soil and full sun. Plant them where they will not be disturbed for a number of years. Their deep foraging roots should not have to compete with the invasive root systems of shade trees such as dogwoods, beeches, and maples. This majestic flower deserves to be shown off in a prominent place. Plant it in an entrance garden, by an ornate garden gate, or in a decorative container.

ZONE 8

BULBS

HOW TO PLANT

Thoroughly prepare a new bed by double-digging to break up compacted soil layers. This will help your amaryllis sink deep roots into the bed and increase its chances of surviving severe winters. Gather compost, aged sawdust, or shredded leaves; mix these into the soil to enrich the bed. A dusting of lime or an application of wood ashes will help sweeten the soil if needed for an ideal pH of 6.0. When planting, use a bulb-booster fertilizer at the rate given on the label. The rule of thumb for planting bulbs: the planting depth should be 2 to 3 times the length of the bulb from nose to basal plate. But in this case, plant your amaryllis 4 to 6 inches deep. Cover the bulbs with the prepared soil and water well to settle the bed.

CARE AND MAINTENANCE

New plantings will benefit from a little attention the first season. When the round bare stalk breaks ground in May or June, begin watering amaryllis regularly during dry periods. Once the beds are well established in the gardens of the Southeast, they require very little attention. Fertilize the bulbs once or twice monthly after the foliage appears. This will strengthen the bulbs for succeeding years. The foliage will turn yellow as the plants go into dormancy. At that time the flower stalks can be cut down and plants divided if necessary. Where they can be grown outdoors, a thick winter mulch should be applied after frosts.

ADDITIONAL INFORMATION

I have seen very few amaryllis in Triad area gardens, though I believe there are a few lucky gardeners near Winston-Salem with small patches outdoors. (Most likely these are not Dutch hybrids but the St. Joseph's Lily.) When you cut amaryllis blooms for flower arrangements, leave a few inches of stem above ground.

ADDITIONAL SPECIES, CULTIVARS, OR VARIETIES

There are scores of hybrid cultivars. Popular varieties include 'Appleblossom' (pink), 'Byoux' (salmon), 'Red Lion' (scarlet), and 'Christmas Gift' (white). Heirloom cultivars are *H. puniceum* (belladonna lily) and *H. × johnsonii* (St. Joseph's Lily).

49

Autumn Crocus

With the first crisp days of October comes a fall-blooming bulb that will snap you to attention with its sudden burst of color. What an exciting time it is when autumn crocus appears. The rosy-lilac flowers are 3½ inches wide on 3-inch stems. Depending on the species, autumn crocus may start blooming as early as September and continue blooming well into November. The coarse foliage emerges weeks after the crocus-like flowers fade. Autumn crocus is a member of the lily family. It is not a true crocus like the spring-blooming variety sold at all garden shops. Though there are some true crocus that bloom in the fall (such as the saffron crocus), these should not be confused with the colchicums. Autumn crocus is purchased as a rather plump, wrinkled bulb called a corm. Asheville gardener and author Peter Loewer writes that 'Water Lily' is the loveliest cultivar of colchicums, and that "few variations can hold a candle to this one." The large pink double flowers of 'Water Lily' are long lasting. Another of Loewer's favorites is meadow saffron (*C. autumnale*), called "wonder bulb" The nickname refers to its tendency to bloom on a windowsill before being planted. Clearly, autumn crocus should not be judged by its size alone!

WHEN TO PLANT

Autumn crocus bulbs should be planted in late summer, or as soon as they arrive from the mail-order nursery. Keep the bulbs cool and dry until you are ready to plant them, or you may be in for an early-blooming surprise!

WHERE TO PLANT

Autumn crocus is best naturalized in a woodland garden. When they are happy with their location, they will thrive for many years unattended. Since these autumn beauties are relatively small in size, they are best appreciated close-up. Plant them along a path, near a sidewalk, or by a patio sitting area. Autumn crocuses are especially beautiful at the foot of a rock or in front of a perennial garden.

How to Plant

Autumn crocus thrives when planted in rich, well-drained soil. Amend poor, coarse soil with aged compost or sphagnum peat moss. Broadcast bulb-booster fertilizer and spade it into the soil before planting the bulbs. Excavate a planting pit that is at least 18 inches square and 6 inches deep. Return some of the amended back-fill soil to the pit. Plant the bulbs 2 inches deep (measured from the top of the corm) and space them at least 6 inches apart. Water the planting area to settle the soil. Mulch with a light mulching material such as pine needles or shredded leaves.

Care and Maintenance

This cormous lily is not a heavy feeder. Apply bulb fertilizer in early September each year to energize the plants for the next growth cycle. Autumn crocuses planted near shallow-rooted trees will need watering during the fall months while blooming. Irrigate them weekly or as needed. The leaves should not be cut back or damaged while they are lush and green. This foliage is necessary for replenishing the bulb's food reserves to insure flower bud development in the coming months.

Additional Information

Ants are especially fond of the seed coats of autumn crocus and often help in naturalizing the plants. This bulb is also attractive to the bees that work the flowers diligently from dawn to dusk. In spring, the spent yellow foliage can be trimmed back. Look out for nurseries that sell colchicums dug from the wild—conservationists frown on this practice!

Additional Species, Cultivars, or Varieties

'Water Lily' has pink double flowers that are suitable for cutting. 'Album' is a late, white-flowering cultivar. 'The Giant' blooms early with big lavender-pink blooms. 'Roseum' is a rose-pink color. C. speciosum is rose to purple, and grows to 5 inches high with blooms that are 4 inches in diameter. C. cilicicum is a deep lilac color and has foot-long leaves that appear soon after flowering.

Bearded Iris

OTHER COMMON NAME: German Iris

*T*hese sensational showy plants are among the most useful and widely grown perennials. The flower is named after the Greek Goddess of the Rainbow, and there are indeed iris flowers in every color of the rainbow. Not only are irises prized today in the land-scape, but they are also greatly valued for their decorative qualities as cut flowers. The bearded iris is made of 2 sections, an inner section consisting of 3 upstanding petals called "standards," and 3 outer drooping petals called "falls." The name comes from the dense, hairy line seen along the midrib of the outer "falls." Bearded iris ranges from 18 to 42 inches in height and has leaves that are sword shaped. Its stiff foliage and upright form contrast well with the rounded form of many border perennials, and it is available in standard and dwarf forms. These lovely late-spring bloomers are easily grown under ordinary garden conditions provided the soil does not stay wet. There are hundreds of named varieties of this marvelous flower.

WHEN TO PLANT

The ideal time for the division of the bearded iris is the period immediately after flowering. New root growth is made at this time, and new plants will have an opportunity to become well established before winter. These plants will usually produce blooms the follow-ing year. Late-autumn planting is not advisable because the plants won't have a chance to establish.

WHERE TO PLANT

Bearded iris should be planted in a location in full sun or where they will receive at least a half-day of sun. If they do not receive enough sun they seldom thrive, and the weak plants will produce flowers of inferior size. Bearded iris can be interplanted with other perennials for a striking textural contrast. Most gardeners plant entire beds of iris either in a border or alongside plants in the vegetable garden.

ZONE
6,7,8

HOW TO PLANT

Bearded iris grows from rhizomes, thickened underground stems from which roots grow. Rhizomes may be planted singly or in groups of three. Iris may be planted on a mound or in a raised bed, but this is not necessary. Be careful never to plant too deep, or the plants may not bloom. When dividing iris, cut the leaves back to 6 inches. Lift the entire clump out of the ground and remove the soil. With a sharp knife, cut the clump so there is a rhizome and a fan of leaves in each division. Inspect each rhizome for signs of insects or decay. The most serious insect is the iris borer. If you see them, remove the pinkish 2-inch larvae with a pencil and destroy them.

CARE AND MAINTENANCE

Prepare the iris bed with fertilizer and lime for a 6.5 pH. Fertilize with 5-10-10 in spring before bloom time. A second application one month after blooming is needed to stimulate foliage and rhizome growth. Do not mulch iris. Iris plants require an abundance of moisture during the blooming season, but they are able to endure long periods of drought at other times. The best blooms are usually produced the second to fourth years after planting. Most remain in good blooming condition for up to five years before it is necessary to divide them. Overcrowded clumps bloom poorly, so divide them if they become too dense.

ADDITIONAL INFORMATION

In my area, bearded iris are popular for gifts on Mother's Day. The plants can be divided while in bloom to ensure the correct flower color is selected. When planting, cut off the old flower stems. When planted properly, the top of the rhizome can be seen above the ground. If iris fail to bloom, they may have been planted too deeply; if this is the case, hose off the extra garden soil.

ADDITIONAL SPECIES, CULTIVARS, OR VARIETIES

Some favorites are the coral pink 'Beverly Sills,' the powder blue 'Codicil,' and 'Edith Wolford' with its bicolor or yellow standards and blue-violet falls. Others are the white 'Laced Cotton' and 'Plum Delight' with its large plum-colored blooms. Some dwarf irises are 'Baby Blessed,' a yellow rebloomer with a white spot, the late, peach 'Bright Vision,' and 'Michael Paul,' which has dark-purple ruffled petals.

Caladium

*C*aladiums put most other bulbous plants to shame with their large flamboyant leaves. These beautiful plants prove that blooms are not everything in the Tar Heel garden. Caladiums are found in many shapes, sizes, and color combinations. Generally these tropical plants are grown from tubers, and they come in 2 types. Fancy-leaved caladiums have heart-shaped leaves. Strap-leaved varieties have narrow, arrow-shaped leaves. Both types are available in shades of red, burgundy, pink, or white. There are sun-loving and shade-loving caladiums. The shade-loving types are more common. Heights range from 10-inch dwarfs to tall 30-inch plants. Caladiums are the perfect plants for partial- to full-shade gardens. Forty to sixty percent shade is ideal for most varieties. The white varieties will make a strong visual statement in a shady nook or dull green area of the garden. Caladium's colorful leaves are a great asset, as flowers are hard to find in the summer shade garden. Caladium tubers are inexpensive. They can be planted outside after the middle of May across North Carolina. This plant is not winter hardy and must be lifted each fall.

WHEN TO PLANT

Plant caladium bulbs in the garden when the soil temperatures are above 70 degrees Fahrenheit, or after all danger of frost has passed. Tubers purchased from the garden center can be potted in early spring and held in a warm room until they sprout. They can then be planted in the garden. For the best bargain, buy the largest tubers.

WHERE TO PLANT

If you start your caladiums indoors, wait for the temperatures to rise outside before setting them in the garden. Soil for caladiums must be porous and well drained. These summer beauties are versatile plants for containers or beds. Caladiums make great backdrops for shady borders of impatiens and forget-me-nots. Consider using these bulbs in containers with cascading ivies, or even in windowboxes.

How to Plant

To force the tubers indoors, plant 2 or 3 per 6-inch pot; use a sterile soilless seed-starting mix. Plant the tubers 1 inch deep in the pots and place the pots in a warm, well-lighted room. Water sparingly twice each week. When the pointed shoots emerge, apply a soluble plant fertilizer weekly until the caladiums are ready to set in the garden. Transplant your plants outdoors in May or June after the last frost. At that time, bulbs can be planted directly into the garden in a well-drained site. It is usually necessary to spade in organic matter where soils are sandy or contain clay. Mix in 2 pounds of 10-10-10 or bulb fertilizer before planting. Bury the bulbs 1 to 3 inches deep and water well.

Care and Maintenance

Water container-grown caladiums 2 to 3 times a week in summer and fall. Plants in the ground need watering once a week, though they may need watering more often during the hot summer months. Look for signs of wilting as an indicator that watering is needed. If you remove the insignificant bloom pods during the growing season, you will have much better foliage production. Fertilize with 1 pound of garden fertilizer every 6 weeks during the growing season by broadcasting the fertilizer on top of the soil, then watering promptly. Once frost has "melted" back the tops, the leaves can be cut back and the tubers lifted. Store them indoors.

Additional Information

Be sure to dust bulbs with sulphur or a similar fungicide before storing them for winter dormancy. Make sure the bulbs are dry before placing them in an old potato sack or brown bag to store. Dry peat moss can be used in the bags. Most gardeners just leave the tubers in the ground to rot instead of digging them for re-use the following season.

Additional Species, Cultivars, or Varieties

Fancy-leaf cultivars include the white 'Aaron,' 'Candidum,' and 'White Christmas'; the pink 'Carolyn Whorton' and 'Fannie Munson'; the red 'Mrs. Nehrling,' 'Postman Joyner,' 'Red Flash,' and 'Scarlet Pimpernel'; and 'Rosebud,' which is rose with a green border. Strap-leaf cultivars include 'Miss Muffet' (cream with red spots), 'Red Frill,' and 'White Wing.'

Canna

When you are traveling down the highway at 65 mph, there are few herbaceous perennials that will catch your eye the way cannas do! Interstate 40 between Winston-Salem and Raleigh displays numerous mass plantings of this terrific tropical-looking bulbous plant. The red, yellow, pink, or bicolor canna flowers are large and showy and grow on upright plants that resemble miniature banana trees. Cannas continue their flowering frenzy right up until November when they can be blackened by a hard frost. Canna was slow in making it to the highway engineer's list of flowers that are suitable for North Carolina Department of Transportation plantings. Planners were perhaps overly cautious, and there was a concern that the plant's inordinate height, ranging from 2 to 6 feet, would obstruct motorists' view. Canna reached stardom when it was planted to prepare for the Olympic Festival in the '80s. It was not a problem for motorists, and thousands have been planted since then, beautifying our roadsides. Visitors to North Carolina remark on the marvelous floral displays planted by Department of Transportation horticulturists, especially when canna and crape myrtle bloom periods overlap. New cultivars have dazzling leaf colors as well as bicolored flowers. Cannas are seeing a revival and they are here to stay!

WHEN TO PLANT

Cannas are planted successfully after the soil has warmed in mid-spring. Seed of the 'Tropical Rose' variety can be sown indoors in late winter for planting in the garden in April.

WHERE TO PLANT

Cannas are most effective when planted in groups or massed in single colors against a solid background. Their coarse foliage is a good backdrop for finer textured perennials and ornamental grasses. Canna can serve as a seasonal screen in a border. Plant cannas in full sun where the soil drains well.

HOW TO PLANT

Cannas are planted from rhizomes (stocky root pieces). They are tender bulbs, and they may not overwinter in the Mountain region.

Plant canna in ordinary garden soil that is well tilled. Mix 10-10-10 fertilizer into the soil at a rate of 2 pounds per 100 square feet, or use a bulb-booster product during soil preparation. Cover the rhizomes with 2 inches of soil, or use 4 inches of well-aged compost for backfill. Firm-in the rhizomes by hand or foot, then water the bed thoroughly. Keep the soil moist until the stalks reach 1 foot in height. Do not overwater your cannas. It is best to water only lightly until the shoots break the ground.

CARE AND MAINTENANCE

Water cannas generously once the leaves are full-grown. The North Carolina Department of Transportation uses a deep mulch of leaf compost for maintaining island plantings. If the planting will be irrigated, fertilize with a general garden product every 6 weeks until early September. Cannas are not finicky plants. These rugged garden favorites are resilient despite weather-related stresses. The biggest canna concern in the western half of the state is winter hardiness. Cold-damaged rhizomes often send up weak sprouts later in the season. From Statesville westward, dig up the rhizomes in November and store them inside at 45 degrees Fahrenheit.

ADDITIONAL INFORMATION

'Nervosa,' the yellow-veined variety I grow, is apparently irresistible to Japanese beetles—or perhaps the roses planted nearby attract beetles to my canna bed. I shake the foliage routinely in June and the beetles roll right off into a pail of soapy water.

ADDITIONAL SPECIES, CULTIVARS, OR VARIETIES

The Seven Dwarfs strain grows 18 inches high and is suitable for small gardens. Pfitzer's Dwarf grows to 36 inches. Red-flowered cultivars include 'The President' (the most common variety) and the dwarfs 'Crimson Beauty' and 'Firebird.' Two yellow-flowered dwarfs are 'Lucifer' and 'Primrose Yellow.' 'Black Knight' and 'Wyoming' have bronze foliage with red blooms. 'Chinese Coral' is pink. 'Pretoria' has multi-colored foliage and brilliant blooms. 'Tropical Rose' was the first seed-grown introduction.

Crinum

*C*rinums are great summer-flowering bulbs that are found in old homesteads throughout the South. This member of the amaryllis family is one of the more cold-hardy bulbs, and it can be safely planted in the eastern regions of our mountains. The coarse sword-like foliage of crinums is lustrous and statuesque, providing a pleasing contrast to finer textured ornamentals. The long-necked bulbs of this beauty can grow as large as footballs! The flowers of crinum resemble those of the common Easter lily, yet they are half the size. Each long-tubed pink bloom is about 4 inches long and has a characteristic rose-red stripe on each petal. Up to 15 flowers are borne on each rigid 2- to 3-foot-tall stalk. The white form 'Album' and the wine-red 'Rubra' are choice garden plants. The South African crinum, *C. moorei* 'Schmidtii,' a white-flowering variety, is especially adapted to the heat and summer rainfall of Zone 9. The pink-blooming *C.* 'Fred Howard' is a fragrant hybrid of *Amaryllis belladonna* that blooms in late summer. You will be delighted with numerous late-summer surprises when you plant crinums in a moist garden spot.

WHEN TO PLANT

Plant crinums in the warmer months, beginning in April. You can continue to plant them through late October. They produce both seed and off-sets (suckers). The off-sets can be removed from the mother plant in summer and early fall. In my opinion, seed propagation of crinum and most other bulbs is best left to the professionals.

WHERE TO PLANT

Crinums will thrive in sun, provided the soil is moist, or in filtered shade. When planted facing the south sun, the foliage will yellow, looking rather shabby as the crinums go into late-summer dormancy following bloom. Because of this, plant crinums in the middle of the border. The species *C. mooreii* grows well in a woodland shade garden along with such perennial companions as *Canna, Caladium,* ferns, and *Agapanthus.*

HOW TO PLANT

Find a location for crinums that is naturally moist, or add large quantities of organic matter (sphagnum peat moss, compost) to sandy or gravelly soils. The bulbs are easy to grow, and once they're planted, they should be left undisturbed for many years. The bulbs are quite large, requiring a deeply spaded planting hole. Spade up an area that's a minimum of 1 square foot and mix in some bulb-booster fertilizer as the label directs. Plant the bulb with its long neck prominently visible above ground, much as you would plant a Dutch amaryllis for forcing in a flower pot. Watering is not necessary at planting time. If planted in the sun, use a thin layer of mulch around crinum.

CARE AND MAINTENANCE

Newly planted crinums will need to settle in for a season or two before they begin blooming freely. Crinums are not demanding; they require only some handweeding. Apply a high-phosphorus fertilizer (for example, 10-20-20) in mid-May each year after the first flowering season. Water faithfully during the bloom period if there is a lack of rainfall. After 4 to 5 years, remove the off-sets and replant them to enlarge your collection or share them with a gardening friend. Master Gardeners at the Extension Center will be glad to take a few off your hands if you don't know what to do with them.

ADDITIONAL INFORMATION

Crinums don't like to be disturbed! Can you think of a better endorsement of a perennial flower? In the far west regions of North Carolina, crinums should be grown in containers and taken inside for the winter.

ADDITIONAL SPECIES, CULTIVARS, OR VARIETIES

Many of the crinum cultivars are age-old hybrids that were developed even before much was known about hybridization. Most are crosses of *C. bulbispermum* and *C. moorei*, such as *C. × powellii* and *scabrum*. Cultivars include white-flowering 'Schmidtii' and 'White Queen,' pink 'Houdyshel' and 'Roseum,' red 'Carnival,' and bicolor 'Milk and Wine' types.

Daffodil

If you must choose between tulips and daffodils for a landscaping project . . . go for the daffodils! Because they are not
bothered by critters such as voles and squirrels, these hardy spring-
flowering bulbs are quick to naturalize in woodland gardens. Daffodil
bulbs grow larger each season. They can adapt to tight-clay soils much
better than most other bulbous plants. They adapt to a wide range of
climates in North Carolina, and their yellow, white, or bicolored trumpet flowers have become the symbol of spring. By choosing varieties
that bloom in different months, you can have daffodils flowering from
late winter until early summer. The miniatures make stunning rock garden plants. Some cultivars, like 'Ice Follies,' can be potted for forcing
indoors during the winter months. If you're looking for fragrance, look
no further—the paper-whites (tazettas) are intensely aromatic and are
terrific for potting or for planting in borders. You can purchase daffodils by the bushel for fairly inexpensive, magnificent spring floral
displays. Spring is not complete in a Tar Heel garden without a
wonderful bed of daffodils.

WHEN TO PLANT

Daffodils should be planted after the first frost in October. Most
bulbs do poorly if planted later than early December. Bulbs for
forcing can be planted a little earlier, but they should be held in an
unheated garage or shed until cool weather arrives. Narcissus can
be potted, then set in a trench in the garden until time to bring
indoors where the heat will induce blooming.

WHERE TO PLANT

Plant your daffodils in full sun or partial shade. While rich, friable
soil is preferred, these workhorses will grow amazingly well in
some pretty terrible bulb locations. Naturalizing varieties should be
planted in irregular drifts along stream banks and in wide borders.
Play around with a color wheel to plan some great beds that combine daffodils with pansies, thrift, and candytuft. Try planting some
bulbs in groundcovers.

How to Plant

It is important to purchase high-quality bulbs—only the largest and firmest—to achieve success in planting. The bulbs that have 2 or 3 noses will produce more blooms the first year. Shop early at the garden centers in the fall. Or do as many people do, and buy from mail-order nurseries. These mail-order nurseries do the lion's share of the business. Who can resist the titillating photographs in the catalogs? Plant daffodils much as you do tulips, with good soil preparation. Add lime and phosphate to the soil if needed, and incorporate large quantities of ground pine bark into poorly drained beds. Plant daffodils in masses. The bulbs should be covered with 4 to 6 inches of topsoil and mulched.

Care and Maintenance

Newly planted bulb beds should be watered weekly during dry fall weather. Fertilize the beds in January or when new shoots appear, and again in early fall. Use 2 pounds of 10-10-10 fertilizer for a 100-square-foot bed. After flowers fade away, snip off the old heads to prevent seedpods from forming. This will keep the energy flowing into bulb growth for the next season. To make the faded plants look better, many local gardeners fold the leaves and secure them with a rubber band. I never have the time to do this, nor do I think it is a good practice. However, it does beat having to mow down the foliage before it dies naturally.

Additional Information

Crowded beds of narcissus can be divided when the foliage yellows. Plant the clumps of bulbs back immediately or dry them in the sun. Store them until fall in mesh onion or apple bags in a cool, dry location. I have been known to move them green, soon after flowering, but only when I needed the bed space. Grape hyacinths can be planted to mark the spots where bulbs grew.

Additional Species, Cultivars, or Varieties

The American Daffodil Society recognizes outstanding cultivars with its Wister Award. These award winners should be the first ones to try if you are a novice. Some of the winners are 'Peeping Tom,' 'Sweetness,' 'Ceylon,' 'Salome,' 'Ice Follies,' 'Stratosphere,' and 'Accent.' 'St. Kerverne' and 'Rapture' are heat-resistant cultivars. Lists of dependable cultivars are available at County Extension Centers.

Dahlia

*I*f you are most excited by big flowers in the garden, then dahlias can give you the ultimate high! Though the iridescent blooms of dahlia can be as small as a nickel, some grow larger than the biggest dinner plate. Their jewel-toned brilliance is unmatched among tender perennials. This tuberous-rooted ornamental varies tremendously in color, form, and size. The *Classification Handbook of Dahlias* contains more than 1500 listed cultivars of all styles. The most popular styles enjoyed by gardeners range from Decorative and Informal Decorative to Straight Cactus and Semi-cactus. Combinations of these double-blooming types are good for cut flowers and displaying in exhibitions. Some dahlia flowers are perfectly ball-shaped. Singles are known as anemones, water lilies, or miniatures. Flower colors are numerous, ranging from basic yellow and white to red, purple, and pink. The stunning blended or bicolor blooms are the result of decades of hybridization. The fast-growing succulent dahlia stems can mature at 1 foot or top out at over 6 feet in height, depending on the variety. Dahlias are native to Mexico, so they do well in North Carolina's warm weather and intense sunshine.

WHEN TO PLANT

Dahlias are planted from bulb-like rootstock called tubers. In North Carolina, the tubers can be planted directly in the garden soil soon after the danger of frost has passed. Some cultivars are grown from seed and are handled like annuals. The seeds are best started indoors in late winter. Transplant the seedlings into the garden after hardening-off.

WHERE TO PLANT

Dahlias prefer rich, well-drained soil, but they will grow in ordinary loam. They are considered cool-season flowers. Like roses, dahlias prefer a sunny location, so keep this in mind when deciding where to plant. Some of the short varieties make excellent choices for borders, windowboxes, and containers. Most, however, will probably be planted as background plants or grouped together for the pleasure of cutting.

How to Plant

Many gardeners start dahlia tubers indoors a month before the last anticipated frost date. The tubers are placed in 1- to 3-gallon nursery pots that contain professional potting soil. The soil is kept semidry until the tender shoots emerge. Then the pots are moved outdoors to a protected area and kept moist until time to transplant. Other gardeners prefer to wait until the soil warms sufficiently and plant the tubers directly into well-prepared garden soil. Amend tight soils with compost or pine-bark soil conditioner. Cow manure or slow-release flower fertilizer can be spaded into the soil as well. Tubers are placed sideways about 3 inches below the soil line. Do not water before shoots appear!

Care and Maintenance

Dahlias require consistent watering during dry periods; if they are not irrigated during a drought, it is often impossible to get them to flower later in the season. It is advisable to mulch dahlias to conserve moisture. Dahlias are greedy feeders. Apply a 10-20-20 fertilizer or similar analysis every 4 to 6 weeks during the growing season. (Always water the day before fertilizing!) Periodically apply foliar applications of a soluble fertilizer containing micronutrients. To produce more blooms, pinch back often. Pinch the dahlia shoots back to the third joint soon after the shoots first emerge. The plants grow tall and they require support by staking.

Additional Information

Dahlias will die back from a hard frost. When this occurs, cut the canes back to 3 inches from the ground. Using a spading fork, lift the tuberous roots from the soil. Hose off the clinging soil and dip the tubers in a fungicide solution. Let them dry thoroughly; then store them indoors for the winter in dry peat moss at 40 to 50 degrees Fahrenheit. The tubers can be separated in spring.

Additional Species, Cultivars, or Varieties

Dahlia cultivars are too numerous to list. It is best to first select a flower style, then consult the American Dahlia Society for nursery sources. Many garden centers offer prepackaged dahlias. In the bedding plant flower trials conducted by Dr. Bailey each year at North Carolina State University, seedling dahlia varieties have not survived well.

Gladiolus

OTHER COMMON NAMES: Glads, Sword Lilies

This is a group of fast-growing and durable summer-flowering bulbs whose ease of care makes them ever-popular with gardeners. Every color in the rainbow is represented in the group, including dazzling bicolor and tricolor varieties. The plants have rigid sword-like leaves that grow up to 3 feet high, and flower stalks ("scapes") that may require staking. These plants are grown from flattened bulbs called corms. Glads are tender plants and will often freeze in the ground during winter in western North Carolina. I have had them come back for years in the Piedmont where they were planted on raised rows in a vegetable garden. In my garden here in Winston-Salem, however, I always harvest the showiest varieties and store them in cardboard boxes in the garage. As a kid, I remember buying glads at Woolworth's for pennies and never being disappointed with the outcome when I dropped them in our clay soil. Generic glad varieties can still be bought for small change in bulk by mail order or at garden shops. Amateurs and professionals like gladiolus equally well, never failing to find a place for them in their gardens. Glads are wonderful for cutting,

WHEN TO PLANT

To extend the flowering period, plant gladiolus several times during the growing season. The first planting should be done after the soil has warmed up, in April down east and in May in other areas. Corms can be planted monthly in Zones 8b and 9. They usually take 8 weeks to flower; there are early and late varieties.

WHERE TO PLANT

Plant gladiolus in full sun in well-drained soil. Clay soils may require "bedding up" to insure perfect drainage. These spectacular plants are a must for the cutting garden. There are dwarf varieties that can be used in flower borders, especially following spring-flowering bulbs. Keep in mind that some varieties may need staking. Plant them in groups, using several corms of a single variety for a floral accent.

How to Plant

Dig up or rototill the soil to a depth of 6 to 8 inches before planting. Apply a bulb-booster fertilizer or garden fertilizer, such as 5-10-10 to the planting hole and mix it in thoroughly. Place several bulbs in the planting hole at least 5 inches apart. Cover with 2 inches of topsoil, and water well. If you are planting dwarf glads in a large container or urn, be sure they have adequate drainage and are potted with a loose potting soil. In tight clay soils, incorporate several inches of pine-bark soil conditioner to improve soil aeration and drainage. Plant a row of glads in your vegetable garden to enhance its beauty and to provide a source of fresh cut flowers for decorating.

Care and Maintenance

Gladiolus requires a minimum of care, mostly weed control. Planting in poorly drained sites may result in bulb rotting diseases. Weed glad plantings by hand, or consult with an Extension agent or garden center operator about herbicides that are available for large plantings in the garden. Do not dig around the plants with a hoe, as you may disturb the roots. Glads are tolerant of drought, but they will have stronger flower scapes if irrigated as the blooming period begins. Mulch glad plantings only lightly to maintain moisture. Cut down the plants after the foliage dries and, if you live in one of the colder areas, dig the corms.

Additional Information

Staking gladiolus is required unless you plant dwarf cultivars. I have seen a few insect pests eating the flowers. Both Japanese beetles and thrips are common pests, and their presence may make it necessary to cut the glads early for use indoors. The stage for cutting glads is set when the first few flowers open.

Additional Species, Cultivars, or Varieties

There are hundreds of varieties of gladiolus and new ones appear every gardening season. Unless you have specific colors in mind for your flower garden, it is best to start with a mix of varieties. A companion plant is *Acidanthera*, referred to as "Orchid Lily" in some catalogs.

Magic Lily

*T*here is always a rush to purchase spring-flowering bulbs when they arrive at the garden shops in fall. It is unfortunate that only on a rare occasion will the buyer happen upon a package of magic lilies. (The "magic" in the name must in part refer to the euphoria experienced when you find the blessed little bulbs at a garden shop!) One of the first signs of life following a mid-July rainstorm is the sudden appearance of the long, green leafless stems of magic lilies. The flower stems grow to 24 inches and bear up to seven 3-inch trumpet-shaped pink flowers. These showy blooms are not only visually spectacular, but are mildly fragrant as well. Magic lilies are cold-hardy bulbous plants that can survive 20-below-zero winters in states to the north. Unlike the common red spider lily (*L. radiata*) that produces fall foliage after blooming, magic lily waits until winter to leaf out. The 2-foot-long dull green leaves wither and die as the warm days of May appear. Magic lilies are quite elegant, whether planted in groups or naturalized in beds of groundcovers. The sight of a few of these lilies popping out of mum beds in summer is truly . . . magical!

WHEN TO PLANT

Plant magic lily bulbs in August and September. If you are fortunate enough to have a gardening friend with a large patch of magic lilies, show up at this friend's house about the time the plant's leaves yellow in spring. Fading foliage is a good indication that the magic lily is dormant and ripe for transplanting.

WHERE TO PLANT

Magic lilies will thrive in sun to filtered shade. Like other bulbs, this plant would prefer a deep rich soil, but any well-drained soil should do fine. This *Lycoris* member should be planted where it can be observed frequently as the blooming drama unfolds. Plant in an entrance bed or by a sitting terrace or patio, or naturalize along a walk in a woodland area.

ZONE
6,7,8

How to Plant

Spade up an area that is 15 inches by 15 inches. Plant 3 bulbs in this space. Magic lilies like quick-draining soil. The addition of bark soil conditioner or granite screenings will improve the texture of tight clays. Mix the amendment and bulb-booster fertilizer into the planting area to a depth of 10 inches. Place the bulbs in the planting hole, spacing them 6 inches or more apart. Cover the bulbs with 4 to 5 inches of friable soil. Water well after planting the lily bulbs in order to settle the ground. In difficult, shallow soils, build the soil by stockpiling leaves in the beds. Add topsoil to the decomposing leaves, a practice that will raise the soil level and increase the life expectancy of your planting.

Care and Maintenance

Magic lilies do not like to be disturbed for many years after planting. They may be left in the ground for as long as 8 years or more without dividing. The best time to divide magic lilies is after the foliage dies down in late spring. They can be lifted at that time, air dried for several weeks, and replanted in June. Fertilize the bulbs in October, using a complete fertilizer such as 10-10-10, scattering it over the bed at a rate of 2 pounds per 100 square feet during the bloom period. If using bulb-booster fertilizer, apply at a rate of $1/2$ cup per 10 square feet. Water magic lilies as needed during bloom and in the winter months.

Additional Information

The long strap-like leaves of magic lily can add interest to the garden in winter. Prune back the foliage after the leaves yellow in warmer weather. Magic lily's flower stalks can be removed after the blooms fade if the stems are unsightly.

Additional Species, Cultivars, or Varieties

According to some experts, magic lily may be a hybrid. *L. haywardii* is a pink lily that is similar but is shorter and more adapted to warmer regions. *L. africana* 'Golden Hurricane Lily,' a yellow cultivar, blooms later. The airy red-flowered *L. radiata* 'Red Spider Lily' blooms in September. *L. albiflora* has pearl-white flowers on 14-inch stems and blooms in August.

Lilium spp.

Oriental Lily

" $\mathcal{C}$ onsider the lilies of the field . . ." This flowering bulb is a rare beauty. As far back as 1550 B.C., lilies have been revered for their exquisite flowers and heavenly fragrance. Artists have painted the likeness of the Madonna lily, *L. candidum,* for several millennium. The appeal of lilies is timeless. Oriental lilies are fast-growing tender bulbs that produce erect stems of narrow lustrous leaves. During the summer months in North Carolina, this stately plant produces up to 10 spectacular flat-faced blooms on 3- to 6-foot stalks. My favorite is 'Stargazer,' which I have grown both in a perennial border and in containers. When grown in the landscape in filtered sun, 'Stargazer' grows to 3 feet and produces wonderful freckled wine-colored blooms edged in white that measure up to 8 inches across. The Asiatic hybrids are considered simple to grow. Before the 1930s, lilies were thought to be the province of the wealthy, much like orchids. Only skilled plantsmen could revive the desiccated planting stock that was imported from the Far East. Today, with our modern storage capabilities and new hybrid lily varieties, these delightful bulbs are available to all gardeners, all year long.

WHEN TO PLANT

Lily bulbs can be planted in late fall or in early spring as soon as the ground thaws. Unlike tulips, lily bulbs are true bulbs with fleshy scales. They should be planted promptly, not left lying in the open to dry out. Container-grown lilies can be planted even while in bloom. Divide and transplant old established lily beds in the fall.

WHERE TO PLANT

Lilies will tolerate full sun in western North Carolina, but as you travel east, it is best to limit them to morning sun. Provide them with light shade, especially the pastel-colored lilies. Trees can provide the necessary shade, but their roots can rob them of moisture, so it is best to use other shade sources. Lilies prefer moist conditions, but avoid poorly drained planting sites. Plant them in groups for the best effect, and interplant them with perennials for color.

How to Plant

Lilies require a well-drained, moist, organic-rich soil. That's asking a
lot of any region in the Tar Heel State! The soil type is not as important, however, as is good drainage. Do not lime the soil for lilies, as
they prefer an acidic soil. Large amounts of sphagnum peat moss or
a little sulfur will acidify marginally alkaline soils. In areas where
sticky clay soils predominate, lilies do well in raised beds or berms.
To insure good planting conditions, especially in clay soils, double-
dig the bed. This means that you remove the top 6 inches of soil
and spade soil conditioner and bulb fertilizer into the 6 inches or
so of soil beneath. Plant the bulbs 3 to 5 inches deep. Cover them
with soil, water well, and mulch.

Care and Maintenance

Provided you have enriched the soil with compost or pine-bark soil
conditioner, your lilies will not need much in the way of nutrients
during the first growing season. In fact, too much nitrogen is harmful to lilies. Water them weekly during the flowering period, at the
rate of 1 inch of water per week. Don't overwater, as this will rot the
bulbs! Oriental lilies require staking in windy locations. Most garden
shops carry green bamboo stakes and "twist'ems" for this job. After
a hard freeze, cut the stalks back and mulch the beds.

Additional Information

When planning a bed, remember that lilies like "their heads in the
sun and their feet in the shade." Too much heat will cause the flowers to be short-lived. Most gardeners grow Oriental lilies for cut
flowers. When cutting the flowers, leave at least half the stem and
leaves to nourish the bulb for the next year. Remember that lily
pollen will stain clothing!

Additional Species, Cultivars, or Varieties

The American Lily Society developed a system of 9 divisions to clas-
sify the extensively hybridized lily family. Oriental lily is in Division
7. 'Stargazer' grows to 3 feet and offers carmine blooms in June.
'Jamboree' grows to 6 feet and has rose to white fragrant flowers.
'Black Beauty' grows to 7 feet and has recurved red flowers with
green centers. The flowers of 'Imperial Silver,' which grows to 6 feet,
are white with maroon spots.

Tuberose

*W*ant an old-fashioned garden favorite with a fragrance to beat the band? Look no further—tuberoses are tops! This member of the lily family is a tender bulb that grows in clumps of grass-like leaves similar to *Liriope*. From July to October, 2- to 3-foot-tall spikes emerge and white, waxy flowers appear. The individual I-inch flowers open from the bottom upward. Cut the spikes when the flowers are 1/3 fully open. Prized by florists, the cut flowers are intensely fragrant and long-lasting. A double-flowered variation exists, and though it may be a conversation piece, it has a poor-quality flowerhead and is less aromatic than the single-flowered variations. While working in the Wilmington area some years ago, I discovered that country folks in the Coastal counties often plant a short row of tuberoses alongside asparagus and strawberries. In western North Carolina and in the Piedmont, tuberoses are dug out of the garden in November and stored in boxes inside for the winter. The tuberose's roots can be divided and replanted the following spring.

WHEN TO PLANT

Plant tuberose in the spring after the last frost in your area. You will know the soil has warmed up sufficiently when oak leaves are reaching full size.

WHERE TO PLANT

Tuberose will flourish in any well-drained garden soil from clay to sandy loam. For continuous flowering, full sun is important. While most Tar Heels grow tuberoses in rows, they can be planted in groups of 3 to 5 clumps in the perennial garden. As with gladiolus, the planting dates can be staggered by a month or so to spread out the blooms.

HOW TO PLANT

Tuberose can be purchased from mail-order nurseries in packets of a few bulbs. Consider yourself lucky if you can buy them by the bushel from a local grower or gardener. (Check the North Carolina Agricultural Review Newspaper for farm sources). Plant tuberose in soil that is spaded deeply and enriched with 5-10-10 or bulb

BULBS

fertilizer. Overwintered clumps can be separated easily in the spring after the soil on the roots has dried. Clumps that are fist-size are preferred for good flower production. (As is true of diamonds, bigger is better when it comes to buying tuberoses!) After opening the planting hole, place the clumps in it, pointed tops up. Cover with 2 inches of soil and firm the clumps well.

Care and Maintenance

After planting your tuberoses, keep the soil moist until they grow 4 inches high. Water weekly as flowering begins. Sidedress with 10-20-20 fertilizer in midsummer (1 pound per 100 square feet). Do not use a borated fertilizer, as this will spoil the blooms. Tuberoses are tolerant of pre-emergent herbicides, making weed control a snap. Tuberoses are generally planted in rows in the garden. Pine needles or leaf mulch can be used between rows to keep the plants clean. When the middles are mulched well, it is easier to get into the garden following a rain. Carry a bucket of water with you when you cut flowers, and put the flower stems promptly in the water to condition them.

Additional Information

Keep your tuberose flower spikes cut as they bloom out by removing the stems all the way back to the foliage. Water during dry periods. When storing for the winter, spread the clumps out in single layers in cardboard boxes that are left open or perforated for air vents.

Additional Species, Cultivars, or Varieties

The species, *P. tuberosa*, is the variety used in the trade and shared by gardeners. Though the double-flowered form is unique, it is not held in high esteem by growers. Another tuberose species occasionally mentioned in the literature is *P. geminiflora* (Florida's twin flower). It is a red species with low fragrance that is generally grown south of North Carolina.

Tulip

*T*here was a time when 3 tulip bulbs could be sold to pay for a house. That time was in the 1630s in the Netherlands, a time when elitist Europeans lusted for exotic garden flowers. Nowadays, sensational tulip bulbs sell 3 for a dollar, a bargain any way you look at it. With hundreds of Dutch bulb varieties to choose from, the color opportunities are boundless. Varieties include peony-flowered, singles, fringed, parrot, and the diminutive species tulips which grow to only 6 inches tall. The biggest and showiest of all the tulips are the Darwin hybrids which flower through April and May in North Carolina on stems to 24 inches high. Studies conducted at North Carolina State University in the 1980s by my former professors, Doctors Nelson and DeHertogh, helped unravel the mystery of why tulips have a high mortality rate in the warm Tar Heel State. It was long felt that it was just "too hot" in the South for tulips to perennialize. The wise professors made some discoveries that led to the formulation of a special bulb fertilizer and a list of tulip cultivars that are dependable when planted in our gardens. We now know that fabulous tulips can be enjoyed in gardens for years when we pay attention to bed preparation, varieties, and fertilization.

WHEN TO PLANT

These bulbs should be planted when the soil cools in the fall, that is, from the time of the first frost until Thanksgiving. An adequate root system must develop before the ground freezes. Tulip bulbs can be divided in early summer after the foliage yellows and dies.

WHERE TO PLANT

Tulips are generally very easy to grow. Like all bulbous plants, they need sunlight and fertile, well-drained soil. It is more important for tulips than for most other bulbs that the soil be loose and well drained—the mother bulb disintegrates after flowering, and a complete new bulb must form for the plant to bloom again or perennialize. The best practice is to plant tulips in raised beds or in borders.

BULBS

How to Plant

Keep in mind that tulips don't survive in poorly aerated soils. This is the reason I do not own a bulb planter. (A bulb auger for an electric drill may be an acceptable tool for fracturing clay soils when planting small numbers of bulbs.) For durable tulip plantings, it is important that the soil be tested and adjusted to a pH of 5.4 to 7.0. To aerate the soil, work it to a depth of 12 inches and add quantities of pine-bark soil conditioner (for example, spade under a 3-inch layer of pine bark). At planting time, use a bulb-booster fertilizer at the rate given on the label. Tulips can be planted in a trench in the border or in groups of 9 to 15 for the best effect. Plant the bulbs 4 to 6 inches deep and 5 inches apart. Water the bed and mulch well.

Care and Maintenance

The most important maintenance chore is to fertilize bulb beds twice each year. The first application should be in mid-September, the second application when the plants emerge from the soil in late winter. A general fertilizer such as 10-10-10 can be used at a rate of 2.5 pounds per 100 square feet of bed. For large bulb plantings, one application of bulb-booster in early fall will suffice. Water bulb beds during a drought. Don't cut the foliage of tulips until the leaves yellow naturally in June! You may cut tulips for fresh flower arrangements, but leave as much foliage on the plant as possible.

Additional Information

After several years, dig the tulips from the bed when the foliage dies. Spread them in the sun for a week to or so to dry. Toss out the weak ones after dividing. Store your tulips in a cool basement until fall planting time. Many gardeners have lost bulbs to voles. Methods to combat voles include the use of snap traps, poisons, or gravel in beds.

Additional Species, Cultivars, or Varieties

Your Extension Center can provide you with a list of dependable cultivars cited in the 1980s tulip study. Early tulips include Fosterana and Greigii, which have striped leaves. Midseason tulips include the Darwin hybrids 'Parade' and 'Golden Parade.' Late-season tulips are Lily Flowered, Fringe, Parrot, and 'Double/Peony.'

Deciduous Trees

IN STUDIES OF RESIDENTIAL REAL ESTATE VALUES, building lots that had trees brought market prices that were twenty to thirty percent higher than prices of similar lots without trees. Strategically placed trees can significantly reduce the cost of cooling a home by providing much-needed shade during the summer months—these are nature's air conditioners, absorbing heat as they transpire. In addition to the natural beauty they provide, shade trees can be a financial asset!

With increasing concerns over air quality, the public should recognize that planting trees is a cost-effective way to clean the air in urban communities. Carbon dioxide production is a major factor in global warming, and a single mature tree consumes thirteen pounds of carbon dioxide every year.

Deciduous trees, the trees that drop their leaves in autumn, are often selected because they allow the winter sun to warm our houses in the Old North State. The largest specimens, like the oaks, are known for their long lives and majestic forms, while others provide spectacular fall color and ornamental appeal. Still others, like the gingko, are ancient trees with a history as rich as that of humankind. Shade trees can frame a house the way a beautiful picture frame enhances a lasting work of art. While North Carolina is represented by the longleaf pine, a superb evergreen tree with endless utility, most residents are more passionate about the dogwood, our State Flower. The dogwood is a native flowering tree whose spring beauty is unsurpassed. Though a fungal disease known as dogwood blight has caused concerns about the dog-

Chapter Three

wood's survival, the climate in North Carolina continues to be favorable for this marvelous tree. New introductions of dogwoods ensure that this deciduous tree will be found in our gardens for many decades to come.

Spring announces its arrival in this state with a parade of redbuds, Japanese cherries, saucer magnolias, and, of course, dogwoods in full, resplendent bloom. Fall mirrors the floral display of spring with dazzling colors of other hues. The fall show that envelops the Tar Heel State begins in early October on the lofty peaks of the Blue Ridge Mountains and gradually winds its way across the Piedmont to the Coastal Plains by month's end. The seasonal spectacular displays by deciduous trees ensure that tourism will remain a strong influence on North Carolina's economy.

During the dreary winter months, many of these prized ornamentals provide colorful berries for our enjoyment and for the sustenance of migrating birds. The seedpods and berries that follow the handsome flowers are a special treat in the garden. Boughs laden with snow provide a "photo op" for gardeners anxious to capture a cardinal feasting near a window.

One characteristic often overlooked among deciduous trees is exfoliating bark. The visual appeal of a crape myrtle is often not apparent until the winter season. Learn to recognize the characteristics that are subtle on many landscape trees, and plant them where these traits can be appreciated.

Bradford Pear

For more than 2 decades, Bradford pear was the prima donna of North Carolina landscapes. Its reputation as a durable landscape tree has of late been tainted because of the numerous damaging storms and hurricanes striking the state. But in spite of its brittle wood and poor branch structure, Bradford pears continue to be planted like there's no tomorrow. Bradford pear is a hard tree to walk away from at the nursery—it has very rich, green foliage and is unsurpassed in beauty when in bloom. It matures to 45 feet in height and 20 feet in width, and bears magnificent clusters of white flowers each spring. Its exceptional red fall color is second only to that of our glorious red maples. Bradford pear is the last tree to come into full autumn coloration. It holds its blazing coat well into mid-November in the Piedmont region. Bradford pear is a rapid grower with few pest problems. If the tree is carefully selected and given remedial pruning while it is still young, much of the branch splitting can be avoided.

WHEN TO PLANT

Plant Bradford pear during the dormant season in fall or late winter. Container-grown trees can be planted whenever the ground can be prepared.

WHERE TO PLANT

Your Bradford pear needs a lot of room to grow, as it is not a small tree. Find a location that gets full sun and has good soil drainage. This pear makes an excellent lawn, street, or background tree. Many residents use it as a "tall privacy" screen. Please do not plant Bradford pears under power lines, unless of course, you appreciate topped trees. The spring color is especially attractive in bulb beds.

HOW TO PLANT

Loosen the roots of pot-grown plants so they can be straightened out in the planting hole. Prepare a wide hole 3 times as wide as the rootball. Pack the soil from the hole firmly around the sides of the rootball. Water twice while backfilling and firming the soil. Stake the tree with 2 8-foot stakes driven deeply into the soil just outside the planting hole. Form an earthen mound in a circle right at the edge of

the hole. This will help channel water to the rootball during a rain and facilitate irrigation of the tree. Then water well. Apply a 3-inch layer of mulch. Avoid planting when soil is frozen or when soil is wet enough to form a mudball.

CARE AND MAINTENANCE
Using a handheld open-ended hose, water newly planted trees for 10 minutes every third day for the first 2 or 3 weeks. Once the roots are established, water deeply as needed, usually every 7 to 10 days. Any pruning should be performed in summer or late winter. Remove double leaders on young trees to avoid problems later. Use a slow-release fertilizer formulation with a 12-6-6 ratio at the rate of 2 cups per 10 square feet in April. Broadcast it under the canopy of the tree and a little beyond. Watering is extremely important for newly planted trees during the first couple of summers. Maintain a ring of mulch around the roots to help conserve moisture.

ADDITIONAL INFORMATION
When planting balled-and-burlapped trees, cut away the burlap. Remove nylon string or synthetic burlap. Plant with the wire baskets, but cut the top vertical wires. A Bradford pear is grafted; often thorny suckers will sprout up from the base. Keep these removed or they will overtake the top of the plant. Purchase only high-quality pear trees!

ADDITIONAL SPECIES, CULTIVARS, OR VARIETIES
Because it is resistant to fireblight, a fatal bacterial disease, 'Bradford' is the best cultivar of *P. calleryana*. 'Aristocrat' has an oval crown with orange-red fall color and is tolerant of heavy soils. The narrow 'Red Spires,' which has a yellow fall color, is susceptible to fireblight. U.S. Arboretum selection 'Capitol' is very columnar and has a burgundy fall color.

Halesia tetraptera

Carolina Silverbell

This attractive understory tree is a North Carolina gem. It is a small deciduous tree that is found growing in moist, rich soil along streams and bottoms in the western regions of the state. The name silverbell comes from the early spring clusters of white bell-shaped flowers that adorn this small rounded tree. Its small leaves are a deep green color. Carolina silverbell offers a low-maintenance alternative to the popular Japanese cherries found in most residential landscapes. Its abundant beautiful white flowers with golden centers are reason enough to find a suitable place for this lovely tree in your garden. Growing to a mature height of near 40 feet, Carolina silverbell can become an impressive specimen tree in partially shaded areas. To be successful in planting Carolina silverbell, it is important to find a location where the soil will stay moist during the growing period. Many gardeners find the tree does well on the north side of a house or in the shadows of large majestic oaks. Most ornamental trees prefer drier soil, but this beauty can have wet feet and thrive. Carolina silverbell makes a beautiful picture when planted with spring-flowering bulbs, saucer magnolias, and Kurume azaleas.

WHEN TO PLANT

Carolina silverbell can be planted successfully between November and March. When I purchase it as a balled-and-burlapped specimen, I prefer to plant it before the ground freezes in winter. Many garden centers offer small container-grown seedlings that will transplant well even while they are flowering.

WHERE TO PLANT

Carolina silverbell should be planted in rich, moist soil that is well drained. It will grow slowly in full sun, but it is happier in partial shade. When designing your color garden, remember to choose early-flowering plants as companions to your silverbell. Use silverbell as a lawn tree or as an accent specimen.

HOW TO PLANT

Dig a shallow hole that is twice as wide as the rootball's diameter and 3/4 as deep (for example, the planting hole for a 20-inch rootball

DECIDUOUS TREES

should be 40 inches wide and 15 inches deep). Cut the twine from the trunk, but leave the burlap on the ball, cutting it back when you plant. There is no need to loosen the roots. If you have a container-grown tree, however, untangle the roots and spread them out in the planting hole. Make a mix of ⅓ coarse organic humus and ⅔ existing topsoil for the backfill. Pack firmly around the sides of the rootball. Water well and finish by covering the top of the exposed roots with the mix. A 3-inch layer of leaf compost or mulch can then be applied.

CARE AND MAINTENANCE

Carolina silverbells are well adapted to our garden soils. The key element in maintenance is moisture. Water newly planted trees twice weekly for the first month, and later during periods of drought. Well-mulched trees need very little fertilizer—in fact, you can kill a young tree during the first several years by overfertilizing it. Consider applying a slow-release nursery special fertilizer if you notice the tree is lacking its rich, green color or is not growing vigorously. Apply this product as the flowers fade. Because dropping blooms make a slippery surface, plant your silverbell at least 10 feet from a walk or patio.

ADDITIONAL INFORMATION

You may wish to prune your silverbell to train it to a desirable form for cosmetic purposes. As the tree matures, prune out weak branches, especially on the lower half. Seedpods may form on the tree, adding more seasonal interest. There are no serious insects or disease pests to justify spraying.

ADDITIONAL SPECIES, CULTIVARS, OR VARIETIES

'Rosea' is a beautiful pink cultivar. *Halesia diptera*, "two-winged silverbell," is a smaller tree that grows to 25 feet; it is named for the 2-inch winged fruit it produces. This species is being evaluated in sites across North Carolina as part of an Urban Tree Evaluation Study started in 1994. *H. monticola* 'Mt. Silverbell,' suited for Zones 5 and 6, grows to 70 feet.

Crape Myrtle

Crape myrtles are striking landscape trees, the glory of summer in North Carolina. Because of their long period of bloom, they are called the "flower of one hundred days" in China. In July, their terminal clusters of flowers are dense with brilliantly colored ruffled petals. Crape myrtles are at their zenith when grown as multitrunk specimens. Not unlike birches, their peeling bark reveals creamy shades of tan and twisted, muscle-like wood. The *L. fauriei* 'Townhouse,' a North Carolina State University Arboretum introduction, has outstanding dark-red bark and pure-white flower clusters. It makes an excellent focal point in the winter garden. Standard crape myrtles grow in a vase shape to a height of 15 to 25 feet; dwarf crape myrtles remain under 4 feet. Crape myrtles thrive in hot, sunny locations and will grow in almost any type of soil that drains well. They are very drought resistant. These lovely trees flower on new growth formed in the spring. Remove the fading flower clusters before the seedpods form in late summer, and you will be rewarded with another flush of colorful blooms. The small, rounded leaves are dark green and glossy.

WHEN TO PLANT

Plant field-dug balled-and-burlapped crape myrtles in early spring. Container-grown specimens can be planted any time from spring through fall. If transplanting established plants from one place to another in the landscape, do it in late winter or in spring. Seeds are available for the dwarf crape myrtles; sow these in late spring.

WHERE TO PLANT

Unless your crape myrtles have plenty of sun, there will only be sparse flowering. Shady locations may also mean problems with powdery mildew disease. These trees like moist, slightly acidic soils (pH 5.5) and good soil drainage. Crape myrtles are frequently planted in groups that are underplanted with groundcovers. For a contemporary look, use them judiciously in foundations, in courtyard gardens, and in color borders.

How to Plant

Spade up an area that is twice as wide as the diameter of the root-ball and equal in depth to the diameter. In heavy clay soils, plant the rootball so 1/2 is above the soil level. Position the rootball in the planting hole and backfill with the original soil. Fill the hole halfway with the soil, tamping out air pockets. Pour 4 gallons of water to settle the soil. Complete backfilling with the soil and form an earthen watering dam at the edge of the planting hole. Pour on another 4 gallons of water, then mulch with 2 inches of hardwood or bark mulch. There is no benefit to pruning crape myrtles at planting time other than to remove broken branches. Fertilizer planting tablets can be used with large specimens.

Care and Maintenance

Lack of water during the first growing season is a major cause of tree loss. Until they are well established, crape myrtles have a high moisture requirement. Fertilize the trees in May each year or as new growth begins. A general garden fertilizer or nursery product is acceptable; use 1/2 pound per inch of trunk diameter. Most people prefer to train their crape myrtle into a small single or multitrunk tree. In this case, prune off the side branches on the lower half to expose the trunk. Remove basal suckers as they appear. Never top these trees or you will ruin their form. Remove seedpods!

Additional Information

Prune crape myrtles in April by cutting below the former seedheads. The wood you remove will be pencil-size or slightly larger. To prevent cold injury, do not overfertilize or prune hard in the fall. Blackening leaves in the summer is an indication of an aphid infestation. Use an oil spray or registered insecticide in early summer as a preventive measure.

Additional Species, Cultivars, or Varieties

The United States National Arboretum has released many disease-resistant crape myrtle cultivars, most carrying names of Indian tribes. The Greensboro Arboretum has a great collection of labeled crape myrtles. Cultivars include 'Cherokee' (red), 'Natchez' (white), and 'Potomac' (clear pink). Dwarfs are 'Victor,' 'Hope,' and the unusual-flowered 'Peppermint Lace.'

Cornus florida

Dogwood

Many residents think this tree is our state tree, when in fact dogwood is the state *flower* of North Carolina. Dogwood deserves the accolades it receives from its admirers. In general, it is a small low-branching tree with spreading horizontal limbs, but in the wild it can grow up to 40 feet. When grown in a shady area, it will grow flat on top and the blooms will have a layered effect. The dogwood is probably our most popular flowering tree. Most gardeners feel that spring has arrived when the dogwoods bloom. They make beautiful understory trees that bloom in the spring in abundant white and some pink. Though dogwood blooms mean spring to us in the South, we also enjoy the fall color change that slowly occurs from September through October. Because of the big scare over the fatal "dogwood blight" (Discula anthracnose), it is reassuring that there are some new introductions coming on the market—most notably the 'Stellar' series and many fine cultivars. If it is important to you that your landscape be distinguished as truly Southern, it could be argued that having a dogwood in your yard is just as important as having a southern magnolia.

WHEN TO PLANT

Unlike most deciduous trees, the dogwood is best planted in spring rather than fall. This is particularly true of balled-and-burlapped plants. Purchase healthy grafted trees, and leave the seedlings in the woods. Container-grown trees are readily available and can be planted in the spring or fall.

WHERE TO PLANT

Plant your new dogwood in an area with well-drained, highly organic acidic soil. If your tree has been nursery grown, it will tolerate full sun or partial shade. Plant this tree as a specimen, or in groups of trees for a truly spectacular spring accent. It is a native understory tree and is perfect for the woodland garden. Use dogwoods in mixed borders of spring-flowering bulbs and ornamental shrubs such as azaleas.

ZONE
6,7,8

How to Plant

Dig a hole that is ³/₄ as deep and twice as wide as the rootball (for example, a 24-inch ball's hole should be 48 inches wide). Cut the twine from the trunk, but leave the burlap on the ball when you plant. There is no need to loosen the roots. Firm the soil around the sides of the rootball. Form an earthen mound on the edge of the planting hole to facilitate irrigations. The properly planted dogwood will be 5 inches or more above the soil line. Plant it even higher in poorly drained soils. Add 2 to 3 inches of mulch on top of the ball. Water well following planting and twice each week for one month. Avoid planting when the ground is frozen or muddy.

Care and Maintenance

For a new tree, use a slow trickle of water from a hose for a period of time equal to one minute per inch of diameter of the rootball. Repeat twice that week and, thereafter, weekly until the tree is firmly established (usually one growing season). Dogwoods can be pruned immediately following bloom. It is best to avoid pruning during the borer season in June and July. You may want to remove crossing branches and some inner branches to promote an appealing shape and good airflow. Fertilize every 2 years or so with 10-10-10 at a rate of ¹/₂ pound per inch of trunk diameter.

Additional Information

Spotted leaves will indicate the presence of "Spot Anthracnose," a disease that is unsightly but not life-threatening. The dogwood borer is a major threat to weak or scarred trees under stress. Look for holes the size of pencil points to indicate this condition. The new 'Stellar' series like C. 'Rutdan' offers beautiful trees that are resistant to Discula disease.

Additional Species, Cultivars, or Varieties

'Cherokee Princess' is the best white-flowering cultivar and has an upright form. 'Cherokee Chief' has ruby-red flowers. The precocious 'Barton' has large white blooms. White 'Fragrant Cloud' has a slight fragrance. 'Cherokee Daybreak' is a variegated white. 'Cherokee Sunset' is a variegated red. The rare 'Pluribracteata' has double flowers. 'Rubra' has rose-colored flowers.

Eastern Redbud

*R*edbuds in full bloom are among the most striking sights of spring. Occasionally in the wild you find flowering dogwood growing alongside them. What a sight these companions make! Redbud's lavender pea-like flowers herald the arrival of spring as they often burst into bloom slightly ahead of its compatriot's flowers. This small, vase-shaped tree forms a dense round canopy of heart-shaped leaves by early summer. With a height to 25 feet, redbud is recommended by Duke Power Company as a good choice for planting under power lines. When "limbed up," it creates a marvelous oasis for outdoor lounging when you want to be shielded from the summer sun. Multitrunk specimens of the outstanding *Cercis reniformis* 'Oklahoma' redbud are real show-stoppers; this redbud is rated higher than the eastern redbud by some authorities. The J. C. Raulston Arboretum in Raleigh has the largest collection of redbuds in the world.

WHEN TO PLANT
Plant seedlings during the dormant season before bud swell. Container-grown trees can be planted successfully in spring or fall as well.

WHERE TO PLANT
Redbuds grow well in light shade to full sun, in moist soils from clay to loam. They are fairly adaptable, as evidenced by the wide range of native habits. Redbuds are perfectly at home on the fringes of a woodland garden where there's protection from the south sun. A backdrop of evergreens will cause the redbud's lavender flowers to leap out visually. Avoid waterlogged locations where water stands following a rain.

HOW TO PLANT
Dig a shallow hole that is twice as wide and 3/4 as deep as the diameter of the rootball (for example, a 20-inch ball's hole should be 40 inches wide and 15 inches deep). Cut the twine from the trunk, but leave the burlap on the ball, cutting it back when you plant. There is no need to loosen the roots. When planting on new urban homesites

DECIDUOUS TREES

make a mix of 1/3 coarse organic humus and 2/3 existing topsoil for the backfill. Pack firmly around the sides of the rootball. Water well, then cover the top of the exposed roots with the mix. A 2- to 3-inch layer of mulch can then be applied.

CARE AND MAINTENANCE

Redbuds are very adaptable with little care. As long as the leaves are a rich green color, do not be concerned about fertilization. In the spring following the first full growing season, apply a slow-release nursery fertilizer at the rate of 1 pound per inch of trunk diameter (measure the trunk at 4 feet above ground, or chest height). Do not fertilize for another 2 or 3 years. Prune out wild shoots arising from the trunk, or prune to shape the young tree. Water twice weekly for the first 6 weeks and, after that, during dry weather. If a fungal dieback occurs, prune out individual branches promptly.

ADDITIONAL INFORMATION

Large redbuds from the woods struggle to survive transplanting unless root pruning is done correctly. Begin root pruning by August for spring plantings. Fruit pods on this tree may be unsightly to some folks, while they are an interesting landscape feature to others. Beauty is in the eye of the beholder!

ADDITIONAL SPECIES, CULTIVARS, OR VARIETIES

'Forest Pansy' has deep-purple lustrous leaves. 'Oklahoma' (*C. reniformis*) has glossy foliage that is burgundy in the spring. 'Texas White' (*C. reniformis*) offers a profusion of white flowers. The floriferous 'Avondale' (*C. chinensis*) is a shrubby Chinese redbud.

Flowering Crab Apple

*F*inding a disease-resistant crab apple will be the start of a life-long relationship with this member of the rose family. Noted for its beauty when in spring bloom, crab apple is wrongfully maligned for premature leaf drop caused by chronic leaf spot diseases. Today these leaf spot diseases are avoidable; there are literally hundreds of named varieties and more disease-resistant introductions appear every year. Although they range from 6 to 40 feet tall, most grow to about 15 to 20 feet tall. Growth habits vary from rounded to upright to weeping, with few exceptions. As evidenced by their popularity in the Midwestern states, these trees are extremely cold hardy. Like their close cousins the apples, crab apples are found in every county in the state. This is a testimony to their tolerance of a wide range of soils, including heavy clay soils. When in flower, this spectacular tree is covered with white, pink, or rosy-red apple blossoms. Though the flowering period is 10 days or less, the trees don't succumb to borers and short-life problems as do Japanese cherries and flowering plums. Varieties with persistent fruit add winter interest and a food supply for wildlife in the colder months.

WHEN TO PLANT

Plant your new crab apple from late winter through fall. Container-grown trees may be planted any time the soil is prepared and care can be provided.

WHERE TO PLANT

Locate a spot where there is plenty of sun and good air circulation. The soil must drain well to prevent shallow roots, or worst yet, root rot. Crab apple is good for specimen planting, especially the weeping forms. This tree is nice for mass planting in large yards or in parks. Avoid planting by a walk or patio where the fruit can create a hazardous mess.

HOW TO PLANT

Dig a hole that is equal in depth to the rootball and twice its width. Cut the twine from the trunk, leaving the burlap on the ball. Fold the burlap back into the hole after positioning the ball. There is no

need to loosen the roots. Use the soil from the hole for the backfill. When planting containter-grown trees, make a mix of 3 parts topsoil and 1 part bark mulch for backfilling. Pack firmly around the sides of the rootball. After planting, construct an earthen dam 4 inches high around the dripzone area of the tree. Water will collect in this saucer and move down into the rootball area. Add 2 to 3 inches of mulch on top of the ball. Water well.

CARE AND MAINTENANCE

For a new tree, slowly trickle water from a hose for a period of time equal to one minute per inch of diameter of the rootball. Repeat each week for the first month and biweekly thereafter until the tree is firmly established, which usually happens after one growing season. During the early years, some light pruning will be needed to train the tree. Once your crab apple begins to mature, pruning is a must for best flowering appeal. It's best to prune in late summer to prevent switches of suckers from appearing in the pruning cuts. Always prune back to the main trunk or to the branch's point of origin.

ADDITIONAL INFORMATION

Crab apple can be fertilized between November and March, but the best fertilizing time is in spring. Use a general fertilizer such as 10-10-10. Fertilizer application should be figured at a rate of one pound per inch of trunk diameter. Beware of Apple Rust and Apple Scab diseases. If fungicides are used, they must be applied just as the leaves are unfurling.

ADDITIONAL SPECIES, CULTIVARS, OR VARIETIES

'Narragansett' is a white, disease-resistant National Arboretum introduction with carmine buds. 'Donald Wyman' tops the list for disease resistance; it is white and has red fruit. 'Prairiefire' has a round form and burgundy fruit. 'Callaway' is white and has 1-inch red fruit. 'Louisa' is pink with yellow fruit. The weeping 'Red Jade' has white flowers and cherry-red fruit. White 'Sugar Tyme' has red fruit.

Fruitless Sweet Gum

OTHER COMMON NAME: 'Rotundiloba'

Gardeners in North Carolina have very little that is good to say about our native sweet gums. In fact, most curse these trees with their 2-inch spiny gumballs. This common hardwood tree does have its place, but it should be relegated to a natural area where the gumballs will not be a source of aggravation. There is, however, a new premier cultivar for sweet gum lovers: 'Rotundiloba.' This stately tree has all the beauty and luster of the species but it lacks the awful fruit. The fruitless sweet gum grows to 60 feet in height and has the signature 5-lobed starlike leaves of the species. Its fall color is brilliant with yellow and dark burgundy. You can distinguish this variety from the native sweet gums by the rounded lobes on its leaves. 'Rotundiloba' is quite columnar in form when young, but it takes on a wide-spreading pyramidal shape as it matures. Give it a couple of years to establish itself, and it will grow "to beat the band"! If you have an area that is constantly moist, you have a good spot for sweet gums. The wonderful fall color and large glossy leaves of 'Rotundiloba' are the stuff that memories are made of, and these trees outlast the best.

WHEN TO PLANT

Plant the fruitless sweet gum in late winter or early spring. Container-grown specimens have a longer planting season, and they can be put in the ground almost any time of the year. These sweet gums are grafted on native rootstocks. If you have had good luck grafting fruit trees in winter, you might give this one a try.

WHERE TO PLANT

Sweet gums are tolerant of a wide range of soil conditions. Though they prefer a moist, well-drained location, I have seen them grow well in drier upland sites. 'Rotundiloba' grows into a large specimen tree and should be planted at least 20 feet from a house. It can be used to provide marvelous shade for a patio or deck. Plant it in a sunny place so that the most intense fall color will develop.

HOW TO PLANT

Most of the 'Rotundiloba' sweet gums are sold in large containers. Field-grown balled-and-burlapped stock will eventually be readily available. At planting time, dig a hole that is 1 to 2 feet wider than the rootball. (A larger hole is always preferred, as this will encourage roots to forage out more quickly.) No amendments are necessary. Loosen the soil in the bottom of the hole, then firm the bottom soil before setting the tree. See that the tree sets at the same level as it was in the container, or a few inches higher. Frill out the roots that are circling. Fill around the roots with the backfill soil, firming with your foot as you add topsoil. Form an earthen dam, then water thoroughly with 8 gallons of water.

CARE AND MAINTENANCE

Following tree planting, water deeply with a garden hose set at a slow trickle. Each week, water for 30 minutes or until the soil is saturated. Using leaf compost or hardwood bark, mulch to form a ring in a radius to 3 feet from the trunk. Maintain this 3-inch-deep ring indefinitely. After the first year, prune your new tree to train it: eliminate double leaders and very narrow branch crotch angles. Given plenty of room to grow and develop, your 'Rotundiloba' will need practically no maintenance other than raking leaves in the fall. Fertilize your tree with a nitrogen fertilizer (16-4-8) in March every 3 years.

ADDITIONAL INFORMATION

Though an occasional caterpillar or a few aphids may be found on any plant, pests particular to fruitless sweet gum don't exist. Wash minor pests off the tree with a garden hose. When pruning mature trees, be sure to remove the branches properly. Prune outside of the branch collar for tree health. Always prune back to a side limb, or take a limb off at the trunk.

ADDITIONAL SPECIES, CULTIVARS, OR VARIETIES

There are many wonderful cultivars of the native sweet gum, but the only fruitless variety is 'Rotundiloba.' Good cultivars include 'Levis' (good fall color), 'Festival' (an upright form), 'Burgundy' (deep-red fall color), 'Gumball' (a round shrub form, cold sensitive), 'Palo Alto' (orange-red in fall, pyramidal shape), and 'Moraine' (rapid grower with glossy leaves).

Ginkgo

OTHER COMMON NAME: Maidenhair Tree

*I*t is impossible to talk about ginkgo without the topic of sex coming up. Why sex? Because only the male ginkgo tree is suitable for the home landscape—its mate produces large, foul-smelling fruit. I have seen the females in commercial plantings and can verify that when it comes to *ginkgoes*, females are the weaker sex. Ginkgo is a native of China. Though it is a deciduous broadleaf tree, it has ancestral ties with conifers. It is an excellent slow-growing landscape tree with brilliant yellow fall color. Its distinctive fan-shaped leaves are 2 to 4 inches wide. The leaves bear a striking resemblance to those of maidenhair fern, the tree's namesake. The leaves drop abruptly and can be quickly removed for composting. Ginkgo tolerates urban conditions. It is highly acclaimed as a street tree, growing to a height of 70 feet. The finest old specimens are scattered across the state from town squares to grand Southern estates. And yes, this is the plant that serves as a source for the ginkgo "health supplement." The seeds are an Oriental delicacy.

WHEN TO PLANT

The best time to plant your ginkgo tree is from November through March. A tree that has been dug while dormant, healed in, or conditioned may be planted at any time.

WHERE TO PLANT

Ginkgos like full sun and fertile soils for fastest growth. Once established, they will adapt to poor, dry soils, but they will grow very slowly. These stately trees are used as specimen plants for a formal accent in the garden. Their open canopy casts fragmented shadows on the ground below, which is ideal for many shade-loving perennials.

DECIDUOUS TREES

How to Plant

Avoid planting when the ground is frozen or muddy. Dig a hole that is twice as wide as the diameter of the rootball and half as deep. Cut the twine from the trunk, but leave the burlap on the ball when you plant. There is no need to loosen the roots. The loose soil should be used as backfill. Pack firmly around the sides of the rootball and form an earthen basin after filling the hole. Add 2 to 3 inches of mulch on top of the ball. Water well by pouring on 4 gallons of water at planting.

Care and Maintenance

Water your ginkgo tree with a slow trickle of water from a hose for a period of time equal to 1 minute per inch of diameter of the root-ball. Repeat this watering 2 times each week for the first month and every 2 weeks thereafter until the tree is firmly established. This usually takes one growing season. When in doubt, check the soil's moisture before watering by digging down through the mulch into the backfill soil. The ginkgo needs very little pruning, but if it is needed, prune in winter or summer. Fertilize in November or March using a fertilizer high in nitrogen, one with a 3-1-2 analysis or similar.

Additional Information

The best feature of your new ginkgo is that it is virtually pest- and maintenance-free! Sit back and enjoy. Your tree will be the envy of your garden club and neighborhood when it matures.

Additional Species, Cultivars, or Varieties

'Aurea' has bright yellow leaves. 'Fastigiata' has an upright form. 'Laciniata' has leaves that are deeply divided. 'Pyramidalis,' a patented tree, is strongly pyramidal.

Heritage River Birch

*M*any people think river birch needs a wet site to flourish, but many gardeners have discovered this is not true. Provided there is space for this beautiful native tree, we can enjoy its marvelous features practically anywhere in the home landscape. 'Heritage' is the most desirable birch cultivar since it has showy grayish-white bark like its Northern cousin, the European white birch. Though this cousin is short-lived in North Carolina, Heritage river birch will tolerate our summer heat and does not have problems with bronze-birch borers. Heritage river birch is not a small tree. With a height of 40 feet and a spread of 18 feet, it is not the tree to plant among a home's foundation shrubs! It is a vigorous grower and has dark-green leathery leaves. Most birch trees are grown as multitrunked specimens whose exfoliating bark looks especially nice in the winter landscape. The birch's graceful branching habit is most appealing when the tree is used in natural areas. It will take a couple of growing seasons for the salmon-colored bark of a young Heritage birch to turn white, but it is certainly worth the wait.

WHEN TO PLANT

Container-grown birches can be planted in winter, spring, or fall. Trees dug from a field nursery and sold as balled-and-burlapped plants are best planted in late winter or early spring. Small specimens are quick to establish and frequently outgrow their larger counterparts in a few short years.

WHERE TO PLANT

Heritage river birch likes a moist site with at least a half-day of sun. Hot, windy locations may cause premature leaf drop in the summer. The irregular growth habit of this tree lends itself to an informal setting such as a courtyard, a patio, or along a property line. Because it has low-hanging branches, plant it at least 10 feet from a structure or patio.

HOW TO PLANT

Dig a planting hole that is as deep as the rootball and 3 times as wide. Birch is tolerant of our native soils and derives very little benefit from soil amendments provided the tree is mulched. Planting tablets of slow-release fertilizer (available at many nurseries) can be used in the planting hole. Loosen the rootball of container-grown plants and eliminate circling roots by forcing them out. Firm-in the roots with the backfill soil and form an earthen ring around the edge of the rootball to help direct water to it. Water with a garden hose for 20 minutes at a slow trickle, or pour 4 gallons of water from a bucket. Complete the job with a 2- to 3-inch layer of mulch.

CARE AND MAINTENANCE

Water newly planted trees twice the first week, then weekly thereafter for the first 10 weeks. Additional watering may be needed during dry periods. Fertilize birch trees each year in early spring with a complete fertilizer. Using 1/2 pound of fertilizer for each inch of trunk diameter, scattering the fertilizer on top of the ground. In deep, rich soils, fertilizer is not important during the early years of establishment. A birch produces many sprouts or suckers at the base of its trunk. These should be removed in late summer. Late summer is also a good time to prune birches since the cuts will close quickly.

ADDITIONAL INFORMATION

Birches have shallow roots that can be a problem when planted in a lawn. It's best to plant the trees where they can be mulched to their driplines. Their roots can also cause problems in septic fields, so be sure to keep them 20 feet or more from septic lines. Do not prune birches in the winter because they "sap" or "bleed" profusely.

ADDITIONAL SPECIES, CULTIVARS, OR VARIETIES

There are numerous cultivars. Heritage birch is a classic tree for hot climates. Most nurseries offer our common native river birch as well. Its tan, exfoliating bark is handsome, but the tree can reach gigantic proportions. Another borer-free one is Japanese birch, *B. platyphylla*. *B. pendula* and *B. papyrifera* are white birches that grow only in the Mountain region.

DECIDUOUS TREES

Prunus spp.

Japanese Flowering Cherry

herry-blossom season is a high-energy time each spring from Washington, D.C., south to the Tar Heel State. There's a sort of frenzy to grab a camera and jump in the family car to see the show. And wow, what a show it is! Starting with a few sparse blooms, Japanese flowering cherry quickly unloads with a fury until a light pink wash of color dominates the April landscape. Except for the weeping variety, most Japanese cherries are upright in form and have strong ascending branches that reach a height of 15 to 35 feet. Though fruitless, this outstanding ornamental produces both double and single flowers. The large double pink blooms of 'Sekiyama' are very popular in the western North Carolina, while 'Yoshino,' the white flowering Japanese cherry seen at the nation's capitol, is the one found thriving in the east. Unfortunately, these trees often fail to harden-off properly for the winter, resulting in twig dieback and a short life expectancy in Zone 7b and south. The ungrafted weeping higan cherry is a large long-lived tree that is popular with nursery owners in the Winston-Salem area.

WHEN TO PLANT

Japanese cherry is cold sensitive and should be planted in the spring before bud swell. Balled-and-burlapped trees can be planted any time during the dormant season. Trees planted in summer are subject to borers and heat stress decline.

WHERE TO PLANT

Japanese cherry is best used as a specimen tree in a sitting area, or as part of a formal landscape design. Planted near the corner of a large house, the larger varieties can soften the lines of the structure. Find a protected site out of the south sun where the soil drains well. The weeping forms naturalize well in woodland gardens, but they can dominate a landscape.

How to Plant

This is a tree that benefits from being planted on a berm. Excellent soil drainage is imperative, as root rot diseases are acute in heavy soils. In friable soils, dig a hole twice as wide as the rootball and half as deep. Pull loosened soil up to the rootball, firm-in, water, and apply a 2-inch mulch. If more soil is needed, make a backfill soil using screened topsoil with thirty percent or more compost or bark mulch conditioner. In mass plantings of Japanese cherry, plastic drainpipe can be used under the bed for water drainage. Keep the soil moist through spring.

Care and Maintenance

Japanese cherry is a low-maintenance tree when planted in the right location. Give it plenty of space, 20 feet between trees. Fertilize in mid-March and prune during the dormant season or in early August. Watering is a must during the early years; apply an inch of water per week or 10 gallons of water per tree. Cherry borers can be controlled with 2 borer spray applications in June. Treat again on September 1. Avoid pruning during the borer season. Heavy fertilization or pruning in the fall may encourage late-season growth, increasing the chances of winter injury. Ungrafted trees appear to be better adapted to the climate in North Carolina.

Additional Information

Remove sucker growth at the base of the tree or by the graft union any time of year. Occasionally the rootstock will produce a vigorous shoot that can overtake the desirable top. Keep a watch out for webworms, tent caterpillars, and Japanese beetles. These pests can be removed by hand or chemically. Don't burn them out!

Additional Species, Cultivars, or Varieties

Hardy 'Yoshino' (*P. × yedoensis*) grows to 40 feet and is delicate white to pale pink. Vigorous, heat-tolerant 'Okame' (*P. × incam*) grows to 20 feet and has early bell-like flowers. Pink weeping 'Pendula' (*P. subhirtella*) grows to 35 feet and grows true from seed. 'Shirofugen' (*P. serrulata*) grows to 20 feet and has large double soft-pink flowers.

Japanese Maple

*F*ew ornamental trees are as useful for landscaping as the Japanese maple. The outstanding features of this tree are its intricate foliage and its varying leaf types, colors, and shapes. From the seedling varieties to the grafted cultivars, Japanese maple is a superb tree. In spring the leaves burst into color with intense red hues that later fade to green. The grafted cultivars like 'Bloodgood' maintain a steady burgundy color throughout the growing season. The Japanese maple captures the essence of fall color with a brilliance that is unparalleled by other small deciduous trees. 'Osakazuki' has flaming red fall color and 'Nuresagi' has white striated bark that gives it winter interest. Japanese maple trees range in height from 4 feet to over 30 feet. The seedlings become the largest trees. This maple can be grown in a foundation planting or used as a specimen in a court-yard. When planted at curbside, these small trees will not interfere with power lines.

WHEN TO PLANT
For best results, plant your new Japanese maple any time from November through March. Trees grown in containers can be planted up until early summer.

WHERE TO PLANT
Japanese maple grows well in a range of soils provided the soils are not waterlogged. Filtered shade is preferred to direct sun—some maples will sunburn. Plant Japanese maple as an accent or in small groves to create a Japanese garden. The dwarf forms fit nicely into foundation plantings. Place the lacy-leaf dissectums in close quarters where the lacy foliage can be touched and appreciated.

HOW TO PLANT
Japanese maples prefer moist, rich soils. When planting small container-grown trees, amend planting sites by spading compost or soil conditioner into the soil before planting. Transplanted balled-and-burlapped trees do fine without amendments. Add a little superphosphate or seed-starter fertilizer if needed during the plant-ing hole preparation. After removing from the container, free up the

roots so that girdling roots will not strangle your maple years later. Plant the Japanese maple in a wide hole at the same depth it was grown at the nursery. Form a soil dam at the edge of the planting hole to help collect water during rains, or to facilitate irrigation.

CARE AND MAINTENANCE

For quick establishment, it is very important to water and mulch your new Japanese maple. Water regularly each week for the first month, using a slow trickle from a garden hose for 30 minutes for each application. Apply 10 gallons of water every week if there isn't sufficient rainfall. Water deeply in the summer. Maintain a 2- to 3-inch mulch ring with a minimum diameter of 3 feet; increase the size of the ring with time. Keep an eye out for Japanese beetles and spray early.

ADDITIONAL INFORMATION

Leaf tip burn is a chronic problem with Japanese maples, though this condition is not life-threatening. If you are looking for a tree that has stable foliage throughout the summer months, purchase a named cultivar, or shop for your tree in August when true leaf color can be assessed.

ADDITIONAL SPECIES, CULTIVARS, OR VARIETIES

'Bloodgood' and 'Crimson Queen' have burgundy foliage from spring to fall. The strong-growing 'Osakazuki' grows to 20 feet, has green summer foliage, and is brilliant crimson red in fall. 'Hogyoku' has green leaves in summer and a rich, deep orange color in fall. 'Sango Kaku' is yellow with apricot overtones. *A. palmatum* 'Tamukeyama' and 'Burgundy Lace' are spreading forms.

Japanese Zelkova

The new home buyer would be well advised to plant a Japanese zelkova for some fast shade and fine cooling. This large deciduous beauty grows to 80 feet, a perfect size to thwart the hot afternoon sun. Plant this specimen tree by a deck or patio to create the perfect place to enjoy a cold drink in the summer. Shade the southeast or southwest roof with Japanese zelkova and save a bundle on your power bill! First introduced as a replacement for the disappearing American elm, zelkova has found its way from the city street to the suburban backyard. Its foliage closely resembles Chinese elm with its pointed tips and serrated leaf margins. What it lacks in fall color, it makes up for with its rich-green, sturdy stature. Its vase shape and upright growth make it the perfect tree for the person in charge of mowing the lawn. Zelkovas thrive in full sun or partial shade. This wonderful shade tree is a rapid grower and will reward you with 2 or more feet in height each season. Japanese zelkovas are popular with city arborists, and they are showing up in large numbers in parks and on neighborhood streets.

WHEN TO PLANT

Zelkova is readily available at all wholesale nurseries in large containers up to 2-inch caliber. Plant these when the ground is workable in fall or in spring, certainly in May. Balled-and-burlapped trees are usually available at planting time in the dormant season, January through March.

WHERE TO PLANT

Find a sunny location with a good view and put your zelkova there. One day you will find it has become a good spot for a summer retreat. For maximum growth, plant where the soil is moist and deep. Once established, your prize zelkova will do just fine in droughty weather.

HOW TO PLANT

One reason zelkova is growing in popularity is that it transplants well. Spade or till up an area that is 2 to 3 times as wide as the rootball. Dig a hole for the rootball that is 75 percent of its depth.

Remove the tree from the plastic container and free up circling roots. For balled-and-burlapped trees, fold the burlap into the bottom of the planting hole, removing twine or nails. Soil amendments are optional for container-grown trees. Follow soil test recommendations for new home sites. After setting the tree properly in the hole, shovel in the soil backfill only halfway before firming in the soil with your foot. Water at this time and drop in a couple of planting tablets. Continue filling the hole.

CARE AND MAINTENANCE

If the zelkova is planted properly, it will grow well with little care. Watering during the first 2 growing seasons is a must if the summers are dry. A soaker hose is a good investment. In late September, applying fertilizer will help build a stronger root system. Light pruning of weak twigs is important as the main scaffold limbs develop. Maintain a mulch ring equivalent to a 4-foot-diameter circle around the tree at all times. This discourages weeds and protects the thin-barked tree from weed-eater or mower injury. Its upright growth sometimes entices mowers to get too close!

ADDITIONAL INFORMATION

Keep a watchful eye out for the Japanese beetles which are occasional zelkova pests in the Carolinas—but even if you do not spray, a beetle injury is of minor importance. Always maintain mulch rings to prevent equipment injury to the trunk—but don't heap the mulch up on the trunk! Leave a couple of inches of open space next to the trunk.

ADDITIONAL SPECIES, CULTIVARS, OR VARIETIES

'Green Vase' has vigorous growth and golden-yellow to bronze-red fall foliage. 'Village Green' is the most readily available cultivar. It is an excellent tree with a smooth, straight trunk and dark-green foliage that turns wine-red in the fall. 'Green Veil' has pendulous branches. 'Parkview' has a good vase shape.

Red Buckeye

*R*ed buckeye is another great North Carolina native that is certainly worth looking for. Some landscape plants have to be pampered once installed, but this small tree does not. Red buckeye grows 15 to 25 feet tall and has dark-green glossy leaves; each compound leaf consists of 5 to 7 leaflets arranged palmately. The flowers are just as distinctive as the leaves. Appearing in 6-inch clusters, the red tubular flowers emerge in April and May just in time to herald the return of ruby-throated hummingbirds to the Carolinas. The red buckeye located in Sarah P. Duke Gardens in Durham is always a pleasure to behold during spring bloom! Red buckeye is a graceful tree with a tropical look. The nuts, or buckeyes, are brown, and they ripen in October. Though the buckeyes are poisonous, the Indians used to soak them and grind them for flour meal. (Perhaps soaking them diluted the toxins.) Another interesting member of the family member is the bottlebrush buckeye, *Aesculus parviflora*. It is a wide-spreading shrub that produces long, showy white flower panicles. Both of these buckeyes are terrific low-maintenance ornamentals for Tar Heel gardens.

WHEN TO PLANT

Plant red buckeye when dormant in late fall or winter. Even container-grown plants will occasionally die if transplanted after they leaf out in spring. The buckeyes can be planted soon after they are harvested in early fall.

WHERE TO PLANT

Red buckeye is best planted as a specimen tree in sun. It will also grow as an understory planting among mature woodland trees. Buckeyes appear to be at their best on the edge of a forest where the roots can enjoy a humus-rich soil. Plant them in front of an evergreen hedge or in a border of rhododendrons.

HOW TO PLANT

Locate a site where the soil drains well. Prepare a planting hole that is 2 to 3 times larger than the rootball. Spade in $1/2$ cup of superphosphate fertilizer or bonemeal and a half-bushel of compost. Do not disturb the roots of container-grown plants unless the plants are

heavily rooted or potbound. Firm the soil around the rootball, and position the red buckeye tree to plant it slightly higher than grade. Water well, using 4 gallons of water to settle the soil. Mulch with leaf compost or aged hardwood mulch. Water twice weekly, and regularly in dry periods during the first spring. In woodland plantings, wrap a foot-long strip of hardware cloth around the lower trunk to protect the tree from rabbits and voles.

CARE AND MAINTENANCE

Few native trees are as adaptable or as pest-free as red buckeyes. Once established, these trees will thrive on neglect; but keep newly transplanted specimens watered well the first growing season with weekly irrigations during late summer. A slow-release fertilizer can be applied in September the second season, and as needed in following years. Pruning is usually not necessary for this fine ornamental, except if desired for cosmetic reasons. Buckeyes are quite drought tolerant once established, but expect some leaf scorch in very dry periods. This is, of course, not life threatening to the trees.

ADDITIONAL INFORMATION

Young red buckeye plants will flower when 2 to 3 years old. (The one I transplanted from a 3-gallon pot bloomed the second season.) The nuts of buckeyes are reported to be poisonous, so keep this in mind if young children play in your garden. Bury the nuts as they drop, or cart them off with the trash.

ADDITIONAL SPECIES, CULTIVARS, OR VARIETIES

'Splendens' has scarlet flowers. 'Atrosanguinea' has dark-red flowers. 'Humilis' is a low shrub form. *A. glabra* 'Pyramidalis' is an Ohio buckeye with an upright growth habit.

Red Maple

*R*ed maple is the "Rolls Royce" of maples. This native tree reaches a height of 50 feet in a relatively short period of time. It displays brilliant red or orange fall color and has medium-sized 3-lobed leaves and striking gray bark. Exquisite new cultivars include 'Red Sunset,' 'Autumn Blaze,' and 'October Glory.' Its strong, upright growth habit and broad spreading crown make red maple the perfect shade tree for suburban landscapes. Columnar and compact forms like 'Armstrong' can be used by homeowners with smaller lawns.

When to Plant

Red maples are available as both container-grown and field-dug balled-and-burlapped trees. Plant balled-and-burlapped trees during the winter, or perhaps in early spring if healed in and irrigated properly. Plant container-grown trees any time the soil can be prepared.

Where to Plant

Red maple grows naturally in a wide range of conditions. It grows best in moist locations in full sun or light shade. Place red maple as a specimen tree where there is ample room, certainly not closer than 18 feet to the house. Some homeowners use red maple as an alley of trees lining a driveway.

How to Plant

Rototill or spade an area at least 3 times the diameter of the rootball and 3/4 the depth. Incorporate lime and superphosphate if need is indicated by a soil test report. Dig the hole for the rootball; in well-drained soils, the hole can be deeper than indicated above for setting the tree at grade. Remove any twine, synthetic materials, or wire basket. If you have a container-grown tree, remove the pot and free up circling roots with a handtool or knife. If the soil is gray or sticky, add soil conditioner and plant the tree "high." Place the tree in the hole and shovel in half the backfill soil. Firm the soil and water with 4 gallons of water. (Several fertilizer tablets can be dropped into the hole at this point). Complete the backfilling process and pour in 4 more gallons of water. Mulch with leaf compost or 3 inches of aged hardwood mulch. Stake your new red maple if you have planted it in a windy location or if it is quite large.

CARE AND MAINTENANCE

Water is the key to survival for newly planted shade trees. There are few challenges in getting red maples to grow other than summer and fall irrigation. Your tree will need water regularly during the growing season for the first 2 years. Using a bucket is acceptable, but using a soaker hose or a slow trickle from the garden hose (30 minutes at least) is better. For the first 2 months, irrigate twice a week; after that, every 10 days will do. As the red maple matures, remove weak branches and those with narrow crotches at the trunk. Try to develop a strong framework with a single leader (trunk) and branches growing at 90-degree angles to the trunk. Fertilize your tree every 3 years in March or November.

ADDITIONAL INFORMATION

Maples can be pruned during the late summer months if limbs hang too low to the ground or if some thinning is necessary. Pruning while the trees are dormant is also acceptable, but the trees may "sap" ("bleed") profusely. Follow correct pruning practices. Do not make flush cuts at the trunk, and remove limbs in a way that leaves the branch collars intact. Maples have shallow root systems, and trees planted close to walks and driveways may "heave up" pavement.

ADDITIONAL SPECIES, CULTIVARS, OR VARIETIES

'October Glory' has lustrous crimson leaves that hold later than those of most maples. Pyramid-shaped 'Red Sunset' has orange-red fall color. 'Columnare' has a dense, upright growth habit. Another fine cultivar is 'Autumn Blaze.'

Red Oak

Oaks are generally stereotyped as slow-growing trees that take a lifetime to create shade. This stereotype is true of white oaks, but not of the red oak. Red oaks are excellent landscape trees which grow rapidly and tolerate urban conditions well. They can reach a height of 75 feet with a spread half the height. When planted in deep, well-drained soil, it is not uncommon for a red oak to grow 2 feet in a year. Red oaks mature into symmetrical specimens with rounded crowns. They add a majestic touch to any landscape planting. Tender reddish buds open up in spring. During the summer months, the large pointed leaves of red oak foliage are a lustrous dark green, but they change to a deep red in autumn. In older trees, the black, deeply fissured bark adds texture to the landscape. Many older neighborhoods have mature white oak trees that are in stages of decline due to old age and urban stress. My colleague, Dr. James McGraw, North Carolina State University Extension Forester, recommends a program of replanting these urban forests with red oaks. The rapidly growing red oaks would make a good start before the aging heirloom trees came down. Red oaks are tolerant of air pollution, always a concern in urban areas.

WHEN TO PLANT

Plant red oaks from November through March. Smaller trees are more successfully transplanted, either as balled and burlapped, or as container stock. The absence of a taproot makes these oaks relatively easy to transplant. Seedlings can be transplanted as bareroot stock. Trees can be grown by planting acorns as soon as they fall from a tree.

WHERE TO PLANT

Red oaks do best in full sun, and they are widely adapted to a range of environmental conditions. While white oaks must have a dry site, red oaks tolerate moist clay soils as well as dry areas. They prefer slightly acidic (pH 5.5 to 6.5) sandy loam soils. They are good choices for urban landscapes such as homes, parks, streets, and commercial sites. Their height allows for underplantings of shrubs.

HOW TO PLANT

Dig a hole that is twice as wide and 30 percent deeper than the diameter of the rootball. Replace up to half the soil and place the rootball in the planting hole so that 1/3 of the rootball is above grade. When the rootball settles after planting, the object is to have it several inches above grade to avoid drainage problems. Cut the twine from the trunk of balled-and-burlapped stock, but leave the burlap around the roots. Be sure to cover all burlap with soil. Backfill the planting hole with native soil, tamping in place, and form a shallow well around the perimeter of the hole to hold irrigation. Larger specimens may need staking for 6 months. Add 2 to 3 inches of mulch on top of the rootball. Water well.

CARE AND MAINTENANCE

Newly planted trees should be watered deeply at planting, then every 10 days during the first growing season. Using a garden hose, fill the shallow well formed at planting time with water. Allow water to seep deeply into the ground with each irrigation. Do not prune young trees except to remove narrow angled branches and broken twigs. Trees with double leaders (twin trunks) should be pruned to one central leader. Red oaks can be fertilized any time in late winter to early spring. A balanced fertilizer such as 10-10-10 can be used and applied to the dripline zone. If possible, allow leaves to accumulate under the tree.

ADDITIONAL INFORMATION

Red oaks have very few problems. It is common to encounter trees in decline where there has been construction damage around homes. A tree's root system may have been crushed by heavy equipment or destroyed by topsoil removal and grading. Many of these trees can be salvaged by the addition of a thick layer of organic matter to the root zone area.

ADDITIONAL SPECIES, CULTIVARS, OR VARIETIES

Seedling red oaks are an important source of landscape trees. Other species with landscape potential that transplant easily include *Quercus shumardii* (shumard oak); *Q. palustris* (pin oak), *Q. nigra* (water oak), and *Q. acutissima* (sawtooth oak, a non-native species). Other oaks, *Q. alba*, the white oak, and *Q. coccinea*, the scarlet oak, are difficult to transplant.

Saucer Magnolia

Saucer magnolias have one major flaw: they don't stay in bloom long enough for this horticulturist. When they are at the zenith of their glory in early March, they create a magnificent spectacle. Gardeners rush to the nurseries in search of this large-flowered beauty, commonly referred to by locals as a tulip tree. The latest introductions of saucer magnolias are very floriferous and flower sporadically throughout the growing season, especially when there's adequate rainfall. During the primary bloom period, the high fleshy flowers burst open before leaves emerge. Flower colors range from white and yellow to pink and rose. Unlike the evergreen southern magnolia, the coarse-textured leaves of saucer magnolia do not create a litter problem in the landscape. A mature tree can reach 35 feet high and has a wide ascending form. This magnolia offers seasonal interest with its smooth gray bark that contrasts with the dark-green foliage and ostentatious flowers. The best thing about this hardy magnolia is that it requires very little work to keep it in full splendor.

When to Plant

Saucer magnolias are planted from containers any time from late winter to fall. Plant balled-and-burlapped trees while they are dormant.

Where to Plant

Great saucer magnolias are grown in partial shade or full sun. Moist soil will insure strong, rapid growth. Trees that are planted in sheltered sites often escape our late spring frosts that periodically spoil the floral display. Saucer magnolias will grow large enough to provide some good shade.

How to Plant

Thoroughly loosen the roots of plants grown in pots. Prepare a wide, shallow hole 3/4 as deep and 3 times as wide as the rootball. Make a mix of equal parts existing soil and soil conditioner. Pack firmly around the sides of the rootball. Water slowly, applying 4 gallons of water to settle the plant. Add 1 to 3 inches of mulch on top, staying clear of the crown of the plant. Water every 3 days for 3 weeks. Avoid planting when soil is frozen or when soil is wet enough to form a mudball in your fist.

Care and Maintenance

A single-trunk specimen will benefit from training in order to develop a strong framework of scaffold branches. Prune saucer magnolias while young and keep the basal suckers removed. Multiple-trunk specimens can be limbed up in summer or immediately following bloom. Keep saucer magnolias well mulched and water them routinely during the summer and fall months. Apply a slow-release fertilizer (with high phosphate) in the spring.

Additional Information

While southern magnolia is spectacular in a courtyard or patio garden, the old flower petals that drop onto walks can be slippery. Any cold-damaged twigs should be pruned off when noticed.

Additional Species, Cultivars, or Varieties

'Betty' has abundant flowers. 'Speciosa' blooms late. 'Galaxy' has cup-shaped, rosy-purple flowers. 'Butterflies' has bright yellow flowers. 'Elizabeth' has soft yellow precocious flowers. 'Susan' blooms twice. 'Waterlilly' has pale pink, star-shaped flowers. *M. stellata* has early double white blossoms. Another fine cultivar is 'Jane.'

Sugar Maple

here are many varieties of maple recommended for planting in North Carolina landscapes and gardens, but none produces more wonderful fall color than the sugar maple. An October ride down Reynolda Road in Winston-Salem will make you a lover of this "sweet" tree. If it is given plenty of room to mature, sugar maple is almost unsurpassable as a shade tree. It has large 5-inch leaves and produces a rounded canopy perfect for shading a patio or sitting garden. Maturing to a height of 60 feet or more, this tree will reduce your cooling bill by blocking the afternoon sun. A sugar maple is not for the courtyard or small residential property—it may reach a spread of 40 feet! This maple has dull-green leaves in summer that turn to gorgeous orange-and-yellow fall color with the first frosts. It is hardy under a wide range of conditions from full sun to light shade. It is a slower growing tree than are red and silver maples, but it is desirable for its symmetrical form. Its strong branches hold up well in ice storms. Sugar maple, like Norway maple, is better adapted to the Piedmont and westward. It is distinguished by its smooth gray bark and spectacular fall color.

WHEN TO PLANT

Container-grown sugar maples are available, and so are field-dug balled-and-burlapped trees. The balled-and-burlapped trees should be planted during the winter, or possibly in early spring if healed in and irrigated properly. Plant container-grown trees any time that the soil can be prepared. Seeds sown in late fall will produce seedlings by summer.

WHERE TO PLANT

Sugar maples grow naturally under a wide range of conditions. They grow best in moist locations where there is full sun or light shade. Plant sugar maple as a specimen tree where there is ample room, certainly not closer than 18 feet to the house. This is a good tree for large yards and parks, or it may make an alley of trees lining a driveway. It does not perform well as a street tree because it is adversely affected by air pollution.

How to Plant

In clay soils, dig a hole that is at least twice as wide and ³/₄ as deep as the diameter of the rootball (for example, for a 20-inch rootball, the hole should be 40 inches wide and 15 inches deep). Cut the twine from the trunk of balled-and-burlapped trees, but leave the burlap on the ball, cutting it back when planting. There is no need to loosen the roots on balled-and-burlapped trees, but loosen them on container-grown plants. For poor soils, make a mix of ¹/₃ coarse organic humus and existing topsoil for the backfill. Pack soil firmly around the sides of the rootball. Water well and finish by covering the top of the exposed roots with the mix. Form an earthen dam around the edge of the hole, and apply a 2- to 3-inch layer of mulch.

Care and Maintenance

Sugar maples are very adaptable with little care. Fertilization is not necessary as long as the leaves remain a rich green color. After the first full growing season, apply a slow-release nursery fertilizer in the spring at the rate of 1 pound per inch of trunk diameter. (Trunk diameter measurement is taken at 4 feet above ground, or chest height.) Do not fertilize for another 2 or 3 years. Prune out wild shoots rising off the trunk or prune to shape the young tree. Water twice weekly for the first 6 weeks, and after that, during dry weather. Maple worms and aphids may occur infrequently, though they are not serious problems.

Additional Information

Unless they are root pruned in the fall, large sugar maples have to struggle to survive transplanting. Begin root pruning by August for spring plantings. Fruit pods on this tree may be unsightly to some, while they are an interesting landscape feature to others. It is difficult to grow decent turfgrass under mature maples. Try using a mulch tree ring.

Additional Species, Cultivars, or Varieties

'Green Mountain' is the best tree for hot, dry sites; it has good scorch resistance. 'Bonfire' has excellent red fall color and is a rapid grower. 'Monumentale,' 'Temple Upright,' and 'Columnare' are narrow, upright cultivars that are good for small gardens. 'Globosum' is a round shrub-like form. Others are *A. platanoides* (the Norway maple), 'Emerald Queen,' and 'Summershade.'

Willow Oak

Of the 22 oak species that grow in North Carolina, our native willow oak is by far the most popular. It is an excellent landscape tree of the white oak group that has virtually no disease problems. It grows rapidly and tolerates urban conditions so well that it is the predominant oak planted in most major North Carolina cities. Many of these oaks have survived for 60 years under rather harsh conditions. Willow oaks can grow to a height of 80 feet and a spread of 75 feet under good conditions, maturing into nearly rounded symmetrical specimens. The huge willow oak is not the best choice for a cottage garden! From parking lots to porches, this oak reigns as king in the heat of our Southern summers. It is a good tree on which to hang the hammock when you want to stay cool in the shade. Willow oak is well-liked in nurseries because it is easy to transplant. Gardeners like it because it can grow to a respectable size in a decade or less, growing 2 to 3 feet per year once established. Willow oaks produce a consistent annual crop of half-inch acorns that can be a nuisance to rake up in the fall, but these acorns are a delight to the wildlife every season. It does not rank high on fall color as do the pin oak or shumard oak.

WHEN TO PLANT

Plant willow oaks from November through March. The absence of a taproot makes a willow oak relatively easy to transplant. Smaller trees are more successfully transplanted than larger, either as balled-and-burlapped or container stock. Seedlings can be transplanted as bareroot stock. Trees can be grown by planting acorns as soon as they fall from the tree.

WHERE TO PLANT

Willow oaks do best in full sun. They prefer slightly acidic (pH 5.5 to 6.5) loamy soils and tolerate polluted air in city gardens. For landscape plantings, use them as specimen trees. If properly sited on the southeast or southwest sides of the house, they will shade the roof, saving you big bucks on your cooling bills.

HOW TO PLANT

Dig a hole that is as deep as the rootball and 3 times as wide. Replace up to 1/3 of the soil so the rootball will be at least 1/3 of the way above grade when planted. If it is several inches above grade, drainage problems will be avoided. Cut twine from the trunk of balled-and-burlapped stock, but leave the burlap or wire basket with the rootball. Loosen the burlap and cut it back. Backfill the planting hole with native soil, tamping in place. Form a shallow well around the perimeter of the planting hole to hold irrigation. Stake topheavy trees with two 6- to 8-foot stakes for 4 months. Add 2 to 3 inches of mulch on top of the rootball. Water well.

CARE AND MAINTENANCE

Remove broken or dead twigs at planting time. As the tree grows, remove branches that arise from the trunk with narrow crotches. Eliminate codominant leaders (double trunk or forking upright branches) as well. Protect the trunk from mower or string trimmer damage. Spring fertilization is suggested: apply the material as the buds begin to swell. During the first year or two, the most important task is to water routinely. A 4-foot-radius ring of mulch starting out 6 inches from the trunk will encourage the young tree to establish. Maintain and replenish this organic material.

ADDITIONAL INFORMATION

The major insect of willow oak is the orange-striped oakworm. The excrement from these pests can be annoying, and so can the caterpillars crawling all over the yard. Fortunately this insect does little harm, other than to remove leaves that will drop anyway a few weeks later. Red oaks don't appear to be plagued by this pest.

ADDITIONAL SPECIES, CULTIVARS, OR VARIETIES

Seedling trees are the main source of planting stock.

Cladrastis kentukea

Yellowwood

 his excellent landscape tree is native from North Carolina to Kentucky, but it is still unknown by most Tar Heel gardeners. It is as scarce at garden shops as it is rare in the wild. Yellowwood is valued for its foliage and flowers, but it is named for the bright yellow heartwood that is visible when the tree is cut. It will grow to 40 feet, maturing gracefully with a rounded, spreading crown. It makes a fine yard tree since it develops deep roots which permit planting or sowing turfgrass beneath its branches. Discovered in 1796 by French botanist André Michaux while on a plant expedition in the Carolinas, yellowwood was later collected and used as a source of yellow dye. Because of its graceful form, year-round seasonal interest, and lovely fragrance, it is considered by many to be a nearly flawless ornamental. In June in alternating years, yellowwood blooms profusely, bearing 14-inch-long chains (drooping panicles) of 1-inch pea-like white flowers. By autumn its bright-green compound leaves turn a clear, rich yellow. During the winter it is distinguished by its smooth silvery-gray bark.

WHEN TO PLANT

Plant yellowwood in its dormant season from December through March.

WHERE TO PLANT

Yellowwood is a choice specimen tree for small properties or for patio and courtyard gardens. If space permits, plant a background of evergreens to show off its bright foliage and gray bark. Transplant into a full-sun to lightly-shaded location where the soil is well drained. Because of yellowwood's deep root system, a bed of shade-loving annuals or bulbs can be planted beneath.

HOW TO PLANT

Yellowwood grows naturally in rich hardwood forests in western North Carolina. The home gardener should amend the soil with copious amounts of aged compost or commercial cow manure. Spade or till an area that is 3 to 5 times larger than the diameter of the rootball. Plant the tree a few inches higher than grade to allow for settling over time. Firm the soil around the rootball and water

thoroughly. Yellowwood likes moist soil—keep this tree well watered! Invest in a soaker hose, and mulch the tree with leaf compost every year.

CARE AND MAINTENANCE

Be patient with yellowwood; it is a slow to moderate grower. It will take 6 to 10 years to reach a mature age before flowering. Once it establishes itself in the landscape, it is a low-maintenance shade tree and is quite drought tolerant. Be sure you prune yellowwood to a single trunk while it is still young. It can develop weak branch forks which will split apart in ice or severe windstorms when left untrained. Apply a tree-grade fertilizer to the dripline every other spring to maintain the health of the tree.

ADDITIONAL INFORMATION

Yellowwood tolerates a wide range of soil types. It is most important to remember to water the tree in hot, dry weather from June to September. That time of year is also the recommended season for pruning yellowwood since it "saps" freely ("bleeds") when cut during winter or spring.

ADDITIONAL SPECIES, CULTIVARS, OR VARIETIES

Most yellowwoods are planted as seedlings or rooted cuttings of the species. One interesting cultivar, 'Rosea,' is a beautiful pink-flowered form. The original tree is located at the Perkins School for the Blind in Watertown, Massachusetts, according to Dr. Michael Dirr in the *Manual of Woody Landscape Plants.*

Evergreens

FROM THE HIGH PEAKS OF THE APPALACHIANS, where Fraser firs grow naturally, to the Coastal Plains, home of long-leaf pines and yaupon hollies, evergreens are important to the North Carolina landscape. Gardeners may choose from an abundance of tall growing native evergreens to use for privacy screening or for the wind abatement that will conserve on heating bills. During the dreary winter months, the home grounds can be upgraded with some much-needed greenery.

Most evergreens are planted as specimens, but the most frequent request we receive at Extension offices is for a list of plants that can be used for screening. A homeowner may want to hide an ugly utility area, or possibly create a sense of privacy for a swimming pool or a sun-bathing deck. In a few cases, the intent is to keep the Joneses from knowing every detail of the family's daily routine.

This group of woody landscape plants includes both broadleaf and narrowleaf evergreens that offer diversity in texture and growth habit. Our most notable evergreens in the Old North State are the eastern red cedars and the southern magnolias. The red cedars are despised by apple growers because they are a host for the infectious cedar-apple rust. Though cedar seedlings are planted by the thousands each year, they are not welcome near the backyard orchard! Magnolias are as much a Southern tradition as grits and greens, but it does take a large area for them to mature to perfection.

Chapter Four

Planting mixed borders of several species of evergreens is sound advice when planning a hedge or screen in this state. Over the last fifteen years we have seen the rise and fall of *Photinia* (red tips) as a durable screening shrub. Most gardeners replanted their diseased hedges with Leyland cypress, a magnificent evergreen. Consequently, we are now fielding calls from disenchanted home-owners who didn't know that Leyland cypresses are vulnerable to bagworms and the potentially fatal seridium canker fungus. There may not be a perfect evergreen, but the 'Nellie R. Stevens' comes close, and it should be included in a mixed border when designing a privacy screen.

The entries in this book include some lower-growing shrubs that make fine choices for the garden. Some, like the camellias, will delight you with enchanting blossoms; others can be planted as a backdrop for deciduous spring-flowering shrubs. This state is rich in marvelous evergreen plants, and I have only presented a few out-standing ones. Check with a nurseryman before making your final selections.

American Holly

*A*ll through the Carolinas and up the Eastern seaboard, American hollies are found growing in the wild. This wonderful native evergreen has a rich history, and it has been a symbol of friendship for centuries. The Ilex family has been hybridized repeatedly and offers some of the finest woody ornamentals for landscaping. More than 300 varieties of *I. opaca* have been named, and over 60 of these are commercially available. Most of us know this evergreen as the pyramid-shaped tree with spiny leaves that is seen on estate grounds and in public parks. This is the stately holly that evokes memories of Christmas Past with holly berries on the mantel. But American holly should not be kept out of sight until the yuletide season—these hollies offer character and interest throughout the year. Like the English holly, American holly varies in leaf shape, form, and growth habit. The 3-inch leaves of this evergreen are dark-green, stiff, and leathery. Most have an upright growth habit with light gray bark that is exposed as the horizontal branches develop. There are male and female plants, and fruit production is dependent upon having both sexes.

WHEN TO PLANT

Balled-and-burlapped specimens of American holly should be planted in late winter and spring. Container-grown trees can be planted in the spring and in the fall. Native hollies or those established in the landscape can be moved or transplanted in early spring. Always root prune established hollies in late summer before moving 4 months later.

WHERE TO PLANT

American hollies will thrive in a full-sun to part-sun location. They prefer a well-drained, moist soil. They will tolerate dry landscape sites if irrigated during the establishment period. Hollies grow relatively slowly in the early years, but they need ample space as they mature into specimen trees with spreads of 15 feet or more. Plant as a large accent or in groups for a dense privacy screen.

How to Plant

Plant your American holly in a wide shallow hole that is 3/4 as deep and twice as wide as the rootball. (In sandy loam soils, plant balled-and-burlapped trees at the same depth as grown in the nursery.) The tree is pH adaptable but it appreciates a dusting of limestone at planting and a slow-release phosphate fertilizer. Cut the twine of balled-and-burlapped trees after positioning them in the planting hole, and cut back the burlap. Backfill with the native soil and firm-in the soil with your foot, watering thoroughly with 8 gallons of water. American holly appreciates a 2- to 3-inch-thick mulch of compost or aged hardwood bark. Water twice weekly for the first several weeks, and irrigate during droughts.

Care and Maintenance

If you are planting a holly tree for its bright red berries, select a female tree—one with good fruit set—and plant it in a sunny location. Prune only sparingly in the winter, as the flowers, and ultimately the berries, appear off the previous season's growth. It is best to do any shaping and shearing after the berries are large enough to spot in June or July. Re-mulch established American hollies every summer to alleviate drought stress. Leaf miner insects are recurring pests on this plant. They can be controlled with a June insecticide application. Check with your Extension agents for the appropriate chemical.

Additional Information

Fertilize your American holly every few years with a specialty product that contains iron and magnesium. This will keep the foliage a rich green color. Epsom salts or azalea fertilizer will do as well. Our winter weather will often scorch the leaves of holly. Fortunately, they do recover, though the hollies in partially shaded locations fare much better.

Additional Species, Cultivars, or Varieties

There are many interesting cultivars, including a yellow-berried one I planted called 'Canary.' 'Croonenburg' has good berry production. 'Greenleaf' is popular with North Carolina nurseries since it is fast growing and takes shearing well. 'Jersey Knight' has great-looking foliage and is very hardy. 'Carolina #2' has profuse fruiting. Another good cultivar is 'Rotunda'

Colorado Blue Spruce

Although a slow grower outside of the mountains and foothills of North Carolina, Colorado blue spruce is worth planting in large gardens. The blue glaucous color is what attracts most gardeners to this stately pyramid-shaped evergreen with stiff horizontal branches that sweep the ground. In selecting blue spruce, you should consider the grafted cultivars that have outstanding color. Among these are 'Foxtail,' 'Fat Albert,' 'Hoopsii,' and 'Thompsonii.' A group planting of blue spruces can be a striking landscape feature. Unfortunately, the farther east you go in the Tar Heel state, the less blue color do you see on the blue spruces. They have difficulty with hot summer weather and with the heavy clay soils in the Piedmont. The cultivar 'Foxtail,' with its bushy blue branch tips, is your best bet for survival. It is heat tolerant and a rapid grower, according to J. C. Raulston, late Director of the North Carolina State University Arboretum. There are some 60-foot blue spruces tended by patient gardeners in the Triad area that have thrived in full sun and dry soil conditions. Seedling spruce trees are readily available from mail-order nurseries. But beware, because they may not have what all gardeners like: blue genes!

WHEN TO PLANT

Colorado blue spruces that are field grown should be planted in the dormant season, from November to March. Container-grown spruces can be planted any time they are not in an active growth stage. I prefer the fall planting season, for this reason: following summer's heat, the true color of a blue spruce can be assessed.

WHERE TO PLANT

Blue spruces need full sun, or at least some direct sun for several hours of the day. They appreciate moist soil, but avoid poorly drained soils since the trees will be vulnerable to root rot diseases. Though blue spruce can be overpowering in a garden, it is a major player in the winter landscape. Plant it as a specimen or in a grouping for accent.

HOW TO PLANT

When planting individual specimen Colorado blue spruce, prepare a planting hole that is equal in depth to the diameter of the rootball

and 3 times as wide. For all evergreens, there should be 8 inches of loosened soil outside of the rootball in which new roots can forage. For container-grown plants, bark soil conditioner can be mixed with the soil, but for the field-grown ball-and-burlapped ones, no amendment is necessary. Firm the soil around the roots and water to settle the soil. Form an earthen saucer on the perimeter of the planting hole to facilitate irrigation. Spruce like moist soil and need watering every 3 days for the first 2 weeks if there is no rainfall. Apply a 2- to 3-inch mulch layer.

Care and Maintenance

Watering during the first 2 growing seasons is the most important task to keep your blue spruce thriving. If you need to shape your tree, shear in mid-June after the flush of growth has appeared. Remove only 1/3 of the new needles, or remove entire branches that are crowded or rangy. To maintain good color, use a high-nitrogen slow-release nursery fertilizer every year in March. In dry locations, spider mites can become a nuisance in the summer. Control them with a miticide or insecticidal soap spray application. The spruce spider mite can be controlled with a fall miticide treatment in late September. Maintain mulch in mulch rings.

Additional Information

Some gardeners in the hotter regions of the state syringe their blue spruces with water from the garden hose during July and August. This probably does help the plants by cooling them and controlling mites. In the Mountain area, adelgids (white bark aphids) should be controlled to protect the Christmas tree trade. Beware—oil sprays can remove the blue!

Additional Species, Cultivars, or Varieties

Most blue spruces grow to 60 feet and have a spread of 10 to 20 feet. There are a few, like 'Glauca Pendula,' that can make a 3-foot-high sprawling, weed-resistant groundcover. 'Hoopsii' is very blue and is the choice of Dr. Michael Dirr of the University of Georgia. 'Thompsonii' is a whitish-blue color. *P. glauca* 'Conica' (dwarf Alberta spruce) is often planted by doorways or gates.

Cedrus deodara

Deodar Cedar

*M*ention "cedar" in North Carolina and most residents think of the rows of lanky eastern red cedars that line farm fence rows or the dark conical evergreens that dot our highways. Veteran gardeners know that those cedars are actually junipers. The "true cedars" that thrive in our hot, wet climate include deodar cedar and 2 lesser-known species, *C. libani* (cedar-of-Lebanon) and *C. atlantica* (atlas cedar). These cedars are native to Asia and the Middle East where they become massive, reaching 80 feet in height. Deodar cedar is a marvelous tree for the landscape on larger properties where ever-greens are not cramped for space. Mature specimens look like distant mountains on the horizon. These trees mature at 50 feet, often with flattened tops that were frozen back by North Carolina winters. The bluish gray-green foliage of deodar cedar and the blue foliage of atlas cedars offer cool shade in the garden during the hot summer months. Their fine texture and needle-like leaves are a pleasing backdrop for broadleaf shrub borders. Deodar cedar has a wide-spreading pyramidal form and makes a statement wherever it is planted.

WHEN TO PLANT

Because they are sensitive to cold, deodar cedars should be planted as the soil is warming in early spring. There must be enough time to allow their root systems to establish before cold weather arrives in the Tar Heel state. Container-grown specimens can be planted from spring right on through early fall. In the Mountain region, plant only in the spring.

WHERE TO PLANT

Give deodar cedar plenty of space, at least 2000 square feet for its canopy to spread. It needs full sun to grow densely, but it will grow in a half-day of morning shade. In the colder regions of the state, plant this evergreen where it gets some protection from the winter winds. Deodar cedar is almost unequivocally a specimen tree due to its size. It can occasionally be used in groups, or planted as a screen and sheared.

How to Plant

I prefer to plant evergreens grown in large containers. But if you do use field-grown trees, be sure the rootballs meet the American Association of Nurserymen (AAN) standards that ensure an adequate rootball for the tree's size. Dig a planting hole that is as deep and twice as wide as the rootball. I like to take a mattock and break up the soil to a depth of an additional 6 inches for a couple of feet of radius around the rootball (this practice is more important when planting in compacted Piedmont clay soil). Position the deodar cedar in the planting hole and backfill with the soil excavated from the hole. A fertilizer planting tablet can be added to the hole, or add 1/4 cup of superphosphate. Water thoroughly and mulch well.

Care and Maintenance

Newly planted deodar cedars will need watering 3 times the first week, twice the second, and once every 7 to 10 days until they begin growing strongly. Do not prune or stake the trees unless there is good reason to do either. More fertilizer will not be necessary until the spring of the second growing season. These evergreens grow relatively fast once they get acclimated to a new site. In the Mountain region, spray the tree with an anti-transpirant for cold protection during the first few winters. A general garden fertilizer can be applied in the spring every 2 or 3 years.

Additional Information

As the deodar trees mature, some lower limbs will inevitably die, more than likely because of heavy shading from the upper canopy. This is normal; remove the lower limbs to make lawn-mowing easier. Forget growing grass inside the dripline of this evergreen—leave it mulched. Harsh winters can take the tops off these trees.

Additional Species, Cultivars, or Varieties

Grafted plants and seedlings of deodar cedar are available from nurseries. 'Shalimar' is the most cold hardy. 'Nana' is a dwarf mounded form with silver-gray foliage. 'Pendula' is a weeping form. *C. atlantica* 'Glauca' (blue atlas cedar) and 'Glauca Pendula' are popular, though the latter needs a trellis. *C. libani* (biblical tree) is hard to grow.

Japanese Cedar

*J*apanese cedar, a beautiful evergreen conifer, was introduced from Asia in 1861. It quickly became a standard in American gardens. The appearance of Japanese cedar, a cousin to the giant sequoia, is quite different from that of our native red cedars. Its soft sprays of foliage are spirally arranged along drooping branches. The individual needles of juvenile Japanese cedars are spinelike and prickly. As the tree matures, the older needles, held closely together, look like fingers on the wide-spreading branches. *Cryptomeria* can grow quickly to a height of 60 feet with a spread of 30 feet. Old specimens have attractive reddish-brown bark that peels off in long shreds. Once newly planted trees are established, they will shoot up quickly, producing 2- to 3-foot tender growth in late summer. Many nurseries now carry dwarf species such as 'Elegans Nana' that are suitable for placing in foundation plantings. These 2- to 3-foot-high dwarf cultivars do not look like the species; they resemble blue false cypress. Japanese cedars were such an important part of the design at Reynolda Gardens in Winston-Salem that cuttings from the early 1920 plantings were rooted for replanting during the recent garden restoration project.

WHEN TO PLANT

Container-grown Japanese cedars are well adapted to planting any time the ground is workable. In the Mountains and Piedmont, fall-planted evergreens need 6 weeks to establish before the ground freezes. Field-grown trees should be planted in early spring.

WHERE TO PLANT

Japanese cedar thrives in deep, rich soil to light clay soil in open sun. When used as a specimen in full sun, this narrow upright tree will draw the eye toward a landscape feature you want to highlight. Have you noticed that too many Leyland cypresses are being used for screening? Japanese cedar is a viable alternative. Its bronze hue in winter is not as obvious when it is planted in partial shade.

HOW TO PLANT

In well-drained soils, plant Japanese cedars at the same depth that they were grown in the nursery; plant them slightly higher in clay

soils. Loosen the roots of container-grown plants so they can be spread out naturally in the planting hole. The addition of compost or organic matter is recommended for poor soils. Dig holes that are at least a foot larger than the rootball, though the planting hole should be no deeper than the depth of the rootball. A neutral pH is acceptable for this evergreen, so a little liming or the addition of wood ashes is encouraged. Firm the soil around the roots and pour 4 gallons of water over the rootball. Finish backfilling with the soil and apply a 2-inch layer of mulch.

CARE AND MAINTENANCE

Beginning the second season after planting, Japanese cedars grow moderately fast. To keep them in bounds, light shearing is acceptable. Cutting the central leader (trunk) is not recommended. A slow-release fertilizer applied in September will keep the cedar looking good all winter long. Unlike most conifers, Japanese cedars cannot tolerate long periods of drought. Keep them mulched and watered and you will be amazed at the rich, new growth in the late summer months. Don't be reluctant to prune lightly during the Christmas season—Japanese cedar's greenery is attractive for decorating.

ADDITIONAL INFORMATION

To prevent winter winds from topping the new installation, it is wise to stake fall-planted Japanese cedars. Once established, however, they can be used as windbreaks and privacy screens throughout North Carolina. The newer dwarf conifer cultivars need well-drained soil; consider grouping them for an accent planting.

ADDITIONAL SPECIES, CULTIVARS, OR VARIETIES

There are over 70 cultivars of Japanese cedar, all far superior to the old seedling trees available decades ago. In his book *The Year in Trees*, J. C. Raulston recommended 2 full-sized Japanese cedars, 'Yoshino' and 'Ben Franklin.' The latter has blue-green foliage and is tolerant of salt spray. 'Elegans' is a smaller plum-colored form that grows to 20 feet.

Leyland Cypress

In urban counties across North Carolina, Leyland cypress has become a household word. There are few evergreens that grow so vigorously when planted as a privacy screen. Leyland cypresses are often planted by the Department of Transportation along highways where they are sometimes mistaken for eastern red cedars because of their upright, columnar form. Leyland cypress is a blue-green narrowleaf evergreen that is readily available in containers from all our garden centers. It is a hybrid of 2 Pacific Coast species, Monterey cypress and Alaska-cedar. It was introduced to our state in the mid-1970s by the North Carolina State University Arboretum. It was an immediate boon to nurserymen who were searching for an alternative to the red tip photinia as a hedge shrub. Weather conditions in the state have favored this magnificent evergreen over the photinia and other shrubs. Once established, the Leyland cypress can grow 2 to 4 feet each year. It rarely needs pruning and it can reach a height of 50 feet or more. This remarkable evergreen is currently being over-planted; there are some concerns about the appearance of a cypress canker disease.

When to Plant

Plant Leyland cypress any time the ground can be worked. I prefer to plant in early spring or late fall to avoid significant cold damage to foliage.

Where to Plant

Plant Leyland cypress in well-drained soils. This plant prefers full, open sun. Partial shade is acceptable provided it gets strong afternoon sun. Shady locations will cause the plant to become topheavy, likely to topple over in windstorms. This is a great evergreen for formal hedges or as a specimen plant that can be enjoyed for its soft, rich foliage.

How to Plant

Thoroughly loosen the roots of plants grown in containers. Prepare a wide planting hole as deep as the rootball and 3 times as wide. Make a mix of 2/3 soil and 1/3 soil conditioner. Pack this backfill soil

mix firmly around the sides of rootball. Water slowly, applying 4 gallons of water to settle the plant. A Leyland cypress that is larger than 5 feet should be staked with a single stake on the windward side. This is of particular importance on banks or other windy locations. Add 1 to 3 inches of mulch, staying clear of the crown of the plant. Avoid planting when soil is frozen or when soil is wet enough to form a mudball in your fist.

CARE AND MAINTENANCE

When planting during the winter months, Leyland cypress should be sprayed with an anti-transpirant to prevent sunscald. This evergreen prefers moist soil, so water it diligently, especially during the summer months in its early years. Begin fertilizing the second spring after planting. A slow-release fertilizer can also be used in September to increase the growth rate. Leyland cypress can be topped or pruned severely in late winter through early summer. Do not remove more than 1/3 of the foliage in a season. When used for hedges, space the Leyland cypress 3 to 5 feet apart.

ADDITIONAL INFORMATION

The cypress is being grossly overplanted, and horticulturists are concerned about recent instances of Cypress Canker reported in North Carolina. We don't know how severe or widespread this acute fungus disease may become. *Caution:* Branches that suddenly turn brown and die should be removed promptly.

ADDITIONAL SPECIES, CULTIVARS, OR VARIETIES

'Naylor's Blue,' with grayish blue foliage, is cold hardy to Zone 5. 'Castlewellan' is hardy and has yellowish new growth. 'Leighton Green' is readily available; it is currently the Leyland cypress being used by Christmas tree growers in our state. The species is very tolerant of salt spray in Coastal regions.

Longleaf Pine

*L*et's hear it for longleaf pine, the State Tree! When I go to speak at civic clubs, I find it amusing to ask the group for the name of the State Tree. Nine times out of ten the instant reply is, "Dogwood." And what a fine State Tree it would be if it weren't already the State Flower! The longleaf pine is one of the most distinctive Southern pines. It matures into an 80-foot evergreen. It is appreciated most for its 12-inch needles that provide the marvelous mulching material we North Carolinians call pine straw. The dense needle tufts of the longleaf pine are held at the ends of its branches, as are its 10-inch cones. As the tree approaches 20 years in age, the coarse, scaly bark becomes a prominent feature; the trunks of the mature trees show off rough plates of bark. In sandy Coastal soils, the tree produces a deep taproot with very developed laterals. In the northwest Piedmont's clay soils, it has relatively shallow roots like other shade trees. This amazing tree will survive flooded soils but it is subject to wind-throw. Our winter ice storms in the west are longleaf pine's biggest threat. The storms often leave these trees in shambles.

When to Plant

Container-grown longleaf pines may be planted any time that soil conditions allow. The tree seedlings are available bareroot from some nurseries. Plant them immediately upon receipt, or heal them in and plant them in February or March as spring approaches.

Where to Plant

Plant your longleaf pine in full sun. A distinct feature of this variety is that it can be "limbed up" to allow planting activities under the canopy of the tree. This pine makes an interesting specimen tree when use as a backdrop for broadleaf evergreens. A popular place for planting indica azaleas is in the shade of longleaf pines. Plant these trees a distance from the house.

How to Plant

Dig a hole that is as deep and twice as wide as the rootball. Position the tree and backfill with an amended soil, allowing the ball to sit slightly higher than the existing soil. It will settle a bit over time.

Mulch to a 2-inch thickness, but do not place mulch against the trunk. Water the newly planted pine with 4 gallons of water; repeat this every week for a month. During the first year, it is best to stake trees that are over 6 feet in height. Staking will prevent winds from uprooting the trees. When planting a row of longleaf pines, space them 15 to 20 feet apart to allow for mature growth. They can be planted closer if a wind or privacy screen is desired.

CARE AND MAINTENANCE

Water your longleaf pine weekly until the tree is firmly established; water more often as needed during the first growing season on a dry, sandy planting site. You can prune this tree any time except when new growth is developing—wait until new candleshoots have had a chance to harden-off. Your longleaf pine should be fertilized any time from November through March. Use a complete fertilizer that is high in nitrogen (for example, a 2-1-1 ratio) at the rate of 1 pound per inch diameter of the tree trunk. Broadcast the fertilizer on top of the ground out at the dripline and several feet beyond this point.

ADDITIONAL INFORMATION

The longleaf pine rarely suffers any serious problems. Sometimes the pine beetle and fungal rust can occur. If these do become a problem, consult your Extension Center for proper advice. The biggest threat comes from ice and heavy snowfalls in western North Carolina, so don't plant longleaf pines in this area. There are some beautiful specimens growing as street trees in the Winston-Salem area.

ADDITIONAL SPECIES, CULTIVARS, OR VARIETIES

Seedlings are the main source of commercially available longleaf pines. State nurseries operated by the North Carolina Forest Service are responsible for collecting high-quality seeds and growing improved seedlings. These are distributed through that agency each winter via seedlings applications that can be picked up at the county offices. These seedlings are a fraction of the cost of those that come from most mail-order nurseries.

Nellie R. Stevens' Holly

A conical hybrid holly, 'Nellie R. Stevens' has become the choice of landscape designers for formal hedges and screens. This magnificent holly is stately in appearance as it matures to 20 to 30 feet. The foliage is a glossy dark green and is quite compact. The bright-red fruit are not as prominent as they are on some of the American hollies, but the plant's rapid growth rate is a true advantage. 'Nellie R. Stevens' has the beauty of its English holly parentage and the drought tolerance of the Chinese holly family. Certainly it is a favorite choice for a screen or a specimen evergreen tree. It serves as the backdrop for the renowned perennial border at the North Carolina State University Arboretum in Raleigh. A similar hybrid that is popular with nurserymen is 'Mary Nell' holly. *I.* 'Mary Nell' has glossy, very spiny, toothed leaves. It reaches 15 feet in height and is a dense ornamental for a privacy screen. A new NCAN (North Carolina Association of Nurserymen) introduction is *I.* 'Carolina Sentinel.' It is a tight, upright holly that is perfect for screens and hedging, and it needs no shearing. Some nurserymen are saying it will replace the Foster's holly because it stays in bounds and is naturally dense.

WHEN TO PLANT

Plant container-grown 'Nellie R. Stevens' holly any time the ground permits and supplemental watering can be applied. Large balled-and-burlapped plants meant for hedges should be planted in late winter through spring.

WHERE TO PLANT

'Nellie R. Stevens' should be planted in a full-sun location to ensure good berry production and compact foliage. The plant is quite adapted to clay soils, but avoid poorly drained conditions. Consider planting in a mass for screening purposes, spacing 4 to 8 feet apart.

HOW TO PLANT

Spade up an area twice the diameter of the rootball. Soil conditioner can be used with individual container-grown hollies; balled-and-burlapped hollies can be planted directly into well-prepared soil. Open a planting hole in the middle of the prepared bed and set the

rootball slightly higher than the original grade. (Rootballs often settle in too deeply with oversized plants.) Backfill halfway, firm-in the soil, and pour in 4 gallons of water. After the water drains out, finish backfilling and water again. If a specimen tree is over 5 feet, stake it for 6 months or longer in windy locations. Water 2 or 3 times each week, using a minimum of 12 gallons of water over each 7-day period.

CARE AND MAINTENANCE

Keep the newly planted 'Nellie R. Stevens' watered well during the first 2 seasons. Mulches and soaker hoses are wonderful for irrigating thoroughly in hot summer weather. 'Nellie R. Stevens' responds well to a slow-release fertilizer applied in early fall. Don't overfertilize or you will be pruning regularly, especially when the plant reaches maturity. Any heavy pruning should be done in late winter or early summer. Some shaping of a young holly is important during the early years, particularly if it is grown singly as a specimen tree. Few pests other than scale insects will bother this holly.

ADDITIONAL INFORMATION

Planted 4 to 5 feet apart and left unpruned, a row of 'Nellie R. Stevens' makes a perfect screen. To use as a specimen, limb up the lower branches to expose the smooth gray trunk. Multiple-trunk specimens are especially nice to anchor the corners of a 2-story house. Old foliage that has dropped should be raked up before reapplying mulch.

ADDITIONAL SPECIES, CULTIVARS, OR VARIETIES

'Mary Nell' is a similar hybrid holly that has foliage that is more showy but has very spiny leaves. 'Carolina Sentinel' is narrow and upright, and may be used as a specimen or screen. 'Foster #2' holly has a loose upright form and a profusion of red berries, and it requires shearing. 'East Palatka,' with glossy leaves that have few spines, should be planted in protected sites. 'Hume' offers heavy berry crops.

Palmetto

*T*his Southeastern native is the hardiest palm species known. Once established, it can withstand temperatures of 10 degrees Fahrenheit. Palmetto can be recognized by its straight single trunk and compact crown covered with persistent leaf bases. Surprisingly, palmetto is seldom encountered in Piedmont landscapes, primarily because it is unavailable at nurseries west of the Coastal Plains. Palmetto appears as an evergreen shrub in its juvenile form, but it should be expected to grow to a height of 20 feet or more. It is an excellent street tree or specimen plant for the seaside, as it is very tolerant of salt spray. Dwarf palmetto (*S. minor*) is very hardy even into the Piedmont area, withstanding temperatures to minus 10 degrees Fahrenheit. This palmetto has lustrous blue-green foliage and can be used as an accent shrub for an unusual tropical effect in the landscape. Another interesting evergreen palm is the needle palm, *Rhapidophyllum hystrix*. This lovely palm tolerates the cold of Zone 7 and matures to a 4-foot-tall shrub. Both palms are found naturally in moist soil conditions, but they will adapt to much drier conditions throughout much of North Carolina.

WHEN TO PLANT

Container-grown plants can be planted any time in late spring or summer. They transplant easily from May to July in Zones 7 and 8. Small plants have a higher percentage of roots than do larger palms, so don't feel deprived if you are offered a small-sized plant.

WHERE TO PLANT

Palmetto is an excellent specimen tree which can be used as an accent in a patio or terrace garden. It creates interesting shadow patterns against walls. Give it plenty of space (it has a 10-foot spread) and a sunny location. This palm makes a terrific street tree in the Coastal counties. It is very tolerant of a wide range of soil types from clay to sand, but it does love moisture.

EVERGREENS

How to Plant

Using a hand-held cultivator, carefully loosen the roots of plants grown in pots. Prepare a wide, shallow hole that is twice as wide and 3/4 as deep as the rootball. Work plenty of aged compost into the planting hole, especially in heavy soils or pure sand. Firm the soil around the sides of the rootball, then water well. Continue back-filling with loose soil until the rootball is entirely covered. Form an earthen saucer with some of the backfill soil to create a watering well. Apply a 2-inch layer of mulch around the base of the newly set plant. Keep its roots moist during the establishment period.

Care and Maintenance

Plant palmetto in late spring so it can get well established before winter. Keep it mulched well year-round in Zones 8 and 9. Extremely cold winters can sometimes cause leaf burn, but this is usually not a major problem. In Zones 7 and 8a plantings, a deep winter mulch applied within the dripline area will provided added protection in harsh winters. (I have constructed a 2-foot-high cylinder of welded wire fence, placed it over young plants, and filled it with leaves.) Mulch can be removed in March. As the tree grows, old leaves will deteriorate and should be pruned away routinely.

Additional Information

Keep well watered the first 2 summers until the palmetto is established. Fertilize every few years with a slow-release product. Pest problems are minimal; however, palmetto weevil and palm leaf skeletonizer may warrant some control. This palm is considered a moderate grower. It is marginally hardy in the foothills of North Carolina

Additional Species, Cultivars, or Varieties

There are no known cultivars of *Sabal palmetto*. Another palm recommended highly by our North Carolina Association of Nurserymen for Zone 8 is *Butia capitata*, the Brazilian butia palm. It has long 5-foot leaves that are pinnately compound with conspic-uous fiber strings. It is very hardy in a wide range of soil types.

Southern Magnolia

*S*outhern magnolia is a champion among fine evergreen trees. In North Carolina, magnolias are revered for their large shiny green leaves and 10-inch pure-white flowers. The sweet fragrance of a magnolia blossom in May is distinctive, a Tar Heel heritage. Southern magnolia is native to the South from North Carolina's southeastern counties to the Gulf states. It is a large conical tree maturing at 60 feet with a spread half the height. Most urban landscapes are marginally small, and magnolia is an immense species, cramped if tucked into close quarters. The most magnificent specimens can be found at county courthouses and on university campuses like Duke's in Durham. Many homeowners choose 'Little Gem' magnolia, thinking it is a dwarf shrub form—and it is not! It is an excellent choice, though, since it is precocious and blooms soon after planting. There are many excellent cultivars available, all great for holiday decorations and quick down-home arrangements.

WHEN TO PLANT

Southern magnolia has a fleshy root system. It should be planted in late winter or spring to insure its survival. Container-grown trees have a longer planting season.

WHERE TO PLANT

This delightful tree grows naturally in North Carolina in rich, moist soil along river swamps. It can be grown as a specimen ornamental throughout the state in drier sites. Southern magnolia does best in high-organic soils with a medium level of fertility and a pH of 4 to 6. The North Carolina State University Faculty Club in Raleigh has a driveway lined with magnolias in full sun. They are doing fine, but the foliage usually looks better on magnolias grown in partial shade. Large southern magnolias are stately and add a feeling of grandeur to any estate.

HOW TO PLANT

Break out the bag of Black Cow or cottonseed meal to enrich the ground before planting a southern magnolia! Spade in the manure and amendments or rototill an area 4 to 5 times larger than the root-

ball. Open a planting hole in the middle of the prepared bed and set in the rootball at grade (same depth as rootball). Backfill halfway, firm-in the soil, and pour in 4 gallons of water. After the water drains out, finish backfilling and water again. If the tree is over 5 feet and in a windy location, stake it for 6 months or longer. Water 2 to 3 times each week with a minimum of 12 gallons of water over a 7-day period.

CARE AND MAINTENANCE

Remember to keep the newly planted southern magnolia well watered during the first 2 seasons. Mulches and soaker hoses perform wonders. This evergreen responds well to organic fertilizers applied at the dripline in late winter. Some homeowners mix equal parts by volume of cottonseed meal and 10-10-10 fertilizer. Use 1 pound per inch of trunk diameter. Most of the pruning of magnolia is done to get holiday greenery. There is nothing wrong with selectively pruning overgrown trees, and this can be done in March and August. Make cuts back to third-year growth to make a bushier tree. Use a commercial tree spade to transplant large magnolias.

ADDITIONAL INFORMATION

Train a young magnolia for a full pyramidal shape. As the tree matures, allow the lower branches to sweep the ground. This will hide the leaves and unsightly seedpods that drop routinely, and the low cascading limbs create a wonderful natural tree house for children and grandchildren.

ADDITIONAL SPECIES, CULTIVARS, OR VARIETIES

Lustrous-leaved 'Bracken Brown Beauty' is the most cold-hardy cultivar. 'Goliath' has exceptional large flowers. With a height to 30 feet, small-flowered 'Little Gem' is the most compact cultivar. 'D.D. Blanchard' transplants well and has shiny, rounded leaves.

White Pine

*T*he white pine is primarily a mountain tree in North Carolina. It grows best where the climate is cool and humid and the soils are well-draining. Planted east of a line that runs roughly between Winston-Salem and Gastonia, white pines will be short-lived, dying one by one as they approach 20 years old. But where white pines can be grown, they should be planted! This is a beautiful evergreen and a fast screening plant, growing 3 feet or more each season once established. The gray-green foliage is soft to the touch. Its symmetrical growth habit makes a fine specimen tree where there is a large growing area. White pine matures to 80 feet in height with a spread half that. Gardeners frequently plant the inexpensive tree seedlings offered by the North Carolina Forest Service every winter. These are popular for quick windbreaks when used on the north and west sides of a yard; they will also define the property line. They can be planted as a large evergreen hedge and sheared in June to keep the hedge bushy. White pines are also popular Christmas trees and do well for this use when planted in the Piedmont.

WHEN TO PLANT
White pine seedlings are sold by the North Carolina Forest Service every winter for windbreaks. The bareroot seedlings are inexpensive and should be planted any time the ground is not frozen. Balled-and-burlapped trees are available from the Christmas season until spring; these can be planted as soon as the ground is workable.

WHERE TO PLANT
White pine is best planted in full sun or partial shade to keep the trees densely foliaged. This evergreen makes a handsome ornamental when used as a specimen plant. Remember, wherever you plant it, the soil must be well draining, not saturated with moisture.

HOW TO PLANT
Determine whether the soil drains well by digging a hole 15 inches deep with a posthole digger. Fill it up with water and check to see if it drains out in 6 hours or less. If it does, you can plant white pine in that spot. Spade up an area twice the diameter of the rootball, but

only half as deep. Add 1/2 cup of superphosphate fertilizer to the planting hole. Place the rootball squarely in the middle of the hole. Rake the amended soil up to the rootball, firm-in the soil, and water well. In questionable soils, plant white pines on a berm of soil to insure positive drainage. Apply a 2- to 3-inch layer of mulch. Water regularly throughout the spring and summer using 10 gallons of water per week.

CARE AND MAINTENANCE

Water white pines during dry periods the first 2 growing seasons. Two pests occur in white pine: weevils and aphids. Pine weevils cause new shoots to wilt. Control them by pruning out infested shoots. The white pine aphid exudes sap, and the needles can blacken from a sooty mold fungus that is secondary. This sap can fall onto patio furniture and cars parked below, so beware! Control the aphids with a forceful stream from the water hose or with horticultural oil sprays. White pines may develop root rot disease; prevent this by planting properly and avoiding wet sites. Remove weak and dying trees.

ADDITIONAL INFORMATION

Let white pine grow naturally if you have the space. Shaping is a common practice, however. Shear this tree when new needles are 2/3 their mature size, normally in late June. Low-hanging limbs can be removed any time of year. White pines can be severely damaged in ice storms, as happened in the winter of '96.

ADDITIONAL SPECIES, CULTIVARS, OR VARIETIES

Most white pine plantings come from seedlings, but there are a few good cultivars in existence. These include 'Pendula,' a good specimen plant with a 30- to 40-foot weeping form that must be trained to develop a leader and the bluish-green var. *glauca*, planted in the Arnold Arboretum. 'Compacta' is a dense rounded form.

CHAPTER FIVE

Fruits

$\mathcal{G}$ROWING FRUIT IN THE HOME GARDEN CAN BE
REWARDING, but it can also be challenging because of pest-
control problems. There are many varieties well suited to our
temperate climate in North Carolina. Choosing recommended varieties at the start will ensure good fruit quality and help prevent
serious insect and disease problems later.

The easiest fruits to grow are the "small fruits." Raspberry, blackberry, blueberry, even strawberry plants can be found growing in
the wild in many regions of the state. Although these native small
fruits are inferior to the cultivated varieties, they manage to produce small berry crops in spite of formidable pest problems and
diverse soil types. You will find these fruits offered at most grocery
stores, but the quality is rarely as good as those that can be grown
at home with virtually no chemicals.

"Tree fruits" require a little more attention to pest control than
do the brambles or blueberries. Late frosts, high humidity, diseases,
and cross-pollination concerns make it imperative that variety selection and pest management be given a high priority when planning
a fruit garden. Apples are worth growing, particularly the dwarf
and spur-type trees. The "stone fruits" such as peaches, nectarines,
and plums are not for the amateur gardener. They are still quite
affordable at the supermarket or, better, at the farmers' market.
Considering the spraying costs required to get an annual harvest
and the short life of stone fruits, it is hardly worth the effort in the
Piedmont and Mountain regions.

Chapter Five

Fruits can replace ornamentals in many landscape designs provided there is plenty of sunlight and air circulation to minimize disease problems. You can choose among dwarf blueberry or pink panda strawberry plants for groundcovers, or use dwarf apples and Japanese persimmons for specimen trees. Kiwi makes a fast-growing vine, and brambles will create a rugged screen. Planting fruits allows you to be creative while enjoying an "edible landscape"!

Apple

The search for a small flowering tree suitable for the home land-scape need not be restricted to ornamentals. There are some excellent fruit trees for Tar Heel gardens, most notably apples. They have attractive pinkish white blooms in April, and the better varieties have consistent crops of delectable fruits. Everyone knows that picking an apple fresh from your own tree is not only a rewarding experience but gives you an apple that is second to none in flavor. Growing apples at home can be very successful if recommended varieties are selected and attention is given to pest management. Full-sized apple trees require about the same amount of space as many ornamental trees. Dwarf trees are preferred because of their manageable height, which means greater ease in spraying and harvesting. Dwarf trees grow to a height of 6 to 10 feet and begin bearing normal-sized fruit sooner than do standard apple trees. They can be grown in planters or in raised beds, or along a property line to serve as a summer privacy screen. The most common varieties recommended for North Carolina gardens are 'Stayman,' 'Winesap,' 'Golden Delicious,' 'Mutzu,' 'Gala,' and 'Empire.' If planting only one tree, select the 'Golden Delicious' for its larger crops.

WHEN TO PLANT

Mid-January until the end of March is the best time to plant apple trees, especially bareroot trees ordered through mail-order nurseries. I have planted container-grown apple trees in the summer, but this is risky unless you water carefully. Many nurseries sell surplus inventory in summer; an apple tree in good condition can be a bargain for fall planting.

WHERE TO PLANT

Plant apple trees where there is full sun and good air circulation for disease prevention. A southern exposure is a good location, though morning shade is acceptable. The soil must be well drained and limed if acidic. Avoid areas where water tends to stand following a rain. If the soils are questionable, plant apples in a raised bed or on a berm. Dwarf trees can be planted in containers or used judiciously in a foundation planting.

FRUITS

How to Plant

Soil testing is very important before planting permanent fruit trees like apples. The ideal soil pH is 5.8. Limestone, phosphorus, and potassium should be mixed thoroughly into the soil before planting. Dig a wide planting hole that is a minimum of 2 feet wide and 1 foot deep. For bareroot trees, soak the roots 24 hours before planting. Trim off any broken roots. Spread the roots in the planting hole and cover them with half of the backfill soil. Pour 3 gallons of water over the roots and continue filling the hole with soil. The tree should be set no deeper than the depth it was grown at the nursery. Stake your fruit tree by placing 2 stakes in firm soil outside the planting hole.

Care and Maintenance

Do not add fertilizer at planting time except for what may be recommended in a soil test report. Water weekly if there is a shortage of moisture in late winter. New trees frequently need a little pruning to train them; this can be done over a 3-year period following planting. When in doubt, do not prune dwarf fruit trees, except to remove a broken branch. Most apple trees are grafted, and any sprouts coming from the graft union or the base of the trunk should be removed promptly. It is very important to water during the first growing season, especially in the hotter months. Fertilize your apple tree in early spring each year.

Additional Information

When selecting fruit trees for planting, it is better to buy a small healthy tree than an over-sized one. Apple trees require cross-pollination for a good fruit set. 'Golden Delicious' is a good pollinator for most varieties. When buying dwarf apple trees, compare the rootstocks to determine the ultimate size of the tree. The better rootstocks are 'MM 111' and 'M7.'

Additional Species, Cultivars, or Varieties

Many cultivars of apple trees are available as spur-type trees. These fruit earlier and keep the tree height down. Heirloom varieties of apples and disease-resistant varieties rate very high for home gardens. Disease-resistant varieties include 'Liberty,' 'Priscilla,' and 'Prima.' Other varieties include 'Gala,' 'Empire,' 'Golden Delicious,' 'Stayman,' 'Rome,' and 'Winesap.'

Blueberries

*B*lueberries can be grown in gardens in all 100 counties across North Carolina. A small planting of this indigenous fruit can produce an abundance of deliciously sweet berries. The wild berries (huckleberries) that are commonly harvested in our woodlands bear only light crops, but the commercial blueberry varieties are very prolific, bearing 8 to 12 pounds of fruit on each plant. This woody shrub makes a fine hedge in sun or shade. It is likely to catch the attention of numerous songbirds when the berries ripen in June or July. Its brilliant-red fall foliage is an added bonus. Both the highbush (*V. corymbosum*) and the rabbiteye (*V. ashei*) types can be grown in the Coastal Plain and Piedmont regions. Only the highbush will consistently survive the winter temperatures below 10 degrees Fahrenheit that regularly occur in the Mountains. The rabbiteye is more resistant to heat and drought, and it tolerates a wider range of soil types. Rabbiteye is the type to plant in the clay soils of the Piedmont. The secret to success in growing blueberries is to select the variety carefully and prepare the soil properly.

WHEN TO PLANT

It is best to plant blueberries in late winter (February to March) as soon as the soil can be worked for bareroot plants. Be sure to keep bareroot plants moist if planting is delayed. Plant 2- to 3-year-old container-grown plants from March through spring. Fall planting (October to November) is acceptable in Zone 8 gardens.

WHERE TO PLANT

Full sun is desirable, but up to 50 percent shade is usually acceptable for good berry harvests. Space rabbiteye blueberries 6 feet apart and highbush types 4 feet apart at the minimum. Blueberries are often planted in rows for cross-pollination; rows should be 8 feet apart. Plant blueberries on the north side of a vegetable garden, or plant them as a border or deciduous hedge. A grouping of blueberries for fall color will serve as an accent.

HOW TO PLANT

Soil for blueberries must be more acidic than for most other plants. Garden soils are usually limed to raise the pH for other fruits—

recently limed soils should be avoided. Have the soil tested before planting. If it is too alkaline, apply sulfur to lower the pH (ideal pH is 4.5 to 5.3). This small fruit likes moist soil but is susceptible to root rot in poorly drained sites. Consider bedding up the soil so the plants can be set well above grade. Incorporate necessary nutrients and about 1 cubic foot of decayed pine sawdust or peat moss into the planting hole by rototilling. Spread out the roots into the amended soil and firm-in as you backfill. Water well and mulch with 3 inches of sawdust.

CARE AND MAINTENANCE

Do not fertilize newly set blueberry plants until the first leaflets have reached full size. Apply 1 tablespoon of special azalea fertilizer or 10-10-10 in a circle 1 foot from the plant. Repeat at 6-week intervals through mid-August. Blueberries are shallow rooted, so cultivate around them carefully. Maintain a 3- to 5-inch mulch over their roots at all times. At planting time, prune off 1/2 the twiggy growth of your new shrubs in order to force strong new shoots. In succeeding years, winter pruning will be necessary to increase fruit production. Water regularly.

ADDITIONAL INFORMATION

Blueberries should receive a minimum of 1 1/4 inches of water per week from a combination of rainfall and irrigation during the growing season. Drip irrigation and soaker hoses in combination with mulching are sufficient. As the fruit ripens, spray the plants with grape Kool-Aid (no sugar) to deter the birds!

ADDITIONAL SPECIES, CULTIVARS, OR VARIETIES

Plant more than one variety to ensure cross-pollination and high yields. Rabbiteye varieties include 'Climax,' an upright cultivar; 'Premier,' which is disease resistant; 'Tifblue,' the standard cultivar; and 'Powderblue,' which has a long season. Highbush varieties include 'Bluechip,' an early cultivar; 'Jersey,' late season; and 'Patriot,' a mid-late cultivar. The new Southern Highbush varieties should be tried in the Piedmont.

Fig

*T*his temperate zone plant is scattered throughout the Carolinas where it bears at least 1 and sometimes 2 crops of fruit each year. Gardeners in our area are quick to plant figs because they require no spraying. The fig is a true connoisseur's fruit. It is not as hardy in the harsh winters and late spring frosts of the western region of North Carolina. Following a couple of seasons of mild winter weather, these multistemmed wonders can approach tree size. Their exotic-looking foliage and smooth pale-gray bark is distinctive. The self-pollinating cultivars are the trees for backyard fig growing in North Carolina. 'Brown Turkey' reigns as the best all-around variety, although there are other deserving cultivars on the market. What a thrill it was for this Tar Heel native to see super fig trees growing like weeds while touring the Middle East! To my surprise, the figs found in London, England, were no small cookies either. Given winter care and a protected site, figs are a versatile fruit plant for Tar Heel gardens. The fruits are wonderful when eaten fresh, right from the plant; but dry them and you will be even happier in the winter.

WHEN TO PLANT

Plant container-grown figs in early spring when the soil begins to warm. You can plant figs throughout the summer months if you are willing to water them for several weeks. Dormant cuttings can be wrapped in a paper towel and stored in the refrigerator for planting in the garden in the spring.

WHERE TO PLANT

Figs are not very demanding, so plant them where you like, as long as there's plenty of sunlight. They do prefer moist, well-drained soil. In the eastern part of North Carolina, plant them in full sun alongside the fruit trees and strawberry beds. In the west, figs may need a little protection from winter winds. Large fig shrubs are often found thriving on east and north sides of garages.

How to Plant

Rooting cuttings of a neighbor's productive fig tree is a sure way to get a fruitful plant. The cuttings can be rooted in winter and set out in spring. Most full-service garden shops offer container-grown figs which are usually available in February. Figs prefer a well-drained soil that has been thoroughly tilled. Add superphosphate to the area before tilling and several caps of dolomitic limestone. After removing the container, frill out the tangled roots and plant with the roots placed shallowly in a wide planting hole. Firm the soil and water well afterwards.

Care and Maintenance

Figs are not finicky about pruning. To keep them productive, it is important to renew old canes by removing them completely every few years and allowing a new shoot to mature. Following winter dieback, pruning out cold-damaged branches will keep decay to a minimum. Thin out suckers from the base of bushes annually. Late-spring fertilization with manure or 10-10-10 fertilizer is beneficial, but not always necessary.

Additional Information

Figs bear fruit on previous season's growth. To control the height of figs, do not prune back more than 1/3 when pruning in early spring. In the mountain region of North Carolina, wrap figs with frost blankets for cold protection in December. A cylinder of chicken wire around the fig bush filled with leaves or straw will provide extra insulation.

Additional Species, Cultivars, or Varieties

Some 250 cultivars are found in America. In North Carolina the best cultivars are 'Brown Turkey' (Texas everbearing), 'Brunswick,' 'Celeste,' and 'Hardy Chicago' (early variety). 'Brown Turkey,' originally from Britain, is the workhorse in our state, and is favored for its resistance to souring.

*A*nyone who has ever eaten a store-bought kiwi from the produce counter will be interested in the advertisements touting hardy kiwis—but I have yet to see more than a few successful kiwi plantings west of the Coastal Plains in North Carolina. They do make fabulous vines for fences and arbors, if you can live with the fact that you won't get a lot of fruit at harvest time. Kiwi is tropical in nature. It grows rapidly in a warm, long growing season. It is a long-lived, perennial deciduous vine that grows vigorously until it reaches a length of 15 feet or more. Much like bunch grapes, the fruit is born on horizontal fruiting arms with lateral shoots. Kiwi fruit is oval in shape and may be smooth or, more often, covered with a brownish fuzz. (*A. deliciosa* is hairy, while *A. arguta* lacks hair.) The flesh is bright-green and seedy. It is valued as a rich source of Vitamin C. Kiwis have male and female plants, both with cup-shaped flowers. The pistillate (female) flowers are larger than the staminate (male) flowers. If you are planning to grow kiwis, be warned that it will take patience and some desire to learn how to manage them properly.

WHEN TO PLANT
Plant kiwi in early spring after all danger of frost is past. Kiwi can be grown in temperate climates with care. Generally, it takes 3 to 5 years for kiwi vines to bear fruit.

WHERE TO PLANT
Plant kiwi in well-drained soil in a protected area. Full sun is required, as direct light is needed for fruit development. Avoid heavy clay soils and very sandy soils. The soil should be slightly acid with a pH around 5.5 to 5.7. A sturdy fence or trellis should be constructed before planting this fruit. Though deciduous, the vine will provide a privacy screen during the summer months.

How to Plant

If planting in a large garden, space kiwis 12 to 15 feet apart in rows with 15 to 20 feet between rows. This will provide plenty of space for root development. A trellis is required for the support of kiwi vines. Check with an agricultural Extension Agent for details on trellis construction. To assure adequate pollination, both male and female plants must be planted. Use only strong, robust plants. Because of its size, vigor, and longevity, kiwi must be trellised. The soil should be tested before planting. Amend the soil following the soil test recommendations for your locality.

Care and Maintenance

Kiwi plants require regular amounts of water (up to 25 gallons per week). Daily watering may be necessary. A complete fertilizer such as 10-10-10 should be applied just before active growth begins in the spring, after all danger of frost is past. If too much fertilizer is applied, there will be too much growth, affecting flowering and fruit yields. Fruiting arms should be pruned and replaced every 2 to 3 years. The trunk and main branches are maintained permanently on the trellis. Keep weeds and grasses under control by mulching or with herbicides.

Additional Information

Kiwi plants are cold-sensitive and need special protective structural devices for guarding against winter injury. Providing irrigation in some form is necessary for steady growth. *A. arguta* is recommended for hardiness Zones 3 through 7. To really grow successfully, however, the plants require 220 frost-free days.

Additional Species, Cultivars, or Varieties

'Hayward' is the cultivar planted most often, and it is perhaps the most productive for southeastern North Carolina. A number of other cultivars of both *A. delicosa* and *A. arguta* are available. The cold-hardy variety 'Issai' holds the most promise for Tar Heel gardeners. It is more compact and self-pollinating.

Vitis rotundifolia

Muscadine Grapes

uscadine grapes grow well in all but the westernmost counties of North Carolina. Vines of some of the hardier muscadine varieties survive temperatures that drop to 10 degrees Fahrenheit. In mountainous regions where early winter temperatures may drop below zero, considerable injury or death of muscadine vines is likely. In 1584, Sir Walter Raleigh's colony found this grape "growing to the tops of every shrub on Roanoke Island." In 1810 the original scuppernong vine was later discovered growing wild in northeastern North Carolina by Dr. Calvin Jones, a noted naturalist and editor of *The Star*, a Raleigh Newspaper. Since then, many improved varieties have been developed by researchers at North Carolina State University. Muscadine grapes make excellent and distinctive jellies, jams, and juices. Most of the leading varieties develop an exceptional fruity flavor that is different from bunch grape varieties. Unlike bunch grapes, muscadine grapes require a minimum spray program for disease control. In spite of the heat and humidity in our state, this grape will grow and produce. A mature muscadine grapevine can yield 20 pounds or more in the home garden.

WHEN TO PLANT

Plant muscadine grapes in late winter, before the buds swell. Some retail garden shops sell potted grapes. These should be planted in early spring, shortly after the last freeze.

WHERE TO PLANT

Muscadine grapes are adapted to almost any well-drained, moderately fertile soil. Muscadine grapes will not tolerate "wet feet." Never plant where the surface water stands more than a few hours even after the most severe storms. Where soil drainage is poor, plant on a raised row on the north side of the vegetable garden. Space your grapevines 10 to 20 feet apart. This grape can be used on an arbor as a specimen vine.

HOW TO PLANT

The soil pH for muscadine grapes should be 6.0. Before planting vines, broadcast and work fertilizer and lime into the soil as indicated by a soil test (usually about 2 pounds of fertilizer and 5 pounds of dolomitic limestone per 100 square feet). Prepare a planting hole that is twice as wide as the diameter of the root mass. If you have bareroot vines, spread the roots out and prune back damaged or weak roots. Firm-in the soil around the roots and water thoroughly. Apply 4 gallons of water twice a week for the first month after planting. For weed control, a pre-emergent product can be used. Many gardeners use mulch or clean straw for individual plantings.

CARE AND MAINTENANCE

After setting the vines and just before growth starts, apply ¹/₂ cup (¹/₄ pound) of 10-10-10 fertilizer in a 20-inch circle around each vine. Repeat monthly until July 15. In the second year, double the first-year amounts but follow the same time schedule. For bearing vines, scatter 1 to 2 pounds of 10-10-10 fertilizer per plant over the area. Repeat with 1 pound per vine in mid-June. Watering is crucial the first season or two in order to get the vine growing quickly and trained onto a trellis. A vertical trellis can be constructed using 7-foot treated posts set 2 feet into the ground. Use 9-gauge galvanized wire and set posts 20 feet apart.

ADDITIONAL INFORMATION

It is advisable to build the trellis before planting your grapevine. Train 1 main trunk up the trellis. Prune to develop fruiting arms that go in opposite directions on the wire. This gives your vine better exposure to sunlight and ensures higher yields. It is important to select self-fertile varieties for the home garden, particularly if only 1 vine is planted.

ADDITIONAL SPECIES, CULTIVARS, OR VARIETIES

The newer perfect-flowered cultivars serve as both male and female for pollination. For best results, plant 1 of these cultivars within 25 feet of female vines. The best bronze grape varieties are 'Carlos,' 'Dixie,' 'Magnolia' (cold hardy), and 'Sterling.' The best black grapes are 'Nesbitt' (cold hardy), 'Noble,' and 'Regale.' 'Scuppernong' is a female grape.

Oriental Persimmon

It is hard to categorize Oriental persimmon, for it has both ornamental appeal and delicious fruit. The beauty of its large orange fruit and bright-red color in fall make it an attractive landscape plant. It is adaptable to much of North Carolina, though it does have a strong preference for the warmer regions of the state. In general, Oriental persimmons do not tolerate temperatures below 10 degrees Fahrenheit, though some cold-hardy cultivars are now being tested. This compact tree grows to 18 feet and has a spreading habit and lustrous, dark-green leaves. It is considered a low-maintenance fruit. Unlike the stone fruit, it has few serious insect pests and disease problems which require routine spraying. Fruit begins ripening in September. There are two major types of Oriental persimmon fruit. One group, the non-astringent types, may be eaten while the fruit is still firm and newly ripened. The other type, astringent, will turn your mouth inside out unless it is softened. (Remember waiting until frost to eat a wild persimmon?) The non-astringent varieties are the best for home gardens. Seeds are normally not produced in these varieties. This fruit has one flaw: many gardeners complain of the alternate-year bearing.

WHEN TO PLANT

Oriental persimmons sold bareroot should be planted in their dormant season from December through March. This type of tree should be planted immediately upon arrival from the nursery. If this is not possible, heel-in bareroot plants in the garden after soaking the roots for several hours. Container-grown trees can be planted in winter, spring, or early fall.

WHERE TO PLANT

This fruit tree will grow in a wide range of soils, although it prefers loamy, well-drained soil. Plant Oriental persimmons away from walks and patios where the fruit can create a problem. Since the plants are deep-rooted, find a permanent location for them while they are young—they are fussy about being transplanted or relocated later. If you need 2 trees for pollination, space them 15 feet apart in full sun.

How to Plant

Before planting, have the soil tested to ensure an optimum level of fertility and a pH of 6.0 to 6.5. Care should be taken when planting—this persimmon has a fragile root system. Rototill an area 10 square feet in size and 9 inches deep. Amend the soil with the nutrients suggested by a soil test; if you do not perform a soil test, add 1/2 cup of bulb fertilizer and 1 pint jar of limestone to the planting area. Turn the soil over several times to thoroughly mix in the nutrients. Carefully straighten the roots of the Oriental persimmon and firm them in with the loosened backfill. The tree should be planted at its original nursery depth. Pour 4 gallons of water over the roots. Form an earthen saucer at the edge of the hole.

Care and Maintenance

Persimmons are trained to a central leader system (1 main trunk). The first branch should be 4 feet off the ground. Whorls of 3 to 5 branches develop on the trunk with 2 feet between the whorls. A strong framework is important for the heavy fruit load. The leader should be topped off each year to keep the height down and to allow sunlight to penetrate for better fruit production. Prune mature trees only minimally and then to remove weak limbs and root suckers. Oriental persimmons need nitrogen fertilizer annually at a rate of 1 ounce per year of tree age. Harvest the fruit when it's in full color.

Additional Information

Light pruning is required to renew fruiting wood every 2 years. Rootstock selection is important when buying this fruit tree. Oriental persimmons are grafted onto seedlings of the native American persimmon (*D. virginiana*). The main advantage of using this rootstock is that these seedlings will tolerate excessive moisture and drought quite well.

Additional Species, Cultivars, or Varieties

Non-astringent cultivars include 'Fuyu,' a red, flat fruit; 'Jiro' and 'Hanagosho,' both early; and 'Yamagaki,' the most cold-hardy cultivar and also a good pollinator. Astringent cultivars include 'Korean,' which has a medium-sized orange, flat fruit, and 'Hachiya,' bearing a red oblong-conical fruit. 'Tanenashi' does not require a mate for pollination as do the others.

Pawpaw

Pawpaw is an interesting native tree with 8- to 12-inch leaves that turn a brilliant yellow in fall. The large leaves of this deciduous tree and the pyramidal shape are reminiscent of magnolia. Pawpaw is frequently found growing in bottomlands along streams throughout North Carolina in small groves of slender multitrunk trees up to 30 feet in height. Pawpaw can make a nice landscape tree. Planted in full sun, it forms a small tree with wide spreading branches much like sassafras. The unusual flowers which appear in April are a dark maroon color and must be appreciated close-up. Two different varieties are required to cross-pollinate. Once pollinated, 5-inch-long stubby banana-like fruit will form, ripening from late summer through fall. When eaten fresh, the delightful fruit tastes like a creamy blend of banana, pineapple, and mango—tropically delicious! The fruit is ripe when it is soft to touch. Wildlife, especially raccoons, seem to relish the fruit of pawpaw. If you have deep, moist soils, this carefree native is certainly worth growing in your garden.

WHEN TO PLANT

Many nurseries carry unnamed pawpaw varieties. They should be planted in late winter from bareroot seedlings or small balled-and-burlapped trees.

WHERE TO PLANT

Plant in sun to partial shade for consistent fruit production. Pawpaw prefers deep, moist, acidic soils. Though the fruit is loved by many, most horticulturists agree that pawpaw has limited value as an ornamental. These trees can tolerate sub-zero temperatures!

HOW TO PLANT

If planting for fruit, be sure to purchase a named cultivar. If fruit quality is unimportant, the brown lima bean-like seeds can be planted in fall. They will have to go through a winter before germinating. Young potted plants can be purchased in spring. Pawpaw is somewhat difficult to transplant. It has a long taproot and should be planted carefully so as not to disturb the roots. Incorporate 1/2

bushel of compost and 1 cup superphosphate into the planting hole area. Plant pawpaw at the same level it was grown at the nursery.

CARE AND MAINTENANCE

The plants respond well to an all-purpose fertilizer and should be fertilized at least once a year in spring. They tend to be slow-growing the first year or two and grow rather quickly thereafter. Pawpaw will grow in a more moisture-retentive soil than will most fruit trees. It is found along stream banks and moist woods through-out most of the Eastern United States. Keep trees well watered for the first couple of summers and then during hot, excessively dry summers that follow.

ADDITIONAL INFORMATION

During its first year of growth, pawpaw should be partially shaded. But for fruit production, it should be placed in as much sun as possible. Keep the soil moist at all times, especially while fruit is present.

ADDITIONAL SPECIES, CULTIVARS, OR VARIETIES

All varieties are selected for good-quality fruits. 'Sunflower' is self fertile. 'Wells' has the largest fruit. 'Davis' is an old cultivar with good fruit. 'Overleese' has large fruit of excellent quality. 'Mango' has fruit that tastes much like . . . mango. 'Mitchell' has medium-sized fruit with excellent flavor.

Pecan

I grew up in a neighborhood where pecan trees were the predominant shade trees. You could not count on a good crop of nuts every year, but it seemed that there were always a few pecans that the squirrels left for us for Thanksgiving. Climbing these massive trees—as well as cleaning up the mess they certainly made—will always be among my cherished childhood memories. The pecan tree is a large hardwood tree that can grow to heights of 90 feet. Most of the trees are pruned at head-height while they are young so they will develop multiple trunks. Their large dark-green leaves are pinnately compound and have a characteristic odor that resembles that of walnuts and hickories. Pecan wood is brittle and susceptible to wind and ice damage. The pecan is native to America and has been grown commercially for well over 100 years in the Southeastern and Southwestern regions of the United States. The first pecan was grafted in 1846. All commercial pecan cultivars are grafted or budded. Pecans can be planted for shade, but their fall color is not exciting. The new cultivars grow to bearing age rather quickly.

WHEN TO PLANT

Pecan trees are normally planted during the dormant season (January to March). Budded trees are planted primarily as bareroot trees or as container-grown trees. The nuts can be planted in the fall, and they will usually come up by June. Seed production usually results in small-sized nuts and disease-prone trees.

WHERE TO PLANT

Pecan trees require plenty of space for adequate growth. Their spacings should be 60 feet by 60 feet when planting in groups or establishing small orchards. Plant so the trees will not touch when they reach maturity. Do not plant close to houses since the spoiled nuts and debris will end up in gutters and on walks or patios. Pecans produce better in eastern North Carolina, but they will grow anywhere in well-drained soils.

ZONE 7,8

How to Plant

Pecan trees are shallow-rooted and need good soil preparation at the time of planting. When planting, do not bury the graft-union. This swollen joint should be 6 or more inches above grade. Dig planting holes 3 to 3^1/$_2$ feet deep and 2^1/$_2$ feet wide to allow for sufficient root expansion and development. The soil pH should be at least 6.2. Backfill with the native soil, firming in the roots with your foot. Water well when the hole is backfilled halfway. Finish the backfilling, and form a basin at the edge of the planting hole to facilitate watering. To assure quality, be sure your pecan trees are ordered from a reputable nursery.

Care and Maintenance

Annual applications of a complete fertilizer are needed to keep nut production high. Fertilize according to your soil sample reports, or use 1 pound of 10-10-10 fertilizer for each inch of trunk diameter. Apply the fertilizer in March each spring. Training and pruning are critical to the development of pecan trees. Prune trees to a central leader system similar to apple trees. Young pecan trees require water in their early years. Do not let trees experience drought conditions. During dry conditions, apply 10 gallons of water per week. Remove webworms with a cane pole, but don't burn them out!

Additional Information

Monitoring for selected insect pests is important. Major insects include the pecan weevil, twig girdler, hickory shuckworm, and fall webworm. Follow good sanitation practices such as disposing of fallen branches, twigs, and nuts. Scab disease is a common concern, but because these trees are so large, it is not prudent to spray for diseases. Plant 2 varieties for cross-pollination.

Additional Species, Cultivars, or Varieties

Cultivars recommended for North Carolina are 'Cape Fear,' 'Stuart,' 'Pawnee,' 'Forkert,' 'Kiowa,' 'Desirable,' 'Sumner,' and 'Gloria Grande.' Proper selection of cultivars is important for pollination. Our state is not a big nut producer because of weather problems.

Raspberry

*I*t's called the King of the Berries, a fitting name for a bramble that demands a royal price at the market. Raspberries have red, yellow, or black fruit, and they grow best in cool climates. Red raspberries are best suited to the Mountains of western North Carolina Black raspberries, which can tolerate heat, are more suitable for the Piedmont and Coastal Plain areas. There are at least 7 varieties recommended for Tar Heel gardens, and it is important to select the ones better adapted to your geographical region—for example, the 'Dormanred' raspberry is a trailing type that tolerates the conditions of the Coast. There are 2 distinct growth habits of raspberry: erect bush types and trailing varieties. The berries are borne on biennial canes formed the previous season; a second light crop of berries is produced on an everbearing raspberry like 'Heritage.' Be sure to start with certified plants from a reliable nursery to guarantee freedom from diseases. Make the decision to plant either red or black raspberries, as the two must be kept separate. Our long growing season makes it quite easy to grow an ample supply of raspberries from just a few plants.

WHEN TO PLANT

Plant raspberries in March as soon as the ground thaws. Plants from established beds can be transplanted in late summer. New raspberry plants should be purchased every 5 to 7 years to avoid disease problems.

WHERE TO PLANT

Raspberries should be planted in a sunny or semi-sunny location. Orient the rows or bed in a north-south direction for better light exposure. Choose a site that has both good soil drainage and air circulation. You may wish to plant a hedge row of raspberries as a background for a perennial border. A trailing variety makes an interesting specimen on an attractive trellis or it can be used as a deciduous screen.

HOW TO PLANT

Raspberry prefers a soil pH of 6.0 and a spacing of 30 to 36 inches, with rows 8 feet apart. Eliminate sod and perennial weeds the sum-

mer before planting. Deep-till the garden in the fall and incorporate lime if needed. In spring, rake in 10-10-10 fertilizer at a rate of 1 pound per 100 square feet. Mound the soil so the rows are 6 inches higher than grade level. Set the plants 1 inch deeper than they were grown at the nursery. Water well, and continue with 1 inch of water each week from a sprinkler. Bareroot plants are the most commonly purchased raspberries. They should be kept moist and cool until planting time. The bareroot plants can be heeled-in if the ground is too wet when the new plants arrive.

CARE AND MAINTENANCE

The way you maintain your raspberries depends on the type you grow. The bush types have erect, thorny canes that do not require support. A simple wire trellis, however, will make harvest easier. These plants multiply by sending out suckers from the main roots, so thinning of the row is imperative. In general, remove old fruiting canes immediately after harvest. If growing the everbearers, cut back the canes after 2 crops are harvested. The trailing types and black raspberries are vinelike and must have a double wire trellis for support. Using 1 pound of 10-10-10, fertilize the plants in May and repeat in July.

ADDITIONAL INFORMATION

Pruning and thinning are important tasks; raspberries are susceptible to diseases when they get crowded. Close attention should be given to summer weed control. Some weed-preventer herbicides are labeled for home gardens, but mulching is the preferred method. For bigger berries, irrigate routinely during the harvest season. A raspberry plant should yield up to 4 pounds of delicious berries. Raspberry is self-pollinating.

ADDITIONAL SPECIES, CULTIVARS, OR VARIETIES

Red 'Dormanred' is a trailing type. It has large-sized fruit and a fair flavor. Dark-red 'Heritage' is erect and everbearing and has medium-sized fruit with good flavor. 'Autumn Bliss' is another red—it is erect and everbearing and has good flavor. 'Titan' is for trial use only. A black raspberry with excellent flavor is 'Cumberland.' 'Allen' is another good variety.

Thornless Blackberry

rue Southerners must have their blackberries! When talking with some old-timers in this part of the country, it doesn't take long to scare up a few good stories about "berry-pickin'." And most of the stories have some truth in them, especially the parts about black snakes, sharp thorns, and chiggers. When it comes to tromping through a meadow, I'm the first one in, but a batch of wild blackberries is another matter. Give me a few trellised blackberries—the thornless variety—and I'm one happy camper. Thornless blackberries were God's gift to the South. They are a bit seedy and tart, but that's a small price to pay for blackberry cobbler. If you have a sunny spot in your backyard with average soil, thornless blackberries will do well for you, though they need a support. They are native to the Tar Heel State, so you can't find an easier fruit to grow. The only problem you will have is keeping them in bounds. I have grown the newer thorny, erect varieties from Arkansas such as 'Shawnee' and 'Cheyenne.' Though delighted with their sweeter berries, I was unhappy with the prickly thorns. 'Navaho' is a good choice for an erect type. It is thornless and does not require a trellis.

WHEN TO PLANT

Early spring planting of dormant blackberry plants is best. Thornless blackberries propagate themselves by producing suckers which can be dug up in late summer and planted. The tips of branches that lie on the ground will take root naturally (these are called "tip-layered" plants and can be planted in summer). Tip-layered plants are usually available from November to March.

WHERE TO PLANT

A full-sun location is desirable for heavy fruiting, although blackberry plants will thrive in partial shade. Frost is normally not a problem for this fruit since it flowers later than many fruit crops. To avoid virus diseases like double blossom, the erect type should not be planted within 300 feet of wild blackberries. Plant erect blackberries as a border, and plant the trailing types as a privacy fence or on a rustic splitrail fence.

How to Plant

Perennial weeds and established sod should be destroyed in the spot where you will plant your blackberries. A glyphosate herbicide can be used to eliminate the weeds; spray in late summer before planting. A soil pH of 5.8 to 6.5 is ideal. Plow or spade up an area to a depth of 12 inches. Compost or a similar organic material can be mixed with the soil. Mix 1/3 cup of 10-20-20 fertilizer into the planting hole. If the dormant blackberry plants are dry upon arrival by mail, soak the roots for several hours before planting. Trim off broken roots. Set the plants in the garden a few inches higher than grade to allow for settling. Use leaf mulch or pine needles to help protect the soil. Water well.

Care and Maintenance

Blackberry plants produce new shoots from the crown of the original set plant and possibly from the buds formed on the roots. These shoots grow one season and produce laterals (side branches). The second year, small branches grow from the buds on the laterals. Fruit is borne on the tips of these small branches. After the 2-year canes have borne a crop, the cane dies. These are removed to the ground as soon as the berries are harvested. The plants are fertilized at that time with 1/2 cup of 10-10-10 fertilizer per plant. New canes will soon appear from the soil. Keep the plants watered during late summer. Fertilize in May as well.

Additional Information

Space the erect-type plants 3 feet apart in rows. When these plants reach 3 feet high, cut off the tips of the canes so the canes will branch and support heavier crops. The trailing types are vigorous and should be set 6 to 10 feet apart. Align plants carefully in the row to accommodate the trellis which will be constructed for trailing blackberries. Tie the plants to the trellis.

Additional Species, Cultivars, or Varieties

Blackberries exist in 2 major forms, erect and trailing. The erect bush-like 'Navaho' from the University of Arkansas has excellent size and flavor. Semi-trailing types are 'Boysenberry,' 'Dirksen,' 'Loganberry,' 'Tayberry,' 'Hull Thornless' (USDA), 'Chester Thornless' (USDA), 'Smoothstem,' and 'Carolina.' USDA releases are often the best cultivars.

CHAPTER SIX

Groundcovers and Ornamental Grasses

*O*NCE ONLY TURFGRASSES WERE USED TO PREVENT SOIL EROSION and to provide the "green color" in the home landscape. In the New American Garden, groundcovers and ornamental grasses can be used for these purposes. Huge flowing beds of these two groups of ornamentals can be strategically spaced to create interesting contemporary designs.

Why would anyone install these two plant materials when turfgrasses are the most familiar groundcovers in use? For most gardeners, one of the big advantages of planting groundcovers is the savings in "sweat equity." More and more, gardeners want to reduce the time they spend mowing their lawns. (Not only does mowing equipment affect air quality, but it creates noise pollution in suburban neighborhoods.) Some groundcovers are the best choice for shady yards—there are few turfgrasses adapted to shaded conditions. Groundcovers are also ideal for steep slopes, rocky sites, and open areas where tree roots make gardening difficult. They help define shrub beds and are essential in woodland gardens.

There is growing interest in using ornamental grasses in a similar fashion. While there are few ornamental grasses that tolerate shade, there are endless ways to use these native plants in the home landscape. If you have a wet or dry site, there are grasses that will thrive in your garden. There are virtually no pests that bother these unique plants. Ornamental grasses such as blue clump fescue can

Chapter Six

be used as groundcovers, while Japanese blood grass should be used in mass groupings to echo the colors of choice perennials planted nearby. The taller ornamental grasses will create movement in the landscape as they sway rhythmically in the wind. To add another dimension to your garden, allow the dormant foliage to remain throughout the winter months.

Whether you are planting ornamental grasses or groundcovers, it is important to choose the varieties that will flourish in your particular garden. Purchase vigorous plants and prepare the soil thoroughly as you would for other ornamentals. It will take a year or two for these plants to get firmly established. Once they have settled in, your patience will be rewarded with low-maintenance plantings.

Ajuga

OTHER COMMON NAME: Bugleflower

When spring bulbs are blooming in North Carolina landscapes, the deep blue flower spikes of the durable groundcover ajuga come shining through. And these blooms are terrific—but it is ajuga's foliage that sets it apart year-round. Ajuga plants or crowns consist of somewhat oval, waxy, 2- to 4-inch-long leaves that form a low, thick mat. The leaves are a burgundy color in the cooler months, but in late summer and in shady locations they acquire a forest green color. My favorite is 'Burgundy Glow,' which has variegated foliage in sunny gardens. Its wine and white colored foliage is stunning in rock gardens, or when used as an edging with other perennials that have rather coarse uninteresting features. Ajuga is a hearty performer in the landscape. It spreads readily by stems that root on contact with the soil. It is so hardy that it sometimes escapes from a bed to a moist area or lawn. If not properly controlled or restrained, the species variety can become a nuisance. I have not had a problem with the named cultivars.

WHEN TO PLANT

Plant ajuga any time that container-grown plants are available. Late summer to December will give good results. You can transplant the crowns of plants in late winter or immediately after their flowering period. It is difficult to kill ajuga plants when planting, but if this does happen, you probably didn't move any of the roots with the plant, or perhaps you let them dry out!

WHERE TO PLANT

Plant ajuga in full-sun to partial-shade areas in rich, moist soil. Shady locations are best as you go toward the Coastal Plains. Because of its low-growing, fast-spreading habit, ajuga is especially adapted for use in woodland gardens. If it is too dry to grow lawn grasses under a particular shade tree, you can bet that ajuga will thrive there. Plant this pretty groundcover where the blue flower spikes can be appreciated.

ZONE
6,7,8

HOW TO PLANT

Prepare the soil by working in ample compost or bark soil conditioner to a 4-inch depth. Apply 1 pound of 10-20-20 fertilizer (or similar analysis) per 100 square feet of bed, and rake it into the soil. Ajuga plants are purchased in cell packs and are easily set into the ground using a hand planter or a short-handled army shovel. Space the individual plants 1 foot apart on a grid pattern. It helps if you mulch beforehand and plant groundcovers through the mulch. Water thoroughly after planting, and keep the soil moist for the first month.

CARE AND MAINTENANCE

During the spring each year following bloom, apply a granular balanced fertilizer like 10-10-10. Be sure to water-in the fertilizer after applying, or time your application to precede a forecasted rain. Ajuga is an aggressive groundcover that spreads relatively quickly. If the plant's runners invade unwanted areas, just cut them back, or dig out the crowns. Use a garden hose for watering individual plants in new plantings, but an oscillating sprinkler is more practical in beds. Apply 1 inch of water per week if rainfall is short. Once established, ajuga is practically invincible. Dig out dying plants if dead spots appear in spring.

ADDITIONAL INFORMATION

Ajuga beds are occasionally injured by a soil-inhabiting fungus called rhizoctonia. There is no good control for this short of removing infected plants. The bed usually fills in a month or so later. It is difficult to kill established ajuga plants with herbicides, except in a lawn. Enjoy its unique leaves while keeping an eye on its growth habits.

ADDITIONAL SPECIES, CULTIVARS, OR VARIETIES

'Burgundy Glow' has deep-red to pink-and-white leaves and true-blue flowers. 'Atropurpurea' has bronze-purple foliage and purple flowers. 'Alba' has white flowers. 'Rubra' has purple-red blooms. 'Silver Beauty' has white-and-green foliage and blue flowers. Slow-growing Geneva ajuga makes a good floral show. 'Metallic Crispa' has unusual stiff-leaved wrinkled crowns that are dark brownish purple!

Blue Rug Juniper

There are few junipers the average homeowner knows by name. But mention blue rug juniper and the lights go on. From southern California to the coast of North Carolina gardeners love blue rug, a class of woody evergreens we sometimes call "creeping junipers." This cultivar is the finest prostrate juniper in its class. Unlike many other popular covers, blue rug juniper hugs the ground with an intense blue-green foliage that reaches 4 to 6 inches in height. Its trailing habit makes it especially suitable for use on banks or as an edging plant. This variety is a moderate grower, and a single specimen will spread to a diameter of 5 feet. Blue rug juniper sporadically forms blue berries. When planted in full sun, it takes on a plum color during the winter months. When you plant it in the proper location, you can enjoy a soft-textured living carpet that is nearly weed-free. A similar cultivar is 'Bar Harbor,' a very hardy juniper with silvery-green wispy branches. It has a purplish winter color. The taller cultivars of creeping junipers are Japanese Garden, Sargents, 'Prince of Wales,' 'Blue Pacific,' and Andorra Compacta, which is maroon in winter.

WHEN TO PLANT

Plant blue rug and similar groundcovers during warm months since they are native to the hot, arid regions of the country. I recommend planting from spring to late fall when soil temperatures are favorable for root growth. *Note:* Keep in mind that some creeping junipers turn a purplish red color in winter. 'Prince of Wales' does not.

WHERE TO PLANT

The creeping junipers are adaptable to a variety of soils, from light sands to heavier clay soil. Because they are desert plants, they should be planted in areas that receive full sunlight. If you plant blue rug junipers in poorly drained soils, you can expect big problems! They can actually take a little shade better than they can tolerate wet feet. Use blue rugs in mass plantings and as groundcover for soil stability on embankments.

HOW TO PLANT

Blue rugs and other creeping junipers are best planted in large beds rather than individual holes. This is of particular importance in clay

soils where a hole may be something like an "in-ground aquarium," suitable not for junipers but for aquatic plants! In sandy loams and well-drained sites, dig a hole as wide and twice as deep as the container. Remove the plant from the container and shake off most of the soilless medium to expose the feeder roots. If the plant is potbound, free up the roots by making several vertical slices in the rootball with a spade or knife. Position in the prepared hole, and backfill with the loosened soil. The upper roots should be visible when planted. Water well, apply a weed-preventer, then mulch the bed.

CARE AND MAINTENANCE

Water your newly planted junipers for 20 minutes twice each week for the first month, using a garden hose adjusted to a low flow. Afterwards, water only during dry periods in summer for the first growing season. For better color and faster growth, fertilize with a slow-release product (for example, an 18-6-12) in spring and early fall. Prune blue rug juniper only to contour the shape. Other creeping junipers such as the shore junipers may be trimmed year-round, but early spring is always best. Selectively remove individual shoots. Junipers can withstand hot, dry weather! Grassy weeds can be removed with herbicides; otherwise, handweed.

ADDITIONAL INFORMATION

Common diseases and insects include juniper blight, branch die-back, and spider mites, each of which may become serious on some species. Blue rugs tend to be the most resistant to these problems when planted in full sun where there is good air circulation. Watch for declining foliage color and, if necessary, call the Extension Service to address these problems correctly.

ADDITIONAL SPECIES, CULTIVARS, OR VARIETIES

J. procumbens 'Nana' (Japanese garden) is my favorite for use in edging sunny beds or borders; it stays in bounds well and is great for Japanese gardens or as a dwarf specimen plant. Another important groundcover species is *J. conferta* (shore)—the best of this group is 'Blue Pacific.' In shade gardens, try *Microbiota*, Siberian cypress.

English Ivy

*E*nglish ivy must hold this state together! Some variety of this plant is found growing in every county of North Carolina. This ubiquitous groundcover is one of the most popular vining evergreen covers for Tar Heel gardens. If you notice a groundcover uniformly covering the foundation of a home, it is likely to be English ivy. One reason it is so popular is that it has many uses and does well in heavy shade, although it will adapt to sunny conditions without much problem. When growing near trees it will take on a shrub-like form as it works its way up a tree, attaching itself with root-like tendrils. English ivy will go 40 or more feet up a tree and into the canopy and crown, especially if it is in a moist location. While old trees appear to cohabit well with ivy, young trees can become stunted. Another potential problem with English ivy arises when it is trained onto the wall of a house. Wood rot and birds nesting in the ivy are regular complaints heard at Extension offices. With over 200 cultivars available, including the lustrous dark-green ones and the curly-leaved or variegated ones, there are endless ivies from which to choose.

WHEN TO PLANT

Most references recommend planting English ivy in spring through early fall, but I say plant ivies any time a shovel can be pushed in the ground. As with many groundcovers, be patient, because ivy will do very little in the first year. Cuttings from ivies are best planted in spring after the soil warms a bit, but root divisions can be planted in winter.

WHERE TO PLANT

English ivy can be planted in full sun to deep shade, but to avoid foliage sunburn, it is better in partial- to full-shade areas. It is planted for its traditional groundcover qualities and is also used to cover walls, giving a regal feeling of formal gardens from the past. Try using ivy in mixed containers and urns, cascading over the sides for a full lush look, or use it on a lamp post. I grow white-leaved ivy and caladiums in pots.

ZONE
6,7,8

How to Plant

Garden centers sell the ivies as rooted cuttings in multi-cell flats, or in containers from 4-inch to 1-gallon sizes. Space rooted cuttings 6 inches to 1 foot apart in beds on a grid pattern—the trick is to prepare the bed and mulch it before planting. Space potted plants 2 to 3 feet apart. Prepare groundcover beds by working in ample organic matter, aged compost, or bark soil conditioner to a 4-inch depth. Rake out the rocks and clods, then mulch. Potted ivies can be planted in planting holes that are 50 percent larger than the containers. Use bulb fertilizer at planting, or use a 5-10-10 product. Water well and keep the planting bed moist for 3 to 5 weeks after planting.

Care and Maintenance

English ivy can be fertilized in spring or early fall with a slow-release product or with 10-10-10 garden fertilizer. Water well after fertilizing; in established beds, take a broom and sweep the fertilizer granules off the foliage to avoid beige burn-spots. Prune English ivy with shears as needed to maintain growth in desired areas. In naturalized beds, both bush-whackers and push mowers can be used to invigorate overgrown matted ivy. English ivy planted in full south sun may develop sunburned leaves which can lead to secondary leaf spot diseases.

Additional Information

Vigorously growing English ivy usually overcomes any pest problems. But if there is a buildup of scale insects, you may want to chemically control the problem. Keep ivy away from the bases of young trees. It is a "fierce competitor of trees," says Dr. Tom Perry, Raleigh Consulting Arborist. Remember the old saying: "Ivies creep, sleep, then leap."

Additional Species, Cultivars, or Varieties

'Glacier' is grayish with silvery patches. 'Gold Child' has yellow leaf margins. 'Gold Heart' displays a gold spot in each leaf center. 'Ivalace' has wavy leaf margins. Dwarf 'Minutissima' has 1-inch pointed leaves. 'Spetchley' (gnome), good for planters, grows to 3 inches and has tiny leaves. Boston ivy is grown on walls for fall color.

Hardy Iceplant

With a name like iceplant, you would think this groundcover would melt in our summer heat and flourish in the harsh winter weather of western North Carolina. Fortunately, the opposite is true! This wonderful plant is a member of a family of low-growing succulents native to the deserts of South Africa. Hardy iceplant is a relatively new semi-evergreen groundcover introduced to the Triad area by our local perennial plant expert, John Heitman, who told me he was given the plant by a botanist from a botanical garden in Colorado. He observed this sedum-like plant for a number of years and decided to propagate it for sale. Its popularity has been more than gratifying. The round fleshy leaves of hardy iceplant are 2 to 3 inches long and the dense foliage grows quickly in a hot, sunny garden spot. The long creeping chains of its succulent stems lie flat on the ground. No doubt the thickened leaves conserve the plant's moisture, allowing it to thrive in dry desert-like conditions. This groundcover is a show-stopper when it breaks loose with quarter-sized magenta or yellow blooms in summer.

WHEN TO PLANT

Plant hardy iceplants from containers during the warmer months of the year as soil conditions permit. I have divided the plants throughout the summer months and transplanted these 4-inch stem segments with virtually 100 percent success rates. In most cases, I covered the severed ends with an inch of mulch and they rooted promptly.

WHERE TO PLANT

For fullness of growth and to prevent root rot, plant hardy iceplants in full sun in well-drained soil. The plants will survive in poor soils and they are pH adaptable. Use iceplant as a low groundcover in front of beds of shrubs or other perennials. It offers a colorful solution to soil erosion problems on sloping ground and banks. *Caution:* because it is a succulent, its fleshy leaves are crushed easily by foot traffic and pets.

How to Plant

For individual plantings, dig a hole that is twice the width and 3/4 the depth of the rootball. Remove the plant from the container and position in the hole. There is no need to disturb the rootball, as the plants are not normally potbound. The new plants are somewhat fragile, so be careful when handling. Mix compost or pine-bark soil conditioner into the existing soil if it is a tight clay soil, using amendments in a quantity equal to 1/3 of the soil removed from the planting hole. If the soil is loamy and well drained, no soil amendments are needed. Carefully backfill around the rootball with the soil. Mulch with 1 inch of crushed pine bark. Soak the plant thoroughly with water after planting to settle the soil.

Care and Maintenance

Fertilize in the spring just before new growth starts each year. Use a commercial shrub fertilizer for best results. Water during the establishment period by irrigating lightly once a week. Keep in mind that this is a desert plant and too much water is detrimental to its health. Don't water if the ground is moist to touch. There is no advantage to winter mulching except in the cold western counties; in those counties, use pine needle mulch. Pruning is not needed by this groundcover except following the autumn frosts when the fleshy foliage "melts down." A pair of hand shears and a rake will do this winter cleanup chore.

Additional Information

Remember that the iceplant is not winter hardy in the Mountain Region and it can look shabby from December to April. My plantings have taken a lot of abuse by dogs and kids on bikes, but they have always grown back fully. This amazing groundcover is sure to become an all-time favorite with gardeners in the Old North State. It is evergreen in the east.

Additional Species, Cultivars, or Varieties

The species is vegetatively propagated and sold by nurserymen as rooted cuttings available with neon yellow and magenta-colored flowers. The foliage can be a blue-green in the cool periods of fall and spring.

'Homestead Purple' Verbena

*T*his semi-evergreen groundcover has risen to stardom in an incredibly short period of time since its introduction by Dr. Allan Armitage of the University of Georgia. Part of its success can be attributed to its ease of propagation and its resistance to pests. 'Homestead Purple' is a vigorous perennial bearing showy 3-inch purple flowerheads. The rich royal purple blooms appear from early spring to fall on the terminal ends of 1- to 2-foot stems. Homestead verbena is certainly a "must-have" if there's a sunny bank that yearns for a splash of color. In spring at my house, it is in bloom when the Japanese maple is leafing out, and it is outstanding growing at the foot of the goldthread cypresses that flank my foundation planting. When the yellow variegated flag iris pops up through the homestead verbena, I get a "gardener's rush." And how can such a great groundcover be so incredibly durable? I have had dogs run through the plantings, even sleep in them, without any lasting damage. Try this Southern gem interplanted with spring-flowering bulbs such as yellow daffodils.

WHEN TO PLANT

Plant 'Homestead Purple' from early spring through early fall. Clumps can be dug up and separated during the warmer months as well. I have taken cuttings during the summer and easily rooted them in a shaded bed of builders sand. The prostrate growing branches root while lying on the ground and they can be removed for transplanting.

WHERE TO PLANT

This verbena likes a warm, sunny location, especially in western North Carolina. It may appear a little tattered following a hard winter or drought. Fortunately, this native rebounds quickly since it is a strong grower. Space plants in the bed 5 to 6 feet apart. Try planting with a colorful evergreen as a backdrop or interplant in bulb beds. Beds of homestead verbena will provide a nice accent to entrance plantings.

HOW TO PLANT

Small pots of verbena are often potbound, so be sure to force the roots apart before planting in a bed. A hand-cultivating fork works well to frill loose the tightly held roots of many hefty growers. Plant groundcovers into a well-tilled bed that has been amended with lime, super phosphate, and soil conditioner. Backfill around the newly set plants while firming in the soil around the roots. A thorough watering after setting is critical. Water every third day for several weeks, then once weekly in the summer. Plant divisions can be made from early spring to midsummer and again in late fall. If this is your first experience with homestead verbena, you should know that you don't need to buy many starter plants.

CARE AND MAINTENANCE

In western North Carolina counties, do not remove cold-damaged foliage of homestead verbena in winter, for it will provide a little added protection from harsh wind and cold. In other areas, moderate pruning and cleaning of this plant is acceptable in December when it has gone dormant. On the Coast, this verbena will be evergreen during most winters. Shear it at will in order to keep it in bounds and increase the flower display. After cold has passed, apply a general garden fertilizer like 10-10-10 in the spring, and again in the summer if growth is slow. This is a free-blooming perennial; as is true of wildflowers, it should not be overfertilized. Occasionally lop back rangy wild stems to keep the plant compact.

ADDITIONAL INFORMATION

The biggest gardening chore in the western half of North Carolina is the winter cleanup after serious cold hits. I use a pair of lopping shears to reach into the plant. I suppose you could use a weed eater and a rake!

ADDITIONAL SPECIES, CULTIVARS, OR VARIETIES

In my opinion, 'Homestead Purple' verbena is king of flowering groundcovers. Most of the annual verbenas give mediocre results. V. 'Texas Appleblossom,' has a pink-and-white flower. V. 'Ultraviolet' is the most vigorous and has dark-purple blooms.

Lavender Cotton

Lavender cotton is a member of the daisy family, though this silver-gray perennial does resemble the herb lavender. Two varieties of *Santolina* are available at garden centers: lavender cotton and *S. virens*. Lavender cotton is the most cold-hardy of the species and offers more interest in the landscape than does the emerald-green *S. virens*. In summer, disk-shaped flowers appear as a nice contrast to the foliage. This herb is a tough, drought-resistant perennial that is native to the dry hillsides along the Mediterranean. Its attractive juniper-like foliage is quite aromatic; oil from its leaves is sometimes used in perfumes. Lavender cotton grows to 2 feet in height with an equal spread. It has a loose growth habit and is a good choice when you are looking for a plant that will spill over slopes, walls, or ledges. It can be used as an edging in both perennial and herb gardens—the dwarf form is especially nice for this purpose. I have seen this plant used very effectively in decorative planters on the streets in down-town Durham and in similar settings in other urban landscapes. Lavender cotton thrives in sunny, well-drained locations even in poor sandy soils.

WHEN TO PLANT

Container-grown plants are available year-round at garden shops. These can be planted any time the ground can be worked. Propagate lavender cotton in the spring by plant divisions, layering, or cuttings.

WHERE TO PLANT

Lavender cotton does best when planted in full sun. It will tolerate a poor soil, and even light shade, as long as the soil is well drained. When planted in a shady location, it loses much of its gray color, turns green, then gets leggy. For the best foliage effect, plant laven-der cotton in rock gardens, containers, herb beds, or anywhere an edging plant is needed. Taller herbs like rosemary and perennials such as sedum make fine companion plants.

HOW TO PLANT

Lavender cotton will not tolerate wet soils, so rototill the entire bed where clay soils predominate or drainage is questionable. A coarse soil amendment such as bark soil conditioner can be added. Do not use fertilizer at planting time except for superphosphate and a dusting of limestone. For individual plantings, dig a hole that is 3/4 the depth of the rootball and 3 times its diameter. Loosen the rootball thoroughly before planting and firm the soil around the roots with your hands. When used as a groundcover, allow ample room for the plants by spacing them 4 plants to the square yard. Water thoroughly, and mulch plantings that are installed in the summer or fall months.

CARE AND MAINTENANCE

Summer plantings of lavender cotton may need watering weekly for the first month. Once the plant has established in the bed, it will be virtually care-free. Too much water and fertilizer are detrimental to this herb. A sign of too much fertilizer is greening of the grayish foliage. Apply an organic nitrogen product such as cottonseed meal each spring if needed for faster growth. Older plantings will open up and should be pruned severely (cut back halfway) in late spring every 3 years to revitalize the plantings and keep them compact. Flowers are produced, but they are not especially handsome and can be removed before (or certainly immediately after) they fade. Do not over-mulch this perennial since it is accustomed to droughty conditions.

ADDITIONAL INFORMATION

What a terrific plant for gravelly or exposed drier gardens! And lavender cotton is the "couch potato's" dream come true. In the colder zones of North Carolina, this groundcover may lose some foliage in winter, but it bounces back in the summer. High humidity and summer rains are its worst enemies in Zone 8, where it may struggle to survive.

ADDITIONAL SPECIES, CULTIVARS, OR VARIETIES

S. chamaecyparis nana is the dwarf form that makes a 1-foot compact mound. *S. virens*, green santolina, has a lovely forest-green color that is most appreciated in the winter garden. It is, however, susceptible to leaf diseases in our wet climate. The flowers of *S. virens* are small and pale-yellow in color.

Liriope

OTHER COMMON NAME: Monkey Grass

Liriope, also known affectionately as monkey grass by Tar Heel gardeners, is extensively planted throughout our state. It can be seen planted in every imaginable location in the landscape from container gardens to perennial borders. Liriope is an evergreen grass-like member of the lily family, and it is popular for its ease in growing. You don't need a "green thumb" to grow liriope, just a hatchet to divide its dense clumps of foliage. This plant matures to 12 to 18 inches in height and grows in tufts of foliage that can be either solid green, variegated green-and-white, or bright white. In midsummer, violet blooms appear on 8- to 12-inch spikes, followed by small green berries that later ripen to black. This clump-forming grass is perfect for borders, edging sidewalks, and beds, and is most effective when used as a groundcover. Creeping liriope, *L. spicata*, is especially suited for steep banks, where it will tolerate deplorable conditions and drought. My favorite is the variegated cultivar, which is fabulous when used with a grouping of dwarf nandinas or crimson pygmy barberries. In mass plantings under a river birch, liriope creates a soft texture in the landscape during the winter months.

WHEN TO PLANT

Since monkey grass is grown in containers, you can plant this perennial herb any time the ground is not frozen. It is best to divide parent plants in late winter or fall. Seeds can be planted fresh in early fall after the pulp has been removed for 90 percent germination.

WHERE TO PLANT

Liriope will thrive in most soil conditions, but if it is planted in a bed of good topsoil, it will respond with dramatic results. The flowers are showy and can be a real asset in borders or when planted as an accent. Liriope is used to soften the transition from the lawn to a shrub bed. In shade gardens, liriope can be used as a turfgrass substitute. Plant this groundcover in sun or shade.

ZONE 6,7,8

HOW TO PLANT

When planting single containers of liriope, dig a hole as deep and twice as wide as the width of the rootball. Remove the plant from the container and score the rootball with a knife or hatchet. Most plants are severely potbound when brought home from the nursery. Position the plant in the prepared hole. Backfill with the original soil and firm the rootball with your foot. Water thoroughly to settle the soil. A liquid starter fertilizer can be used at planting time or one week later. To stave off a crabgrass problem, apply a weed-preventer in March to large beds before mulching. Mulch to a depth of 1 to 2 inches. Large established clumps can be divided into 3 sections before transplanting. Space 15 inches apart.

CARE AND MAINTENANCE

Water liriope generously, especially when plants are young and during prolonged droughts the first season. There is no need to prune this groundcover during the growing season. In late winter, however, it needs to be trimmed to within 3 inches of the ground to remove burned brown foliage. It is important to do this before the emergence of new growth. In shade gardens, there is no need to shear back the plants. Fertilize in the spring with a slow-release product (for example, 2-1-1 analysis). A supplemental summer feeding is recommended to maintain the health of the plant. Sometimes rabbits will chew liriope down to the ground! Control weeds by spraying the bed with a "grass killer."

ADDITIONAL INFORMATION

There are no major problems with liriope—it can "monkey" around for years without any attention. There is one thing that will kill this plant, and that is wet soils. You will be warned of this first by its stunted growth. If you notice scale insects or vole damage, consult with your Extension agent for advice concerning their control.

ADDITIONAL SPECIES, CULTIVARS, OR VARIETIES

'Majestic' has wide, dark-green leaves; use it in borders. 'Monroe White,' dark green with white flowers, is best in shade. 'Variegata' is considered a catch-all term for all the yellow-and-white-striped liriope varieties. 'Big Blue' has large flower spikes. Dwarf white-striped 'Silvery Midget' grows to 8 inches. Beware, L. spicata can be invasive!

Pachysandra

OTHER COMMON NAME: Japanese Spurge

*P*achysandra is an evergreen groundcover that is grown in shade gardens throughout the world. Large naturalized beds of pachysandra make a stunning addition to the landscape whether there is a soil erosion concern or not. It has veined oval leaves, 2 to 4 inches in length, that grow in clusters at the top of upright stems. This plant may not be as exciting as many other groundcovers, since it doesn't produce showy blooms, but its redeeming quality is its aggressive growth in full-shade conditions. For the best growth, pachysandra needs moist soil with plenty of organic mulch. It grows by means of stolons (above-ground stems) that flourish when there is a layer of humus to enrich the soil. A mulch layer will encourage faster growth since these stolons don't have to fight their way into tight or compacted soils like the soils throughout most of North Carolina. The new variety 'Green Sheen' will tolerate some sun and has glossy, dark-green foliage. Pachysandra is not restricted to one color—there is a variegated variety with white leaf margins. The larger-leaved handsome native, American pachysandra, can be seen at Duke Gardens.

WHEN TO PLANT

For best results, plant container-grown pachysandra in spring or early fall. New plants can be started from divisions in spring. With the use of 2 spades, almost any clump of perennials or groundcovers can be easily separated.

WHERE TO PLANT

This unusual plant has a preference for full shade and moist, acidic soils like those in much of North Carolina. Pachysandra is one of our most effective evergreens for difficult-to-cover areas such as shady embankments where erosion is a problem. It is suitable for large-scale planting projects, or in small gardens for a lush look. You don't have to worry about this groundcover cracking a sidewalk or climbing a tree!

ZONE
6,7,8

GROUNDCOVERS

How to Plant

Since a groundcover comes as close to being a permanent planting as anything in the landscape, it makes good sense to prepare beds for large-scale plantings. Cell packs or flats of pachysandra are readily available at garden centers. After tilling the bed, mix in 2 inches of organic matter or bark soil conditioner and some organic fertilizer or cow manure. Mulch the beds before planting. For individual plants in small gardens, dig a hole twice as wide and just as deep as the container. Remove plants from the containers and position in the planting hole. For large projects, apply a weed-preventer. Water very well after planting and keep the soil moist throughout the first growing season.

Care and Maintenance

Pachysandra is not a heavy feeder and it should not need fertilizer the first year. In fact, if the color looks good in summer, I would not fertilize the bed at all. Every few years an application of slow-release fertilizer can be made in March. Fertilizer can kill sections of the bed, so go easy! Unless your personal taste dictates, pachysandra never needs pruning. Water as needed to maintain health in the drier years. The biggest challenge will be in removing leaves from the beds in the fall. A leaf blower does wonders if you start early in the autumn season before rain packs down the leaves. Scatter aged leaf compost over old beds.

Additional Information

Pachysandra flowers are a golden color and are not very showy. These can be removed at any time if they are not appreciated. Scale is sometimes a problem, but it is not considered life-threatening. Consult your garden center or Extension Center for proper advice. If your plants turn yellow in winter, they're getting too much sun.

Additional Species, Cultivars, or Varieties

The standard pachysandra is a fine variety in shady locations. For more pizzazz, try the newer glossy cultivar 'Green Sheen' that adapts well to partial-sun sites. A nice variegated cultivar, 'Silveredge,' will brighten up a dark corner in the garden with its green-and-white foliage. 'Green Carpet,' a dark-green groundcover, offers more flowers.

Vinca

OTHER COMMON NAME: Periwinkle

*W*hether you call it vinca or periwinkle, this rapidly spreading groundcover is popular anywhere there is a shaded garden in North Carolina. It sends out vine-like shoots ("trailers") that root readily, making the 6-inch periwinkle quite attractive to gardeners. Once established, this durable perennial will resist drought like a champ. It is a dark-green plant with 1- to 2-inch narrow leaves that hold their outstanding color in the cold of winter. In the spring it delights the gardener with a wonderful show of nickel-sized blue flowers. What could be more peaceful than large shade trees surrounded by a forest-green groundcover dotted with soft blue flowers? Though there are 2 periwinkles commonly found in the Carolinas, this species is by far the more docile and compact. The other, *V. major* (big periwinkle) is somewhat invasive, and it has a coarse texture. It acts more like a prostrate vine, growing to 2 feet high and difficult to contain in a bed. But you will not be disappointed with *V. minor*, particularly if you have a location where there is some shade. Though periwinkle is capable of overrunning a bed, it partners well with many of our spring bulbs and foundation shrubs.

WHEN TO PLANT

Plant this popular plant in the spring, summer, or fall. Dividing clumps or separating trailers in late winter or summer are methods of successfully producing more plants to enhance your landscape. Passalong plants account for more periwinkle beds in the Tar Heel state than do all the nurseries combined!

WHERE TO PLANT

Plant your periwinkle in light shade in a location where the soil is moist. In woodland gardens where the humus layer is deep with decaying leaves, the groundcover gallops across the forest and steep banks. Many of us have large shaded areas where it is difficult to grow anything. Periwinkle prospers in these areas. Plant this evergreen for its spring flowers, and use it as an edging for shrubs or borders.

How to Plant

Prepare a bed for periwinkle by spading the ground 3 to 5 inches deep. Mix organic matter or bark soil conditioner into the soil. Our native acid soils are fine for this groundcover. Mulch beds before planting when large beds are required. For small gardens, dig a hole as deep and twice as wide as the container. Remove the plants from their containers and position them in the prepared hole. The top inch of the rootball should be above grade when planted properly. Water-in the plants well and cover the surface roots with loamy topsoil or bark mulch. A weed-preventer can be applied in spring for large plantings. A soluble starter fertilizer can be applied using a watering can or hozon injector.

Care and Maintenance

Fertilize periwinkle only every few years, using a slow-release product (for example, 18-6-12). In older beds of periwinkle, maintain the plant's growth by mulching periodically with a fine layer of compost or bagged cow manure. Always irrigate before and after fertilizing if dry products are used. Periwinkle is virtually maintenance-free. Trimming is only necessary if your personal taste dictates it. During the first 2 summers, water as needed. Occasionally a stem blight disease strikes periwinkle beds, and plate-sized areas die and brown out. A preventative fungicide can be used in early spring. Prune out dead patches early.

Additional Information

Fortunately, this great groundcover doesn't climb trees; this is good, because it is popular for planting within the dripline of shade trees. Don't plant periwinkle in an azalea bed or among newly planted trees unless those areas are under irrigation. This groundcover can use some selective thinning when the bed gets too crowded.

Additional Species, Cultivars, or Varieties

The common periwinkle is readily available commercially. Improved cultivars include 'Alba' with white flowers, 'Bowle's Variety' with light-blue flowers, 'Gertrude Jekyll' with abundant white blooms and small leaves, 'Sterling Silver' with lavender-blue flowers and leaves with cream-white margins, and 'Dart's Blue' with dark-green leaves and 1-inch dark-blue flowers.

Festuca ovina var. *glauca*

Blue Clump Fescue

OTHER COMMON NAME: Sheep's Fescue

Blue clump fescue is one of the more diminutive ornamental grasses; it can also be considered a groundcover. It is a densely tufted, blue-colored ornamental grass. Blue clump fescue has icy-blue leaves that are up to 10 inches tall and retain their coloring through the heat of summer. During early summer, blue clump fescue displays soft, buff-colored flowers on 15-inch stalks. It forms 10- to 12-inch-wide clumps, making it ideal for use as a border or as an edging plant. With close spacing, the icy-blue blades will grow together, forming a low mass planting. Blue clump fescue would be an interesting choice for a turfgrass-like edging along a perennial or shrub bed.

WHEN TO PLANT

Since blue clump fescue is container grown, it can be planted spring and fall as long as the soil is not too wet. Establishment in summer plantings is poor due to its dormancy in hot weather.

WHERE TO PLANT

Plant in full sun or in partial shade, but you must plant in an area that drains well. Wet soils in summer or planting too deep will create problems with crown rot, a fatal condition for blue clump fescue. Plant blue clump fescue in mass groupings as a landscape accent or use it as an edging along a walk.

HOW TO PLANT

Dig a hole as deep and twice as wide as the container. Remove the plant from the container and position in prepared hold. Add a starter fertilizer if needed. Backfill with a loosened or amended soil. Apply a weed-preventer to large beds, or control weeds with mulch and handweeding. Apply a shallow mulch to a depth of 1 inch. Water well to get this grass established. Use a handtool, spade, or bulb planter to check the soil moisture during the summer months before watering.

CARE AND MAINTENANCE

Fertilize in the spring with a slow-release product (example: 2-1-1 analysis). A supplemental fall fertilization is suggested to maintain the plant's health and encourage good root development. This species needs very little pruning, but you should head back blue clump fescue in early spring to remove winter-damaged foliage. Water every 3 days for the first week to jump-start your new planting.

ADDITIONAL INFORMATION

If scale insects are a problem, they can be taken care of with very little effort. Consult with your county Extension Agent or garden center. Water only as needed, and you will have a wonderful landscape plant.

ADDITIONAL SPECIES, CULTIVARS, OR VARIETIES

'Elijah Blue,' a dwarf, intensely blue cultivar, is one of the most striking small blue grasses. 'Rainbow Fescue' is particularly attractive. Other interesting cultivars are 'Blue Finch' and 'Blue Ember.' There are apparently quite a few others available in European garden centers.

ORNAMENTAL GRASSES

Blue Oat Grass

*E*very garden can use some vertical accent plants in the perennial garden. Blue oat grass can fill this need while providing a pleasing contrast with the gray foliage of such gems as sages and santolina. Blue oat grass forms dense mounds of showy silver-blue foliage. These 2-foot-tall puffs of wiry leaves produce delicate stalks of oatlike seedheads. In early summer, these striking pale-blue flowers are displayed on long arching stalks which become a golden color with time. Garden designers appreciate the fine color and texture that blue oat grass contributes to a contemporary garden. This compact grass is cool-natured and prefers the colder months of the year. During a prolonged drought, you will be glad you have it in your landscaping plan, since it will go into a semidormant state. This characteristic is especially attractive if you irrigate from a well, or you just prefer not to spend your leisure time watering the garden. The fact that blue oat grass is almost care-free adds to its desirability. It is a showy ornamental grass that is hardy in even the coldest North Carolina regions. In warmer climates, this grass will remain an evergreen during the winter months.

WHEN TO PLANT

For best results, plant any time from early spring to late summer. Those in Coastal areas can plant blue oat grass right on through fall as soil conditions permit.

WHERE TO PLANT

Blue oat grass should be planted in full sun where there is good soil drainage. This grass can stand alone as an accent plant, but it is best appreciated when planted in groups or masses. Gray-foliaged ornamentals such as the artemisias, lavender-cotton, and sages make wonderful companions for blue oat grass. The flowers of butterfly bush or bluebeard make a stunning background.

ZONE
6,7,8

How to Plant

Dig a hole as deep and twice as wide as the rootball. Remove the plant from its container and position it in the prepared hole. Backfill with a coarse soil mix amended with compost (this is only necessary in gardens where the soil is tight and feels sticky). The key to success with blue oat grass is good soil drainage. Water-in well to settle the soil around the roots. Two weeks after dormant grasses green up in spring, or when late summer growth begins, apply a garden fertilizer (for example, 1/4 cup of 10-10-10 per plant). Using a soluble plant fertilizer is always best during the drier months. Apply a weed-preventer and mulch to a depth of 1 to 2 inches.

Care and Maintenance

Use a slow-release fertilizer (3-1-2 analysis) in late summer to stimulate growth of the blue oat grass. You may choose to provide a liquid feeding in early spring on heavy soils. In September, or before any new growth appears in late February, you may need to prune back as close as 3 to 5 inches to the ground. This eliminates old weathered foliage while invigorating your blue oat grass. The grass is a medium grower and prefers moist soil conditions. Water as needed to maintain the health of the plant but only during the active growth cycle. Remember, this plant is very drought resistant!

Additional Information

Blue oat grass prefers cool weather for active growth, so you will find it most vigorous in early spring and fall. Don't overwater your ornamental grasses! Do water during extreme drought or in the growing season and your blue oat grass will provide years of enjoyment.

Additional Species, Cultivars, or Varieties

There are none available.

Fountain Grass

ountain grass lends a unique appearance to the landscape. It works quite well as an anchor for the ends of a planting area, and is also suitable as a single specimen within the landscape. The fountain grasses are well named. Their narrow leaves form graceful fountains of broadly arching foliage. In July, stems carrying foxtail-like flower plumes rise above these 3- to 4-foot clumps of leaves. The "New American" landscape design makes use of this fabulous grass mass planted in undulating beds sweeping through the landscape. The foliage of fountain grass turns a golden-yellow in autumn. "The Rose" fountain grass bears beautiful rose-tan plumes at tips of the flowering spikelets. The foxtail plumes eventually begin to deteriorate by early winter, but only after many weeks of providing enjoyment. This garden keepsake can add movement to a lifeless planting of ornamentals.

WHEN TO PLANT

Fountain grass can be planted at any time, spring through fall, as long as the soil is not frozen or too wet.

WHERE TO PLANT

Fountain grass requires full sun for optimum growth. Average to good soil is suitable for this plant. Use as an accent specimen, or as multiples planted together in a group. Group planting can have a breathtakingly beautiful effect: the wind catching the foliage creates a symphony of movement.

HOW TO PLANT

Dig a hole as deep and twice as wide as the container for individual plantings. Rototill entire beds 1 foot deep for planting en masse. Remove from containers and position in prepared hole or bed. Space the plants at least 5 feet apart. Mix a starter fertilizer or rotted manure into the soil. Backfill with the loosened soil mix. Apply a weed-preventer before mulching or be prepared to handweed later. Mulch to a depth of 1 to 2 inches. Water well at planting and for the first few weeks following planting.

ZONE
6,7,8

CARE AND MAINTENANCE

Fertilize in the spring with a slow-release product (for example, 2-1-1). A summer feeding is also recommended to maintain the plant's health. Fountain grass requires no regular pruning during the growing season. It should be cut back to ground level in early spring, however, before new growth begins. It requires regular watering for vigorous growth, and will flower more fully and for a longer period with adequate moisture. This plant is attractive even in drought seasons once it becomes well established.

ADDITIONAL INFORMATION

Fountain grass is relatively trouble-free and has no serious problems. The species *Pennisetum* often self-sows freely in the warmer zones. The black-seeded annual variety can become a weed problem even in Zone 7.

ADDITIONAL SPECIES, CULTIVARS, OR VARIETIES

'Cassian' is a strong golden autumn color. 'Hamelin,' a reliable performer, is a dwarf form that grows to 3 feet. 'Little Bunny' is a miniature cultivar that grows to 8 inches high. Late-blooming 'Moudry,' medium height, has glossy, dark-green leaves and dark-purple plumes on stiff erect stalks.

ORNAMENTAL GRASSES

Imperata cylindrica 'Red Baron'

Japanese Blood Grass

*I*f you are looking for an unusual plant for a vertical accent or just a conversation piece, Japanese blood grass is your plant. The blades of this ornamental grass are a blood red to burgundy color. It is is a low, clump-forming grass that reaches no more than 20 inches in height. It puts out underground stems or rhizomes that are not at all invasive. Soon, small colonies of red grass tufts pop up to enlarge the planting to 2 feet in diameter. The blades are erect and are reminiscent of those of an oversized tall fescue plant. Few plants catch the eye of a gardener like a plant with red foliage. While visiting Islei's nursery in Oregon, I remember seeing this grass for the first time, and a dwarf red juniper as well. Both were displayed in Japanese gardens and made an indelible impression on me. Plants like these can be used sparingly to create an effect, and they are certainly worth using. They can get lost in a garden if not planted in groups. I have grown Japanese blood grass in a partially shaded bed, though I know it is happier in a sunny border. It will thrive in poor garden soils, and is attractive when flanked by a rock. Japanese blood grass is an interesting choice for a small garden.

WHEN TO PLANT

Japanese blood grass can be planted successfully from spring through fall. It can be divided in early spring before new growth begins, or in September following the dry season. This plant needs to get established before winter weather arrives.

WHERE TO PLANT

For the best effect, plant Japanese blood grass in full sun. This plant likes a well-drained, hot site, but it will tolerate partial shade and moist soil. Though it will survive drought, the tips of its blades will brown. Plant Japanese blood grass for its colorful foliage and its low-growing habit. It is a good choice for a meadow or Japanese garden. Use it to accent groundcovers or perennials. It is also a nice rock garden plant.

ZONE 6,7,8

How to Plant

Container-grown blood grass is easily transplanted. Dig a hole that is ³/₄ as deep and twice as wide as the container. If the plant is pot-bound, loosen the roots by hand and shake the soil from the lower half of the rootball. In most cases, blood grass is not heavily rooted and can be planted directly into the planting hole without disturbing the roots. (Bareroot plants shipped by mail should be soaked for 4 hours before planting.) Firm the soil around the rootball and water thoroughly to remove air pockets. Do not drown this grass with mulch; an inch of mulch is adequate. Water twice weekly for the first month after planting.

Care and Maintenance

After the first month, your blood grass should be fairly well established. It will not need watering more than every 10 days throughout the first summer. By fall it will be on its own, and from then on this ornamental grass is a low-maintenance selection. This grass prefers moist soil, but a poorly drained site during the winter months will certainly do it harm. By December the plants will have been ruined by cold and should be cut back level to the ground. This is not a messy plant—unlike other ornamental grasses, there is little effort required in cleanup. Fertilize with a garden fertilizer such as 10-10-10 in early May after new shoots appear.

Additional Information

There are no messy seedheads formed or any need for pruning this plant during the growing season. The plant is virtually disease- and pest-free. Remember to water during periods of extended drought.

Additional Species, Cultivars, or Varieties

The cultivar 'Red Baron' is available commercially. This plant is a fairly new grass compared to other ornamental grass varieties.

Maiden Grass

aiden grass is one of the most popular ornamental grasses in the South. It is completely hardy all across North Carolina, maturing to a height of 6 to 8 feet. Maiden grass forms a clump of finely textured silver-green blades that are ¼ inch in width. The upright arching leaves have a white midvein that is distinctly visible close-up. Maiden grass is most useful as a naturalizing grass where it can be used in groups for vertical accent and texture. In autumn, the leaves are topped with large, fan-shaped, delicate silver-white blooms. These flowerheads are at first reddish, then they become a silvery fall spectacle, greatly desired for floral arrangements. The autumn foliage is a vivid golden-bronze. Maiden grass is most striking when the sun streams through its multiple tall blades. Considered by some to be the most elegant of all grasses, it is often the subject of landscape paintings by Japanese artists. For the gardener who is looking for season-long color and texture change, maiden grass is an appropriate choice.

WHEN TO PLANT

Hold off the urge to plant this grass in the winter; wait until the spring thaw to plant. Maiden grass can be planted any time during the spring through fall season as long as the soil is not frozen or too wet.

WHERE TO PLANT

If you have a need to block an objectionable view of your neighbor's "yard art" or garbage cans, maiden grass is an excellent choice as a screening plant. Multiple plants with close spacing can form a dense barrier. Or it can be used effectively as an interesting specimen, or single plant, in a sunny area of your landscape.

HOW TO PLANT

When planting maiden grass, dig a hole as deep and twice as wide as the rootball. Remove the container and disturb the rootball. Use a knife to loosen the roots of potbound plants. Make several vertical slits in the rootball, and shake some of the soil off into the planting hole. Position the plant in the prepared hole. Backfill with the soil

removed from the planting hole. When doing group plantings, till
the entire area instead of planting in holes. Water well to settle the
soil. Apply an approved weed-preventer in large beds before
mulching. Mulch to a depth of 2 inches.

CARE AND MAINTENANCE

Fertilize in the spring with a slow-release product (example: 3-1-2).
A supplemental summer feeding the first 2 years will help to get the
new plant established. Once established, it will not need fertilizing
every year and will thrive on neglect. Cut back only during the early
spring before new growth emerges. You may cut the grass as close
as 6 to 8 inches to the ground. Prune vigorous grasses using power
hedge shears or handheld lopping shears. Water on a regular basis
until the grass is established. Afterwards, reduce your watering to
the amount needed to maintain the health of the grass.

ADDITIONAL INFORMATION

Maiden grass is basically disease- and insect-free. Just keep it
watered in hot, dry summers and you will have a new garden friend
for life. When you are in need of more plants, remove a few of the
suckers or daughter-shoots from the base of the grass in late spring.
Thinning may help rejuvenate old plantings.

ADDITIONAL SPECIES, CULTIVARS, OR VARIETIES

There are numerous *Miscanthus sinensis* cultivars commercially
available such as 'Silver Banner Grass,' colorful zebra grass with
its horizontal yellow bands, and 'Little Kitten,' a new dwarf.
This genus tolerates many soil conditions from wetlands to dry,
rocky slopes.

Pampas Grass

*P*ampas grass is the grandfather of ornamental grasses. It can grow 8 to 10 feet tall, with blades over 1 inch wide. The foliage in summer is light green, turning beige to light tan in the winter season. In the fall, pampas grass develops its signature feature: 2-foot-long 8-inch-wide flowerheads. These flower plume-panicles are striking, very useful for dried flower arrangements. The fluffy plumes are wonderful in front of the red fall foliage of 'Sunset' maples. They remain throughout the winter, providing visual appeal. They are striking especially in windy conditions or in Coastal gardens where the tall plumes are continuously on the move. In addition to its dominant presence in the landscape, this large clump-forming grass is often a choice for its low maintenance requirements and high tolerance of drought conditions. A compact variety of pampas grass, 'Pumila,' is really not a small plant—it can reach 5 feet in height.

WHEN TO PLANT

Container-grown pampas grass may be planted any time the soil is not frozen or too wet during the spring through fall seasons. When transplanting from one location in the garden to another, wait until the grass is showing some green leaves in mid-spring before digging. Most grasses make a completely new root system in early spring!

WHERE TO PLANT

Plant in full sun in well-drained soil. Pampas grass is quite adaptable to a range of soil conditions from the foothills to the coast. It may be used effectively as a single specimen, or planted in groups, 6 to 8 feet apart. Use it as a wind screen on the coast, or as a backdrop for a border of herbaceous perennials. The plumes are showy and can be cut for drying. Plant in front of burning bushes or maples for a fall delight.

HOW TO PLANT

When planting pampas grass, dig a hole that is as deep and twice as wide as the container. Mix some bulb fertilizer or bagged cow manure into the soil. Remove the plant from its container and posi-

ORNAMENTAL GRASSES

tion it in the prepared hole. Backfill with the original soil if it is loamy or use the amended soil. Water well to settle the soil around the roots. Mulch to a depth of 2 inches. In large-group plantings, a weed-preventer may be practical for the first year or two. Consult with the Cooperative Extension Service before applying a herbicide around newly planted grasses. Seed of pampas grass is available from the seed catalogs; it takes 3 to 5 years, however, to get a flowering plant.

CARE AND MAINTENANCE

Water your newly planted grass twice a week for the first month. Apply a slow-release lawn fertilizer (example, 2-1-1) when your pampas grass has greened up slightly in the middle of spring. A supplemental feeding is recommended during the summer to promote healthy growth. Cut back the entire plant in late winter or early spring before any new growth begins. In the Piedmont and western regions of North Carolina, delay pruning the spent foliage until the worst of the cold has passed. The old leaves will give added winter protection. *Note:* the female plants produce the large showy plumes.

ADDITIONAL INFORMATION

It is customary to burn the dried foliage in the eastern part of the state. This is not a recommended practice as it can cause irreparable damage to the crowns and root systems. A machete or lopping shears will get the job done. (I tried a chain saw once—for about 1 minute!) Plant pampas grass to enjoy its unmistakable form and fall plumes.

ADDITIONAL SPECIES, CULTIVARS, OR VARIETIES

C. selloana 'Pumila,' compact pampas grass, is the only dwarf form recommended. R.G. Halfacre's "Landscape Plants of the Southeast" lists other cultivars: 'Argenteum,' which grows to 12 feet, 'Gold Band,' which has yellow-striped leaf margins, 'Rendatleri' and 'Rosa Feder,' which grow to 9 feet and have pink plumes, and 'Sunningdale Silver,' which grows to 8 feet and has silvery plumes.

Zebra Maiden Grass

OTHER COMMON NAME: Zebra Grass

*Z*ebra grass is a clump-growing ornamental grass that grows to 6 feet in height and 4 to 5 feet in width. Its unusual horizontally striped yellow foliage is its signature feature. In the fall, beautiful flowering plumes appear, and they remain throughout the winter. Zebra grass is terrific when planted as a single specimen in a sunny location or in a site where you want to catch the eye of the onlooker. This plant works quite well when planted in masses, as in a border or privacy screen. If a mass grouping is desired, be sure to allow for rampant growth by planting zebra grasses at least 5 feet apart. This grass is effectively planted near water features where the breezes can create movement and rythm. Many gardeners find that the ornamental grasses add color contrast, texture, and form to the landscape. As one of our Master Gardeners put it, "These plants are tough, and they require so little maintenance." I am sure the trend toward using more ornamental grasses in Tar Heel gardens will become even stronger.

WHEN TO PLANT

Plant container-grown zebra grass during the spring, through the fall season. Transplant or divide established plants in mid- to late spring, certainly after spring greenup.

WHERE TO PLANT

Zebra grass is most vigorous when planted in full sun in moist soil conditions. Plant as a specimen plant for its unusual striped foliage; or plant by a gate for an accent; or plant intermittently throughout a perennial border in groups of 3. The first zebra grass plant I ever saw provided a backdrop for a bed of *Rudbeckia* 'Goldsturm' at a garden center in Chapel Hill. What a sight it was!

HOW TO PLANT

When planting zebra grass, dig a hole as deep and twice as wide as the container. Remove the plant from the container and score the rootball if it is potbound. Otherwise, shake off part of the medium into the planting hole. Add some bulb fertilizer to the planting hole,

ZONE
6,7,8

and position the rootball in place. Backfill with the soil you removed from the hole. It is best to have the rootball slightly higher than grade to allow for settling. Water-in the rootball with 4 gallons of water. (Add a liquid starter fertilizer to the water if the soil is sandy.) Mulch to a depth of 2 inches. Water twice each week for the first 3 to 4 weeks, then every 8 to 10 days during the growing season.

CARE AND MAINTENANCE

After pruning in early spring, apply a slow-release lawn fertilizer (example, 2-1-1). A supplemental feeding is recommended during the summer to promote healthy growth during the first few seasons. In late winter or early spring, before the emergence of new growth, cut back the foliage to 12 to 18 inches from ground level. For new plantings, use a handheld garden hose equipped with a watering wand for watering your plants and seedlings. The wand prevents washing the soil away. Zebra grass likes water, so keep this in mind during dry periods. Zebra grass is very tolerant of neglect.

ADDITIONAL INFORMATION

This ornamental grass has been popular in North Carolina for a number of years. Specimens are found in some of the most out-of-the-way places and gardens. While zebra grass is somewhat similar to pampas grass, it is not as forgiving when it comes to drought. Zebra grass requires ample moisture to perform satisfactorily.

ADDITIONAL SPECIES, CULTIVARS, OR VARIETIES

M. sinensis 'Zebrinus,' zebra maiden grass, is the only cultivar with the horizontally striped leaves. A variety that is often confused with zebra grass is 'Variegatus,' striped maiden grass, which has vertical white stripes and grows to 6 feet in height.

ORNAMENTAL GRASSES

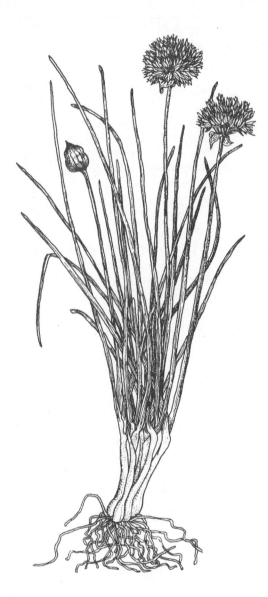

"The single most

important factor in

longevity of life

is...Joy.

Garden for the joy

of it!"

The North Carolina Gardener's Guide
Photographic gallery of featured plants

Abelia
Abelia grandiflora

Ajuga
Ajuga reptans

Amarylis
Hippeastrum

American Holly
Ilex opaca

American Yellowood
Cladrastis lutea

Apple
Malus sylvestris

Aster
Aster novae-angliae

Aucuba
Aucuba japonica

Autumn Crocus
Colchicum byzantium

Autumn Joy Sedum
Hylotelephium spectabile

Bearded Iris
Iris germanica

Black-eyed Susan
Rudbeckia

Blanket Flower
Gaillardia

Blue Clump Fescue
Festuca ovina glauca

Blue False Indigo
Baptisia australis

Bluebeard
Caryopte

Blue Oat Grass
Helictotrichon sempervirens

Blue Rug Juniper
Juniperus horizontalis wiltonii

Blueberry
Vaccinium ashei

Bradford Pear
Pyrus calleryana

Butterfly Bush
Buddleia davidii

Caladium
Caladium x hortulanum

Camellia
Camellia sasanqua

Canna
Canna

Carissa Holly
Ilex cornuta 'Carissa'

Carolina Jessamine
Gelsemium sempervirens

Carolina Silverbell
Halesia

Cherry Laurel
Prunus laurocerasus

Chinese Trumpetvine
Campsis grandiflora

Chives
Allium schoenoprasum

Christmas Fern
Polystichum

Clematis
Clematis x hybrida

Climbing Hydrangea
Hydrangea anomala

Climbing Roses
Rosa

Colorado Blue Spruce
Picea pungens

Columbine
Aquilegia

Coral Bells
Heuchera

Coriander/Cilantro
Coriandrum

Cosmos
Cosmos bipinnatus

Cottage Pink
Dianthus plumarius

Crabapple
Malus

Crape Myrtle
Lagerstroemia indica

Creeping Juniper
Juniperus horizontalis

Crimson Pygmy Barberry
Berberis thunbergii

Crinum
Crinum x powellii

Cyclamen
Cyclamen hederofolium

Daffodil
Narcissus

Dahlia
Dahlia

Deodar Cedar
Cedrus deodora

Dogwood
Cornus florida

Dwarf Burning Bush
Euonymus alata

Dwarf Nandina
Nandina domestica

English Boxwood
Buxus sempervirens

English Ivy
Hedera helix

Exbury Azalea
Rhododendron(A.) exbury

Fig
Ficus carica

Firethorn
Pyracantha coccinea

Floribunda
Rosa

Forsythia
Forsythia x intermedia

Fothergilla
Fothergilla gardenii

Fountain Grass
Pennisetum alopecuroides

Fruitless Sweet Gum
*Liquidambar styraciflua
rotundiloba*

Garden Mums
Chrysanthemum

Garden Phlox
Phlox paniculata

Gardenia
Gardenia jasminoides

Geranium
Pelargonium

Ginkgo
Ginkgo biloba

Gladiolus
Gladiolus

Ground Cover Roses
Rosa

Hardy Iceplant
Delosperma

Hemlock
Tsuga canadensis

Heritage Birch
Betula

Hinoki Cypress
Chamaecyparis obtusa

Homestead Purple Verbena
Verbena canadensis

Honeysuckle
Lonicera sempervirens

Hosta
Hosta

Hummingbird Summersweet
Clethra

Hybrid Teas
Rosa

Impatiens
Impatiens wallerana

Indian Hawthorn
Raphidepis indica

Inkberry
Ilex glabra

Japanese Anemone
Anemone x hybrida

Japanese Blood Grass
Imperata cylindrica 'Red Baron'

Japanese Cedar
Cryptomeria japonica

Japanese Cherry
Prunus serrulata

Japanese Holly
Ilex crenata

Japanese Iris
Iris kaempferi

Japanese Maple
Acer palmatum

Japanese Privet
Ligustrum japonicum

Japanese Spirea
Spiraea x bumalda

Japanese Spurge
Pachysandra terminalis

Japanese Wisteria
Wisteria floribunda

Kiwi
Actinidia arguta

Koreanspice Viburnum
Viburnum carlesei

Kurume Azalea
Azalea hybrids

Lacecap Hydrangea
Hydrangea macrophylla

Lady Banks Rose
Rosa banksiae

Lamb's-Ear
Stachys byzantina

Lavender
Lavandula

Lemon Balm
Melissa officinalis

Lenton Rose
Helleborus

Leyland Cypress
Cupressocyparis leylandii

Liriope
Liriope muscari

Longleaf Pine
Pinus palustris

Longwort
Pulmonaria saccharata

Lycoris
Lycoris squamigera

Maiden Grass
Miscanthus sinensis gracillimus

Marigold
Tagetes

Miniatures
Rosa

Mint
Mentha spicata

Moonvine
Ipomoea alba

Mountain Bluet
Centaurea montana

Mountain Laurel
Kalmia latifolia

Muscadine Grape
Vitis rotundifolia

Nellie R. Stevens Holly
Ilex

Nippon Daisy
Chrysanthemum nipponicum

Oakleaf Hydrangea
Hydrangea quercifolia

Obedient Plant
Physostegia virginiana

Old Garden Roses
Rosa

Oleander
Nerium oleander

Oregano
Origanum vulgare

Oriental Lily
Lilium

Ornamental Pomegranate
Punica

Palmetto Palm
Sabal palmetto

Pampas Grass
Cortaderia selloana

Pansy
Viola

Parsley
Petroselinum crispum

Paw Paw
Asimina triloba

Pecan
Carya illinoensis

Peony
Paeonia officinalis

Periwinkle
Vinca minor

Persian Lilac
Syringa x persica

Persimmon
Diospyros

Petunia
Petunia x hybrida

Pieris
Pieris

Pink Loropetalum
Loropetalum chinese

Pinkshell Azalea
Rhododendron vaseyi

Pittosporum
Pittosporum tobira

Plum Yew
Cephalotaxus

Porcelain Vine
Ampelopsis

Purple Coneflower
Echinacea purpurea

Red Buckeye
Aesculus pavia

Redbud
Cercis canadensis

Red Maple
Acer rubrum

Red Oak
Quercus rubra

Red Raspberry
Rubus idaeus

Redtwig Dogwood
Cornus sericea

Rhododendron
Rhododendron

Rosemary
Rosmarinus officinalis

Sage
Salvia officinalis

Santolina
Santolina chamaecyparissus

Saucer Magnolia
Magnolia x soulangiana

Shrub and Hedge Roses
Rosa

Sourwood
Oxydendrum arboreum

Southern Indica Azalea
Rhododendron indicum

Spreading Zinnia
Zinnia angustifolia

Stella De Oro Daylily
Hemerocallis

Sugar Maple
Acer saccharum

Sunflower
Helianthus annus

Sweet Basil
Ocimum basilicum

Tarragon
Artemisia dracunculus

Thornless Blackberry
Rubus allegheniensis

Thyme
Thymus vulgaris

Tickseed
Coreopsis

Tuberose
Polyanthes

Tulip
Tulipa

Variegated Sedge
Carex morrowi

Victoria Salvia
Salvia

Wax Leaf Begonia
Begonia semperflorens

Wax Myrtle
Myrica californica

White Pine
Pinus

Willow Oak
Quercus phellos

Witch Hazel
Hamamelis

Wormwood
Artemisia

Yarrow
Achillea

Yaupon Holly
Ilex vomitoria

Zebra Grass
Miscanthus sinesis zebrinus

Zelkova
Zelkova serrata

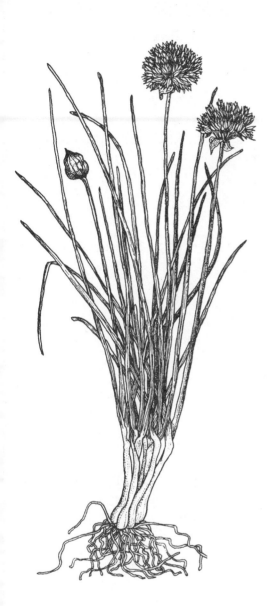

"The love of

gardening is like

a seed...

Once sown it will

grow forever."

CHAPTER SEVEN

Herbs and Perennials

*P*ERENNIAL GARDENS ARE THE BIGGEST BOON TO THE NORTH CAROLINA FLORICULTURE industry since the craze for hanging baskets peaked in the 1970s. Perennials grace our gardens with a plethora of colors and textures. These gardening gems are versatile in the landscape. They can be used in foundations, borders, and containers, and they will stand alone as accent specimens. By choosing varieties with overlapping bloom seasons, your garden can become a tapestry of beauty from early summer until autumn.

When growing perennial flowers, you are not limited to sunny borders, since many perennials flourish in the shade. Some of the best perennials, like the hostas, lungworts, and ferns, can be used to create a showstopper garden when the garden is overshadowed by majestic oaks. The more familiar garden-variety perennials produce their showy floral displays in the sunniest beds.

Herbs are God's gift to the earth. Herbs have so many benefits and uses for daily living. For centuries humankind has grown and collected herbs for their medicinal and culinary benefits. The Bible makes frequent reference to ancient herbal traditions. In modern times there has been a resurgence of interest in using herbs for health and pleasure. These plants add a natural ornamental dimension to any garden, and maybe even a "cure for what ails you."

Many herbs are classified as herbaceous perennials; some, like rosemary, are woody ornamentals that form small hardy shrubs. Whether planting herbs for their medicinal, culinary, or ornamental value, they make a worthy addition to the Tar Heel garden. They are easy to grow and great to share.

The biggest problem that I have encountered in growing herbs is coming up with enough ways to use them. There is always an over-abundance—and the more they're harvested, the bigger the yield in the weeks to come! Fortunately, these plants are easily preserved. I have sundried them on the dashboard of my car, hung them to dry on a coat hanger in the attic, and even frozen fresh sprigs in ice trays for use in cold beverages.

Combine herbs with perennials in the garden. The flowers of the perennials will complement the foliage of the herbs. Certainly the entire text of the *North Carolina Gardener's Guide* could have been dedicated to these two groups of wonderful plants!

Chives

When many plants have peaked and faded, the garden is still graced with the fluffy lilac ball-like flowers of chives. This plant is a versatile perennial herb that adds great vertical contrast and drama wherever it is planted. It is a must in any flower, herb, or windowsill garden. When compared with most herbs, the flowers of this species are quite noticeable. Chives have showy lavender globe-shaped blooms on slender, rounded stems that grow to a height of 10 inches. The blooms can be enjoyed in the perennial garden or in fresh arrangements. The most common use for chives is for scattering on top of a baked potato. I prefer the faint taste of onion that this herb provides in a fresh tossed salad. The garlic chives, *A. tuberosum*, has white starlike blooms that soon turn to heavy green seedpods that should be removed. Chives is easy to grow from seed or from divisions. Maintenance-free and very showy, this plant will thrive in your herb garden for many years to come. The blooms can be dried and enjoyed in everlasting arrangements in the home or office.

WHEN TO PLANT

The best time to plant chives is the early fall or spring, although you can plant any time the ground is not frozen. Container-grown plants are available from garden centers in the spring. The seed can be sown in August or old plants can be divided at that time.

WHERE TO PLANT

This little herb is wonderful in a patio or windowsill container. Be sure to give it at least a half-day of sunlight, and well-drained soil if planted in the ground. Chives can tolerate a variety of soils from sands to clay loam, as well as many moisture levels. It has done best for me in hot, drier garden sites in loamy soil. If you want to use it fresh in the kitchen, plant it close by for easy picking.

HOW TO PLANT

Plant chives directly in the ground by digging a hole at least the size of the plant's rootball. It is best to work up the soil a bit and add a little soil conditioner such as leaf compost in dry sites. Limestone is beneficial for raising the soil pH to 6.0. Firm-in the plant's rootball.

Choose a clay pot for container planting. Use a rich but porous soil and be sure the pot has good drainage. Water well to settle the soil and remove the air pockets. Don't overwater in the early weeks; in fact, it would be best to err on the dry side at first. A soluble plant starter fertilizer can be used every 4 weeks if you just want the foliage for cutting.

CARE AND MAINTENANCE
Allow the plant to dry out slightly between waterings. If this is its first year, water at least once every 2 weeks during spring and fall, and more often in a drought. Those planted in a container need to be watered every third day if outdoors on a patio. You may cut or snip the onion-like foliage any time you need chives in the kitchen. After a hard freeze, remove dead growth and mark the location with a label. Chives do not need much fertilizer if they are planted in good soil. If you choose to feed, use a mild organic food like blood meal or cottonseed meal, and limit to 2 feedings during the growing season.

ADDITIONAL INFORMATION
Be sure to select a spot that has good drainage and gets a half-day of sun, preferably during the intense afternoon period. Some varieties self-seed freely, so there are plenty of plants to share. To prevent seeding, remove the faded flowerheads promptly. There are no pests that bother chives. The plant may droop in hot weather or go semi-dormant, but that is all right.

ADDITIONAL SPECIES, CULTIVARS, OR VARIETIES
Three species are described in the *National Arboretum Book of Outstanding Garden Plants* (Heriteau and Cathey, 1990), two in addition to *Allium schoenoprasum*. *A. fistulosum*, Japanese bunching onion, has clumps to 24 inches and white flowers. *A. tuberosum*, garlic chives, grows to 18 inches in spreading clusters and has flat leaf blades and white starlike flowers that are attractive to bees.

Coriander

OTHER COMMON NAME: Cilantro

Coriander has been described as a plant that appears in a "series of acts." The first act is a display of broad, bright green leaves that unfold from a low-growing rosette. Act II in the drama features the development of fern-like foliage that is similar in appearance to dill or fennel. In Act III, lacy white-flowered umbels burst forth. These umbels resemble those of Queen Anne's lace and other members of the carrot family. The final act before the curtain drops presents the formation of small 1/8-inch berries that bear edible seeds. Coriander thus serves as both herb and spice. The leaves are harvested fresh and called cilantro by Latin Americans. Asians and Mexicans make frequent use of coriander in salads, soups, and sauces. Though the leaves have a strong aroma, once cooked they add a deep flavor to special dishes. The seeds are used in pickling and hot spiced drinks. Most people say that a little coriander goes a long way! This herb is easy to grow in any sunny location. It can be planted from seed or with small transplants from the garden center. Coriander is an erect annual that can grow to a height of 2 feet.

WHEN TO PLANT

Coriander is grown as a cool-season herb in North Carolina. You can sow seeds of this plant indoors in February, and transplant outdoors in March. Most avid gardeners will wait until late August or September and sow seeds directly into the garden. Or you can grow coriander in the fall garden from the berries produced in your spring garden.

WHERE TO PLANT

Whether in the ground or in a container on a deck or patio, coriander prefers a bright, sunny location. It will grow in very dry to moist soils. Soil quality is not crucial, but a loose soil makes it easier on both the gardener and the roots of the plant. If you are growing it to harvest its foliage, plant coriander as an edging plant in the border. In a fall garden, give this herb its own row so it will have ample space to bloom.

HOW TO PLANT

Prepare the garden row by mixing limestone and several inches of compost or peat moss into the soil. The optimum pH is 6.5. You may also mix some organic fertilizer into the soil. Sow coriander seed in rows directly in the garden. When this herb is grown for its leaves, thin the seedlings to 4 inches apart; when flowers and seed are desired, thin or plant transplants 9 to12 inches apart. Some gardeners, especially those with small spaces, plant 2 or 3 transplants purchased from a garden center. Select large transplants in 3-inch peat pots. Plant these at grade in loose garden soil and water well every 2 days for the first 10 days. To encourage quick establishment, always remove peat pots before planting transplants.

CARE AND MAINTENANCE

Water-in new transplants with a soluble fertilizer every 2 weeks. Coriander prefers weekly watering, twice weekly in extreme heat. Harvest coriander/cilantro as often as you need it. If drying and storing it for later use, then harvest the entire plant in late summer. Just pull up the plants and hang them to dry using clothespins on coat hangers. (In the summer months, herbs can be dried in cardboard boxes placed in the trunk of your car.) Coriander seeds can be gathered and stored; toast them lightly and store in jars.

ADDITIONAL INFORMATION

Coriander is practically maintenance-free. If you are growing the plant for foliage, you should trim potential blooms to prevent seed production. If you want seeds, however, let them bloom and enjoy the seeds' orange flavor in pastries and fruit dishes. *Note:* The taprooted seedlings cannot be transplanted.

ADDITIONAL SPECIES, CULTIVARS, OR VARIETIES

Two types of coriander are cultivated, *C. sativum* var. *sativum* with 1/3-inch berries and *C. sativum* var. *microcarpum* with 1/16-inch berries (sometimes called "small-fruited coriander"). 'Leaf Santo' and 'Long Standing' are slower to flower and may produce more foliage for cutting. Cilantro (*Eryngium*) offers a similar flavor. The newest is Park's 'Festival,' a cilantro that is 2 weeks earlier than other varieties.

French Tarragon

arragon is essential for cooking tasty green beans and for flavoring fish. I have grown this delicate-looking herb for a number of years now, since first buying a plant from the Tippetts at Rasland Herb Farm near Dunn. The plant is not at all aggressive by nature, and its 2-inch-long, narrow, grayish green leaves are reminiscent of dianthus foliage. What this herb lacks in stature it makes up for in aroma. French tarragon is widely known for its distinctive licorice-like flavor and aroma. Don't confuse it with Russian tarragon, its close relative, which is much less flavorful. According to my friends at Foothills Nursery in Mount Airy, Russian tarragon is plentiful since it is easy to grow from seed. The more flavorful French tarragon has sterile seeds and must be propagated by cuttings, a process that is more time consuming for growers. French tarragon is native to southern Europe; it was known by the Greeks as early as 500 B.C. It is a slow-growing perennial that spreads by underground rhizomes and grows to 2 feet in height. Its flowers are inconspicuous and may not show up at all. French tarragon is a versatile herb. It is good in salads and soups and is a great addition to marinades.

WHEN TO PLANT

This herb is best planted from containers during the cooler months, from October to May. You will need to divide the plants in spring, or take stem or root cuttings in the fall or spring.

WHERE TO PLANT

Plant French tarragon in full sun or partial shade in rich, well-drained soil. This plant does not take the heat well, so protection from the afternoon sun will increase its life expectancy. It's best to space plants 2 feet apart because of the natural spreading growth habit. The plant grows well in containers and in hanging baskets. As few as 1 or 2 plants will produce a good supply of tarragon for the kitchen.

HOW TO PLANT

Tarragon is easy to transplant into the garden. Simply spade a hole as deep as and twice as wide as the width of the rootball. Most herbs prefer limestone or wood ashes to sweeten the soil, so mix one of these into the soil as you plant. Score the rootball to free up tightly bound roots. Firm the roots with the soil, and water well using a soluble fertilizer solution such as 20-20-20. French tarragon prefers moist soil, so apply a layer of aged manure or compost after planting. Water twice each week for the first month until the roots establish.

CARE AND MAINTENANCE

In western North Carolina, French tarragon can freeze to the ground, so it is best to protect the roots with mulch when planting in the fall. I have had no problem growing tarragon in the northwest Piedmont. It is important to irrigate regularly in hot weather, especially if your plants are in a full-sun location. Apply a complete garden fertilizer such as 10-10-10 in mid-spring. Since fertile soil is important to French tarragon, I recommend using an organic fertilizer during the summer months. This will avoid stressing the plants in hot weather. Divide the plants every 4 years to keep them growing vigorously.

ADDITIONAL INFORMATION

Shear the plants heavily in early spring to remove cold injury and to rejuvenate the plants. The leaves of French tarragon are much more flavorful when harvested in early summer before flowering. They are better when used fresh, but they can also be frozen or dried. Dry stems of French tarragon by placing them in a frost-free refrigerator.

ADDITIONAL SPECIES, CULTIVARS, OR VARIETIES

Russian tarragon can be rather weedy, though it is commonly available at nurseries. Remember that it is not as flavorful as French tarragon. Texas tarragon, *Tagetes lucida,* is a substitute for French tarragon. It has yellow flowers in fall.

Lamb's-Ear

OTHER COMMON NAME: Woolly Betony

*T*his plant is for the gardener who would like a pet but would rather not put up with all the fuss that goes along with being a pet-owner! Once you stroke lamb's-ear's fur-like leaves, you will find this plant irresistible. The leaves are the shape of a lamb's ear and every bit as woolly. Colonists used the leaves for bandages. This spreading perennial is an ancient herb that is now grown primarily as an ornamental groundcover or "filler" plant. Though it produces thick foot-high seed stalks containing tiny violet flowers, its semi-evergreen silvery foliage is its glory. It is an attractive edging plant in perennial borders, and it can be quite handsome lining a walk. At the National Arboretum in Washington, D.C., I saw a fine bed of lamb's-ear used as a groundcover in the Ornamental Grass display. It was no doubt the compact nonflowering cultivar 'Silver Carpet.' When you use this rapid-growing variety, there is no need to perform the daunting task of removing coarse seed stalks in the hot months of summer. The common passalong variety grows in clumps to 10 inches high, and it can spread to 2 feet in a season or two. As is also true of pet ownership, there are some negatives: this herb is capable of "moving around" in the garden. It can be tamed, though, and quite easily.

WHEN TO PLANT

This herb can be planted from containers in spring, summer, and fall. The seeds can be sown in spring or late fall. Most gardeners propagate lamb's-ear by division as the new growth begins in spring or immediately after the summer flowering period. I have successfully moved the plant when it was in full foliage; if you attempt this, water the plant well and prune it severely.

WHERE TO PLANT

Grow lamb's-ear in full sun to partial shade. It flourishes in moist, rich soils. Avoid poorly drained soils. Plant it where you can enjoy the striking contrast of its silvery foliage against the foliage of other plants. In the moonlight it has its own luminance. It is a coarse-textured plant that works well as a groundcover under trees or large shrubs that are "limbed up." It can be used as an accent edging.

How to Plant

As with all groundcover plantings, it is best to rototill or spade the
entire bed to a depth of 4 to 6 inches. I like to add superphosphate
fertilizer and bark soil conditioner to clay soils. Space the lamb's-ear
plants 2 feet apart. Using a hand spade or hoe, dig holes in the tilled
soil that are just large enough to accommodate the rootballs. Loosen
the rootball by cutting it and shaking the soil mix free. (Root distur-
bance is a good practice with vigorously growing plants such as
herbs.) Firm-in the rootballs with the soil and water thoroughly.
Mulching lamb's-ear is not that important except for enriching the
soil or maintaining soil moisture. Use a thin mulch layer. This herb
will "shade out" unwanted weeds.

Care and Maintenance

Water newly planted lamb's-ear only sparingly, during dry periods.
If your new plants die, perhaps you have overwatered them or they
have been placed in a poor, wet planting site. Fertilize your plants in
early fall with a 1-2-2 analysis slow-release flower fertilizer. Remove
the seed stalks soon after the flowers fade or you will have seedlings
galore. (Spent plants tossed onto the compost pile in the summer
months will often root and reestablish. But the big revelation is that
lamb's-ear seeds sprout readily anywhere!) Cut back the wilted
foliage after the fall freezes; rake out the litter.

Additional Information

What a hardy plant! It is durable, drought resistant, and long lasting. It is bothered by no insects. Only root rot is sometimes a
concern, in heavy wet soils. Plant this herb high if the soil is tight
and moist. Lamb's-ear is a must for the garden if there are children
in the house. They love the soft, furry leaves and the woolly flower
stalks in late summer.

Additional Species, Cultivars, or Varieties

'Silver Carpet' is the best cultivar for foliage. It grows to 8 inches
high and is a nonflowering variety with silvery-gray leaves. It is
an indispensable groundcover for the front of a sunny border.
S. macrantha and S. officinalis are both known as "Betony" and
are mat-forming. They grow in dry soils and range in height from
12 inches to 3 feet.

Lavender

*L*avender has been called the "Queen of the Scented Garden" and has been the backbone of the perfume and soap industry for decades. Now horticulturists are beginning to recognize this wonderful herb as a durable landscape ornamental. Lavender has fine-textured foliage that can be shiny and bright green or a pleasant-looking silver-gray color. As are many herbs, lavender is pest-free and ideal for a low-maintenance border. One of the better varieties, 'Hidcote,' has attractive long-lasting violet flowers borne on 20-inch stalks that are great for drying. The small flowers of some species range in color from white to pink. This is a tough evergreen herb with a remarkable ability to withstand harsh winter exposure. I have a 5-year-old lavender plant the size of a foot tub that stands alone in a south-facing location. Despite neglect, exposure to the elements in winter, and bone-dry summer weather, it still shines on. In fact, it looks prettier in November and December than at other times of the year. Though lavender is rarely used in cooking, it is often used in dried arrangements and potpourris. The silver-gray foliage will add interest to any perennial border.

WHEN TO PLANT

Plant lavender any time the ground can be worked. Cuttings can be taken in late spring and set out in the garden in early fall.

WHERE TO PLANT

Lavender thrives in full sun and alkaline soil. I have seen great-looking beds of lavender growing in the worst soils. My own lavender thrived under the eaves of the house, planted within 1 foot of a brick foundation. For the best floral impact, plant in masses. Plantings that line a walk or driveway are very handsome. The gray lavenders are good companions to wax-leaf begonias and geraniums.

HOW TO PLANT

Lavender can be grown from seed, but this is a slow arduous task. I prefer to buy quart-sized containers of nursery-grown plants. Lavenders like alkaline soil, so incorporate limestone thoroughly

into the bed at planting time at the rate of one pound per 10 square feet. Plant lavender in a shallow planting hole, spreading the roots out horizontally to insure that the plant is set high—or plant in a raised bed or berm. A wet-natured soil can be improved for lavenders by mixing granite screenings or ground pine bark into it. No soil amendments are necessary when planting in well-drained soils. Water weekly the first month, then only in dry weather as needed to promote healthy growth.

CARE AND MAINTENANCE

Lavender will respond well to an early spring shearing to clean the plant up a bit. Trim off foliage sunburned from winter exposure by pruning the tips of stems by 2 to 3 inches. Very little mulch should be used around this herb, and certainly do not place mulch close to the crown. Such a practice would lead to stem and root rot diseases. There are no special lavender problems that require routine care. If you are considering using the flowers for drying, cut the buds as they first open. The aromatic foliage is considered a natural repellent for a few common household pests.

ADDITIONAL INFORMATION

The most important advice for growing lavender successfully is to select a well-drained site. Overwater and you will kill even the most robust lavender plants. Don't be afraid to move a lavender plant if you discover a better location for it. Lavender is incredibly resilient!

ADDITIONAL SPECIES, CULTIVARS, OR VARIETIES

'Hidcote' is 18 inches in height and has gray, needle-like leaves. 'Jean Davis' has pale-pink flowers. 'Munstead Dwarf' is 12 inches and has rosy-purple flowers. 'Alba' is a white-flowered lavender.

Lemon Balm

emon balm is a lemon-scented member of the mint family. But don't let the word *mint* scare you. This mint family member doesn't produce the rampant rhizomes that take over azalea beds and threaten flowers. Lemon balm is an annual in most of the Old North State, but it is perennial in its native Europe where the climate is not too harsh. The plant may reach 2 feet in height in rich garden soils, but it develops many branches and normally stays rather bushy. The leaves of lemon balm are 2 inches long, wrinkled, and oval-shaped with scalloped edges. Its minute flowers are light-blue to white and appear in midsummer. You will enjoy stroking its foliage for a whiff of its delicate lemon aroma. The lemon flavor of this herb is valued for its culinary and medicinal uses. According to Dr. Jeanine Davis, Extension Horticulture Specialist, "The volatile oil in lemon balm contains eugenol, citronellal, and geraniol; both oil and hot-water extracts of the leaves have been shown to possess strong antiviral qualities." This plant is used fresh for garnishes and to top drinks.

When to Plant

Lemon balm is easy to grow from seed sown in the spring or early fall. Cuttings and root divisions, however, are faster and easier ways to establish this herb. Root cuttings should contain at least 3 buds each. In the fall, plant root cuttings early enough that they can establish before the first frost. Lemon balm self-sows freely and may become a weed!

Where to Plant

Lemon balm grows best in moist, fertile soil, but I have grown it in poor, dry soil and it grew fairly well. It will thrive in full sun, but it is one of the few herbs that does well even in shade. Plant lemon balm in the herb garden or vegetable garden where its seedlings can be controlled in succeeding years. In the shade garden, this herb will serve as a filler plant. It has light-green leaves and offers some textural interest.

How to Plant

My first lemon balm plant was given to me in the middle of the summer as a clump jerked right out of a friend's garden. The advice from my friend was simple: "Dig a hole the size of the rootball and drop the darn thing in green-side up. Cut it back to the ground and water it." It worked! If you want to sow seeds of lemon balm, spade up an area and rake out the clods. Scatter 5-10-10 fertilizer, one cup for a 25-square-foot garden space. Rake in the fertilizer and broadcast the seed. (Lemon balm seeds are tiny and should be mixed with sand to help in handling.) Cover the seed thinly with sand or potting soil. Water daily.

Care and Maintenance

Water the seedlings or newly planted lemon balm twice a week until they are 6 to 10 inches tall. They are quite drought tolerant and need very little care. You can begin cutting lemon balm for fresh sprigs any time after the first month. Pruning the plant this way will keep it compact and vigorously growing. Apply a 1- to 2-inch layer of mulch around the plant to control weeds and reduce the need for watering in dry periods. To prevent foliar diseases on this herb and others, water early in the day. This is a deciduous perennial and it should be mulched heavily in winter so that it will return. Pests are no problem on lemon balm.

Additional Information

The biggest challenge in growing lemon balm is to prevent a siege of unwanted seedlings from cropping up in various and sundry places. These are easily plucked by hand. I recommend keeping the flower spikes removed promptly, before the blooms open. The leaves of lemon balm can be air- or oven-dried.

Additional Species, Cultivars, or Varieties

The variety 'Aurea' is an ornamental lemon balm. Its leaves are variegated with yellow, but the color disappears during flowering.

Marjoram

OTHER COMMON NAME: Oregano

*B*oth marjoram and oregano are in the mint family. Marjoram is *Origanum majorana* and oregano is *O. vulgare*. Marjoram is a tender perennial and has a more delicate, sweet flower. Marjoram is an upright 2-foot shrub with reddish stems and small 3/4- to 1 1/2-inch fuzzy leaves. Creeping golden marjoram is an attractive form which is useful in the landscape and has the same fragrance and flavor of marjoram. This variety is propagated by seeds for the most part, but also sometimes by cuttings. It is not winter hardy. Oregano is also known as wild oregano. It is a very hardy perennial with a flavor that is stronger than that of marjoram. It is native to the Mediterranean and grows from 1 to 3 feet in height. The stems of oregano are square, hairy, and usually purple. The flower tops yield a reddish-brown to purple dye that can be used for linen and wool, though it is not very durable.

WHEN TO PLANT

Plant marjoram and oregano in the spring. Plants can be propagated by seed, cuttings, or root division. They self-sow easily.

WHERE TO PLANT

Grow marjoram and oregano in full sun. They need to be planted in somewhat rich, light, well-drained soil. Marjoram and oregano grow very well indoors in a sunny area. Oreganos make attractive fragrant borders in the garden. You may want to try golden oregano as a groundcover in a sunny location, or plant it in containers.

HOW TO PLANT

Spade up a large bed when planting oregano as a groundcover. Following soil test recommendations, amend the garden soil with 1 pound of limestone and 1/4 cup of 5-10-10 for every 10 square feet of area. There is no need to add soil conditioner or to plant "high" unless there is some concern over drainage. Space oregano plants 1 to 2 feet apart. After removing the plant from the container, frill out the roots and set the plant in the prepared soil at its original depth.

Firm-in the roots and water thoroughly. Apply an inch of mulch and water weekly for the first month. Seeds can be sown directly and covered lightly with 1/4 inch of topsoil or aged sawdust.

CARE AND MAINTENANCE

To encourage new, bushy growth, cut back marjoram and oregano before the flowers appear. Plants that are 3 or 4 years old should be thinned out or replaced with newer plants.

ADDITIONAL INFORMATION

Once plants are established, stems can be cut near the soil surface, bundled up, and strung up to dry in an airy place out of direct sunlight. Rub the dry leaves through a fine screen to ready them for culinary uses. Fresh sprigs can be harvested as needed for cooking. Remember, it takes twice as much of a fresh herb as it does of the same herb dried to prepare a spicy dish.

ADDITIONAL SPECIES, CULTIVARS, OR VARIETIES

O. 'Variegatum,' gold marjoram, has gold-spotted leaves and a mild savory flavor. *O.* 'Compact Pink' has dark-green leaves and dark-pink flowers. *O.* 'Aureum' has yellowish leaves that scorch in the sun. There are also crinkled leaf and spreading forms. *O. onites* is the true Greek oregano which is not cold hardy in the western regions of North Carolina.

Mint

$\mathcal{T}$his is a great perennial for a North Carolina garden. Everyone can be a successful gardener with this aromatic, sometimes massive, plant. Mint is maintenance-free if planted in a wet area. There are many varieties and new ones are developed every couple of years. Mint loves damp areas, but it can survive in dry spots as well. It is adaptable to almost any light condition. Some mints are wildly invasive and should be planted where they can be contained. I have lost beds of azaleas to the woolly apple-mint. These invasive varieties can be planted in terra cotta pots or in drainpipes that are set vertically in the soil before planting time. They are good companions for bee balm and other tall perennials. Mint is great to have at arm's reach to put in the iced tea or lemonade you may be sipping under the big oak your grandfather planted long ago. And mint helps to discourage certain pests in the garden. It can even be placed in cabinets or drawers to help repel insects.

WHEN TO PLANT

Early spring or fall are excellent times to plant this popular, fragrant herb. If you get clumps or a start from a friend, you will be able to transplant them at any time of the year as long as the soil is not frozen.

WHERE TO PLANT

Mint is great for covering a large, hard-to-maintain area. It can tolerate soil extremes from a "bog-type" area to dry clay soil. You may want to plant it in a hanging basket or container. Even though mint will tolerate shade, try to choose a sunny spot. Mints are attractive to bees that are essential pollinators for cucumbers in our backyard vegetable gardens.

HOW TO PLANT

Not much preparation is necessary for planting this herb. The soil should be tilled or "turned over." A single plant can be set in a hole that is at least the size of the rootball or a little larger. Add some pine-bark soil conditioner to loosen heavy soils. Terra cotta flue liners or similar in-ground containers can be used to house invasive

mints. Mint has no problem with surviving—it is controlling it that is the challenge!

CARE AND MAINTENANCE

Keep mint moist when first established in the garden. If not planted in a "bog-type" area, mint will need water 2 to 3 times a week. It can survive with less watering, but it will not thrive. Trim mint as needed for teas and culinary uses throughout the growing season. Just snip the stems with small pruners or scissors, making a cut just above a leaf node. Cut back after a hard freeze and mulch lightly. Mint is not a heavy feeder. You can use an organic food such as fish emulsion or a soluble fertilizer if you want to encourage more growth.

ADDITIONAL INFORMATION

'Blue Balsam' and peppermint are favorites for fragrance and teas. Dry some of the sprigs just before the flowers open. They will dry well in a car trunk or frost-free refrigerator. Try dropping fresh sprigs in ice trays and making "mint cubes" for use in a summer beverage.

ADDITIONAL SPECIES, CULTIVARS, OR VARIETIES

M. × *piperita*, peppermint, is popular and aggressive. *M. spicata*, spearmint, is also an aggressive variety. *M pulegium*, pennyroyal, is less aggressive. *M requienii*, corsican, is tiny and a bit temperamental. Also available is chocolate mint, a vigorous spreader, with a chocolate fragrance. Blue calument mint makes delightful hot tea.

Parsley

*T*his bright-green herb with curly leaves comes in several varieties that can grow from 10 to 18 inches high. Parsley is popular in French cuisine and is used as a garnish to decorate our dinner plates in the South. When eaten fresh, it will freshen the breath, and it is especially rich in iron. The Italian variety has gained interest from many chefs. Parsley is a biennial herb of the carrot family and will die the second season after it flowers. It is very easy to grow from container-grown plants. Its growth habit is a nice, compact bushy look with multiple branching stems. The lacy white flower clusters appearing the second year will remind you of its cousin, Queen Anne's lace. Parsley is a great plant that softens the look of the herb garden, and like most herbs, it is quite carefree. Its culinary uses are not as numerous as those of other herbs. However, it is useful in the garden to attract the caterpillars (parsley worms) which turn into black, elusive swallowtail butterflies.

When to Plant

Parsley seed can be sown outdoors in late April or started indoors in late winter. Small starter plants from garden centers can be transplanted almost any time during the growing season with proper care.

Where to Plant

Plant parsley in lots of sun and in soil that is well drained. This is a versatile and rugged little herb that should be placed near the front of the herb garden. Try mixing parsley plants with annual flowers in patio pots and herb bowls for a unique combination. Bring the potted parsley plants into the house for the winter and enjoy this freshly-cut herb right from a sunny windowsill.

How to Plant

Simply follow the directions on the seed packets when sowing parsley indoors for the spring garden. Sow the seed in sterile potting soil or vermiculite. It is slow to germinate and somewhat uncertain from seed. Spade up a spot for potted parsley in good, fertile soil.

Loosen up the rootball carefully and place it into a hole that's a little larger than the ball. Cover the roots with soil and water well. Use a soluble starter fertilizer once a week for the first month. Mulch only lightly (if at all), as this plant has a thick, deeply growing taproot.

CARE AND MAINTENANCE

If you are growing parsley in containers, allow the soil to dry slightly between waterings. After planting parsley in the herb garden or flowerbed, water well once a week during the growing season provided the plant is getting full sun. No pruning is necessary other than the harvesting of fresh sprigs for cooking purposes. Just snip with scissors to bring into the kitchen. No fertilizer is needed for parsley once it is established, as it adapts to almost any garden condition. Handpick the caterpillars if you don't want them to decimate the plant in a few short days. A spray of insecticidal soap will also control them. If you want butterflies in your garden more than you want a big parsley crop, allow the caterpillars to feed on your parsley.

ADDITIONAL INFORMATION

This is quite an ornate herb to have in the garden. It is a nice edging plant and one that can intrigue children that are told the "worm story."

ADDITIONAL SPECIES, CULTIVARS, OR VARIETIES

One of my grower catalogs lists 3 cultivars. 'Italian Dark Green' grows to 12 inches and has flat leaves that are deeply lobed, fine, and rich in flavor. 'Champion Moss Curled' grows to 12 inches, has bright-green curled foliage, and is good for soups and salads. 'Forest Green,' the finest "super-curled" variety, retains its bright green color and regrows well after cutting.

Rosemary

*T*his delightful plant has bridged the gap between houseplants and herbs. You will find rosemary topiaries in every bonafide garden center in North Carolina. Herb bowls containing rosemary command a premium price, as do sachets and bunches of dried sprigs. This ever-popular herb is at home in the perennial border or in the container garden. Rosemary is easy to grow and it has a carefree look. This evergreen member of the mint family has gray-green foliage that forms a clump of fine-textured foliage to 3 feet in height. Depending on the variety, it can be used as a groundcover, foundation specimen, or compact border. Its 1-inch needle-like leaves are intensely aromatic. Its flavor in meat dishes is distinctive and delectable. Once you have tasted broiled chicken or turkey seasoned with fresh rosemary, you are hooked for life! The pale-blue flowers are attractive and are scattered along the terminal shoots of the woody stems. My wife Becky was the first to describe rosemary as "the plant with the Christmas tree foliage." Trying to identify an herb over the telephone is a difficult task, but she drew the perfect word picture for me. Mature leaves of this plant do resemble those of Fraser fir!

WHEN TO PLANT

Container-grown rosemary can be planted from spring through fall in the Piedmont and Coastal regions of the Old North State. In the Mountains, however, where temperatures go below zero, grow it in a container and bring it indoors for the winter. Though a sunny window is adequate, a cold frame or home greenhouse is ideal for its care.

WHERE TO PLANT

This herb is a real sun-lover, though a semishaded location will do. Rosemary will thrive in alkaline soil that is fast draining. It is the plant to grow in hot sites, as it stands up well in heat and drought. If planting in containers, use terra cotta pots and a coarse soil mix. The cultivar 'Arp' is the right one for colder regions. The prostrate forms like 'Renzels' are suitable for groundcovers, or they may be planted in the herb or container garden.

HERBS

How to Plant

In poor soils, spade either bark soil conditioner or compost into the planting area before planting. A soil pH of 7.0 is best for rosemary. Where the soils are acidic, mix limestone or wood ashes with the soil to adjust the pH to the alkaline range. Remove the plants from their pots and pull the roots out onto a horizontal plane. The rosemary should be planted shallow, with its uppermost roots showing after it has planted. Use compost to cover the top inch of roots. Water thoroughly with a gallon of water to which a soluble fertilizer has been added. Water weekly during the next month. Leggy transplants can be sheared at planting time and the trimmings used in the kitchen at mealtime.

Care and Maintenance

Rosemary that is planted in containers or raised beds will need irrigation twice a week during the hot weather. When planting in clay soils, be careful not to overwater. (I would rather err on the dry side with most herbs.) Once your plants are established, normally in 10 weeks, dry weather is not a threat. Rosemary will use a lot of water in gravelly soils! Fertilize rosemary at least once during the year, in April or September. Use a complete garden fertilizer with a 1-1-1 analysis for these applications. If you want more flowers, cut back on the nitrogen. Prune rosemary in early spring and snip sprigs routinely.

Additional Information

You can harvest the leaves of rosemary any time of year; its fragrant oil, however, is at its peak before the flowers open. Dry sprigs in a paper bag indoors. Do not mulch deeply in the winter months. Rosemary is a rabbit-resistant herb. It can be propagated by cuttings or divisions in the summer; seed germination is the slowest method.

Additional Species, Cultivars, or Varieties

'Lockwood de Forest' is the cultivar I grow. It is 2 feet high with wispy shoots and bluish flowers. 'Albus' has white flowers. 'Prostratus' is the dwarf rosemary. 'Collingwood Ingram' grows to 3 feet with curved stems. 'Arp' has dark-blue blooms and can grow 2 feet high, spreading to 10 feet across in 4 years!

Sage

*S*age is so much more than the pungent leaves that flavor a turkey's stuffing. New sage varieties recently introduced are durable bedding plants that are available in a myriad of colors. On a garden tour to England in '96, I was delighted with the great beds of purple sage used in the knot gardens at Hampton Court. What a novel idea: borders of sage! Few other herbs can survive subzero weather or extended drought and still remain evergreen. Common cooking sage is a compact plant that forms a 20-inch-high mound. The grayish green leaves are soft to the touch. Spicy-scented sage has many culinary uses and a few practical medicinal uses (an Arabic friend carries a sprig of sage with her for calming an upset stomach). This herb is beneficial in the treatment of respiratory ailments. The *Salvia* genus includes a wide array of showy ornamentals from the colorful annuals scarlet sage and blue salvia to the vigorous Mexican bush sage with its fuzzy white-and-lavender flower stalks. The variegated sage cultivars are by far the most popular sages for herb bowls and garden beds. The handsome mounds of green-, gold-, or purple-variegated foliage provide a striking contrast with annuals.

WHEN TO PLANT

Quart-sized plants are available almost year-round in garden centers. These can be transplanted successfully any time the soil is warm. Sage seed can be sown in the spring. Clumps of sage can be divided in the summer.

WHERE TO PLANT

All sage varieties love to be planted in well-drained, full-sun gardens. Sage is a tough perennial that adds interest to any herb garden. The plants should be spaced 20 inches apart and placed in a background location. These plants are drought tolerant and non-invasive. The variegated varieties work well with annuals or in container gardens.

HOW TO PLANT

Sage is easy to plant from containers. Simply loosen the soil with your hands, or better still, take a hand spade and break apart the

rootball. Start from the bottom up, slicing through tightly bound roots, so you can open the rootball. It can then be planted in a "pancake fashion" in a shallow planting hole. Unless the soil is very poor or sandy, amendments are not needed in new beds. It *is* important to lime the soil, since sage enjoys an alkaline soil. Mix limestone into the soil at a rate of 5 pounds per 100 square feet. When transplanting sage, loosen the soil and plant at the same depth at which it was growing. Water thoroughly after transplanting.

CARE AND MAINTENANCE

Sage prefers to be left alone, though it is important to water weekly the first couple of months following planting. Apply a light application of 10-10-10 fertilizer in the spring (1 pound per 100 square feet) to get your sage off to a good quick start. Sage can be divided every 2 to 3 years for sharing or enlarging your garden bed. To keep it compact, a little pruning is beneficial. Use the prunings for cooking or store fresh in a reclosable plastic bag in the refrigerator. Sage loves dry soil, so don't overwater this plant in spring.

ADDITIONAL INFORMATION

Don't crowd your sage plant. Give it plenty of room for the necessary air circulation. This will prevent foliar diseases in our humid summers. Avoid root and stem root diseases by planting in fast-draining soils. Herbs can be dried in a frost-free refrigerator. Just place sprigs of your herb in a paper bag or wrap them in dry paper towels.

ADDITIONAL SPECIES, CULTIVARS, OR VARIETIES

'Icertina' is a gold-and-green-leaved sage used as an edging or planted in a mass. 'Tricolor,' a beautiful wine, white, and green, is a compact variety. 'Purpurea' is a dark-purple to burgundy sage, growing 2 to 3 feet high. 'Avrea' is a very nice golden-leaved sage. *Note:* Plant the variegated cultivars in full sun for the best color.

Ocimum basilicum

Sweet Basil

$\mathcal{S}$weet basil is an annual herb with bright-green wrinkled leaves. This European variety can grow to 25 inches in height. Western cooks consider it essential, and Asians, particularly the Thai and Vietnamese, also use basil (the large-leaved Thai varieties) in their cuisines. Basil has wonderful versatility in the garden. The genus name *Ocimum* is from a Greek verb meaning "fragrant." And fragrant it is. Basil is wonderful in Italian dishes, pesto, soups, sauces, and more. There are many new varieties such as lemon, cinnamon, chocolate, and purple. A 1997 All-America Selection winner is a delicious Thai basil called 'Siam Queen.' All the basils are easy to grow and they grow rapidly. There has been much interest in basil for its ornamental uses in perennial and flower gardens. For example, 'Purple Ruffles' has a deep rich purple color and very frilly foliage. 'Spicy Globe' is a wonderful border plant; its small compact growth habit makes it look a bit like a miniature boxwood. Basil can be enjoyed from May through October in gardens throughout the South. Plant it for use as a tasty kitchen herb or enjoy it as an ornamental for its fine foliage.

WHEN TO PLANT

Most basils do fine when seeds are sown directly in the ground after the last killing frost. In North Carolina, this is usually after April 15th. To get a real head start, you can begin sowing seeds indoors in February or March. A sunny window with a bank of fluorescent lights will grow terrific basil for seedlings or for kitchen use.

WHERE TO PLANT

The best location for basil is in the sun. Basil can be planted alone in containers or in herb planters with companion plants and flowers. Basil can also be planted in rows in a vegetable or herb garden. Smaller dwarf varieties can be used for edging a perennial border; or use it when creating a knot garden. Its unique color makes it good for use as an accent planting. Plant it in well-drained soils to avoid crown rot disease.

How to Plant

Till up the soil when planting in the vegetable or herb garden. The addition of limestone at the rate of 30 pounds per 1000 square feet will improve the growth of this herb. Sow the seed according to seedpacket directions. After they reach 3 inches in height, thin the basil seedlings to allow 15 to 18 inches between plants. The thinned seedlings are perfectly edible! Basil plants are available from the garden centers in plastic cell packs. When ready to plant, loosen the roots carefully, and remove peat pots if they are present. After planting small plants, water-in with a starter fertilizer. I like to use fish emulsion for the first 2 weeks. Then I use Peter's 20-20-20 soluble fertilizer every 10 days.

Care and Maintenance

Basils need plenty of water during the beginning of their heavy growing season. Irrigate at least twice a week, more if the basil is in containers. Do not allow it to become dry. Pruning the plant is a must to keep it in bounds. The flowers should be pinched off regularly. Allowing the plant to bloom will slow production of the foliage, and producing foliage is the most common reason for growing basil. When you need leaves for the kitchen, snip the desired amount with scissors and the plant will send out new growth at the cut points. Harvest the entire plant before the first killing frost. Basil is a tender plant, not cold tolerant.

Additional Information

Allow plenty of room in your garden for this vigorous grower. Some varieties will grow to 3 to 4 feet tall with a spread of 2 to 3 feet. Do not transplant new plants into the garden too soon since basil is sensitive to cold temperatures. Beware of planting basils in poorly drained soils. Stem, crown, and root diseases are prevalent in the Piedmont.

Additional Species, Cultivars, or Varieties

'Purple Ruffles' is a deep rich purple and has very frilly foliage. 'Spicy Globe,' a flavorful miniature, is a great border plant. 'Dark Opal,' a purple basil with pink flowers, gives a red color to vinegars. 'Siam Queen,' a 1997 All-America Selection, is a Thai variety that grows to 15 inches. It has showy dense-purple blooms and can be used in the kitchen or as a container-grown ornamental.

Thyme

he Greeks believed that this herb imparted strength to the user. Their word for courage (*thymon*) may have given rise to the name of this plant. Thyme is as useful in the garden as it is in the kitchen. Some species, such as 'Mother of Thyme' (*T. praecox*), are suitable groundcovers, while others are perfect for herb bowls. Thymes have small, tender, aromatic leaves. The semi-evergreen foliage is held closely to stiff, wiry stems. The leaves are generally smooth, but some can be "woolly," or variegated with yellow stripes. Terminal clusters of tiny white- to rose-colored flowers occur throughout the growing season. This herb readily hybridizes, and there are over 60 cultivars available to Tar Heel gardeners. Thyme is easy to grow in average soil and can spread 1 to 3 feet in a year. Its low-growing habit will smother out weeds as it forms a dense mat on the floor of the garden. Harvest sprigs of this herb any time for use in preparing food. Just as the early Greeks discovered, thyme is stalwart in the garden. You will be pleased with its performance in the Old North State.

WHEN TO PLANT

Most garden shops have better selections of herbs in the spring, though thyme can be planted any month of the year from containers. I prefer to plant small potted herbs when the soil is warm from April through October. Seedlings can be produced indoors during the winter months for later transplanting into the garden.

WHERE TO PLANT

Thyme should be planted in a sunny location where there's well-drained soil. In the Mountain region, find a protected site. This plant is a champion for planting along a garden walk among flagstones or rocks. Accent a sidewalk or border with a planting of thyme. Add interest to the garden with masses of thyme cascading over a rock wall or growing in a container. A word of caution: bees are attracted to some varieties.

HOW TO PLANT

Find a sunny spot in the garden and dig a hole that is 3 times the width of the container. Thyme prefers a loose soil with a near-

neutral pH. In the absence of a soil test, add lime and a little phosphorus fertilizer at planting time. Mix the amendments to a depth of 4 inches. After removing the plant from the container, force the roots apart and spread them in the shallow planting hole. Use the soil from the planting hole as backfill. Firm-in the roots and water generously. New plantings should be watered weekly for the first month. A thin mulch of leaf compost will be beneficial when planting during the summer months.

CARE AND MAINTENANCE

Thyme thrives on neglect once the plants are established. For lush growth, an organic fertilizer that is rich in nitrogen can be applied each month. Irrigate your plantings during dry periods in the summer and fall. Plantings in containers will require weekly watering. To keep the thymes bushy and productive, shear them routinely and use the trimmings for cooking and for drying. I have never had problems with pests while growing thyme.

ADDITIONAL INFORMATION

Although thyme can be harvested any time for use in the kitchen, its best flavor is at bloom time. Keep the flowers pruned off for more active vegetative growth. Lemon thyme is less cold hardy than many of the varieties we grow. Thyme is especially good for use in chicken and fish dishes, and for making herbal teas.

ADDITIONAL SPECIES, CULTIVARS, OR VARIETIES

Thymes suitable for groundcovers are woolly thyme, 'Elfin,' 'Minus,' and 'Mother of Thyme.' Taller varieties include lemon thyme, common thyme, French thyme, and oregano thyme. Unique and interesting thymes are caraway thyme, with its rose-pink flowers, 'Aurea,' with its green-and-yellow leaves, and silver thyme, which has silver leaves.

Artemisia

OTHER COMMON NAME: Wormwood

*T*here are hundreds of artemisias, including some annuals like sweet-annie (*A. annua*), an intensely fragrant herb. But it is the ornamental perennials that are gardenworthy. While the flowers are not particularly attractive, the silver-gray foliage of artemisia is quite distinctive and of great value as an accent in the garden. The variation in texture of artemisias is as vast as their variation in height (they grow from 6 inches to 4 feet high). Artemisia foliage is a great contrast for many herbaceous perennial gardens where it can be used as in a border. Ornamental grasses used in the background of a planting of artemisia is quite striking. Plant this perennial herb in dry sites where many flowers dare not grow. Gardeners in rural North Carolina often have problems with deer browsing their gardens. Artemisia is one perennial that deer seem to ignore while they forage through the country landscapes. Some of the larger cultivars like 'Silver King' can become invasive and should be used at the back of the border. The luminescence of artemisias as well as their drought tolerance makes this plant an irresistible choice for the garden.

WHEN TO PLANT

Plant artemisias after the soil has warmed up in late spring (May) and through early November. Divide artemisias for transplanting in spring, and again in September for enlarging your beds, or just to share them with a friend.

WHERE TO PLANT

Most artemisias are strong growers ideally suited to sunny, dry exposures in borders. Poor or rocky soil doesn't seem to faze this determined perennial. Because of its heat tolerance, it is adapted to container gardening as well. Be selective when you choose your varieties since they range widely in height and spread. Spacing of artemisias in a garden can vary from 1 to 6 feet.

How to Plant

Artemisias should not be planted in moist soils but in poor, drier sites. After you have selected a sunny location, loosen the soil. Incorporate large volumes of granite screenings, gravel, or bark mulch into clay soils. Dig a planting hole and place the artemisia so the top roots will be visible on the surface once the plant is firmed in. Planting shallow like this will ensure perfect drainage in the bed. Water thoroughly to settle the soil around the rootball. Don't mulch until the middle of the summer. Remember to find a place where the soil is too poor or rocky for other fine perennials, and plant artemisias in that spot.

Care and Maintenance

During the first growing season, water every 10 days during dry periods. Don't overwater. (I have killed my share of artemisias with kindness!) A liquid plant fertilizer can be used monthly to encourage establishment. They are not heavy feeders. Prune away blighted leaves following a wet summer season. The taller growing artemisias can be cut back severely in late winter to control their height. Shear this plant as needed for arrangements; or just enjoy its colorful and often aromatic foliage.

Additional Information

Artemisias prefer to be left alone once established. But prune them severely in late winter, leaving 6- to 10-inch stems with strong buds for the next growing season. A light fertilizer application once each spring is adequate. Pests are no problem for this rugged perennial— some artemisias will even repel pests.

Additional Species, Cultivars, or Varieties

'Powis Castle' is a non-blooming, shrubby 2- to 4-foot plant with finely cut foliage. 'Silver Brocade' is a beach wormwood that tolerates salty winds. 'Valerie Finnis' is white, has gray foliage to 20 inches, and is not aggressive. 'Lambrook Silver' has great foliage and grows up to 3 feet in height with equal width. 'Silver Mound' is a 6-inch groundcover with delicate foliage.

Gaillardia × grandiflora

Blanket Flower

lanket flower is a fitting name for this multicolored perennial that covers the ground with its foliage and cheery blooms. The yellow-tipped crimson flowers are a common sight in coastal landscapes and seaside gardens. These striking flowers are available as annuals and perennials. Blanket flower is a sun-loving native American wildflower. The annual varieties of blanket flower form clumps of foliage that resembles the hairy leaves of the blackeyed susans. The best annual selection is the All-America Selection 'Red Plume.' These grow easily from seed if sown in well-drained soil, and they flower freely. G. 'Goblin' is the most popular perennial blanket flower. It is compact, growing to 1 foot with 3-inch blooms. It thrives in dry garden sites and can be used in mass beds or for edging a perennial garden. The 5-inch flowered cultivar G. 'Torchlight' grows to 30 inches in height and makes a terrific choice for the cutting garden. Blanket flowers can be erect or spreading, depending on the site and variety. They can bloom most of the summer and into the fall if the plants are sheared lightly after the first flush of blooms fades away.

WHEN TO PLANT

It is best to plant blanket flower in the spring or summer. Both annual and perennial varieties can be seeded early indoors, or sown directly in warm garden soil. Container-grown *Gaillardia* plants are available at the larger garden centers. Plant these whenever conditions permit in the growing season.

WHERE TO PLANT

Plant blanket flower in average to poor soil, as long as it drains well. Crowns tend to die out in heavy clay soils during wet summers. Often they will return the next spring from persistent roots or seedlings. Transplant wayward seedlings back into the perennial bed. Blanket flowers must have full sun to reach their potential. The perennial border or wildflower meadow is an ideal location for this beauty.

How to Plant

Rototill the garden and incorporate pine-bark soil conditioner
into clay soils. Rake the garden to remove rocks and large clods.
Broadcast 5-10-10 fertilizer at the rate of 1 pound per 100 square
feet, and rake again. Sow the seeds of blanket flower and cover with
1/3 inch of sand or soil. Water well using a watering wand attached
to the garden hose. Perennial plants bought in containers can be set
in this well-prepared soil. Good drainage is essential to maintain
blanket flower as a perennial. The seed can be started indoors in
March using flats of sterile potting soil. Harden-off the seedlings for
2 weeks before setting in the garden.

Care and Maintenance

Keep seedbeds moist until the plants are 3 inches in height, then
water twice weekly. Irrigation is not important after the plants begin
blooming. Too much water is harmful to blanket flower, and it does
not require much fertilization. In fact, it will flower better in nonfer-
tile soil. After the first flush of flowers has faded, cut back the bed
with hedge shears or a weed-eater, then fertilize with 10-10-10 to get
the plants started on another growth spurt. Propagate by transplanting stray seedlings and by division in the spring.

Additional Information

For years I was reluctant to plant blanket flowers in my Piedmont
garden because of our clay soils. What a pleasant surprise to discover that they will flourish in our region and weather our unusual
winters like seasoned warriors. Plant this flower with other wildflowers and have a great meadow garden.

Additional Species, Cultivars, or Varieties

'Baby Cole' is bicolored, red and yellow. 'Burgundy' is a solid burgundy red. 'Golden Goblin' is yellow. 'Grandiflora Mix' is yellow,
red, and gold. The University of Georgia recommends *G. aristata*
over *G. × grandiflora* if you are more interested in long-lived plants
than in high-quality flowers. *G. pulchella*, an annual species, includes
'Red Plume' and 'Yellow Sun.'

Christmas Fern

hroughout most of North Carolina, the Christmas fern goes virtually unnoticed until the autumn leaves have fallen and settled into their permanent place. Deep hardwood forests with moist ravines provide an ideal habitat for this terrific Tar Heel native. Entire carpets of Christmas fern can frequently be found naturally, and they are often the focus of plant rescues organized by conservationists or botanists from noteworthy organizations like our North Carolina Botanical Gardens. William Lanier Hunt writes in *Southern Gardens, Southern Gardening*, "It is really hard to understand why we have not taken to Christmas ferns more than we have. They are easy to transplant and will brighten up dark corners where almost nothing else will grow. Ferns make the most elegant backgrounds for wildflowers, especially the smaller ones." Christmas fern is a compact, clump-forming plant growing to a height of 2 feet. Its medium-green evergreen foliage and delicate fronds add perpetual interest to the shade garden. Ferns like a rich loamy soil and a constant supply of moisture. Supplying a suitable habitat is the secret of fern cultivation. Choice ferns for landscape gardening include autumn fern, shield fern, Japanese painted fern, and, on the Coast, holly fern.

WHEN TO PLANT

Ferns can be planted practically all year when the soil can be worked, especially those grown in containers. Transplant ferns in late winter or early spring and fall. I have moved wild Christmas ferns in the middle of the summer, but only to shady locations.

WHERE TO PLANT

Ferns are well suited to city gardens and as companion plantings with native wildflowers. Christmas fern serves well as a ground-cover in shade gardens where it can create a lush, tropical feel. If you do not have a natural stream habitat for ferns, consider planting them where there may be moist conditions, such as by a leaking air conditioner or next to a water garden. Ferns have done fine on my home's north side.

ZONE
6,7,8

How to Plant

Very few ferns will thrive without moist, organic soil and partial shade. Prepare the area for planting your ferns by tilling or spading in large volumes of sphagnum peat moss or my preference, aged leaf compost. The soil mix should be a minimum of 50 percent organic matter so that the soil can be worked by hand during transplanting. Good soil drainage will ensure oxygen gets to the fine, fibrous roots of ferns. Ferns adapt well to most soils, acid or alkaline. Don't add garden fertilizer to the planting hole; a little bonemeal or cottonseed meal, however, is okay. When planting Christmas fern be careful not to break the tender fronds arising from the crown. Plant shallow, water well, and apply a mulch.

Care and Maintenance

Once established, some ferns can tolerate up to 4 hours of direct sunlight. Hardwood forests can be limbed up and saplings removed to accommodate a planting of ferns. Shallow-rooted trees like maples and beeches are not fern-friendly. Dense evergreen forests are also poor places for most ferns due to root competition and subsequent dry soils. There are many deciduous ferns to choose from for the garden; these need to be pruned back after the November freeze. Most of the evergreen ferns require only an occasional light pruning to remove sunburned foliage or injury from weather, pets, and slugs.

Additional Information

Ferns are truly low-maintenance plants, amazingly resilient after they are established. Watering is essential during the first season but only in dry spells in the years that follow. Water 3 to 4 times per week following planting, especially during the growth spurts. Organic mulch from a composter is the best fertilizer. Apply mulch annually.

Additional Species, Cultivars, or Varieties

Evergreen ferns include Christmas fern, autumn fern (*Dryopteris*), holly fern (*Cyrtomium*), 'Rochefordianum,' and arborvitae fern (*Selaginella*). Deciduous ferns include maidenhair fern (*Adiantum*), Japanese painted fern (*Athyrium nipponicum*), southern shield fern (*Thelypteris*), and the new Asian fern from North Carolina State University Arboretum, black-lady fern (*Athyrium japonicum*).

Columbine

Columbine can be classified as both wildflower and herbaceous perennial. In mid-spring the common red-and-yellow-flowered seedlings of *A. canadensis* appear overnight and burst into bloom. This species behaves like a wildflower, throwing seeds by summer that soon germinate in every nook and cranny of the garden. The foliage is delicate, resembling that of the maidenhair fern; it provides an interesting contrast where grown among more coarse garden perennials. My favorite is dwarf-blue columbine, *A. flabellata pumila*, with its 2-inch blue-and-white flowers. This American native forms a clump and has blue-green leaves that are low to the ground. The bloom period is just too short, so I never get enough of this columbine's glowing blue blooms. The stems support flowers that appear poised for flight. The ancient Romans gave this perennial its Latin name "columbae," which means dove. The exotic flowers have spurred petals that resemble a covey of doves in flight. (The petals of hybrids form a cup and saucer.) Columbines will grow well in dry, poor soil without coaxing. Since the new hybrids have appeared, the color combinations are endless!

WHEN TO PLANT

Plant columbines in the fall and in the spring. This group of plants seeds freely, unless you are using the hybrid varieties. The seed can be sown in late autumn for spring blooms. Collect seed of your plants as the pods lose their bright-green color. Transplant established columbines any time in the summer, spacing them 15 inches apart.

WHERE TO PLANT

Columbines will grow in full sun or filtered shade in ordinary garden soil. They are primarily spring-flowering plants, but occasionally the hybrids will produce a few blooms in the fall. Plant columbines in the front of perennial borders since they are small plants. The hybrids are docile plants, and can be used in mass groupings in small gardens and in containers. Plant columbines in combination with annuals.

HOW TO PLANT

Columbine can be handled as an annual or a perennial depending upon where you garden in the state. It is a very easy perennial to grow. Prepare a bed in a sunny location, just as you would for seeding vegetables. Eliminate perennial broadleaf weeds mechanically or chemically several weeks before seeding; and rake in the seeds, barely covering them, in late fall or spring. If planting a potted columbine, dig a hole 3 times larger than the container and plant at grade or slightly higher. Many container-grown perennials are pot-bound when purchased, so score them with a knife to free up the roots. Firm-in the plants and water well. Irrigate twice each week for the first 3 weeks.

CARE AND MAINTENANCE

For new plants and seedbeds, use a watering wand and garden hose to irrigate for several minutes each day. Do this until the roots are established, generally in several weeks, or when new growth emerges. Columbine has a life expectancy of 3 to 4 years; it can be divided during the spring. Purchasing new plants for replacements is advisable. Seedheads can be left to mature and young plants started as replacements. Columbine likes good, rich, loose soil; it benefits from supplementary feeding in late spring using a slow-release flower fertilizer. Mulch in the summer months with 1 inch of compost.

ADDITIONAL INFORMATION

The native columbine will produce unwanted seedlings throughout the garden unless deadheaded (remove and promptly destroy the green seedpods). Another approach is to use columbine hybrids. In a meadow-like garden, it may be desirable to let the plants reseed. You can save seed by placing the ripened seedpods in a paper bag.

ADDITIONAL SPECIES, CULTIVARS, OR VARIETIES

'McKana' hybrids and 'Music' series are widely offered in seed catalogs. These two give the gardener a symphony of color combinations and uniform flowers. *A. caerulea*, Rocky Mountain columbine, grows to 2 feet and has flowers that are similar to those of the sky-blue-and-white *A. pumila*. *A. canadensis* is the wild columbine; it's easy to grow from seed and is very durable.

Echinacea purpurea

Coneflower

OTHER COMMON NAME: Purple Coneflower

*T*his wonderful perennial is a member of the composite family, a group that is recognized by its daisy-like flowers, each having a prominent center core surrounded by a skirt of petals. A native of the North American prairie, the purple coneflower has been widely introduced as a garden plant around the world. This easy-to-grow sun-loving plant produces long-lasting flowers from early summer through late fall. The strong stemmed flowers make excellent cut flowers. A sturdy, rather coarse perennial herb, purple coneflower has showy purplish pink to almost-white flowers. The blooms are borne as solitary heads on stiff stems that reach a height of 2 to 5 feet. The seedpods last for months until discovered by marvelous little songbirds or goldfinches in late summer. The finches quickly devour the dry seedheads, leaving bare stalks to dry in the hot sun. Butterflies are attracted to the large flowers all summer long. Variants of the commercially available cultivars have been observed in natural stands in the wild. Once established, purple coneflower reseeds itself freely and becomes a great passalong plant.

WHEN TO PLANT

Early spring and fall are the best times to plant purple coneflower. You can successfully transplant any time the soil can be worked and good moisture conditions exist. Seed can be started in early spring or summer in nursery flats and transplanted when plants are 1/2 inch in diameter. Direct-seeding also works, but plant yields will be low. Expect flowers the second year.

WHERE TO PLANT

Plant purple coneflower in any location that receives full sun to dappled shade. These plants are tolerant of a wide range of soils provided the soil is well drained. Rich, sandy soils provide the best growth, but mineral and clay soils can also produce fine plants. Coneflower does very well on slopes and hillsides.

ZONE 6,7,8

How to Plant

Purple coneflower can be divided in spring, as several crowns will often sprout from each mature root. Plant in groups with individuals 12 to18 inches apart. Groups of these single-flowered plants will provide a striking focus in the garden and these mass plantings are attractive to wildlife. Some natural seed spread will occur, but the purple coneflower is considered noninvasive.

Care and Maintenance

This plant tolerates thin layers of bark or leaf mulch for the control of weeds and stabilization of soil moisture. Once established, coneflowers are very drought tolerant and do not require fertilization. The plants will bloom continuously if deadheaded. Cutting back the dead stems in the fall and winter does not harm this prolific plant.

Additional Information

Purple coneflower is very disease- and pest-resistant. Once established, it requires no extra care for survival. Japanese beetles will feed on the petals during bloom, and some control might be helpful. During extreme drought, occasional watering will improve the foliage. When buying native wildflowers, make sure they were not collected from the wild.

Additional Species, Cultivars, or Varieties

Three species of coneflower can be found in natural populations in North Carolina. *E. laevigata*, the smooth coneflower, is a federally protected endangered species in the Piedmont of North Carolina. Hybrids include 'Sombrero,' 'Robert Bloom,' and 'Bright Star.' White variants are 'White Lustre' and 'White Swan.'

Heuchera sanguinea

Coralbells

OTHER COMMON NAME: Alumroot

*T*hanks to hybridization, today's generation of coralbells boasts tall flowers, evergreen foliage, and tolerance to hot, humid weather. The parent to many of the improved varieties is a North Carolina native, *H. americana.* Coralbells is a low-growing perennial, with maple-like lustrous foliage that radiates out from a crown called a rosette. The beauty of its foliage is reason enough to grow this semi-evergreen perennial. Some of the showiest coralbells have plum-colored leaves glistening with a metallic sheen. One of these, 'Palace Purple,' was dubbed Perennial Plant of the Year by the national Perennial Plant Association. The airy flower spikes of coralbells, ranging in color from cherry to coral, can be as striking as the distinctive-looking foliage. In early summer, the sway of these 18-inch spikes will create movement in the garden as the delicate bell-shaped blooms ring in the breeze. Coralbells are ideal for most shade situations provided they have adequate drainage. Plant this garden gem for its bold, colorful foliage. Larger, fine-textured plants like plum yews are a good backdrop for coralbells. *Lamium* 'White Nancy' is a good groundcover to serve as a companion in shade gardens.

WHEN TO PLANT

Set out container-grown coralbells in spring. The clumps can be divided in the fall to make root divisions. These dormant root divisions are handled like daylily divisions, and can be planted until early December.

WHERE TO PLANT

Coralbells are traditionally planted as border plants in single file, military fashion. Their real beauty is best appreciated when planted in groups. Variegated flag iris, hostas, ferns, and astilbes are good companions for coralbells. Try planting it with some shade-loving grasses like mondo grass and *Carex.* Few plants are happier in partial shade than this one. To prevent problems, plant coralbells only in moist, rich soils.

How to Plant

Old garden coralbells, and the new releases as well, are intolerant of sticky clay soil. To avoid problems, good drainage is essential. If planting a container plant, dig a hole 3 times the size of the root mass. Work leaf compost or granite screenings into the soil before you firm-in the coralbells. This should help improve the soil drainage. In wet sites, plant on slight berms. Water well to settle the soil around the rootball. Mulching is one way to enrich the soil and improve the survivability of the plants. Coralbells do fine in acidic soils, so there is no need to lime them.

Care and Maintenance

Coralbells prefer sustained moisture, so mulching in summer is important. Water deeply, only 2 times each week, until they are established. In woodland gardens they are durable perennials, especially in the Piedmont and westward. After a hard freeze, remove spoiled foliage. Clumps of coralbells can get quite large over time. They should be divided every 4 to 5 years to invigorate the bed. They are great plants to share with a gardening friend, since they are "tranplanting-friendly." Rake the beds clean in spring to remove old debris—you don't want the winter winds to blow too many leaves over the beds and suffocate the plants. They don't like deep mulches over their crowns.

Additional Information

There are only a few cultivars that prefer full-sun conditions in the Tar Heel state. Most prefer dappled light and good drainage. Some coralbells, particularly the native variety 'Garnet,' will tolerate sandy coastal soils. To improve soil drainage, berm up plants or amend with coarse organic matter like pine bark or screenings.

Additional Species, Cultivars, or Varieties

'Palace Purple' has bronze-burgundy foliage and white flowers in June. 'Mt. St. Helens,' with fiery red flowers, blooms all summer. 'Garnet' (*H. americana*) has bronze leaves and tolerates sun. 'Silver Shadows' has silver iridescent foliage. 'Plum Puddin' is shiny and plum-purple. 'Canyon Pink' is a dwarf form with green leaves and hot-pink flowers. 'Strawberry Swirl' has ruffled green leaves and bicolor flowers.

Cottage Pinks

*D*ianthus has been in European gardens for centuries. The group we call cottage pinks made its way to North America with the English colonists. These flowers were the rage in the nineteenth century. Few old varieties survive today, but the ones that do are delightfully fragrant. Most Tar Heel gardeners will remember a close cousin to the pinks, the sweet-william, *D. barbatus*, of Grandma's garden. Unfortunately, sweet-williams didn't stand up in the heat and were rather short-lived plants. Cottage pinks are much more tolerant of heat and will form mats of silvery foliage that are handsome even when the plants are not in flower. Most cottage pinks bloom in May or June and have a scent of jasmine that is enchanting when they are used as cut flowers. They vary in flower color from white, red, and pinkish to salmon, yellow, and orange. The low-growing habit makes this 8-inch-high perennial an ideal choice for the front of the border or in a rockery. I have had success in starting pinks from seed, and have taken advantage of the new cultivars for spicing up the garden. My favorite is 'Strawberry Parfait,' a bicolored pink with jagged petals. For the aspiring gardener, the annual pinks and carnations are exciting flowers.

WHEN TO PLANT

Cottage pinks and other *Dianthus* can be started from seed indoors in February under fluorescent lights by a sunny window. Container-grown transplants from the nursery can be planted outside in early spring about the time forsythias finish blooming. They like cool weather and can be divided for planting in the fall also.

WHERE TO PLANT

Plant pinks in sun or partial shade; but by all means, plant where their "feet" will stay dry. Root rot is the biggest killer of this great perennial. It will grow in normal garden soil provided it is well-drained and enriched with organic matter. Plant cottage pinks in the front of a border or in masses for vivid color. They are a great companion for santolina, artemisias, and lavenders; or use them to circle a bed of miniature roses.

ZONE
6,7,8

HOW TO PLANT

Cottage pinks will live a longer life when planted in a raised bed. It is important to give them perfect drainage, so in clay soils, mix in large quantities of bark soil conditioner or compost. They prefer an alkaline soil; incorporate limestone at the rate of 7 pounds per 100 square feet of bed along with a phosphorus fertilizer. Some gardeners have found that double-digging beds will give good results with pinks. (Double-digging means removing the top 6 inches of soil, spading amendments into the ground below, then replacing the topsoil layer.) Plant seedlings and potted plants at grade in the thoroughly prepared beds. Water to settle the soil and mulch the beds to conserve moisture.

CARE AND MAINTENANCE

When selecting a garden spot for cottage pinks, choose a location where there is morning sun in an eastern exposure. Protection from the summer afternoon sun is appreciated by this perennial. Fertilize with a complete garden fertilizer in early spring and again in early fall. Newly set plants can be fertilized with a soluble fertilizer every 2 weeks to get them off to a quick start. Consider using a soaker hose and mulch to keep the pinks well watered in hot weather. Promptly remove wilted plants, as root rot can spread in the bed. Divide established beds in early fall. Pinks are half-hardy perennials!

ADDITIONAL INFORMATION

Cottage pinks are relatively maintenance-free when planted in fast-draining soils. Granite screenings or similar coarse, gravelly amendments can be used to fill raised beds. In tight soils, plastic drain tile can be placed under beds. Prune back old flowerheads. Enjoy these delightful, long-lasting flowers in small arrangements indoors.

ADDITIONAL SPECIES, CULTIVARS, OR VARIETIES

'Telstar Picotee' is an All-America Selections award winner, crimson with white-edged petals. The 'Parfait' series includes 'Strawberry' and 'Raspberry.' Other cultivars are 'Snowfire,' 'Spring Beauty' (double , mixed colors), 'Aqua,' and 'Mrs. Sinkins.' *D. barbatus* (sweet-william) includes 'White Beauty,' 'Scarlet Beauty,' and 'Newport Pink.'

233

Cyclamen

yclamen is a great little perennial that grows from tubers. Most people are familiar with the greenhouse cyclamens, but a wealth of notable garden varieties are available as well. There are few garden scenes more beautiful than a bed of cyclamen flourishing in a woodland garden. Many species are hardy in the Middle South. The species bloom at various times. "A gardener with a collection of most of the hardy ones may expect to have at least a few flowers every day of the year," says Nancy Goodwin of Montrose. The white, pink, or crimson flowers have 5 petals connected at the mouth and flung back much like *Dodecatheon* (shooting stars). Many species have fragrant flowers. They require a dormant period but return to active growth when their time comes each year. Attractive leaves beautifully marked with silver appear before, at the same time, or after the flowers. *Cyclamen hederifolium* is the most easily grown species, often producing a flower in summer, but making a splendid display in fall. Flowers appear first, followed by spectacular leaves in October and November. By late summer, *C. graecum* blooms with velvety leaves that are even more beautiful than the flowers.

WHEN TO PLANT

Cyclamen are best planted just as they are breaking dormancy in late summer. Only *C. purpurascens* prefers to be planted in spring, as it returns to growth for the summer.

WHERE TO PLANT

Cyclamen requires a well-drained site and most varieties are happy beneath deciduous trees. But cyclamen does like sun. *Cyclamen coum* and *C. hederifolium* prefer winter sun and summer shade. *C. purpurascens* needs shade.

HOW TO PLANT

Cyclamen wants to be planted near the surface of the soil. Only *C. repandum* should be planted about 1 inch below the soil level. Adding gravel throughout the soil when planting helps with drainage and may deter mice and voles.

CARE AND MAINTENANCE

Cyclamen thrives on benign neglect and requires no extra water. In fact, it should be planted where it will receive no artificial water during the dormant period. A light application of an all-purpose fertilizer just as the plants return from dormancy is helpful, but not necessary. They will benefit from an application of dolomitic lime if planted in very acid soil.

ADDITIONAL INFORMATION

Cyclamen increases by seeds often dispersed by ants attracted to the sticky covering on them. Watch for young plants nearby. These plants may be left in place to mature or transplanted the following year.

ADDITIONAL SPECIES, CULTIVARS, OR VARIETIES

C. hederifolium is pink, with white flowers in fall. *C. graecum* has velvety leaves and lovely flowers. Cold-hardy *C. parviflorum* blooms in midwinter. *C. repandum* is fragrant in spring. *C. pseudibericum* has large, showy flowers. *C. purpurascens* produces fragrant flowers for a long period in summer.

Achillea spp.

Fern-Leaf Yarrow

his garden favorite is tough and reliable. Grandmother's garden certainly included fern-leaf yarrow, the pale-pink variety. Yarrows belong to a large family, but all share the same plant habit. All have basal leaves forming a rosette of gray, finely divided, aromatic "fern-like" foliage. This easy-to-grow perennial comes in a multitude of flower colors from tricolored pastels to the ever-popular sulfur-colored 'Moonshine.' Flower stems will grow from 1 to 3 feet tall, bearing 3-inch flattened flowerheads called corymbs. Plant yarrow in the background and your purple salvias or red cosmos will come alive!

WHEN TO PLANT

Plant yarrow in spring or early fall from divisions and container-grown stock.

WHERE TO PLANT

Yarrow grows easily in average to poor soil. Given a full-sun location, fern-leaf yarrow will bloom in late spring throughout summer. Shade causes tall species to be a little lanky and open. Yarrow is one perennial that can rescue a barren area and cover it with bloom. It has been proven from the dry Southwest to the hard-baked clay soils of North Carolina. Give yarrow plenty of space (25 inches apart) to minimize mildew disease.

HOW TO PLANT

If you have trouble with yarrow, it's most likely due to "wet-feet" syndrome. Prepare the soil so it is loose and friable. Gravel or bark amendments can be added along with a half-cup of superphosphate. Root pieces (2-inch rhizomes) or container pots can be used to get yarrow started. Dig a 1-foot planting hole and place your plant shallow. Berm up the plant in heavy soils to ensure excellent drainage. Water generously the first month only.

CARE AND MAINTENANCE

Once established, yarrow will thrive on neglect. The plant can be pruned back to encourage better foliage. Remove spent blooms (deadhead) routinely. After a hard freeze in November, remove the spoiled foliage. Liquid feed with any general garden fertilizer monthly to increase the plant growth.

ADDITIONAL INFORMATION

In shady locations, leaf deterioration is a common problem when the wet July weather begins. A systemic fungicide or application of sulfur dust may be helpful.

ADDITIONAL SPECIES, CULTIVARS, OR VARIETIES

'Coronation Gold,' a hybrid that grows to 3 feet, is the standard gold yarrow. 'Moonshine,' a light-yellow hybrid, grows to 20 inches. 'Fire King' (*A. millefolium*) grows to 2 feet and has rosy red flowers and sea-green foliage. 'Pastel Shades' is tricolor, in pastels. 'Lilac Beauty' is a rich pink, reminiscent of grandma's yarrow.

Chrysanthemum × morifolium

Garden Mums

eeks before Labor Day, every retailer garden center, grocery store, and mass merchandiser in the country now stocks the shelves high with mums. Their popularity with homeowners is unparalleled in the floricultural trade. And justifiably so—gardeners like flowers that return dependably! The new varieties of garden mums are phenomenal in form and color. The dwarf introductions (cushion mums) such as 'Julia' and 'Bravo' require no pinching to remain compact and full of stunning blooms in September and October. The flowers, either daisy-like or fully double, come in a wide range of colors from the standard yellow and white to hot-pink to red. Though yellow is still the most popular color, the red cultivars are big sellers. Garden mums have few serious pests and are adaptable to almost any site. They can be planted while in full bloom for an instant effect in the tired summer garden. The flowers are long-lasting when cut for fresh arrangements.

WHEN TO PLANT

Container-grown mums can be planted any time the bed is ready for planting. Garden shops are well-stocked with mums in the fall, which is the the best time to select them based on true color. Planting conditions are also good in autumn. Dividing established plants can be done from November to May provided the soil is not frozen.

WHERE TO PLANT

Garden mums need a full-sun to partial-shade location. Planting in full sun will mean less pruning and more compact plants. Mums give the best effect when planted in mass groupings. In border plantings, use light colors in back of the dark-color varieties; this will cause the dark ones to show up well. Mums work well in containers, windowboxes, or any area that needs dressing up for a fall display.

PERENNIALS

HOW TO PLANT

Garden mums are commonly available in 8- or 10-inch mum pans, or as transplants in smaller containers. They are not fussy about soil type, but they need well-drained conditions. Most gardeners plant mums in beds. For single plants, dig a planting hole as deep and twice as wide as the container. Spade or till the bed and mix in nutrients if recommended by the soil test. Mums are vigorous growers and quickly fill the containers with roots. It is imperative that the roots be disturbed before planting to get the plants established. Use a handtool or knife to loosen the lower half of the rootball. Plant the mums at grade in the bed. Water them thoroughly, and apply a layer of mulch.

CARE AND MAINTENANCE

There is no need to fertilize garden mums that are planted in the fall where there is good garden soil. Watering every third day is important during the month after planting. Following a freeze, the mums will yellow and can be cut back to ground level. Rake up the debris and throw in the compost bin. In spring, apply 10-10-10 garden fertilizer at a rate of 1 pound per 100 square feet of bed. Make applications of fertilizer every 6 weeks during the growing season. During the summer months, watering weekly is sufficient. Some varieties of mums require staking, particularly if they are crowded or in shade.

ADDITIONAL INFORMATION

In order to keep your garden mums compact and producing more blooms, you will need to pinch them (shear them) twice. The first pinching is in May, or when the plants reach 8 inches in height. Shear them back to 5 inches with hedge shears. They will branch and will need a second pinching around July 4. Keep an eye out for caterpillars that eat the flowers.

ADDITIONAL SPECIES, CULTIVARS, OR VARIETIES

The Prophets by Yoder are a popular series of cultivars grown by most nurserymen. There are dozens of these from which to choose. Here are my favorites: 'Jessica,' 'Sunny Linda' (yellow flowers), 'Debonair,' 'Megan,' 'Stargazer' (rose/mauve color), 'Dark Triumph,' 'Grace' (orange/bronze), 'Tracy,' and 'Nicole' (white, daisy-like).

Garden Phlox

his family of perennials is old-fashioned, but it remains a garden workhorse. There is a phlox for every location from streamside to open woodlands. These flowers are especially picturesque when found growing wild along the rocky roadsides in the North Carolina mountains. Garden phlox is highly valued for its long bloom period in summer and fall. Many of the showy garden phlox cultivars are most likely hybrids with the *P. maculata*. Flower colors range from purple, magenta, and pink to white. The erect stalks of this perennial often stretch 3 feet high in the August sun. It is a great passalong plant since it is indigenous to the Tar Heel state. Because of our humid North Carolina climate, this garden warrior can require higher maintenance than other perennials. Try garden phlox as a background plant in combination with spider flowers and obedient plant for the look of an English cottage garden.

WHEN TO PLANT

Spring or early fall is a good time to plant garden phlox. They divide well for transplanting during these seasonal windows.

WHERE TO PLANT

Garden phlox will bloom best in full to partial sun. They grow quickly in hot weather and will reach their full potential in moist, fertile soil. Plant them up against a picket fence or in front of an evergreen hedge to appreciate the true brilliance of their flowers. In shady woodland gardens, *Phlox divaricata* is a great blue-colored companion that will enhance your spring daffodils and tulips.

HOW TO PLANT

You don't need a "green thumb" to successfully plant phlox. Spade a little compost or soil conditioner into the planting hole of a garden bed and set your phlox plant at grade. Well-limed soil that's enriched with superphosphate certainly makes for healthier plants and a better floral display. Keep your garden phlox and other perennials watered well during the early part of the season, especially if it's a dry spring. Irrigate in the early morning to avoid chronic leaf diseases.

ZONE
6,7,8

CARE AND MAINTENANCE

Deadhead the garden phlox after peak bloom and you will accomplish two things. First, you will enjoy a second flush of flowerheads; second, you will prevent a rash of unwanted seedlings if you're growing the native species. Garden phlox needs dividing every 2 or 3 years to keep them vigorous. Mildew disease seems almost synonymous with *Phlox* and *Monarda*. Be prepared to spray with a systemic fungicide. Some organic gardeners use horticultural oil as a preventative, especially as we head toward the hot, humid weather of June. Many perennials including phlox are vulnerable to voles when planted in a woodland garden site.

ADDITIONAL INFORMATION

Phlox is not a heavy feeder. A little 5-10-10 or similar fertilizer applied twice during the growing season is sufficient. Avoid wetting the foliage while irrigating phlox. Thin new shoots in the spring, as most plants can only support 5 to 6 strong stems at best. Thinning also increases the air circulation which discourages powdery mildew disease.

ADDITIONAL SPECIES, CULTIVARS, OR VARIETIES

'Blue Boy' has unique lavender-blue flowers. 'Fairy's Petticoat' has large heads of pale-pink flowers. 'Fujiyama' is a vigorous white cultivar. 'Miss Lingard' is a fragrant mildew-resistant white cultivar with a yellow eye. 'Fairyland' is a dwarf, clear-pink cultivar.

Hellebore

OTHER COMMON NAME: Lenten Rose

Hellebores are handsome perennials producing flowers in winter and early spring. Some are deciduous and others have attractive dark-green leaves throughout the year. They grow to 15 to 18 inches and have a similar spread. The glossy foliage of Lenten rose shows forth when everything else is drab during the colder months. The large flowers with showy bracts in colors from white to pink and green to deep purple decorate gardens in the colder months of the year. Many have a central cluster of showy yellow stamens. *Helleborus niger*, the Christmas rose, may bloom with large white flowers from November through March. *Helleborus orientalis*, the Lenten rose, has many forms that bloom in early winter but most plants of this species bloom in February and March. In a severe winter the flower buds may be damaged, but the magnificent foliage throughout summer makes this a worthwhile addition to any garden.

WHEN TO PLANT

Fall is the best time to plant hellebores. These are summer-dormant plants that come into growth as temperatures fall in September. They make new roots at that time and will establish easily.

WHERE TO PLANT

Hellebores grow well in most sites as long as they are well drained. Most books recommend them for shade, but they also grow well with considerable sun and will bloom better for it. Plant hellebores where they can be viewed from an indoor room during the winter, or in an entrance bed.

HOW TO PLANT

Most hellebores are available as seed-grown container plants. Division of established plants may be done in early fall, but this is a slow process. Prepare the area by spading plenty of compost or organic matter into the planting hole. When planted, the crown of the plant should be at ground level or slightly higher. Mulch well and water just after planting. Hellebores seldom require additional artificial water after that time.

CARE AND MAINTENANCE

A general all-purpose fertilizer applied in very early spring will please most species of hellebores. *H. niger* often requires additional magnesium to bloom well, so a solution of 1 tablespoon of Epsom salts (dissolved in a gallon of water and poured over and around the plants) may help stimulate flowering. Although hellebores grow in alkaline soil in their native habitat, they don't demand alkalinity. In western North Carolina, try spraying the foliage with a protective spray during the winter months.

ADDITIONAL INFORMATION

Cut off the old leaves in late winter, for cosmetic reasons and to reveal emerging flowering shoots. When established, hellebores will self-sow freely. Young plants may be transplanted in the fall of their first or second year.

ADDITIONAL SPECIES, CULTIVARS, OR VARIETIES

Other good garden species include: *H. foetidus* (bearsfoot hellebore), which has green pendant flowers in February; *H. argutifolius*, which has spectacular foliage with green flowers that are late; *H. odorus*, with cupped green flowers; *H. multifidus*, with broad green petals; deciduous *H. lividus*; and *H. purpurascens*, which has flowers with purple backs.

Hosta

OTHER COMMON NAME: Plantain Lily

With the continued interest in shade gardening, it is no great surprise that the popularity of hostas is on the rise. Ease of culture, colorful foliage, and low maintenance make hosta the perfect perennial for contemporary gardens. Only a few years ago, the variegated passalong variety was the hosta most commonly sold and shared. Today, gardeners can choose from over 2000 different hosta varieties. Hostas are versatile, ranging from the miniatures such as 'Tiny Tim' and 'Dwarf Bunting' to the huge 7-foot spreading plants, 'Blue Angel' and 'Sum and Substance.' Hostas are grown primarily for their foliage, and there are 4 basic foliage color groups: blues, greens, golds, and variegated. Some selections, such as the fragrant *H. plantaginea* and the double-flowered *H.* 'Aphrodite,' have notable flowers. Both the leaves and flowers are useful in flower arranging. One of the great attributes of hostas is their toughness. If weather conditions become too extreme, they will simply go dormant early. In their native Asian homeland, hostas grow wild in native prairies. Here in the South, plant this broadleaf beauty in some shade and you'll be rewarded with a marvelous, long-lasting ornamental.

WHEN TO PLANT

Container-grown hostas can be planted any time the ground is not frozen. I prefer transplanting and dividing hosta as the new shoots peek out of the ground in early spring or in late summer when they are inactive. I have never botched up a hosta planting effort, regardless of the season.

WHERE TO PLANT

While hostas need some shade from the afternoon sun in North Carolina, it is filtered light that suits them best. Planted in a shade garden, the variegated foliage seems to bounce out at you. Too much sun will make the variegated ones turn green. This tender perennial prefers well-drained soils that are rich in organic matter. Hostas are suitable for a groundcover under a shade tree. 'August Moon' will tolerate full sun.

How to Plant

Hostas are quite adaptable to a wide range of soil conditions. They prefer rich soils, so amend infertile soils with abundant amounts of organic material such as compost, chopped leaves, aged sawdust, or similar products. (Hostas will grow with little planting fuss as long as they are set in the ground green-side up!) Thoroughly loosen the roots of potbound plants. It's better to plant them too high than too deep. Spade up a wide area for a single hosta that is 3 times the diameter of the rootball. Spread out the roots in the hole and back-fill, firming the soil well. Water thoroughly 3 times for the first 10 days. Hostas will live indefinitely in a well-prepared site.

Care and Maintenance

Fertile soils are preferred by hostas, as they are heavy feeders. Broadcast a slow-release fertilizer in the garden each spring to encourage dense foliage. During dry seasons, be diligent in watering your hostas and mulch them well annually. Dry leaf tips and margins are a result of drought stress. Hosta foliage that is torn or weathered may be pruned. In late summer, many of the showy ones send out 3-foot flower spikes that can be unsightly. Remove them completely back beyond the plant's canopy if they are not wanted. Hosta can be divided as needed.

Additional Information

The major pests of hosta are children, voles, and blister beetles. I placed children first on my list of hosta pests, since I can legally poison the other two! (Of course, I could move my plants so the kids would not jump off my porch onto the bed of hostas.) Yellow foliage is a sign of waterlogged soils. Stem rots or root loss is often due to voles.

Additional Species, Cultivars, or Varieties

With more than 2000 cultivars available, the number of hosta selections can be daunting. The American Hosta Society publishes a list of reliable varieties. Some of the exciting ones are 'Sum and Substance' (an extra-large one), 'Gold Standard,' 'Halcyon,' 'Francee,' 'Blue Wedgewood' and 'Elvis Lives' (both with blue foliage), and 'Golden Tiara' and 'Kabitan' (both small plants).

Japanese Anemone

While most herbaceous perennials reach their zenith during the summer months, Japanese anemone makes its debut shortly after Labor Day. This beautiful member of the buttercup family unassumingly takes center stage after a long wait for its competition to fade. These clump-forming plants are wonderful for partially shaded gardens where they will bloom continuously until frost. Japanese anemones produce long 1- to 2-foot flower stalks from low-growing foliage that resembles the leaves of maples. The stalks support small clusters of poppy-like blooms that are mostly white and shades of pink. These long flower stems are ideal for cutting for fresh bouquets. There are many good varieties of this fall-blooming perennial, but none are as popular in North Carolina as 'September Charm.' According to Alan Elvington, curator of the perennials at L. A. Reynolds Garden Showcase, this variety is a very vigorous grower that can be divided periodically to fill garden beds to overflowing. It has 2-inch, saucer-shaped, silvery pink flowers on well-branched stems. 'Honorine Jobert' is the best white Japanese anemone, producing clouds of huge 3-inch blooms that float above 1-foot-high mounds of foliage.

WHEN TO PLANT

The best time to plant container-grown Japanese anemones is in spring through early summer. Both root cuttings and divisions are methods of propagating this garden gem. Use care in dividing the established plants, and transplant them in fall or early spring. The mail-order nurseries sell bareroot plants for spring planting.

WHERE TO PLANT

For the best performance east of the Foothills, plant Japanese anemones in bright filtered shade. They need rich soil that has excellent drainage in the winter months. Plant this perennial in a semi-permanent location since it resents being moved once it has gotten established in a bed. Anemones are good companions for hostas, ferns, lungworts, and cyclamens. They are simple flowers, ideal for cottage gardens.

PERENNIALS

How to Plant

Japanese anemones require a humusy soil with a neutral pH. Add
compost and a dusting of limestone to clay soils. Remove the plants
from their containers and set them in soil that has been tilled to a
depth of 6 inches. If planting individual clumps, dig a hole about
twice the size of the rootball and firm-in the roots with amended
soil. Water thoroughly every 3 days for the first 2 weeks. A garden
fertilizer with a 1-2-2 analysis can be used monthly. Irrigation is particularly important during the first 2 summers until the plants are
established. Japanese anemones will benefit from a 2-inch layer of
mulch. Space the plants 18 inches apart within the bed.

Care and Maintenance

Irrigate the plantings once a week during the summer months and
more often during drought. This is of particular importance while
the Japanese anemones are blooming and for beds that receive full
sun. These plants are very drought tolerant after a few years in the
bed. Remove the dead flower stalks by snipping off their stems near
the base of the plant. During the winter months the foliage tends to
dry up, leaving very little mess for the gardener to clean up. Tidy
the bed by removing all the dead foliage. If mites and aphids appear
in the summer months, apply spray oil to eliminate these pests.

Additional Information

The ideal location for Japanese anemones is where they will receive
morning sun and afternoon shade. Since the flowers appear on tall,
slender stems, these plants can be placed near the back of the perennial border. Anemones are superb for cut flowers in the fall!

Additional Species, Cultivars, or Varieties

A. 'Queen Charlotte,' the best pink, has semi-double flowers on 20-
inch stems and spreads into colonies. 'Honorine Jobert' is a superb
white that grows to 4 feet tall. 'Margarete' has double rosy-pink
flowers and grows to 20 inches tall. 'Alba' has single white flowers
and grows to 20 inches tall. 'Whirlwind' is semi-double, has pure-
white 4-inch flowers, and grows to 5 feet tall. The more sun-tolerant
A. hupehensis var. japonica has early pink blooms.

Japanese Iris

*E*very Tar Heel gardener has a favorite flowering plant that he or she "lives" to see bloom each year. Then comes the magical moment and the flowers appear. For some folks it's the night-blooming cereus cactus; or maybe it's a moonvine, orchid, or evening primrose. My special flower is the Japanese iris. Showy dinner-plate-sized flowers open on this gladiolus-like plant as summer approaches. My garden-variety Japanese irises have pale lavender-blue flowers with prominent veins in their silky petals. Over a period of a week or more, multiple blooms of irresistible flowers form on stiff, single 2- to 3-foot-high stems. The coarse green leaves provide a nice contrast with the luscious flat blooms. You can't have just one Japanese iris! Gardeners who have been bitten by the iris bug will often rearrange their vacation plans to stay home during the blooming period. (Why are the best things in life so fleeting?) Japanese iris can be divided easily, so before long you can have a garden bed devoted to this marvelous perennial. It is wonderful planted beside a water garden where its reflection can be clearly seen!

WHEN TO PLANT

Container-grown Japanese iris should be planted in early spring or in late summer after the flowering period. Established beds can be divided from midsummer through early winter.

WHERE TO PLANT

Japanese irises require sunny locations and moist soils. They will thrive in heavy clay soils that are poorly drained and they are perfect for planting on a streambank. They are most effective when planted in groups of one color. Plant them near a deck or patio where they can be admired for the short period during which they bloom. They grow to 3 to 4 feet and can be placed in a border behind finer textured perennials.

HOW TO PLANT

Unlike bearded iris, this group of irises has a root system like daylilies that can be planted by dividing the parent clump. Japanese iris is easy to plant since it appreciates tight, wet soils that are slightly

acidic (pH 5.5). Dig a planting hole that is several inches larger than the rootball. Mix a little bonemeal or bulb-booster fertilizer in the planting hole. In sandy soils, spade several inches of peat moss or compost into the planting hole or bed. Japanese irises can be potted in clay pots and set into the edge of the water garden. The plants do fine in shallow water with as much as 4 inches of water covering their roots. Mulch heavily!

CARE AND MAINTENANCE

I plant Japanese iris as much for their maintenance-free culture as for their incredible flowers. The key to robust plants is constant moisture, especially as warm weather approaches. The flowers appear in North Carolina after our big spring bloom period, sometime in late May or June. A well-mulched bed means less watering and larger flowers. Apply 5-10-10 garden fertilizer each spring to jump-start the plants. In November or later, the plants will brown out and can be cut back to the ground. These irises are very cold hardy, so there is no need to be concerned about winter protection.

ADDITIONAL INFORMATION

If you like to fiddle with irrigation systems, this durable perennial offers plenty of opportunity to play. Divide the bed after several years to prevent crowding. Space the Japanese irises 18 inches apart at planting time. Keep plenty of organic matter in the beds during the summer months to enrich the soil and improve the health of the plants.

ADDITIONAL SPECIES, CULTIVARS, OR VARIETIES

Cultivars worth having include 'Frilled Enchantment,' 'Snowy Hills' (a white color), 'Storm at Sea,' 'Dancing Waves' (violet), 'Agrippinaella' (deep rose), and 'Variegata' (white-striped foliage with lavender-blue blooms). *I. siberica*, Siberian iris, is another hardy garden iris worthy of growing. It resembles Dutch iris in form and size and is great for cutting.

Lungwort

There is nothing quite as striking in the spring woodland garden as the lungworts. You would think these durable early bloomers with attractive foliage would be grown everywhere, but that's not the case. Perhaps their name is their Achilles' heel. The Latin name *pulmonaria* was given this plant because of its foliage, which is often olive-green with silvery-gray spots, resembling a diseased lung. It grows from a basal rosette, usually no more than 6 to 10 inches tall with a slightly wider spread. It flowers in very early spring beginning around the end of February. The cup-shaped flowers, usually either pink or blue, are held on short stalks that reach just above the foliage. Lungworts retain their foliage through most of the winter, then become completely deciduous just before the new season's growth cycle. In summer their leaves wilt as they take a little siesta from the heat. In general, this perennial has a preference for cool, moist conditions, although there are some species indigenous to dry regions of its native Europe. The most commonly grown of the species is 'Mrs. Moon,' which has spotted foliage and a unique combination of pink and blue flowers. Exciting cultivars are now arriving from the West Coast.

When to Plant

Lungwort is planted from containers in fall and again in late spring following bloom. Frequently they are seeded by nurserymen, producing variable quality in seedlings. When given a choice, always select the well-spotted vigorous ones! Transplant lungwort from established gardens in October.

Where to Plant

Lungworts will tolerate deeper shade than most other herbaceous perennials. The secret combination is moist, rich soil and a little morning sun. This beauty will be right at home with other shade-loving plants such as cyclamen, hellebores, Virginia bluebells, and spring-flowering bulbs. Plant lungwort in the border or by a shaded water garden.

How to Plant

If you provide lungwort with the proper location, it will establish quickly. Amend poor garden soil with aged compost or sphagnum peat moss. When the soil is right, you can easily plant your container-grown plants with gloved hands! Space your plants 18 inches apart. All rootbound perennials benefit from a scoring of the rootball with a trowel or pocketknife. Frill out the roots and dig a shallow hole in the bed. After firming in the roots of your lungwort, water well using a slow trickle from a garden hose. Since this plant likes moisture, a soaker hose buried under the mulch layer will ensure its survival in a woodland garden. An attractive mulch for small plants is coconut shell mulch.

Care and Maintenance

Providing irrigation is critical for lungwort, particularly in an area where hardwood trees spread their shallow feeder roots. Pay attention to moisture during the active growth and flowering periods. Your plants may wilt down in the heat of the summer. This is normal, and overwatering at that time encourages root rot disease. Organic fertilizers such as cottonseed mill or a specialty slow-release flower fertilizer can be used in early fall. Always divide lungworts as the weather cools heading into fall; they will be in bloom very early in the coming months.

Additional Information

Many varieties are prone to powdery mildew disease on the the foliage during our humid summers. While this is unsightly, it seems to cause little problem with lungwort's overall health or survival. Horticultural oils or systemic fungicides applied prophylactically at the first sign of the disease will keep the foliage clean.

Additional Species, Cultivars, or Varieties

'Mrs. Moon' is the standard cultivar. 'Milky Way' is a vigorous grower with great floral display. 'Excalibur' has shiny, silver leaves with green edges. 'Anderson' is a heat-tolerant cultivar for the South. Yellow lungwort is good in dry shade.

Mountain Bluets

OTHER COMMON NAME: Perennial Cornflower

*M*ountain bluets are beautiful low-growing perennials that are closely related to the common annual cornflowers. This semi-evergreen perennial is a native wildflower in many of the Western states. Mountain bluets generally grow to a height of 1 to 2 feet, forming a dense mound of long, soft leaves. Starting in spring, gorgeous spidery purplish-blue flowers are produced, and these blooms continue into the next several weeks. Flowers will suddenly appear sporadically throughout the growing season, though there is a definite tendency to early flowering. In warmer regions of North Carolina, the foliage is evergreen. The plants reproduce freely, so there are plenty of new starts for sharing with friends or enlarging the perennial garden. These "runners" can be planted any time of the year. This tough, versatile perennial withstands extreme drought and poor soil conditions and requires little attention.

WHEN TO PLANT

Plant mountain bluets in the spring, summer, or fall. The best time to transplant is early to mid-spring, though the plants are just as forgiving in midsummer to fall.

WHERE TO PLANT

Mountain bluets love rich, well-drained soil and full sun. They thrive in moist or semidry sites and will flower sparsely even in partial shade. They will be a great asset in your perennial border. These plants are small enough to fit into many gardening locations. Consider using bluets toward the front of the border or as an edging plant in a sunny garden. A solid bed of bluets is quite a show, or use them with daylily.

HOW TO PLANT

Work up an entire bed for these perennials. Or, for single plants, dig a hole that is at least the size of the rootball, preferably another 2 to 4 inches deeper and wider. Backfill using soil mixed with a little organic humus or compost. The addition of lime and phosphorus

fertilizer is suggested for new planting beds. Set the mountain bluets, leaving about one-fourth to one-eighth of the rootball above ground, and cover with the soil mixture. Mulch is not necessary for this perennial, except possibly in dry garden sites.

CARE AND MAINTENANCE

Water newly set plants twice the first week following planting. Once established, mountain bluets need little water. During the first year, however, you will need to water well once a month if rainfall is in short supply. Mountain bluets should be divided every 2 or 3 years. There is no need for much fertilizer, but they should be fertilized lightly with a 1-2-2 analysis fertilizer in the spring. To keep the plants tidy, the flower stalks can be removed, though they tend to disintegrate on their own after a while.

ADDITIONAL INFORMATION

Make sure mountain bluets have good drainage and lots of sun. This perennial is best used as a filler, not as a specimen plant. After a couple of years of growth, you will be able to divide your bluets to share with your gardening friends. This is a great plant for a Master Gardener Plant Sale or garden club sale.

ADDITIONAL SPECIES, CULTIVARS, OR VARIETIES

'Alba' has white flowers. 'Rubra' has dark-rose flowers.

New England Aster

A fall without asters is unimaginable in the Tar Heel state. The hot, miserable summer weather is more palatable when you know that a colorful wave of asters is forthcoming. Gardeners love the daisy-like lavender-to-violet flowers of New England aster, a centerpiece of the perennial garden in autumn. This tenacious plant easily grows from 3 to 4 feet high and will benefit from a pinching by July. I have seen this clumping aster staked in gardens and laden with blooms until November. In the last 10 years, some very nice new cultivars of New England aster have been offered by many North Carolina nurseries. 'Purple Dome' is the first true dwarf form; it never needs pinching or support. 'Fanny's Aster' is a real "looker," with spectacular powder-blue flowers on a compact 18-inch plant. Our native *Aster concolor*, eastern-silvery-aster, was designated Wildflower of the Year in 1996 by the North Carolina Botanical Garden and The Garden Club of North Carolina. This wild aster could be mistaken for a tall blazing-star (*Liatris*) when seen along the roadside.

WHEN TO PLANT

Plant New England aster from spring to fall as soil conditions permit. They can be divided every 2 or 3 years from November to May. Seed of certain asters can be sown either in October or later in March.

WHERE TO PLANT

New England aster prefers full sun and tolerates fairly dry to moist conditions. Generally, this clumping-type aster is native to moist soils from New England to the Rockies. The species plant makes a fine background specimen in the perennial border. It is especially showy when planted near the silvery foliage of artemisias or gray santolina.

HOW TO PLANT

The New England aster requires very limited preparation for planting. Most well-drained soils can be spaded 4 to 6 inches deep, and the soil is ready for planting. Dig a hole that is twice the size of the rootball and sprinkle into the soil a little slow-release flower fertil-

izer. Firm the soil around the rootball and water generously. It is better to err in favor of being too shallow when planting native perennials rather than too deep. Mulch the bed of asters when hot weather arrives. This perennial is very tolerant of weed-preventer chemicals. These should be applied promptly after planting, but before mulching.

CARE AND MAINTENANCE

Water your newly planted aster deeply every 5 days for the first 3 weeks. If rainfall is lacking, water thoroughly every 10 days, particularly during its growth spurt in early summer. An application of fertilizer every 6 weeks from spring until September is more than enough nutrition to keep the plants healthy. You will need to stake most varieties of New England aster, particularly if they do not get direct sunlight. Keep an eye on your garden for powdery mildew disease, which is prevalent in our summers.

ADDITIONAL INFORMATION

Don't be reluctant to prune back the taller varieties when they reach 8 inches in height. This pinching will produce dense plants and more blooms. After a hard freeze, cut New England aster back to within 1 inch of the ground. The plants are extremely cold hardy and do not need mulching to survive the winter. Deep mulching will injure asters.

ADDITIONAL SPECIES, CULTIVARS, OR VARIETIES

'Purple Dome' is a 2-foot plant with l-inch purple flowers. 'Fanny's Aster' is blue, compact, late blooming, and grows to 18 inches. 'Our Latest One' is violet-blue and grows to 2 feet. 'Hella Lacy' has 4-inch royal-purple flowers. 'Alma Potschke' is salmon-colored and grows to 3 feet. 'Harrington Pink' is salmon-pink and grows to 4 feet. 'Treasurer' grows to 3 feet and has huge lilac flowers. A personal favorite is Mongolian Aster, a double, white, airy plant.

Nippon Daisy

Nippon is far superior in foliage quality to its spring-blooming cousin shasta-daisy. Nippon offers the same nostalgia as the field daisy, but the durability of the garden mum. This hardy perennial, reaching a height of 30 inches, has large white daisy flowers and sturdy glossy leaves that glisten in the sunshine. It is a good performer for late summer color that is long lasting.

When to Plant

Nippon is a rugged plant with a long planting season. It is happier planted yearly in the growing season so it can become established before blooming, but a few plants can be popped in the ground any time the soil is prepared.

Where to Plant

As for most members of the chrysanthemum family, give this plant full hot sun and loose soil. This shasta-like daisy is not fussy and will grow in partial shade, but it can get topheavy if given too much shade. Plant Nippon daisies in clusters of 6 or more plants. Use them as a backdrop for more colorful annual bedding plants and garden mums in the flower border.

How to Plant

Dig a hole that is twice the size of the rootball. Add a little organic matter or soil conditioner for heavy soils; mix into the existing soil. Then gently loosen the rootball, expecially if the plants have come in small quart-sized containers. Keep the top of the rootball just above the existing soil level. Do not plant too deep. Water twice each week for the first 3 weeks, then only as needed throughout the season. A dry fall may require additional watering while the plant is in bloom.

CARE AND MAINTENANCE

Nippon daisy, like many herbaceous perennials, benefits from a high-phosphorus fertilizer applied monthly during the growing season. Supplemental watering during the bloom period is important since this plant flowers late in the season. Nippon daisy tends to lose its foliage on the lower third of the plant. This is common and is not related to disease. For this reason, this daisy should be used behind other low, compact border perennials.

ADDITIONAL INFORMATION

In the Coastal regions where this daisy has a long growing season, pinch back the shoots in early summer to promote more compact growth. This also stimulates flower bud production and increases the flower display.

ADDITIONAL SPECIES, CULTIVARS, OR VARIETIES

The traditional daisy found in most old Tar Heel gardens is the shasta daisy, *C. maximum*. This species flowers early in the perennial border, but flops over without staking. Choose a compact cultivar, such as 'Alaska.' The "gold and silver" chrysanthemum, *C. pacificum*, is a smart-looking garden plant, especially when its rich golden blooms appear in late autumn.

Obedient Plant

OTHER COMMON NAME: Obedience

*Y*ou would think that with a name like obedience, this perennial would be the couch potato's dream. But not so: this aggressive plant requires some taming. I have grown obedient plant from my early gardening years, and certainly find it worth the effort required to deal with its little idiosyncrasies. It is great for the cutting garden, since it holds up well in arrangements. The tube-like flowers are attached to long stems by small hinges which will flex "obediently" when moved by hand (thus the name). When the heavy flowerheads are weighed down by the summer rains, they will make a right turn to point upward again. These tall, pale, lavender-pink blooms are reminescent of those of penstemon and snapdragon. Obedient plants reach a height of 2 to 4 feet before they begin blooming in midsummer. The flower's worst enemy is the hot afternoon sun which will scorch the plant if the soil is too dry. The foliage of the obedient is willow-like, a medium-green color. Use this plant in the background of a perennial border where its height is an advantage. Obedience is an old wild-flower, but it is still a workhorse in gardens where there is plenty of moisture.

WHEN TO PLANT

Potted plants or transplants of obedience can be planted from October to May provided the ground is workable. Divide clumps of this durable perennial in early spring or in early fall. I have yanked up flowering stems that had fallen over only to discover that they were rooted and ready for transplanting after a hard pruning. Rooted cuttings plant well.

WHERE TO PLANT

A sunny garden is all that is required. Moist soil will encourage rampant growth of underground stolons, so give this perennial plenty of space. Obedient plants are not finicky about soil type—heavy clay is just fine. The stems will need some support by staking, or plant in the border next to sturdy companions like rudbeckias or garden mums.

How to Plant

Obedient plant is readily available from gardening friends. It is usually given away in big clumps! The clumps are set in ordinary garden soil at the depth they were originally growing. Spade a little 5-10-10 fertilizer or similar analysis into the planting area at the rate of 1 pound per 100 square feet. The clumps are set on 2-foot spacings to allow enough room. Container-grown obedience is planted similarly. There is little benefit to adding organic matter to the soil unless it is a dry-natured or rocky soil. If this is the case, add several shovelsful of compost or rotted manure to the planting hole. Rich, moist soil encourages a leggy plant that requires staking. This plant enjoys mulch.

Care and Maintenance

Other than its need for staking, obedience can be considered a low-maintenance plant. Late-spring pinching may help keep the height down and increase the flower display. If you enjoy the scapes (flowerheads) in fresh arrangements, pinching will shorten the stems. A light fertilizing of 5-10-10 in spring should get obedient plant up and running. If you have a dry site, keep the plant irrigated during bloom or else the flowers will scorch. Cut the plant down to the ground in November or after the killing freeze ruins the foliage.

Additional Information

The flowerheads get heavy and may form a shepherd's crook if left unstaked. Keep an eye out for dwarf cultivars and try these first. Beetles may nibble on the leaves or flowers, though this is normally a minor concern. Cut the scapes freely for decorating and share obedient plant with a gardening friend.

Additional Species, Cultivars, or Varieties

Flower colors range from pink to rose to white. The old passalong variety has a lavender tinge in its pink blooms. Cultivars include rosy-crimson 'Summer Glow,' white 'Summer Snow,' 'Bouquet rose' with its spires of shell-pink flowers, 'Vivid,' and 'Rosy Spire.' 'Variegata' is a variegated form with white leaf margins.

Peony

The peony has long been a favorite of Tar Heel gardeners. It is one of the hardiest and most easily grown of any of the perennials. These outstandingly beautiful garden flowers belong to the buttercup family and are related to the clematis, the columbine, and the trollius. Peonies bloom in colors of whites, cream, pinks, and reds. The delicate blossoms will make fabulous cut flowers for floral arrangements. By selecting varieties with varying flowering times, the blooming season can last for 6 weeks or more. The height of this perennial can range from 2 to 4 feet. There are even yellow singles and wonderful tree peonies for serious peony enthusiasts. All the flowers are large and showy. Gorgeous blooms and pleasant fragrance will grace the garden when peonies are present.

WHEN TO PLANT

Peony may be planted in early to late fall and early spring, with September and October being the most favorable months.

WHERE TO PLANT

Peonies do best in full sun, but they will grow reasonably well in light shade. The more shade, however, the fewer number of blooms, so it is best not to plant in deep shade. They are hardy in cold climates but do not like their winter rest broken—they are not likely to succeed in such warm climates as those of Florida and Southern California.

HOW TO PLANT

Peonies thrive fairly well in almost any soil but do best in a rather heavy clay loam that is well drained. A hole of generous proportions should be dug. The depth of planting is a matter of great importance with peonies; more failures are probably due to planting too deeply than to any other cause. The plant should have at least 3 buds. It should be placed into the hole so that the tip of the buds are from 1 to 2 inches below the surface of the soil. If planted too deeply, it may never bloom. Good topsoil should be filled in about the roots and firmed well, and the plant should be watered immediately after planting. They should be spaced approximately 3 feet apart.

CARE AND MAINTENANCE

Two applications of a complete fertilizer such as 5-10-10 are recommended. Peonies do not grow well in acid soil. The soil should be a neutral one, or one containing lime, but a slightly acid medium is not too objectionable. The first lime application (1/4 cup per plant) should be in the spring when the new shoots are just coming up. The second application should be made after the period of bloom is over. If the second application is missed, an application of bonemeal can be put around each plant after the foliage has died down. When applying fertilizer or bonemeal, it should be sprinkled on the surface of the soil a few inches away from the stem.

ADDITIONAL INFORMATION

Peonies resent being moved; when well established, they may be left undisturbed for many years. For general garden use, they need not be disbudded. If exhibition blooms are desired, however, all side buds on the flower stem should be removed, leaving only the large central bud. Old blooms should be removed as soon as they fade in order to keep energy from being wasted on seedpod development.

ADDITIONAL SPECIES, CULTIVARS, OR VARIETIES

'Heritage' has early dark-red flowers. 'Dinner Plate' blooms in midseason. 'Mister Ed' is double and white. 'Prairie Moon' is yellow. Lightly scented 'First Lady' blooms early and double.

PERENNIALS

Sedum 'Autumn Joy'

OTHER COMMON NAME: Stonecrop

*S*edum 'Autumn Joy' was one of the first herbaceous perennials
that I discovered during my quest to build a perennial garden in
the late '80s. Like many gardeners new to the Winston-Salem area, I
sought out John Heitman, the Perennial Plant Association officer emer-
itus, for advice on plants to include in my gardening venture. He was
quick to suggest this unique, durable succulent. What a terrific plant it
is! Its sturdy family is referred to as stonecrops, which implies that
many of them are rock garden plants. The sedums like hot, sunny
weather, which they certainly find here in North Carolina. In early
spring, this tender perennial pushes gray-green buds out of the soil; as
the temperatures rise, the fleshy broccoli-colored leaves expand. By
summer, the stems and leaves are rigid and dependable flowering
begins. In mid- to late summer, reddish to brilliant carmine flowerheads appear on 18- to 24-inch leafy stalks. As the season progresses,
the show continues as the blooms fade to a coppery color, then finally
to rust by cooler weather. The stalks can be cut and used in decorating. Hard freezes in late October to November blacken the leaves. The
stalks of 'Autumn Joy' should be cut away for its winter rest.

WHEN TO PLANT

Plant 'Autumn Joy' any time of year except when the ground is
freezing. This plant can be divided in March for transplanting as
the new buds begin popping out of the cold earth. Select container-
grown plants that are produced in quart-sized pots. These can be
divided the following season.

WHERE TO PLANT

Plant 'Autumn Joy' in full sun for dense mounds of foliage and
an abundance of large showy flowerheads. The hotter the site, the
better this sedum flourishes. One of the "musts" for growing
stonecrops is sharp drainage. Avoid wet or shady locations. Plant
this rugged beauty in groups in the foreground of the perennial garden or use as an accent. Plant some of the finer-textured spreading
sedums at the base.

How to Plant

Success with 'Autumn Joy' is simple: prevent "wet feet." This can be accomplished easily by mixing coarse aggregates into the soil before planting. Granite screenings, fine pine-bark mulch, or pea gravel are suitable amendments. The soil level can be raised, or plant the plants in containers. Sandy loam soils need no amendments or special preparation. Dig a hole that is the same depth as the rootball and 3 times as wide. Break the ball apart and work the loosened soil in and around the fleshy roots. Trim the longest roots back by one-third. Water just enough to settle the soil. Don't water again for 2 weeks unless you are planting sedums in the middle of the summer.

Care and Maintenance

Once your 'Autumn Joy' sedums take off growing in spring, scatter a little 5-10-10 fertilizer over the bed at the rate of 2 pounds per 100 square feet. This should take care of the nutritional needs of this durable stonecrop for the growing season. Too much nitrogen can cause the flowerheads to flop over in wet summers. Irrigate the planting every 2 weeks in dry weather, but don't overwater! If you mulch the planting, do it sparingly. Also, keep the mulching material a couple of inches away from the base of your plant. After a killing frost in fall, prune back the woody stalks to the ground. Do not mulch for the winter.

Additional Information

The only serious pests encountered with 'Autumn Joy' sedums are termites that can move into the woody stems and roots in dry weather. Control these with a soil drench of insecticide. See your Extension Agent for a product recommendation. An occasional caterpillar or beetle may nimble at the blooms. Enjoy the dried blooms in winter!

Additional Species, Cultivars, or Varieties

S. 'Brilliant' is a bright-carmine flowering cultivar that is preferred over 'Autumn Joy' by many gardeners. Three low spreading cultivars are 'Vera Jameson' with pink flowers and maroon foliage, 'Rosy Glow' with dark-rose flowers and blue-gray leaves, and S. sieboldii, which has pale-pink flowers and grayish foliage and is the latest to bloom. Many sedums attract butterflies to the garden.

'Stella de Oro' Daylily

My introduction to the world of daylilies began with a tour of Dr. Bob Elliott's impressive collection while I was the agricultural agent in Durham, North Carolina. Bob was working on his Ph.D. at the time at North Carolina State, and I was fascinated by the whole process of the hybridization of plants. Bob gave me an insider's look at the procedure from early-morning pollination using a camel's hair brush to the arduous waiting game of watching and selecting suitable candidates for introducing to the gardening public. What commitment and love of horticulture it takes to birth a new cultivar! Since that time I have carried a collection of showy daylily varieties with me with every move. Most Southerners don't have a true appreciation of *Hemerocallis* until they've visited a daylily farm in late spring. The "roadsider" or "outhouse orange" daylilies have tarnished this plant's image. Unfortunately, most daylily cultivars have one primary bloom period. Many of the newer introductions are repeat bloomers in a range of colors from white and yellow to pinks. The best continuous bloomer is 'Stella de Oro' daylily, an 18-inch beauty with golden flowers. It is truly one of the greatest perennials for Tar Heel gardens, since it is durable and resilient.

WHEN TO PLANT

Early spring or late fall are the most desirable times for planting daylilies in the South. Bareroot crowns are shipped for planting immediately upon arrival. Planting in wet summer periods will encourage crown rotting diseases. I have divided 'Stella de Oro' soon after the first flush of flowers and have had no problems with transplanting.

WHERE TO PLANT

Daylilies prefer full sun. They will tolerate part-shade conditions, but they require a minimum of 6 hours of direct sun for free-blooming. Any good soil is appropriate for growing 'Stella de Oro' provided it is well drained. Daylilies perform admirably near and under tall pine trees. This daylily is best used in mass groupings for a color accent. It can also be used near the entrance to the home in the foundation.

How to Plant

In heavy clay soils, bed up the soil for planting daylilies the way you do for certain vegetables in the garden. In good garden soil, plant them with very little preparation other than a wide planting hole that is 10 inches deep. (It is hard to fight the urge to add good compost; oh, go ahead!) When receiving bareroot plants, keep the roots moist until time to plant. Soak the crowns for several hours in a shallow pan of water. Make a mound in the middle of the hole and spread the roots out as you do for roses. Work in the soil around and between the roots. Firm the soil and water well. Space 'Stella de Oro' a least 1 foot apart, farther if you will not be dividing them.

Care and Maintenance

The flowers of this fine daylily seem to last a long time since there are many blooms per stalk and numerous flower stalks arising in the season. Trim back these stalks completely once the blooms fade. Aphids may be a problem on the unopened flowers; use a garden hose to remove them or use an approved insecticide. Mulching daylilies deeply will cause crown rot, especially when the mulch is piled up against the base of the plant. Fertilize in the spring with a general flower fertilizer and again in late summer for fall blooms. Irrigate the plants during the flowering period. Rake out frozen foliage in December.

Additional Information

'Stella de Oro' is unquestionably my favorite daylily. I enjoy its golden blossoms alongside red-leaved coleus and 'Homestead Purple' verbena. I am amazed at all the color you get throughout the season. It divides well, and remains the most versatile perennial in my garden. There has been no improvement over this one in my opinion.

Additional Species, Cultivars, or Varieties

'Black-Eyed Stella' was the first new daylily to receive the prestigious All-America Selection award. It is supposed to bloom longer than 'Stella de Oro,' its parent, but I haven't heard many Tar Heel gardeners giving it rave reviews. The new tetraploid daylilies are huge and lovely. Miniature daylilies have good utility. *H.* × 'Carefree Yellow' (Klehm) is new for 1997.

Tickseed

ickseed is the perennial of choice when you need to draw a little attention to an entranceway or just create a low-maintenance
flower garden. This attractive summer bloomer produces a profusion
of single or double yellow 2-inch daisy-like flowers on sturdy stems.
The long lance-shaped leaves are a light-green color. Tickseed is a
mainstay of the North Carolina Department of Transportation's highway wildflower plantings. It was recognized by the North Carolina
Garden Council and North Carolina Botanical Garden as a Wildflower
of the Year. Many gardeners have had great success in sowing seed of
the improved lanceleaf varieties like 'Early Sunrise' since its introduction a decade ago. This perennial variety will flower the same year it
is sown. 'Zagreb' (*C. verticillata*), a threadleaf cultivar with airy foliage
and compact 18-inch plants, is a personal favorite of mine. It is by
far the best coreopsis for planting in the home garden if compact
foliage is a high priority. Landscape professionals would do well to
try 'Zagreb' in commercial plantings as well. The golden yellow flowers of tickseed will appear all summer long in our gardens and can
be sheared back if they get leggy for more blooms.

When to Plant

Seeds of lanceleaf tickseed can be sown in October for a quick start
in spring as the weather warms. Plants of container-grown tickseed
such as 'Zagreb' and 'Moonbeam' are planted safely after cold has
past in spring.

Where to Plant

Tickseed grows best in full sun and well-drained soil. In moist soils,
the species plant can reach a height of 3 feet in a season. There are
many foliage textures among the available cultivars; flower colors
range from neon-yellow to gold. Threadleaf tickseed is compact and
serves as a candidate for the front of a border. Plant in huge quantities for the best effect or purchase a meadow mixture for seeding
in fall.

How to Plant

Tickseed can be handled as an annual or a perennial depending upon where you garden in the state. It is one of the easiest perennials to grow. Prepare a bed in a sunny location as you would for seeding vegetables. Eliminate perennial broadleaf weeds mechanically or chemically several weeks beforehand. Rake in the seeds, barely covering them, in late fall or spring. If planting a potted tickseed, dig a hole 3 times larger than the container and plant at grade or slightly higher. Many container-grown perennials are potbound when purchased, so score them with a knife to free up the roots. Firm-in the plants and water well. Irrigate twice each week for the first 3 weeks.

Care and Maintenance

Tickseed is a great plant to share with a "brown-thumb" gardener or to use as a gardening primer for children. Plant tickseed where there is at least 6 hours of direct sun and there will be minimal staking. Full-sun sites will ensure 2 bloom periods for most types. Remove spent flowers immediately after the main bloom flush. Water twice each week for new plantings during the first month only. Thereafter, tickseed can handle a major drought. A light application of fertilizer at planting and after the first flush of blooms is sufficient. A "bloom-booster" fertilizer is best for flowering perennials.

Additional Information

Tar Heel gardeners can allow tickseed to do its thing naturally. But you can encourage a more floriferous planting by deadheading with a pair of hedge shears, or try using a weed-eater/string-trimmer in large beds of the hardy species. Don't be afraid of cutting the plants back halfway when blooming ceases in summer.

Additional Species, Cultivars, or Varieties

Short-lived double-flowered 'Sunray' (*C. grandiflora*) grows to 20 inches and self-sows. Dwarf 'Goldfink' (*C. lanceolata*) grows to 9 inches and has a long bloom period. 'Moonbeam' (*C. verticillata*) grows to 18 inches and has delicate lemon-yellow flowers. There is a pink cultivar with a yellow eye, but it is subject to root rot and is not a strong grower in my opinion.

CHAPTER EIGHT

Lawns

*T*REAT YOUR LAWN LIKE A GARDEN AND YOU'LL HAVE
GREAT-LOOKING TURFGRASS!

North Carolinians are blessed with a climate for growing both
cool-season and warm-season grasses. In the western region we can
have success with bluegrass, perennial ryegrass, and tall fescue. On
the Coast, centipedegrass, St. Augustinegrass, and carpetgrass are
fine choices, depending on the location of your lawn. The Piedmont
is the transition zone, where you will find an almost endless number of turfgrass varieties and cool-season blends. The cardinal rule
is . . . don't mix cool-season and warm-season turfgrasses together,
or your lawn will look like a spotted pup!

Often the most important factor in growing a high-quality lawn
is the number of hours of direct sunlight your property receives in
the summer. The warm-season turfgrasses win hands-down if you
have a sunny yard. Unfortunately, there's no way to have a green
lawn twelve months of the year with this class of grasses unless you
overseed with annual ryegrass in the fall—or paint the grass green!
For this reason, most residents in the Piedmont and westward prefer to sow their lawns in tall-fescue mixtures. These cool-season
varieties provide a lush green lawn during the time that our dogwoods and azaleas are at their peak of bloom.

A lawn has more plants per square foot than any garden space
on your property. For a high-quality lawn you must make a commitment to provide the basic needs of the millions of individual
grass plants in your yard. Every grass plant will need room to grow,

air for its root system, water during its active growth stage, fertilization, and proper maintenance.

North Carolina State University turfgrass researchers have developed an establishment-and-maintenance program for every grass variety grown in the state. To have a beautiful lawn, it is important to follow the program. If you ask Dr. Arthur Bruneau, Extension Crop Specialist, for some sage advice on lawn establishment, he will say, "The key to a high-quality lawn is soil preparation." This means soil testing and the incorporation of limestone into the soil before seeding. Poor soils benefit greatly from the addition of nutrients and organic matter during soil preparation.

Once the lawn is established, follow a regime of recommended practices that will ensure a dense sod. This doesn't mean the indiscriminate dumping of pesticides on your property! You must be consistent with your mowing practices, weed control, fertilization, and, on clay soils, core aeration. As for weed control, the best defense is a thick turf.

A high-quality lawn is an asset to your neighborhood and to the environment as a whole. Turfgrasses prevent soil erosion, provide oxygen, filter contaminants, and beautify our landscapes. Your lawn deserves a little attention . . . after all, it is a garden too!

Bermudagrass

ermudagrass is a sod-forming turfgrass. This warm-season grass is dormant during the winter and greens up quickly in April. As temperatures rise, the growth rate of Bermudagrass increases. It is very tolerant of drought and it loves hot, sunny growing conditions. It is available from commercial sources as seeds, sprigs, and sod. If the soil in your yard is less than perfect (shallow or rocky), Bermudagrass is a good choice for your lawn. The premier type is the hybrid Bermudagrass, which has to be sprigged or sodded. The most cold hardy of these hybrids is 'Vamont,' which is used on athletic fields across North Carolina. There are a number of improved Bermudagrasses that are available at garden shops. The advantages of these are not well known, nor have these grasses been well evaluated. Bermudagrass can be overseeded in the fall with ryegrass, providing a green lawn during the dormant season. A major disadvantage of using Bermudagrass in the home lawn is its aggressive nature and tendency to encroach on landscape beds. After it is established, Bermudagrass requires minimal care.

WHEN TO PLANT

In North Carolina, Bermudagrass should be seeded in mid-spring about the time dogwoods are blooming. Sprigging and sodding can be done beginning 2 weeks after the Bermudagrass greens up in spring and continuing into July.

WHERE TO PLANT

Plant Bermudagrass in full sun for best results. It frequently creeps into partially shaded areas by means of its prolific rhizomes (runners). Seeding or sprigging this turfgrass in shady lawns gives poor results.

HOW TO PLANT

A soil test is recommended before you establish any new lawn. The ideal pH for Bermudagrass is 6.0. Improve your soil before planting according to the soil test results. Rototill the soil, mixing in lime and fertilizer. Rake all the clods for the finished grade. Broadcast the seed using a cyclone seeder at the rate of 1 pound per 1000 feet.

Lightly rake in the seed and apply a wheat-straw mulch at the rate of 40 bales per acre. Roll the lawn to firm-in the seed; keep the soil surface moist by watering daily until the grass seed germinates. When sprigging hybrid Bermudagrass, broadcast 3/4 bushel of sprigs per 1000 feet over well-prepared soil. The sprigs are pressed into the top inch of soil by hand or using a disk plow.

CARE AND MAINTENANCE

After seeding or sprigging, soak your new yard with a sprinkler, applying 1 inch of water, measured with a range gauge. Keep the soil moist continuously until the seed germinates or the sprigs begin growing vigorously. The watering can be reduced to 2 irrigations a week until the grass is established. By all means, water your new lawn throughout the first growing season; do not let the soil dry out excessively. This may mean more watering in the late summer months. Fertilize every 4 weeks until mid-August with 1 pound of nitrogen per 1000 square feet (for example, use 6 pounds of 16-0-0 with each application).

ADDITIONAL INFORMATION

For a high-quality lawn, mow your Bermudagrass turf frequently at a mowing height of 1 inch, using a reel-type mower if possible. Suggestions for preparing your lawn for winter include raising the mowing height in fall, controlling insect pests, and boosting the potassium in the soil.

ADDITIONAL SPECIES, CULTIVARS, OR VARIETIES

There are many improved strains of common Bermudagrass such as 'Guymon,' 'Sahara,' 'Cheyenne,' and 'Sundevil.' Some may have better color or density than common Bermudagrass but more data is needed. Hybrid Bermudagrass cultivars include 'Tifway 419,' 'Tifway II,' 'Midiron,' and 'Vamont,' which is best suited for western North Carolina.

Centipede Grass

entipede grass is one of the most popular lawn grasses in south-eastern North Carolina. Since its introduction from southern China in 1916, this fine warm-season turfgrass has found widespread acceptance by homeowners throughout the Carolinas. Major strengths of centipede grass are its low growth habit, its tolerance of acidic soil and shade, and its low fertilizer requirements. Many residents who have Coastal property frequently bring both seed and sod inland for establishment when they return home to the cooler Piedmont region—but one major disadvantage of centipede grass is its susceptibility to winter injury when planted outside of the Coastal counties. This turfgrass is relatively easy to establish, and its seed is readily available from Raleigh eastward. Healthy centipede grass is a lime-green in color. It is a slow grower when compared to hybrid Bermudagrass, which is a sod-forming grass that spreads by means of stolons, horizontal spreading stems. Centipede grass does not produce a dense sod, but it makes a beautiful low-maintenance lawn where it can be planted. It can be planted no farther northwest than the Piedmont Triad region.

WHEN TO PLANT

March through early July is the planting season for centipede grass in the Piedmont and Coastal regions. (It is too cold for this turfgrass in the mountains!) Expect centipede grass to take 2 to 3 years to establish from seed. A quicker method is to plant sod or plugs for a new lawn.

WHERE TO PLANT

Centipede grass is a sun-loving turfgrass, but it will thrive in partially shaded lawns. It is common to see lovely lawns growing in the filtered shade of tall pines as you drive through the Coastal counties. Plant in soil with a pH of 5.0 to 5.5; a higher pH will cause this grass to be perpetually yellow due to an iron deficiency. This is the best turfgrass for someone who does not want to spend weekends in the yard.

How to Plant

Have the soil tested before establishing a centipede lawn. Incorporate recommended amounts of fertilizer and limestone into the soil. Eliminate all perennial weeds and till the soil to a depth of 4 to 6 inches. Use a hand-rake to remove roots, rocks, and large dirt clods. You will have better establishment if you irrigate the lawn a few days before seeding to allow the soil to settle. Use a handheld rotary seeder to sow the seed. The seeding rate is 1/4 to 1/2 pound of seed per 1000 square feet of lawn. Apply clean straw mulch at a rate of 30 to 40 bales per acre. If plugging centipede grass, for every 1000 square feet use 3 square yards of sod cut into 2-inch squares set on 12-inch centers. Water!

Care and Maintenance

Be patient with your centipede lawn the first year; it is slow to establish unless sod is used. Keep the lawn grass irrigated twice each week, more often for seedlings. Fertilize with 1/2 pound of nitrogen per 1000 square feet in June (and again in August on the Coast). Avoid using any phosphorus after establishment. A reel mower is preferred for cutting centipede grass, at a mowing height of 1 inch. Begin mowing when the grass is 50 percent higher than the recommended height. Thatch buildup can be a problem later on, so power raking and core aerification may be necessary annually. Keep mower blades sharpened!

Additional Information

According to my friend and colleague in Wilmington, Dr. Bruce Williams, "More centipede grass is killed by love than by all the environmental, disease, or pest factors combined. Centipede is a *low-maintenance lawngrass*." Overfertilized centipede lawns are a dark-green color, but they are short-lived and liable to succumb to disease and winterkill. *Note:* Do not expect perfection with centipede grass lawns! If you want a high-quality turfgrass, then consider another type of warm-season grass such as zoysia or St. Augustine.

Additional Species, Cultivars, or Varieties

There are no cultivars of centipede grass available.

Kentucky Bluegrass

*I*f you desire a grass that will stay green in the cooler months and a lawn that tolerates some shade, then choose Kentucky bluegrass. It was bluegrass that was underfoot when the term "barefoot lawn" came about. Kentucky bluegrass is a cool-season grass with a sod-forming growth habit. It is finely textured and, unlike the tall fescues, is very tolerant of close mowing. Its deep-green to blue-green color makes a very attractive lawn. This is the turfgrass of choice in the Mountain region and in the states north of us. Kentucky bluegrass is often mixed with perennial ryegrass or fine fescue in western North Carolina to make a beautiful, durable lawn. In the Piedmont, this bluegrass variety adds density to a tall fescue lawn, giving it the appearance of a thick, lush carpet. Many gardeners have recognized that bluegrass requires less mowing than some other turfgrasses. Count yourself lucky if you live where it is cool enough to have a Kentucky bluegrass lawn.

WHEN TO PLANT

For the best results in the western part of our state, plant Kentucky bluegrass in early spring. In the Piedmont region of North Carolina, September is the month for seeding. Bluegrass seed is slow to germinate, so be patient. You will see signs of life in 3 to 4 weeks.

WHERE TO PLANT

This grass species is most often used in mixtures, especially for lawns in the Piedmont of North Carolina. If you want a lawn of 100 percent bluegrass, I hope you live west of Asheville or at high altitudes in the Smoky Mountains. Homeowners in the Coastal region are advised to stick with centipede grass for shady lawns.

HOW TO PLANT

For a new lawn, first determine the soil pH. The ideal range is from 6 to 7. If your soil falls below this, a lime application will raise the pH level. Determine the square footage of the area that you will seed. Apply the seed in an amount equal to 2 pounds per 1000 square feet. Broadcast a starter fertilizer to promote growth. Lightly apply straw to your new yard, at a rate equal to 1 bale per 1000

square feet (or 50 bales per acre). There is no need to rake the straw—just let it decompose. If you are overseeding an established lawn, broadcast one pound of seed per 1000 square feet. For a mixture, use Kentucky bluegrass at a rate of 1 pound combined with 5 pounds of tall fescue per 1000 square feet.

CARE AND MAINTENANCE

When you establish your bluegrass lawn, water it heavily. Irrigate at a rate of 1 inch of water per week. Keep newly seeded lawns constantly moist until it's time to begin mowing. When your lawn reaches 3 inches high, mow one-third of the grass growth. Even though bluegrass will tolerate a lower cut, leaving the grass at this higher level will cause deeper root growth and a healthier lawn. In February, apply a 10-10-10 according to recommendations. In April, apply a broadleaf weed control. In September and again in late November, apply a turf-grade fertilizer at the rate of 1 pound of nitrogen per 1000 square feet of lawn.

ADDITIONAL INFORMATION

You may have a problem with the following insects and diseases: leaf spot, brown patch, Japanese beetle grubs, and sod webworms. If you notice an increase in mole activity or if the grass dies in spots, a soil insecticide can be applied in August. For proper advice, contact your lawn and garden center or County Extension Agent.

ADDITIONAL SPECIES, CULTIVARS, OR VARIETIES

Shade-tolerant cultivars are 'Bristol,' 'Ram I,' 'Glade,' 'Georgetown,' 'America,' 'Midnight,' 'Mystic,' and 'Sydsport.' Other cultivars are 'Aspen,' 'Blacksburg,' 'Monopoly,' 'Nassau,' 'Suffolk,' 'Baron,' 'Kenblue,' and 'Princeton.' Cultivars vary in their availability each year. (Sometimes there are weather-related shortages in seed supply.)

St. Augustinegrass

While zoysia grows at a snail's pace, St. Augustinegrass gallops like a thoroughbred when it is planted. This fast-growing turf-grass is in the same class as Bermudagrass—both flourish in the warm months and go dormant following the first frosts. Residents in the southeastern counties of North Carolina are fond of this coarse grass for its drought and shade tolerance. St. Augustinegrass has broad, rigid leaf blades that are medium-green in color. It spreads aggressively by means of runners (stolons), making a dense sod and beautiful lawn. Anyone growing this grass knows that it will encroach on beds and will require edging periodically. It is best adapted to warm, humid areas that are not exposed to intense periods of cold weather. The 'Raleigh' variety has the best cold tolerance and seems best suited for the eastern Piedmont and Coastal regions of the state. St. Augustine grows best in well-drained soils. On beach-front properties, home-owners will be pleased with the salt tolerance of this warm-season turfgrass. Given proper care, St. Augustinegrass can make a lush, high-quality lawn that prevents soil erosion and beautifies the home landscape.

WHEN TO PLANT

St. Augustinegrass can be sprigged, plugged, or sodded beginning 2 weeks after spring "greenup." In the eastern half of North Carolina, this means an April or May planting season. Since the roots need warm soil to develop, planting too early is a mistake. Repairing damaged lawns and doing small sodding projects can continue until early July.

WHERE TO PLANT

This warm-season grass thrives in fertile, well-drained soils. For the best results, plant St. Augustinegrass in semi- to full-shaded conditions. In areas where this lawn grass continues to die out, replant the area with another grass type, mulch the area, or convert this spot to a natural area. St. Augustinegrass is not tolerant of heavy traffic such as that on playgrounds, nor will it survive in the cold western regions.

How to Plant

When average daytime temperatures are above 60 degrees Fahrenheit, it is time to plant St. Augustinegrass. Begin by having the soil tested to ensure proper fertility for newly planted lawns. In the absence of a soil test, apply 75 pounds of ground limestone and 20 pounds of 10-20-20 (or 20 pounds of 10-10-10 plus 4 pounds of 0-46-0) per 1000 square feet of lawn . Using a rototiller, incorporate the lime and fertilizer into the top 6 to 8 inches of soil. (I prefer to hire a professional to do the initial soil preparation if it is a new lawn.) After leveling out the yard with a rake or harrow, plug or sprig the lawn, using plugs planted on 12-inch centers. Space and plant sprigs at the rate of 1^1/$_2$ bushels per 1000 square feet (1^1/$_2$ square yards of sod).

Care and Maintenance

Irrigate thoroughly the first week following planting. Apply ^{1}/$_2$ inch of water every 3 days. If runoff occurs, stop watering until the water is absorbed. Continue irrigating, keeping the soil moist during the first summer to prevent drought stress. Proper irrigation will also prevent pest attack. Mow the grass before it reaches 4 inches high, and maintain the mowing height at 2 to 3 inches. After a few years, dethatch the grass when the thatch layer gets ^{3}/$_4$ inch thick (check in late spring). Fertilize in May, June, and August with ^{1}/$_2$ pound of nitrogen per 1000 square feet using a 3-1-2 analysis turf-grade fertilizer. Irrigate during periods of drought!

Additional Information

St. Augustinegrass is sensitive to some post-emergent herbicides. Control summer weeds while they are small, and when the grass is not drought stressed. Chinch bugs can kill this turfgrass. Check for these pests in sunny locations by pushing a coffee can into the ground. Treat if you see 20 chinch bugs per square foot.

Additional Species, Cultivars, or Varieties

'Raleigh' can be seeded and is the most cold-tolerant St. Augustinegrass. Common St. Augustinegrass, 'Delmar,' 'Floralawn,' 'Floratam,' 'Jade,' and 'Seville' are cultivars that may not have sufficient cold tolerance. County Extension Centers can provide the latest cultivar information.

Tall Fescue

*T*all fescue is the most widely used turfgrass in North Carolina. When compared with other bunch-type grasses, this cool-season grass has excellent heat and drought tolerance. It is often preferred over the warm-season grasses since it remains green throughout the winter. Though the old standard in the state is 'Kentucky 31,' plant breeders have introduced new cultivars that are lower growing and darker green. These new cultivars, such as 'Bonanza,' 'Rebel 3D,' and 'Phoenix,' produce a dense, high-quality turf in sun or partial shade. There are claims of improved brown-patch disease resistance when a blend of several cultivars are used together. Personally, I like the finer texture of these new introductions. You can have a lush, green lawn without a lot of fertilizer. The dwarf fescue varieties are the deepest green color. 'Kentucky 31' can still be used in hot, dry locations where there is minimal maintenance. But add 15 percent (by weight) of Kentucky bluegrass to get a thicker turf. In my opinion, 'K-31' is best left in the pasture or on a commercial lawn. With the cost of lawn renovation these days, I wouldn't try to economize by buying cheap grass seed. The new tall fescue varieties can make a beautiful lawn that looks professional.

WHEN TO PLANT

Fall is the preferred season for establishing and renovating tall fescue lawns. Lawns seeded in September will have time to develop deep roots by winter. Then when warm weather arrives, the lawn will thrive. In the western region, fair results can be expected with spring seeding. Much of the success in the spring has to do with the summer weather.

WHERE TO PLANT

'K-31' tall fescue requires full sun to survive. The new cultivars, however, are more shade tolerant. They prefer open sunlight, but they can be planted in partially shaded lawns. Spring in the Piedmont region with its tulips, azaleas, and dogwoods wouldn't look the same without a fescue lawn. Plant this grass in dry or moist sites.

LAWNS

How to Plant

The first step to a healthy tall fescue lawn is a soil test. It is imperative that acidic soils and fertility issues be dealt with from the start. According to Dr. Art Bruneau, Extension's Turf Specialist, "The key to a quality lawn is amending the entire root zone to a depth of six inches. Unless this zone is uniformly limed and fertilized, turfgrass roots will not occupy it and will die during periods of stress." For a new lawn, rototill the area and rake out rocks or clods that are larger than a golfball in size. Spread amendments such as compost or peat moss; till these into the soil. Broadcast the seed at the rate of 6 pounds per 1000 square feet. Rake lightly to cover the seed. Spread the fertilizer and straw.

Care and Maintenance

Irrigation is crucial for newly seeded tall fescue lawns, particularly during September when the weather can be hot and dry. Using an oscillating or rotary irrigation sprinkler, keep the soil moist with daily watering. Continue watering until germination occurs (7 to 14 days). At that time, reduce the irrigations to twice each week. Once you begin mowing, water weekly or as needed. Begin mowing the new lawn when it is 4 inches high. Remove only 1/3 of the leaf blade at each mowing. Tall fescue should be fertilized heavily in the fall (2 pounds of nitrogen per 1000 square feet). Fertilize at half that rate in mid-February. Aerate each fall.

Additional Information

The best control for weeds in a fescue lawn is a thick turf that is mowed and fertilized properly. Don't scalp your lawn, and don't worry about removing clippings if you mow regularly. Irrigate in the fall and spring as needed. Core aeration is very beneficial for long-term maintenance and for overseeding tall fescue. Buy clean, pure seed!

Additional Species, Cultivars, or Varieties

Research is ongoing at North Carolina State University, and new cultivars appear each year. Every County Extension Center has the latest information on the variety trials. The publication "Carolina Lawns" contains cultivar and cultural recommendations; it lists 35 very good cultivars. A blend of 2 to 4 cultivars with a little bluegrass and fine fescue serves all lawns.

Zoysia

*P*erhaps you are looking for the perfect summer lawn. Zoysia is compact, making it a lush green carpet under your feet in the hotter months of the year—it is so thick that weeds don't stand a chance! It is not invasive like Bermudagrass, and it can be planted in close proximity to flower and shrub beds. Every spring, Extension offices are deluged by telephone calls that come following the slick advertisements for zoysia grass that generally run during the spring planting season. The ads extol the virtues of zoysia, such as its low-growing habit and its tenacity when competing with weeds. What the ads don't say is that zoysia is brown for as many months as it is green. Consequently, if you plant this grass in your front lawn in a subdivision in the Piedmont or Western region of the state, in the winter you will probably get some disapproving looks from neighbors who have tall fescue lawns. This dormant period can also detract from the early spring garden display, especially if you have bulb beds. Zoysia grasses are cold hardy throughout the Tar Heel state, and they're drought tolerant. They are slow to establish, but they do have tremendous utility.

WHEN TO PLANT

Plant zoysia in spring and early summer, but do not plant it until 2 weeks following its spring "greenup." Most homeowners fall prey to the slick zoysia ads and plant the mail-order sprigs. Professionals use sod, purchased by the pallet for cutting into plugs (2- to 4-inch squares of turf). Zoysia can also be seeded, though the process is slow.

WHERE TO PLANT

Zoysia grasses like hot sites and full-sun exposures. Zoysia will tolerate partial shade, but it will grow very slowly. It is tolerant of a wide range of soil types provided they drain well. In regions where tall fescue is king, many homeowners plant zoysia in their backyards where there is heavy traffic from outdoor activities. Plant it on slopes that are too steep to mow; zoysia prevents soil erosion on banks.

How to Plant

Before planting zoysia have your soil tested. The optimum pH is 6.0. Broadcast lawn-starter fertilizer and limestone according to the report. Rototill the nutrients into the entire rootzone area to a depth of 5 to 6 inches. This is the most important step in establishing a permanent lawn. Rake or harrow the area, leaving the soil as smooth as possible. Sprig the lawn in May, June, or July, using 1/4 square yard of sprigs (1 to 2 bushels of stolons) for every 1000 square feet. Roll or press the sprigs into the top half-inch of soil or cover with a half-inch of topsoil. When plugging, cut the sod into 2-inch x 2-inch or larger squares. Follow the same procedure as outlined above. A few varieties of zoysia can be seeded.

Care and Maintenance

Whether you sprig or sod, keep the zoysia turfgrass in good shape by keeping it well watered. Set up a sprinkler system for daily watering during the first 2 weeks after planting zoysia. Irrigate weekly, applying an inch of water during the first growing season. In succeeding years, zoysia will need irrigation during periods of drought to prevent summer brownout. It will survive, though, once it has established. Mowing is very important. Mow before the grass gets 2 inches high and cut it to a 1/2- to 1-inch height. Fertilize zoysia twice each year with 12-4-8, in May and July. Zoysia will need de-thatching periodically.

Additional Information

Many homeowners plug zoysia into established fescue lawns. This is a big mistake, as these two are very different grass types. Your zoysia will grow at a snail's pace and the lawn will look like a spotted pup in the winter when the zoysia is dormant. Some spray the dormant lawn with a plant paint for a "green" winter lawn!

Additional Species, Cultivars, or Varieties

'Meyer' zoysia is a medium-textured variety that is like Kentucky bluegrass in size. 'Emerald' is a fine-textured dark-green zoysia with good winter hardiness. It is one of the best zoysias for a high-quality home lawn. Z. 'Manilagrass' is better for Coastal areas. Seeded zoysias are 'Sunrise,' 'Zenith,' and 'Panda.'

Roses

*T*HERE IS PERHAPS NO FLOWER IN ALL THE WORLD THAT IS MORE POPULAR than America's national flower, the rose. Its beauty of form, rich pleasing color, delightful fragrance, and incredible versatility have made it a favorite of gardeners and flower-lovers for generations. No wonder it is called the Queen of Flowers.

The rose is a testament to human creativity. Once a wildflower, it has been cultivated and engineered to suit all types of gardens. There is a rose for every region of North Carolina, a form for every location. Varieties are available for borders, for growing on arbors and trellises, and even for bedding plants. The unique specimen tree roses are ideal for container gardening, while the newer groundcover roses adapt well to small spaces. Of course, the hybrid teas are superb for cutting and are the rose of choice for millions of Americans.

People have grown roses for centuries for many reasons. In times past, the rose was revered for its value as food and medicine. The quaint herbal concoctions were believed to cure many ailments. Not until recently have we known that rose hips have as much Vitamin C as citrus fruits.

Today we grow roses mostly for their beauty in the garden. There used to be more reluctance to grow them because of widespread problems with fungal diseases, but with better cultivars, these prob-

Chapter Nine

lems are not as prevalent. New introductions, especially among the shrub roses, allow gardening success without heavy pesticide use. Also gardeners are now re-visiting the heritage roses because of their hardiness, fragrance and tolerance of neglect by well-meaning homeowners.

If treated with proper feeding and maintenance, many roses will bloom continuously for up to seven months in a Tar Heel garden. It would be difficult to find a more delightful ornamental than the rose.

Climbing Roses

*N*othing is more picturesque than a gorgeous climbing rose flowing over a white picket fence or garden gate. Experienced gardeners and novices alike have been constructing trellises, arbors, and even small gazebos as excuses to grow climbing roses. This class of ornamental can literally raise your garden to new heights! Like other roses, they come in a host of colors and forms. Traditionally, the large-flowered climbers are the most popular because of their longer flowering time. While no rose is a true climber, having no tendrils for attaching to a support, these plants do produce long canes that can be trained and tied to a fence or trellis. The climbing rose consists of a single group known as 'Ramblers.' These roses bloom only once, in late spring to early summer, but their full-bloom display is well worth the wait. They have a growth potential of up to 20 feet. Climbers have mixed parentage, and therefore vary in aroma, height, and color. Some can be pruned into cascading bushes or permitted to crawl on the ground. Nothing can compare to the instant "curb appeal" a climbing rose creates when framing an arbor or garden. And the fragrance produced by these beauties is wonderful as it wafts across the landscape.

WHEN TO PLANT

The best time to plant any bareroot climbing roses is mid-January through April. Potted roses can be planted April through June if planting is followed by proper watering practices. Early fall is an acceptable time to plant roses, though they must have time to establish well before the ground freezes.

WHERE TO PLANT

Plant climbers in at least 6 hours of good, intense sun and in well-drained soil. Plant these roses where air circulation is good to minimize diseases. Obviously, they need some type of support, whether from brick walls, fences, arbors, or trellises. The uses of a climbing rose are almost limitless. Varieties recommended for a pergola or trellis include 'Don Juan,' 'American Pillar,' 'Blaze,' and 'Cecile Brunner.'

ZONE
6,7,8

How to Plant

Spade plenty of compost, aged cow manure, or bark soil conditioner into the planting area. Once the soil and amendments are all blended, remove a quantity to create a hole large enough to accommodate the rose's roots. If you are planting a container rose, be very careful when removing the pot. Try to keep the ball intact and place gently into the hole. If you are planting a grafted rose, you will need to make sure the bud union (the swollen bulge at the base of the plant) is just above the soil level. Backfill the hole, firming the soil around the roots. Most roses will benefit from being planted with 1/3 of their rootball higher than grade. Water thoroughly and mulch.

Care and Maintenance

Roses must be planted in well-drained soil since they will be watered heavily the first season or two. They will certainly survive with once-a-week watering, but the more often you water, the better off the plant will be. Drip irrigation and mulching is the secret to keeping roses looking good. These plants prefer 1 to 2 inches of water per week and need the moisture to penetrate deeply. Climbers are eventually less dependent on water and pesticides than are other roses, particularly once they are well established. Prune climbers only to shape in spring. Severe pruning to control growth or to invigorate older plants should be done immediately after blooming.

Additional Information

Climbers' stiff canes tend to need substantial support. Use carefully placed vine supports found at your garden center. For advice on suggested spray schedules for roses, consult a rosarian or the Extension Service. Spray with a dormant oil spray at least once during the winter months.

Additional Species, Cultivars, or Varieties

Available cultivars include 'Blaze,' 'America,' 'Altissimo,' 'Don Juan,' 'Handel,' 'New Dawn,' 'Royal Sunset,' and 'Rhonda.' *Rosa banksiae* 'Lutea,' a Lady Banks rose, is a thornless variety that will naturalize. Lady Banks rose varieties appear to thrive on neglect and they tolerate Coastal conditions including salt spray. Its small, double, yellow flowers are a Southern tradition. 'Normalis' has single white flowers. 'Albo-plena' has fragrant double white blooms. 'Lutescens' has single yellow flowers.

ROSES

Floribunda Rose

During the early twentieth century, this class of roses originated from a cross between the hybrid tea and polyanthas. Floribunda roses have smaller flowers than the hybrid teas, but they produce more flowers on each stem. Their name means "abundantly flowering." Their colors range from snow white to deep crimson. Floribundas are low-growing, densely branched bushes that are quite adaptable to many landscape uses. There are many varieties that yield continuous bloom through the season. 'Europeana' is one that I have grown for years. Its rich-green, glossy foliage and masses of dark-red flowers are wonderful when the plant is used in solid blocks for a color bed. Black spot disease was not as serious a problem for these roses as I had expected. (Like many other gardeners, I am slack on following through with a rigid spraying routine.) My rosarian friend David Pike recommends the varieties 'Cherish,' 'First Edition,' and 'Sunflare.' Roses are among the few plants that can provide constant color and fragrance in the garden from spring through fall. The floribundas provide good cut flowers for bouquets, and they are especially nice as a decorative landscape plant in the border or rose garden.

WHEN TO PLANT

All roses do best when planted in their dormant stage. This is particularly true of the mail-order plants shipped bareroot to your home. Most garden centers are selling container-grown roses that can be planted successfully throughout the growing season. You can root many rose varieties by taking cuttings from new growth in the summer months.

WHERE TO PLANT

Roses must have at least 6 hours of intense sunshine to thrive, and they prefer full sun all day long. They also require organic-enriched soil with excellent drainage. A bed of floribundas needs minimal care and it provides sustained color in your garden. Use these roses en masse in borders or as an edging along the front property lines. They can even be used to disguise an ugly foundation or line a walkway up to your front door.

ROSES

How to Plant

Dig a hole 12 inches deep and 18 inches wide. Blend plenty of organic matter into the backfill soil, and adjust the pH to 6.0 by liming. Once the soil and amendments are all blended, spread the roots of bareroot roses over a mound of soil in the hole. If you are planting a container rose, be very careful when removing the pot. Try to keep the ball intact and place gently into the hole. If you are planting a grafted rose, you will need to make sure the bud union (the swollen bulge at the base of the plant) is just above the soil level. This is where the desirable hybrid rose is grafted onto wild-rose root stock. Backfill the hole and firmly pack the soil until level with the ground. Water-in well and mulch.

Care and Maintenance

Roses love lots of water during the growing season. They will certainly survive with once-a-week watering or even less after getting established the first year. The more often you water, the better off the rose will be. Keep the foliage dry when watering. Try to water in the morning, and keep in mind that roses would much rather have one good soaking than 3 to 4 sprinklings per week. As a rule, roses prefer 1 to 2 inches of water per week and need moisture to penetrate 18 inches deep. Roses love to be trimmed often. Prune lightly in late fall after frost. The final pruning is done in late winter or early spring as the buds swell.

Additional Information

Roses love to be fed. Some folks are successful using all-organics such as composted manures, cottonseed meal, bonemeal, green sand, and compost. Others are equally successful with commercially packaged formulated rose food. A regular fungicide spray to control mildew and black spot diseases is a must for floribundas.

Additional Species, Cultivars, or Varieties

There is an endless list of floribunda varieties for our gardens. American Rose Society selections such as 'Showbiz' or 'Redgold' are a good place to start. Other varieties are 'Papercup,' 'Betty Prior,' 'Circus,' 'Angel Face,' 'Iceberg,' 'Saratoga,' 'Spartan,' 'Rose Parade,' 'Fire King,' and 'Gold Badge,' which is the finest yellow. Tree forms are available!

287

Groundcover Roses

*I*n August 1995, a shade-tolerant rose named 'Flower-Carpet' came to the United States from Germany. More than 2 million of these roses were sold in their distinctive pink plastic pots. Once established, this rose blooms virtually all summer long with pink flowers on a vining shrub that is only 12 to 18 inches high. Imagine a stunning groundcover with beautiful glossy green foliage and bloom throughout the summer. The 'Freedom' series is a new group of exciting groundcover roses hybridized by internationally famous rose breeder J. Benjamin Williams. The 3 creeping roses in this series are both disease resistant and winter hardy. Two of them, 'Dawn Creeper' and 'Ivory Carpet,' will be offered for the first time in 1997. Another series of roses called the 'Meidilands' offers other good cultivars. Some cultivars of groundcover roses have semi-evergreen foliage, making them more adaptable to North Carolina gardens. Many of these roses can offer a colorful alternative to junipers for a steep bank. Groundcover roses are among the few plants that can provide constant color in the landscape without demanding all your leisure time.

WHEN TO PLANT

All groundcover roses sold bareroot do best when planted immediately upon receipt from the nursery. If the ground is frozen or too wet for planting, store your roses out of the sun and keep them moist. Container-grown roses can be successfully planted throughout the growing season.

WHERE TO PLANT

Roses must receive at least 6 hours of intense sunshine to thrive, and they prefer full sun all day. They adapt to average soil provided there is good drainage. The groundcover rose is excellent for planting in masses where a groundcover is needed or where large "pockets" of color can add an accent. You may even use these roses in large planters, urns, and windowboxes.

ZONE
6,7,8

How to Plant

Spade the soil 12 to 15 inches deep, and blend in plenty of organic matter or composted cow manure. Once the soil and amendments are all blended, remove a quantity to create a hole large enough to accommodate the rose's roots. If you are planting a container-grown rose, be careful when removing the pot. Try to keep the ball intact and gently place it into the hole. If you're planting a grafted rose, you will need to make sure the bud union is just above the soil level once it has been planted. This is where the desirable hybrid rose is grafted onto wild-rose root stock. Backfill the hole and firm-in the roots with the soil. Water well, then mulch with bark or pine straw.

Care and Maintenance

Roses must be grown in well-drained soil since they will need irrigation regularly during the growing season. They will survive with once-a-week watering or even less after getting established the first year. When watering, keep the foliage dry. It is best to water in the morning, and keep in mind that roses would much rather have one good soaking than 3 or 4 sprinklings per week. As a rule, roses prefer 1 to 2 inches of water per week and need moisture to penetrate 15 inches deep. Groundcover roses require very little pruning. Some spring trimming will keep them vigorous. Keep a watch out for spider mites in summer.

Additional Information

Roses love fertilizer! There are numerous rose foods designed to create beautiful blooms and lush, green foliage. If you bring a soil test with you, your local garden center or Extension Agent will be able to help determine your plant's specific needs. Be sure to consider fungicide sprays as part of maintenance.

Additional Species, Cultivars, or Varieties

The Freedom series includes 'Dawn Creeper,' which has deep-pink, semi-double flowers; 'Ivory Carpet,' a true dwarf rose with sprays of white double blooms; and 'Scarlet Spreader,' semi-double and scarlet-red. 'White Meidiland' is a white repeat bloomer. 'Sea Foam' is a white flower. 'White Flower Carpet' was new in 1997. The dwarf bush 'Petite Scotch Rose' is a North Carolina Association of Nurserymen introduction.

Hybrid Teas

he hybrid tea is the "aristocrat" in rose societies. This is the rose you bring home from the florist on Valentine's Day for your sweetie. (I've found that it works equally as well other times of the year when you need to get out of the doghouse!) Hybrid tea roses are known for their elegant buds and heavenly scent. The long stems and beautiful blooms make this the queen of flowers, perfect for cutting single buds or a collection for a bouquet. The colors are truly endless and the fragrances can range from sweet and fruity to bold and spicy. Roses are one of the few plants that can provide constant color and fragrance in the garden from spring through fall. Hybrid tea roses are grown more widely in rose gardens than all other roses combined. They are are called "everblooming" roses by some rosarians. Mature bushes reach 6 feet high, depending on your pruning practices. Most of the flowers are double with long, pointed buds. Hybrid teas are winter hardy in most of North Carolina. "The Handbook for Selecting Roses" prepared by the American Rose Society is the place to start when choosing the best varieties for your region.

WHEN TO PLANT

All roses do best when planted in their dormant stage. Container-grown roses are very popular, especially for Mother's Day gifts. These can be planted successfully even in full bloom throughout the summer months provided they are watered regularly.

WHERE TO PLANT

Roses require at least 6 hours of intense sunshine to thrive. Good air circulation through the rose bed is important for disease prevention. Roses also require organic-enriched soil with excellent drainage. Hybrid teas need the most maintenance of all roses. Plant them where you can spray them with fungicides. Most people devote one particular garden just to the hybrid tea roses because of their high maintenance requirements. A single specimen tree rose is a fine accent plant.

ZONE 6,7,8

How to Plant

Have the soil tested before creating a new bed. Work the soil to a
depth of 16 inches and incorporate plenty of organic matter or soil
conditioner into the existing soil. Once the soil is amended thoroughly, dig a hole large enough to accommodate the rose's roots. If
you are planting a container rose, be very careful when removing
the pot. Try to keep the ball intact and place it gently into the hole. If
you are planting a grafted rose, you will need to make sure the bud
union is just above the soil level. Backfill the hole and firmly pack
the soil until level with the existing ground. Water well and then
mulch with pine mulch.

Care and Maintenance

Roses will certainly survive with once-a-week watering, or even
less after getting established the first year. When watering, keep the
foliage dry. Try to water in the morning, and keep in mind that roses
would rather have one good soaking than 3 or 4 sprinklings per
week. As a rule, roses prefer 1 to 2 inches of water per week and
need moisture to penetrate 18 inches deep. Roses love to be trimmed
often. Cut back hybrid teas to waist height after the foliage is ruined
by the fall freeze. In early spring (March), do the final pruning. At
that time, prune to 15 to 18 inches. Remove the oldest and weakest
canes, leaving 3 to 5 strong ones.

Additional Information

The proper way to cut your hybrid tea roses for arrangements is
to remove the flower stems at the second or third leaf node which
contains 5 to 7 leaflets. The remaining bud on the cane will produce
another strong flower stalk. To encourage roses to harden-off for the
winter, stop fertilizing and quit cutting the flowers by late August in
western North Carolina.

Additional Species, Cultivars, or Varieties

My very favorite hybrid teas are 'First Prize,' 'Double Delight,'
'Tropicana,' and 'Paradise.' The most requested varieties are 'Touch
of Class,' 'Keepsake,' 'Olympiad,' 'Crystalline,' 'Pristine,' 'Color
Magic,' 'Elizabeth Taylor,' 'Dublin,' and 'Double Delight.'

Miniature Roses

iniature roses are true dwarf members of the rose family and can easily be grown with a minimum of care and space. These little jewels are North Carolina's best-kept secret in the rose world. Because they are not grafted and grow on their own root stock, they will handle our unpredictable winters like little troopers, peeking their small heads out as spring arrives. Miniature roses are great to plant as a border in a perennial or shrub bed. They are available in a vast selection of colors and cultivars. Like an intricate tapestry, these tiny gems will lend a captivating element to any garden area. They are generally much hardier than other roses and usually do not require winter protection in our area. Light mulching will give some winter protection as well as help conserve moisture during the summer.

WHEN TO PLANT

Roses will do best when planted in their dormant stage, but once the rose breaks dormancy, you can be successful in planting it throughout the growing season.

WHERE TO PLANT

Roses must be in at least 6 hours of intense sunlight. They also require good organic-enriched soil with excellent drainage. The miniature roses may be planted in hanging baskets or patio containers or even as a mass border for your flowerbed. They can also be grown in the house on a sunny windowsill or under fluorescent lights, but they do need more light than the average houseplant.

HOW TO PLANT

Dig up the soil and blend plenty of organic matter and soil conditioner into the existing soil. Once the soil and amendments are blended, create a hole large enough to accommodate the rose's roots. If you are planting a container rose, be careful when removing the pot. Try to keep the ball intact and place it into the hole. If you are planting a grafted rose, you will need to make sure the bud union is just above the soil level. When planting in a container, be sure it has good drainage and a very rich but porous soil. You should move the container to shelter during severe winters. When planting bareroot roses, handle with care. The roots need to be spread out and placed on a small mound.

CARE AND MAINTENANCE

Roses like to be watered weekly. Most rosebeds can be irrigated with the drip watering systems that are available at most garden shops or by mail. This ensures that the foliage stays dry. Prune your miniatures back in late fall. In mid-February, you should cut canes back to active new growth and remove any winter-damaged canes to maintain an appealing and healthy appearance. Rosarians agree that all types of roses need regular fertilization. This can be accomplished with a specialty rose fertilizer or with various organic products. Some of these contain systemic insecticides that are beneficial. Maintain a 2-inch layer of mulch.

ADDITIONAL INFORMATION

Miniature roses are propagated on their root systems, so they can endure difficult weather. Greenhouse-grown roses purchased in early spring should be protected from frost by placing them in a sheltered location or holding them in a sunroom. These miniatures can then be planted after the weather has warmed and the chance of freeze injury is past.

ADDITIONAL SPECIES, CULTIVARS, OR VARIETIES

The American Rose Society includes the following in their list of miniature roses rated 8.5 or higher. Blends are apricot 'Jean Kenneally,' red 'Magic Carrousel,' yellow 'Rainbow's End,' and pink 'Minnie Pearl.' 'Winsome' is mauve. Orange roses are 'Starina' and 'Millie Walters.' 'Rise'n'Shine' is yellow. 'Peggy T' is red. Pink roses are 'Cupcake' and 'Pink Meillandina.'

Old Garden Roses

*T*his group of roses is certainly making a comeback all over the country. In North Carolina gardens, old garden roses are appreciated for their hardiness and disease resistance (unlike the contemporary hybrid teas). The old garden rose category consists of roses that were introduced before 1867. These varieties evolved hundreds of years ago from roses in a region near China. The number of colors is great and heights range from 3 to 9 feet. Old garden roses are often planted because their old-fashioned look is reminiscent of grandmother's garden . . . and they offer gorgeous, fragrant blooms. They are quite rugged during our hot, dry summers and they have few problems with pests. Old garden roses should not be limited to the formal rose garden. They can be worked in the permanent landscape, used as a perennial backdrop, or even grown in a large urn for the patio. Many of the old garden roses can be seen at the National Herb Garden in Washington, D.C.

WHEN TO PLANT

The best time for planting old garden roses is either late winter or early spring. These popular varieties are sometimes not as easy to find as other types of roses. Purchase them early when the selection is best.

WHERE TO PLANT

Roses must receive at least 6 hours of intense sunshine to thrive. Full sun will ensure compact plants and better floral displays. Roses also require organic-enriched soil with excellent drainage. Old garden roses are ideal for a formal rose garden, and they may also be planted in the general landscape or in containers.

HOW TO PLANT

Dig up the soil 16 inches deep and blend plenty of organic matter or bark soil conditioner into the existing soil. Once the soil and amendments are blended, remove enough to create a hole large enough to accommodate the rose's roots. If you are planting a container rose, be careful when removing the pot. Try to keep the ball intact and place gently into the hole. If you are planting a grafted rose, you will

need to make sure the bud union is just above the soil level. When planting in a container, be sure it has good drainage and a very rich but porous soil. Move the container to shelter during severe winters.

CARE AND MAINTENANCE

Roses love lots of water during the growing season. They will survive with once-a-week watering or even less after getting established the first year. Try to water in the morning, and keep in mind that roses would rather have one good soaking than 3 to 4 sprinklings per week. A rose bed with a drip irrigation system installed has the best of both worlds! Prune roses in midwinter or when budeyes begin to swell in the spring. Consider sealing your pruning cuts to prevent rose-borer infestation. Seal each cut with regular household white glue.

ADDITIONAL INFORMATION

There are many rose fertilizers designed to create beautiful blooms and lush, green foliage; some even contain systemic insecticides. Though you have many choices in this arena, all rosarians agree that roses love to feed! You can spray with dormant oil during the winter and repeat in the spring. A single fungicide spray or two in May may be beneficial.

ADDITIONAL SPECIES, CULTIVARS, OR VARIETIES

R. centifolia (cabbage rose) is multi-petaled and light-pink and grows to 5 feet. 'Fantin Latour' is one of the best cultivars. *R.* 'Muscosa' (moss roses) are fragrant, double pink roses. *R. mundi* is striped white-and-red. 'Cardinal de Richelieu' is purplish red. 'York and Lancaster' is a pink-and-white variegated rose.

Shrub Roses

OTHER COMMON NAME: Hedge Roses

The high maintenance demands of contemporary hybrid roses are often not in keeping with the hurried lifestyles of today's gardeners. And a formal rose garden may not conform well to the new less-structured American landscape design. Shrub roses often fill a gardener's desire to enjoy the beauty and fragrance of roses without employing a crew of landscape horticulturists. Easy-care roses like rugosas and old garden roses are a sure bet for superb hedges and informal plantings. They make great barrier plantings or no-shear shrub borders. Rugosa is the name of a species of rose as well as a rose classification. Rugosas, commonly called Japanese roses, are large plants with stiff, spiny canes. They are very adapted to Coastal planting since they can hold down sandy slopes, preventing soil erosion. The flowers of rugosas are primarily singles, in a range of colors including white, pink, and red. These are spring-blooming shrubs with orange-red rose hips. Two other likely candidates for hedge plantings are 'Bonica' and 'Simplicity' roses. These grow to 4 feet high, are very disease resistant, and yield rather large, open pink flowers.

WHEN TO PLANT

Roses do best when planted in their dormant stage, but once roses break dormancy, you can be successful in planting them throughout the growing season.

WHERE TO PLANT

Shrub roses are vigorous and need space in a wide open, sunny location. They are suitable for forming dense barriers and great hedges. Their stiff branches and the spines on rugosas will keep the wanton passerby away. Plant these roses in groups or use for mass plantings. They will "stop traffic" when placed in front of a picket fence or gate.

ZONE
6,7,8

HOW TO PLANT

Dig up 16 inches of soil and blend in plenty of organic matter and soil conditioner. Once the soil and amendments are blended, remove a quantity to create a hole large enough to accommodate the roots of the rose. If you are planing a container rose, be careful when removing the pot. Try to keep the ball intact and place gently into the hole. If you are planting a grafted rose, you will need to make sure the bud union is just above the soil level. Carefully backfill the hole and firmly pack the soil until level with the existing ground. Water well and then mulch with pine mulch.

CARE AND MAINTENANCE

Roses love lots of water and they will survive with once-a-week watering during the first year. The more often you water, the better off the roses will be. When watering, keep the foliage dry. Try to water in the morning, and keep in mind that roses would rather have one good soaking than 3 or 4 sprinklings per week. Roses love to be trimmed often. Cut back in late fall and prune in early winter, leaving enough cane so you can prune off winter damage in the spring. Rosarians all agree that roses love to feed. Your local garden center can help you learn about your plant's need for food.

ADDITIONAL INFORMATION

Shrub and hedge roses require the least amount of care in the "family of roses," but watch for white powdery mildew and black spot disease. If these occur, spray with a fungicide and remove all infected foliage in and around the plants.

ADDITIONAL SPECIES, CULTIVARS, OR VARIETIES

R. rugosa 'Sir Thomas Lipton' is a double-white, fragrant, repeat bloomer; 'Rubra' is deep red; 'Betty Prior' is carmine pink and bushy and has a tea fragrance. Three shrub roses planted in Georgia for the '96 Olympics were 'Bonica,' a 1987 American Rose Society selection with pink blooms; 'Red Meidiland,' which has single red blooms; and 'Scarlet Meidiland,' which has glossy green foliage and bright scarlet blooms.

CHAPTER TEN

Shrubs

*S*HRUBS ARE THE "MEAT AND POTATOES" OF LAND-
SCAPE DESIGN. The landscape would not be complete
without their seasonal interest. We use shrubs in so many ways that
it is hard to list all their wonderful qualities and distinctive habits.

The evergreen shrubs are the ones most sought after for
foundation plantings and screening. Evergreens keep their leaves
year-round. They are either conifers (with needle-like leaves) or
broadleaf evergreens (with flattened leaves). Some broadleaf plants
are deciduous, that is, they lose their leaves in the winter. For example, rhododendrons are broadleaf evergreens, while clethras are
deciduous broadleaf shrubs. We are blessed in North Carolina with
many native woody ornamentals that will thrive in our gardens and
lift our spirits.

Flowering shrubs will always endure in the nursery trade, as
they are loved by gardeners and non-gardeners alike. At my home,
I have camellias that bloom until Christmas time, and Oregon grape
hollies that begin their flowering season on the first warm days of
January. When the forsythia and daphne begin flowering in
February, my excitement for gardening is always rekindled.

There is a debate brewing across the country about the use of
native plants versus the use of introduced ornamentals. Tar Heels
garden in three hardiness zones, and there is no doubt that many
"exotic" landscape shrubs are superior to our natives. A landscape
architect friend, Jones Abernethy, shared his perspective with me:

Chapter Ten

"My clients want low-maintenance year-round beauty and 'toughness' in their landscape plants. Many natives will not thrive in the Piedmont. Our compacted red clay, hot summers, and wildly fluctuating winters put a lot of stress on plants. Many North Carolina natives are best adapted to cool sites and loamy soils. They are good choices only if one is willing to put in the time (and expense) needed to create the necessary microclimate."

Shrubs offer a variety of fine individual traits. Without shrubs such as Koreanspice viburnums and lilacs, you would be deprived of wonderful fragrance in the garden. Many shrubs boast interesting colors from both foliage and berries, and the marvelous dwarf conifers offer a myriad of colorful foliage and forms. Another desirable feature of many shrubs is the attraction they hold for butterflies. What garden is complete without a *Buddleia*?

Foundation plantings of evergreen shrubs serve a dual function. They eliminate the stark look and barreness of our houses' architectural features. Shrubs deflect wind and reduce heat loss for energy conservation. Best of all, shrubs provide winter interest at a time when southerners are wrestling with spring fever!

American Boxwood

merican boxwood is the aristocrat of all shrubs, maturing to 10 to 15 feet in height. When used as an evergreen screen, it creates a look of distinction and historical importance. Boxwoods are associated with the great estates of Western civilization. They have been used in landscapes from the traditional English gardens to plantation estates. You find grand old boxwoods all across North Carolina, from the Biltmore House in Asheville to Old Salem's colonial gardens to the Elizabethan Gardens on the Coast. The American boxwood lends itself to shaping in hedges, as a topiary, and as a specimen shrub. It is also used to anchor the ends of beds, creating quite a regal appearance. The most popular boxwood in foundation plantings is the dwarf species *B. sempervirens* 'Suffruticosa,' called English box by Piedmont residents. This compact boxwood assumes a globular shape with a billowy outline as it matures, and it thrives in the shade. It is less susceptible to the leaf miner insect than is the American boxwood. It is the premier plant for low-maintenance gardens.

When to Plant

American boxwood is very transplantable because of its fibrous root system. It is one of the few plants that can be dug and transplanted year-round with probable success.

Where to Plant

For best results, plant American boxwood in full sun to partial shade in well-draining soil. Though many are planted in full shade, these do thin out a bit. Boxwood planted in fall will most likely turn an orange color from winter sun and exposure, particularly the old English boxwoods. Plant as a hedge or accent shrub in foundations, or use the tree-form boxwood.

How to Plant

Position the rootball in a wide, shallow hole 3/4 as deep and 3 times as wide as the rootball. Mix 1 cup of superphosphate into the backfill soil. Cut twine around trunk and top of rootball. Remove any nails and fold back burlap into the hole; no need to loosen the roots. Pack the soil firmly around the sides of the rootball. Add 2 to 3

ZONE
6,7,8

inches of mulch. Water well, then every 3 days for the first couple of weeks. Avoid planting when soil is frozen or when soil forms mudballs. Always plant "high" in clay soils.

CARE AND MAINTENANCE

It is important to water routinely the first summer. Use a garden hose to water slowly each week, approximately 1 minute per inch in diameter of the rootball, or use a soaker hose. No fertilizer is needed the first year. In the springs that follow, use slow-release nursery fertilizer at the recommended rate, or make your own. Good results on boxwood have been reported using a fertilizer mixture of one-half 10-10-10 fertilizer and one-half cottonseed meal. Spread one cup of this mixture in a circle beginning at the drip zone area and continuing a little beyond. Off-color foliage can be symptomatic of lesion nematodes.

ADDITIONAL INFORMATION

Pruning boxwoods is recommended. They can be sheared lightly each June after the new growth is fully grown. For old overgrown boxwoods, prune back severely over a period of 2 years. The first pruning is done in February; at that time, remove the top third. Cut hard again the next winter, shaping them as you reduce the size.

ADDITIONAL SPECIES, CULTIVARS, OR VARIETIES

'Myrtifolia,' which grows to 5 feet, has narrow leaves. 'Angustifolia' is tree-like and pyramidal. 'Green Mountain' is compact and pyramidal. *B. sempervirens* 'Suffruiticosa' is a dwarf that grows 3 to 4 inches per year. *B. microphylla* (Korean box) grows 3 to 4 feet and has a dense, spreading form; cultivars are 'Tide Hill' and 'Compacta.' *B. harlandii* grows to 4 feet and has bright-green oblong leaves.

Andromeda

Andromeda is an upright evergreen shrub with stiff, spreading branches. It grows to a height of 4 to 6 feet and slightly less in width. It features chains of lightly fragrant flowers which cascade beautifully over the plant's lustrous green foliage. A common name for andromeda is "Lily of the Valley" shrub, as it has tiny urn-shaped flowers which resemble those of the popular groundcover. Often this durable woody ornamental begins blooming before winter has passed. The cool weather sustains the flowers and extends the floral display into spring. There are many cultivars from which to choose. Most exhibit white flowers, but a few feature pink flowers. Still other varieties, like 'Mountain Fire,' have new growth that comes out in spring in an array of brilliant colors. Andromeda offers something of interest for every season. Its features appear in late fall and winter with next season's pendulous flower buds. Spring has showy early-season flowers and bright-red new growth. Summer offers lustrous green foliage and cascading seed capsules. This landscape workhorse is amazingly drought resistant once it becomes established.

WHEN TO PLANT

You can transplant andromedas any time soil conditions allow. Early fall is the ideal time to plant this shrub. When planting in hot weather, provide constant moisture. It might be better to wait to plant this member of the rhododendron family when temperatures become more moderate.

WHERE TO PLANT

Andromeda thrives in a partly shaded location. It grows best when planted in acid, well-drained soils with a pH near 5.5 and is short-lived when planted in wet sites. A soil rich in organic matter is best. This evergreen can be used in a shrub border or foundation bed or as a specimen. When planted in full sun, underplant with a groundcover such as blue rug juniper or liriope.

HOW TO PLANT

In heavy clay soil, prepare a raised bed. Build up around the root-ball with "native soil" mixed with some organic matter. In sandy

soil, amend the entire plant bed with additional organic matter as well—use something like pine-bark soil conditioner, composted manure, or garden compost. Most soils in North Carolina need phosphate in the form of bonemeal, 0-20-0 fertilizer, ground rock phosphate, or 0-46-0 fertilizer added and mixed into the planting soil. Prepare a wide, shallow hole 3/4 as deep and 3 times as wide as the rootball. As with all container-grown plants, thoroughly loosen the roots of the plants. After planting, always water well and apply a 2- to 3-inch mulch layer to enrich the soil.

CARE AND MAINTENANCE

Watering during the first 3 years after transplanting is critical. Andromeda are very shallow rooted and should not be allowed to dry out. Frequent watering will be needed during the summer months when rainfall is sparse. Raised beds will dry out much faster than the native soil. But take care not to overwater—excessive soil moisture encourages root rot diseases. Planting too deeply will kill this hardy plant. Your shrub may not need pruning annually; prune to return the andromeda to its normal growth habit or to remove an occasional dead branch. Cut back individual stems immediately after flowering in the spring.

ADDITIONAL INFORMATION

There are several products which are excellent when used at the recommended rate. Select an azalea-camellia fertilizer or a fertilizer like 16-4-8, and apply in early April. Phytophthora root rot and twig dieback are two diseases that can sometimes be a problem. Lacebugs are the insects that can be a serious pest of this attractive evergreen. Control lacebugs with a mid-April and an August spraying.

ADDITIONAL SPECIES, CULTIVARS, OR VARIETIES

'Compacta' has a compact form and is white and heavy flowering. 'Dorothy Wycoff' has dark-red buds that open to pale-pink. 'Mountain Fire' has fire-red new growth in spring and white flowers. 'Valley Rose' has pastel-pink flowers. *Pieris aiwanensis* 'Snowdrift' is a little-known species of pieris; it is fairly tolerant of heat and of root rot diseases, and has many white flowers.

Aucuba

When it comes to woody plant selections for shade, this shrub is always at the top of the list. Aucuba actually suffers when placed in a hot, open location. It matures to 6 to 10 feet in height, only slightly less in width. Its long, lustrous, leathery leaves provide the coarse texture needed by shade gardens. The attractive red fruit on the female of the species is usually obscured by its thick and heavy foliage. Aucuba cultivars vary from solid green to the old-fashioned spotted variety, 'Gold Dust.' The more contemporary introductions like the male variety 'Maculata' have eye-catching yellow-and-white blotched leaves. This plant has a distinctively tropical look, and at first glance appears to be better-suited to the Florida landscape, but it is exceedingly durable in protected, shady areas in North Carolina. This is a great shrub to consider when looking for a deep-shade plant that produces beautifully colored foliage for fresh arrangements.

WHEN TO PLANT

You can plant aucuba spring through fall as soil conditions permit. Container-grown aucubas are easy to plant at any size. Transplant established shrubs in early spring when they must be moved for a landscaping project. Plant long before the ground gets cold in the winter.

WHERE TO PLANT

Plant aucuba in shade gardens where the the soil drains well. This shrub thrives in medium- to high-moisture situations, and actually prefers our heavy clay soils. Use this plant in shady corners or in planters by a patio. It is a good shrub for a courtyard planting and a good background hedge for shade-loving perennials. A robust aucuba makes a beautiful specimen plant.

HOW TO PLANT

Thoroughly loosen the roots of plants grown in pots. Prepare a wide, shallow hole 3/4 as deep and 2 times as wide as the rootball. Blend organic matter into sandy loam soils, using materials such as compost or bark soil conditioner in a 50:50 ratio for the backfill. In decent soils, use the native soil for planting. Firm-in the soil around

the rootball and form an earthen saucer for watering purposes. Add 1 to 3 inches of mulch on top after planting; then water well. Be sure to avoid planting when the soil is wet enough to form a mudball in your fist.

CARE AND MAINTENANCE

Use an open-ended garden hose to water newly planted shrubs for 10 minutes every third day. Do this until the shrub's roots are established, generally for 2 to 3 weeks. Deep watering is preferred over light watering. When in doubt, check soil wetness with a hand spade before watering. Prune during the spring to shape, and remove any winter-damaged stems. Aucuba does not need much fertilizer if it is kept mulched. For older shrubs, apply a slow-release formulation nursery fertilizer every other spring at a rate of one-half cup per 10 square feet. Broadcast it under the canopy of the shrub and a little beyond. Water during drought!

ADDITIONAL INFORMATION

You should not expect any special problems particular to aucuba other than winter wind-damaged leaves and sunscald. Prune off damaged leaves in the spring. Blackened foliage may be a sign of cold injury or of a soil nematode problem. Check with a County Extension agent for a nematode assay.

ADDITIONAL SPECIES, CULTIVARS, OR VARIETIES

'Crotonifolia' has gold and whitish spots. 'Picturata' has deep-green leaves. 'Nana' is a dwarf form that stays low to 2 feet. 'Longifolia' has long, willow-like leaves. 'Variegata' is a female with yellow flecks on leaves. 'Macrophylla,' a female, has broad, leathery foliage. 'Crassifolia,' a male, has large dark-green leaves.

ℬ𝓁𝓊𝑒𝒷𝑒𝒶𝓇𝒹

OTHER COMMON NAME: Blue Mist Spirea

*T*his lovely tender shrub has aromatic grayish green foliage and long wispy branches that sport rich blue flower clusters every summer. Bluebeard can be classified as a herbaceous perennial in the western region of North Carolina. It reaches a height of 4 feet rather quickly, resembling butterfly bush in its growth habit. The misty, lavender-blue flowers are produced on the new growth and appear in late summer through early fall. Most varieties have grayish foliage which complements the flower color that is unusual that time of year (the yellow and red colors of other plants' flowers tend to predominate). Different bluebeard varieties display height variations from 2 to 4 feet with equal spread. With the autumn freezes, this shrub will die back, and it should be pruned to the ground like most hardy perennials. In late spring, numerous vigorous shoots break the ground as the plant is revived. Bluebeard is a breathtaking plant when in full bloom, especially in the early evening when the bluish blooms seem to glow.

WHEN TO PLANT

Plant container-grown bluebeard any time in spring or fall. In the eastern region of the state, it can be planted practically year-round.

WHERE TO PLANT

Bluebeard prefers full sun to develop to its best potential. It is quite adaptable to a range of soil types. Usually it is placed in a perennial flowerbed or border rather than in a foundation. The compact variety 'Bluebird' makes a nice low-growing hedge. It is striking when combined with the bright yellow and/or orange varieties of mums in the fall garden.

HOW TO PLANT

Plant bluebeard in a sunny area where there is well-drained soil. Compost or bark soil conditioner should be added to the planting hole, especially in clay soils. After removing from the container, score the rootball to free up circling roots. Dig a hole that is equal in depth and twice the diameter of the rootball. Firm the soil around the roots and form a basin to collect water from rain or irrigations. Mulching is very important for this fast-growing tender shrub. Leaf compost or aged manure applied in the spring will be of great benefit.

CARE AND MAINTENANCE

After pruning back to the ground in late winter, no further pruning is necessary. A 2- to 3-inch layer of compost is enough fertilizer for the plant during the entire growing season. A small amount of 5-10-10 or soluble plant fertilizer can be used in early summer. Too much fertilizer causes lanky growth. Keep bluebeard well watered until it gets established. It is quite resistant to dry periods, but a little water during its late bloom period will pay great dividends.

ADDITIONAL INFORMATION

These plants tend not to live very long if the soil is too wet, especially during the winter months. New plants can be reproduced by tip cuttings taken during the summer months.

ADDITIONAL SPECIES, CULTIVARS, OR VARIETIES

The low-growing 'Dark Knight' has dark-green foliage with violet-blue flowers. 'Longwood Blue' grows to 4 feet and has grayish foliage and lavender-blue flowers. *C. incana*, *C. mongolica*, and other varieties of *C. × clandonensis* may be found, but the two named above are among the best varieties.

Spiraea × bumalda

Bumald Spirea

OTHER COMMON NAME: Dwarf Spirea

*V*eteran gardeners in the Old North State have grown spireas all of their lives. The Vanhoutte spirea has stood the test of time in spite of the fact that it can look unsightly after flowering. A new breed of spireas, however, is sweeping the landscape trade. The dwarf spireas are excellent plants for contemporary gardens in which space is at a premium. These deciduous shrubs rarely reach 3 feet in height and offer both flowers and colorful foliage when the old favorites have long since passed their spring glory. 'Limemound,' for example, is a cultivar that provides many months of interest. This dense mounding shrub leafs out in spring with lemon-yellow foliage that turns to lime-green by summer. The long-lasting summer blooms are fuzzy pink clusters held above a canopy of small leaves. These compact shrubs have outstanding fall colors, orange-red or brilliant bronze. The leaf-less twigs are dark and wiry in the winter. The Bumald spireas are responsible for the increased interest in this family of ornamentals in North Carolina. Though they hold up well with contemporary plants, spireas bring a bit of nostalgia to the landscape.

WHEN TO PLANT

As is true of most deciduous woody ornamentals, Bumald spireas can be planted year-round from containers. For summer plantings, keep the roots of container-grown plants moist until they are placed in the landscape. Bareroot plants received from mail-order nurseries should be planted as soon as the ground is workable.

WHERE TO PLANT

Bumald spireas grow quickly to maturity when planted in a sunny location where the soil stays fairly moist. They will tolerate dry sites, however, and they can be used as a groundcover on banks. These plants are pH adaptable and survive well in ordinary well-drained soils. Use them in mass plantings, as fillers in the border, or better yet, as a low grouping in front of evergreens. Plant this spirea for refreshing summer color.

☀ | ZONE 6,7,8

How to Plant

Bumald spireas are tough little cookies! You shouldn't have difficulty getting them established in a new garden site even with
minimal effort in soil preparation. They do well in most soils,
though they are not riparian plants. Wet, poorly draining soils
will stunt them, or worse. When mass planting, prepare a bed by
rototilling the soil. Loosen the roots of container-grown plants and
dig a planting hole that is twice as wide as the rootball. The hole
depth should not be more than 3/4 the depth of the rootball; fill in
with soil if dug deeper. Butterfly the rootball as with azaleas, and
work soil in around the roots. Firm the soil and water thoroughly.
Apply a couple of inches of mulch by summer.

Care and Maintenance

Water newly planted spireas every 3 days for the first 2 weeks, then
go to a watering routine as needed on a weekly basis until they are
established. These dwarf shrubs will reach a height of 2 to 3 feet
with a spread somewhat larger. Pruning is needed only to keep the
growth in check where they are planted on small properties. After a
few years, some late-winter pruning will help open up these plants
and eliminate some of the twiggy growth. This should subsequently
increase the flower display. Spireas are not heavy feeders, but they
perform better if fertilized once in the spring with a nursery fertilizer.

Additional Information

Established Bumald spireas produce suckers and spread out a
bit. Keep this in mind when you are spacing the shrubs in the
foundation planting or in a border. Spacings of less than 3 feet
will ultimately look like a groundcover instead of a low shrub
planting. A light shearing of the old flowerheads in late summer
may encourage sparse fall flowering.

Additional Species, Cultivars, or Varieties

Bumald spirea cultivars in the trade include 'Anthony Waterer,' with
rose-colored flowers; 'Gold Flame,' pink flowers and yellowish
foliage; 'Goldmound,' pink flowers and gold foliage; and pink
'Gumball.' Japanese spireas include 'Snowmound,' 'Little Princess,'
'Lemon Princess,' and 'Shirobana.' New cultivars are S. 'Neon
Flash,' which has red flowers and purple growth, and S. 'Dakota
Charm,' with pink flowers and gold leaves.

Butterfly Bush

OTHER COMMON NAME: Summer Lilac

*T*his is a beautiful deciduous flowering shrub that is highly attractive to butterflies by day and moths by night. The attention-getter is its long trusses of blooms that are up to a foot long and mildly fragrant. (Trusses are clusters of tiny flowers that are borne on the ends of the long stems of new growth. They are 2 to 3 inches wide and resemble lilac flowers.) Though most of the flowers of butterfly bush are lavender-blue with an orange eye, the colors of trusses range from white to magenta. This colorful display continues all summer long and into the fall provided the old blooms are periodically removed. Butterfly bush has narrow leaves to 8 inches long; the foliage is a grayish green. The variety 'Lochinch' is especially gray, and it contrasts well with most evergreen hedges. In general, the species shrub reaches a height of up to 15 feet with a spread of 5 to 8 feet. The "dwarf" butterfly bush that I acquired from Monrovia Nursery grew rapidly, reaching 6 feet high by July. I cut it back severely after the flowers faded for another strong flush of growth and even more blooms! Butterfly bush is a must for the "wildlife" garden since it is so attractive to populations of butterflies, moths, and bees.

WHEN TO PLANT

Containerized plants can be planted spring through fall. You had better buy early at the garden shop before the period of bloom; butterfly bushes are a hot item when the flower trusses are showing.

WHERE TO PLANT

Butterfly bush performs best in full sun. Although it is quite satisfactory in partial shade, it stretches excessively and the flowers will be weighed down in rain. It is a beautiful plant when used as a hedge or border plant and is a good accent specimen in the perennial garden. It is nice near a patio or other outdoor sitting area where all the butterflies can be observed and the honey-like scent of the blooms can be enjoyed.

How to Plant

Butterfly bush thrives in well-drained soil of a neutral pH. Dig a hole that is as deep and 3 times as wide as the rootball. Use a knife to score the rootball and free up the roots, as butterfly bush is a strong root producer. Don't be hesitant about root pruning extremely long roots. Root pruning has been shown to encourage plant establishment by forcing production of new feeder roots at the points where the roots are cut. Firm the backfill soil around the roots, and water as you backfill the planting hole. Mulch with a couple of inches of bark or pine-straw mulch. Butterfly bush is easily grown and quick to establish provided the site is well drained.

Care and Maintenance

Butterfly bush is basically a low-maintenance plant that seems to bloom better in a soil that is not too rich. Fertilizing in spring with 10-10-10 when growth starts and perhaps again following a summer shearing should suffice. The plant should be pruned back to 8 to 12 inches from the ground in late winter. This induces a fuller shrub with plenty of large blooms. If this is not done, the plant will be tall and lanky in growth. Other than removing spent flowers and twiggy shoots occasionally, no further care is needed. In dry locations, supplemental watering will ensure rapid growth.

Additional Information

No major insects or diseases are known. The secret with butterfly bush is to prune liberally throughout the season. I once planted a butterfly bush that had to be moved and transplanted a few months later. To my amazement, the roots remaining in the ground eventually produced 3 small bushes at the first location.

Additional Species, Cultivars, or Varieties

'Black Knight' has dark-purple blooms. 'Lochinch' has fragrant lavender blooms. Blooms of 'Pink Delight' are clear pink, those of 'Sungold' are golden yellow, those of 'Dartmoor' are fragrant and deep lilac, and those of 'Harlequin' are fragrant and reddish purple. 'White Profusion' has white blooms and 'Empire Blue' has blooms that are a rich lavender-blue.

'Carissa' Holly

*T*his variation of Chinese holly is my favorite for foundation plantings on the south side of a house. Like its 'Rotunda' parent, this sun-loving shrub has the lacquered look of the species but only one spine per leaf tip. The evergreen foliage of 'Carissa' holly is leathery and stiff, and the undersides of the leaves are an olive-green color. The plant is similar in appearance to 'Dwarf Burford' holly; it is more compact, however, reaching a height of only 3 feet and a spread of twice that much. 'Carissa' holly has a moderate growth rate and requires virtually no pruning to keep it looking good. I have seen no pest problems with the plant where it is planted in soils that have respectable drainage. When planted in clusters of threes or fives, it can serve as an oversized groundcover in a border on the property line. The shrub's density prevents weeds from penetrating where it planted. Unlike many of the Chinese hollies, this cultivar makes no red berries. You can depend on 'Carissa' holly to weather heat and drought. The lustrous green foliage of this broadly rounded evergreen make it very desirable for North Carolina landscape plantings.

WHEN TO PLANT

This rugged landscape shrub can be planted from a container any time the soil is not too wet or frozen. 'Carissa' hollies that are smaller than the one-gallon size are generally best planted in spring or early fall for maximum root development before winter.

WHERE TO PLANT

Provided drainage is good, 'Carissa' hollies do well in ordinary garden soil with very little preparation. A hot, sunny location is the best spot. It is a good shrub for the foundation or a border where cooler-natured shrubs would struggle to survive. If low maintenance tops your list of requirements for landscape installations, then 'Carissa' will not disappoint you. It is tough and beautiful.

HOW TO PLANT

The stiff roots of 'Carissa' hollies will fill a container at the nursery in no time flat. It is therefore important to score the rootball before planting to ensure good root establishment. Spread the roots out

ZONE
6,7,8

horizontally in the planting hole. In well-drained soils, dig a hole that is the same depth as the rootball and twice the width. Hollies will benefit from the addition of limestone to the planting hole. In poor soils, plant high or on berms! 'Carissa' hollies are more appealing when planted in a bed rather than planted singly. Rototill the entire area and plant the hollies at the same depth they were grown in the nursery. Water the planting well. Cover the bed with 3 inches of hardwood mulch.

CARE AND MAINTENANCE

Water newly planted hollies thoroughly during the first several weeks after planting. Shrubs planted in individual holes can be overwatered, so allow the soil to dry slightly between irrigations. This is one shrub that well tolerate dry conditions after the roots have developed. An occasional light shearing in late spring will help to shape the shrub if a formal look is preferred. (You may want to remove a wild sprig here and there, but enjoy the natural growth form of 'Carissa.')

ADDITIONAL INFORMATION

The only complaints I have heard about 'Carissa' hollies have been about the yellowing foliage that may be seen the first year until the plants are well established. Usually an application of iron or Epsom salts will help perk them up. If the shrubs do not improve after one year, you may have a wet site and need to plant them higher. Wax scale insects should be controlled.

ADDITIONAL SPECIES, CULTIVARS, OR VARIETIES

If you are looking for a prickly foundation shrub for security reasons, try 'Carissa' holly's mom, *I.* 'Rotunda.' (She will eat you alive!) For a hedge, try 'Needlepoint' or 'Burford.' I have seen dwarf 'Burford' hollies in the 7- to 9-foot range. Two beautiful plants to brighten up a garden are 'O'Spring' and 'Cajun Gold'; they have yellow to cream leaves.

Cherry Laurel

*T*his plant species includes some of the finest evergreens for North Carolina landscapes. It has rich, lustrous foliage and may be used as a large privacy hedge or as a dense, spreading foundation shrub. Nurseries are stocking up on this plant now that they have found a way to eliminate the leaf spot disease that plagued them when the plant was grown under constant irrigation. The oldest variety, English laurel, is a massive evergreen shrub commonly found in large estate gardens. Hedges of this plant grow to 15 feet high and 10 feet wide, but they may grow even larger under ideal conditions. Their 6-inch-long leaves are dark green and glossy, accompanied by 2- to 5-inch spikes of fragrant white flowers in the spring. In the summer, the flowers become clusters of blue-black berries. The cherry laurels are the best landscape shrubs, particularly the compact 'Otto Luyken,' which makes a fine foundation planting or low border. The cherry laurels are moderately fast-growing shrubs and have a horizontal branching habit. They will grow to 4 feet with a spread slightly larger. They take well to shearing and thrive in full sun to partial shade. This is a terrific evergreen plant!

WHEN TO PLANT

The smaller cherry laurels are mostly container grown. These can be planted any time the ground is prepared from late winter to fall. The English laurels are less common, but they may be bought as balled-and-burlapped plants for planting in fall or winter. Container-grown plants need a month to establish before cold weather in the western region.

WHERE TO PLANT

Cherry laurels grows best in well-drained, medium-fertile soils. Plant them in full sun or filtered shade. Moist soils will be tolerated if drainage is quick. The English laurel is salt spray tolerant; it is useful as a windbreak, tall hedge, or foundation plant near large buildings. Cherry laurels are best used in groups in the foundation or border. They can serve as a tall group cover in areas where the soil is rich.

ZONE 6,7,8

How to Plant

An acidic soil with a pH of 5.5 is ideal. Plant a balled-and-burlapped plant in a hole that is 3/4 as deep and at least twice as wide as the rootball. Cut any twine around the trunk and rootball and remove nails on the top of the burlap in order to fold back the burlap to the sides of the rootball. Don't remove any wire basket. To the soil taken from the hole add compost or bark soil conditioner to make a 50:50 mixture. Backfill this mixture firmly around the rootball and tamp thoroughly. Flood the planting hole with water and apply 2 to 3 inches of mulch over the site without piling it against the trunk. A container-grown plant can be planted using the same method after removing the pot.

Care and Maintenance

Avoid overfertilization, but fertilize in the spring just before new growth starts each year. Use a prepared commercial shrub fertilizer for best results. Water during the warm months during periods of low rainfall. Use a sprinkler or a soaker hose to water to the depth of the rootball. Use a hand spade or a pipe probe to determine wetness. Cherry laurels respond well to pruning and may receive light prunings year-round. Severe renovation prunings should be done about one month before new growth starts in the spring. Laurels appreciate organic, enriched soil. Mulching helps achieve this and helps control weeds as well.

Additional Information

Laurels may develop winter leaf scorch and sometimes shed foliage when transplanted. They are susceptible to wood borers and leaf spot (or "shot-hole rust") which is worse with overhead irrigation or in areas of heavy rainfall. An insecticide spray for borers in June is beneficial if a problem develops, or just to keep the plants vigorous.

Additional Species, Cultivars, or Varieties

'Caucasida Nana' is a compact, thick shrub. 'Magnoliifolia' is large-leafed and hardy and may be trained as a tree. 'Otto Luyken' is a compact, dark-green, shrubby plant. 'Schipkaensis' is a dark-green, narrow-leaf shrub. 'Variegata' has leaves mottled with creamy white. Compact 'Zabeliana' has willow-like leaves; it is 3 feet high but it spreads to 8 feet.

Common Witch Hazel

*O*ne of the best-kept secrets to help you achieve your goal of a twelve-month garden is witch hazel. This deliciously sweet native bears twisted creamy-yellow flowers along naked stems in late fall. And the ribbon-like flowers of this multistem beauty are not its only interesting feature. Its golden fall foliage is also impressive. In the wild, witch hazel is a slow grower, reaching 8 to 12 feet in height with a similar spread. It is well adapted to ordinary garden soils provided they are enriched with organic matter. Witch hazels are especially nice where they are grown along a garden path or planted at the edge of a shady grove of massive hardwood trees. The shrubs will be more striking in bloom if planted in front of an evergreen border of American hollies. "Early settlers used the forked branches of witch hazel for divining rods," write Tripp and Raulston in "The Year in Trees." Though its name has an eerie history, this rugged ornamental is perfect for the woodland garden.

WHEN TO PLANT

Late fall or spring is the preferred time for planting common witch hazel. Avoid planting within a few weeks of the ground freezing.

WHERE TO PLANT

Witch hazels prefer moist soils and partial shade, but common witch hazel will adapt to a wide range of soil types. A full-sun site is acceptable provided the plant's roots don't dry out excessively. Morning sun is ideal. Plant witch hazel as a specimen, as an understory shrub along a path, or on the fringes of a woodland garden. Good companions for this native are rhododendrons and winter-flowering bulbs.

HOW TO PLANT

Enrich the soil with copious amounts of compost or soil conditioner. High-organic soils that are well drained are the witch hazel's natural soil preference. Position the shrub in a wide shallow hole that is 3/4 as deep and 3 times as wide as the rootball. Fold back the burlap into the planting hole if planting a balled-and-burlapped specimen. Firm-in the roots with the amended soil, and water regularly during

the first 2 months. This native will appreciate a 2-inch layer of mulch or leaf compost. Irrigate the newly planted shrubs during the first 2 summers.

CARE AND MAINTENANCE

Witch hazel will happily bask in the sun only if mulched well or irrigated during dry periods, especially in August and September. A soaker hose or, even better, drip irrigation is useful when maintaining large plantings of moisture-loving ornamentals. Clay soils absorb only 1/4 inch of water per hour, so hand watering is an inefficient method of irrigating moisture-loving natives in big gardens. Fertilize witch hazels in the spring with an organic fertilizer or finished compost. Pruning of these shrubs should be done in late winter to open up the plants or to control their size. They are best left in a natural shape.

ADDITIONAL INFORMATION

Remember to keep woodland natives routinely mulched. Good leaf mulch from a city composting program or from the backyard does wonders for stimulating root activity. This is important in the early years of development for woody plants.

ADDITIONAL SPECIES, CULTIVARS, OR VARIETIES

Vernal witch hazel (*H. vernalis*) is a winter-flowering species. Chinese witch hazel (*H. mollis*) blooms in late winter. The best cultivars of this species are 'Arnold Promise,' which has yellow flowers in early spring; 'Ruby Glow,' which has copper-red flowers; 'Sunburst,' which has 2-inch intense yellow flowers; 'Diane,' which has brilliant-red flowers; and 'Pallida.'

Compact Inkberry Holly

OTHER COMMON NAME: 'Shamrock' Holly

Inkberry hollies show up in the Extension Service leaflet "Qualifiers for Quagmires." They are tolerant of very wet sites where most landscape shrubs would fail. These beautiful evergreens resemble the Japanese hollies except that they are upright in their growth habit. The species plants are large shrubs reaching 8 feet in height, but the compact inkberries grow slowly to 3 feet with a slightly smaller spread. Their leaves are deep-green and glossy, and some bear heavy crops of black berries. The dark fruit conspicuously dots the foliage as if it were touched with an artist's ink pen. 'Shamrock' holly is one of the best compact inkberry hollies for foundation plantings. Its rich, lustrous foliage is sure to be admired. Landscape professionals find that 'Shamrock' hollies can be massed together in sunny sites for a wonderful evergreen border. They serve well as a low screening plant. If you like boxwoods, you will want to plant compact inkberry hollies. You get the same look as boxwoods, but these plants are a better value in semi-shaded gardens, and they don't have the pest problems that are common to the boxwoods. Inkberries are taking the landscape industry by storm.

WHEN TO PLANT

Plant container-grown 'Shamrock' hollies from late winter through fall. Keep the containerized shrubs watered well until they are ready to plant into the landscape.

WHERE TO PLANT

Inkberry hollies are native to swampy regions in the Northeast, where they may be known as gallberries. These shrubs will tolerate full-sun to partially shaded locations. Plant them as a substitute for boxwoods or Japanese hollies. They can be grouped together in a foundation planting or used in a mixed evergreen border. Their rich green foliage can be appreciated in a small evergreen accent planted by a gate.

ZONE
6,7,8

How to Plant

Thoroughly loosen the roots of a plant grown in a pot and shake off most of the soil mix. Prepare a wide, shallow hole 3/4 as deep and twice as wide as the rootball. Pack soil firmly around the sides of the rootball. Form an earthen saucer using the backfill soil at the perimeter of the planting hole. This will direct water to the rootball when it rains. Water the plant well before and after mulching to settle the soil. Add a 2-inch layer of shredded hardwood mulch after planting, staying clear of the crown of the plant. Water twice each week for the first month. Avoid planting when the soil is wet enough to form a mudball in your fist. When planting several hollies, rototill and plant in a slightly raised bed.

Care and Maintenance

For newly planted shrubs, use an open-ended garden hose, watering plants directly for 10 minutes with each irrigation. Do this until the shrub's roots are established, generally in 3 to 4 weeks, or when new growth is evident. This plant is one which enjoys a wet site, so be generous with water. Mulching is important since inkberry likes high-organic soil. This plant will tolerate heavy pruning, which is done in early spring or before the new growth emerges. It can be sheared in midsummer as well. Once each spring, apply a slow-release nursery fertilizer at the rate of 1 tablespoon per foot of height.

Additional Information

Heavy leaf drop and yellowing leaves is a sign that the plants need additional watering. This is a good plant to use with drip irrigation. It is not a heavy feeder, so fertilizing during the early years is not so important. Leaf spot disease is common during wet summers but should not be a serious threat to the inkberry hollies.

Additional Species, Cultivars, or Varieties

'Compacta' is a dwarf female variety similar to 'Shamrock' but with heavy fruit set. 'Viridis' has a burgundy winter color. *Ilex glabra* cultivars are 'Ivory Queen' and 'Leucocarpa,' which grows 6 to 8 feet tall and has white berries. 'Nigra' and 'Viridis' have burgundy winter leaf color.

'Crimson Pygmy' Barberry

*A*s I was finalizing the list of shrubs to be included in this book, I casually skipped over 'Crimson Pygmy' barberry because of its spiny twigs and winter appearance. (Another consideration was that this plant did not show up in my "favorite plant" survey of Master Gardeners.) Then I gave my friend John Edwards, the store manager of Avalon Gardens in Winston-Salem, a call for some sage advice about this shrub and its suitability for home landscaping. John's words were, "For the color you get, and the nice contrast with other landscape plants, 'Crimson Pygmy' barberry is hard to pass over." He's right—this is a fine shrub. 'Crimson Pygmy' grows to 2 feet in height and 3 feet wide. It has a dense branching habit, giving it a full, thick appearance. Barberry has signature purple-red foliage all summer long which then changes to deep amber when cooler weather arrives. Its colorful summer foliage makes it very popular during the summer season when used in masses with gold-variegated shrubs and small flower plantings. Barberry 'Rosy Glow' has pink to wine foliage and is great for a hedge or border. Barberries can provide a wonderful color contrast to the background of the overall landscape.

When to Plant

This shrub is available almost exclusively as a container-grown plant. This makes it possible to plant 'Crimson Pygmy' barberry any time that the soil is workable. In the Mountain region, plant early enough that the roots will establish before the worst winter weather.

Where to Plant

For the best growth and color intensity, plant this variety in areas where there is full sun. 'Crimson Pygmy' is adaptable to most types of soils and growing conditions, though it will not tolerate soggy soils. It can be used as a specimen in a small garden, but in most situations it should be used as a low border in groupings. It will stand out in your garden when used in front of lighter-colored foliage.

How to Plant

Loosen the yellowish-colored roots of the container-grown plants.
There is no need to be gentle; bounce the rootball around and fray
out those roots! Prepare a wide, shallow hole 3/4 as deep and twice
as wide as the rootball. Use the soil from the planting hole for backfilling provided it is not a gray, sticky clay material. It is best to
plant barberries too high than to have them sink deeply into the soil.
Firm the soil around the sides of the rootball, and water thoroughly.
Add a 2-inch mulch layer on top, staying clear of the crown of the
plant. Bareroot plants are easily transplanted into the landscape as
well. Space the barberry 3 to 5 feet apart for a naturally low border.

Care and Maintenance

Use a garden hose to water newly planted shrubs directly for 10
minutes every third day. Do this for 2 weeks, then irrigate weekly
until the shrub's roots are established, generally in 4 to 6 weeks.
(Deep watering is preferred over light frequent watering.) Pruning is
needed only to shape; barberry may be trimmed at any time. Heavy
pruning on old plantings is best done in late winter before new
growth. Fertilize barberries in early fall, every other year. Use a
slow-release nursery formulation at the rate of 1/2 cup per 10 square
feet and broadcast at the dripline of the shrub and a little beyond.

Additional Information

Under normal landscape situations, 'Crimson Pygmy' barberries
have no serious disease and insect pests. To prevent a possible insect
problem. you could spray with malathion or a high-quality horticultural oil in early June. Wet soils will predispose this shrub to root rot
disease. This shrub is terrific for commercial plantings, but it will
collect litter!

Additional Species, Cultivars, or Varieties

'Red Bird' has large leaves and is compact and colorful. 'Sheridan's
Red' is red-purple in August. 'Aurea' has vivid yellow foliage.
'Kobold' has a perfect mound form. Another cultivar is 'Bagatelle.'
The gold-leaved dwarf barberries are lovely, but they have not been
as hardy in my garden.

Dwarf Burning Bush

OTHER COMMON NAME: Winged Euonymus

Whether you call it burning bush or winged euonymus, this excellent landscape plant steals the show in the fall. As the frosty days of autumn arrive, this rather unassuming shrub ignites into a scarlet blaze, snatching all the attention from other flamboyant ornamentals. Burning bush is a deciduous shrub that has 2-inch medium-green leaves on horizontal branches. The dwarf variety 'Compacta' will grow slowly to 6 feet. The individual stems have corky projections, or wings, that add interest in the winter garden. When the leaves drop, tiny orange berries are seen clinging to the bare branches. As the shrub matures, its vase shape takes on a fuller, rounded form with a pleasing texture. Dwarf burning bush makes a wonderful screen or accent specimen in summer, and looks great when left unpruned in a natural setting.

Tar Heel gardeners love fall foliage; needless to say, burning bush makes us salivate! One Triangle area homeowner who was repeatedly asked by passersby for the name of his "red plant" posted a huge sign, Latin name included, right in front of his burning bush for the education of the community. I would have been more impressed if he had posted the correct botanical name! It was a good idea, though.

WHEN TO PLANT

Dwarf burning bushes can be planted from containers any time that the ground is not frozen and is ready for planting. This plant is easily rooted from late summer cuttings, which can be planted in the landscape in the spring. In a hedge planting, space burning bushes 2 to 3 feet apart for a dense screen.

WHERE TO PLANT

Dwarf burning bushes grow well in sun or shade in ordinary garden soil. You will not have the brilliant fall color, however, without a half-day of direct sun on this shrub. It tolerates a wide range of moisture conditions from a near-wet site to a bone-dry site once it is established. Plant burning bushes for a unsheared hedge. For a great fall display, use in mass groupings with heritage river birch and garden mums.

How to Plant

Plant dwarf burning bushes in well-drained soil at the same depth that they were grown in the nursery, or plant slightly higher in clay soils. Loosen the roots of container-grown plants so they can be spread horizontally in the planting hole. The addition of compost or organic matter is recommended for poor soils. Dig holes that are at least 1 foot larger than the rootballs. The planting hole should be no deeper than the depth of the rootball. Slightly acidic soil is acceptable for this deciduous plant, as these plants are pH adaptable. Firm the soil around the roots and pour 4 gallons of water over the rootball. Finish backfilling with the soil and apply a 2-inch layer of mulch.

Care and Maintenance

Use a garden hose or oscillating sprinkler to deep-water the plants in the first 6 to 8 weeks following planting. After that, water every 10 to 14 days. A 2-inch layer of hardwood mulch should be maintained in the beds. This shrub has few pest problems that warrant treatment. Weevils may take bites out of the leaves, but scale insects are the pests that can cause serious injury. Late winter is the best time for heavy pruning of overgrown shrubs. In early fall, apply a slow-release fertilizer such as 12-6-6 at the rate of 1/2 cup per 10 square feet; broadcast at the dripline area.

Additional Information

You will appreciate the low maintenance requirements of burning bushes. I have never watered my plantings since the first growing season, though I do keep them mulched. Keep a watchful eye out for scale insects! A fall dormant oil spraying and a June insecticide application will alleviate an infestation.

Additional Species, Cultivars, or Varieties

'Monstrosa' is a strong grower. 'Rudy Haag' is a round shrub that grows to 5 feet. 'Nordine Strain' is a compact plant. *E. americanus* is our native strawberry bush. *Euonymus japonica* 'Gold Spot' is a variegated evergreen. *E. japonica* 'Microphylla Variegata' grows to 2 feet, has tiny evergreen leaves, and is good for edging or borders.

Dwarf Nandina

*D*warf nandina is hard to beat! It is a virtually pest-free, "no-maintenance" ornamental. These are compact plants with dense foliage that can be a brilliant red if you plant a cultivar like 'Fire Power.' Dwarf nandinas maintain the look of the species nandinas with their compound pointed leaves, though they may reach only 2 to 3 feet in height and their foliage is much smaller. The groundcover variety 'San Gabriel' has thin, delicate leaves. Unlike the common old-garden nandinas that produced clusters of red berries just in time for the holidays, the dwarf nandinas are nearly fruitless—but what they lack in fruit and flowers they make up for in color. The winter color of dwarf nandinas is superior to the colors of other plants during that season of the year. A mass grouping of these small evergreen shrubs fronted by an edging of variegated liriope or pansies is a car-stopper any time during the long, dreary winter months. Dwarf nandinas are easy to grow and tolerate a wide range of soil types and climatic conditions from full sun to shade. The plants grow relatively fast when compared to dwarf conifers.

WHEN TO PLANT

Dwarf nandinas are easier to transplant than almost any woody ornamental in the garden. Plant them from containers when the soil is not frozen. Established nandinas can be moved from one location to another any time you have a shovel in your hand.

WHERE TO PLANT

The dwarf nandinas will be most showy in a bright, sunny location where drainage is adequate. They do adapt to shade and even dry sites, and can be planted near the roots of shade trees. The smallest varieties can be used for edging large shrub plantings to hide their bases. Homeowners often plant dwarf nandinas for accent at entrances where they will draw your eye. They are a substitute for winter flowers in borders.

HOW TO PLANT

Thoroughly prepare the soil by spading an area that is twice the diameter of the rootball and the same depth. Loosen the roots of

plants grown in containers. Shake off some of the soilless media
until the outer 2 inches of feeder roots are exposed. Dig the planting
hole and use the removed soil for planting the dwarf nandinas. If
the soil has a sewage odor or has an oily, gray look, then you have
probably encountered a poorly drained site. Don't plant nandinas,
or for that matter any other ornamentals, in those planting conditions without first berming up the soil, and/or installing drainage
tiles under the bed. (Any time you haul in topsoil for planting,
it should be more coarse than the original soil.) Mulch, then
water well.

CARE AND MAINTENANCE

If you are unsuccessful growing nandinas, you either have a poorly
drained site or have failed to keep the newly planted nandinas
moist until the roots establish. (I am assuming the shrubs were taken
out of the containers and planted green-side up!) The first 2 to 3
weeks after planting is critical to the shrub's survival. Fine-textured
soils like clay loams will literally suck the water out of the rootballs
of potted plants. Water deeply every third day for the first several
weeks in warm weather; don't let the shrubs wilt first. After the new
roots catch, nandinas are tough! Fertilize your plants in the fall or
spring; and water the first summer.

ADDITIONAL INFORMATION

I have seen only one case of disease on dwarf nandina. The Plant
Disease Clinic at North Carolina State University diagnosed the
problem as a virus. In a case like this, the worst plants should be
dug out and the others pruned back severely. You can be sure that if
you plant nandinas, or many other ornamentals, on the edge of the
woods, voles and rabbits will find your plants tasty.

ADDITIONAL SPECIES, CULTIVARS, OR VARIETIES

Dwarf nandinas vary to some degree in foliage color, hardiness,
form, and size. 'Harbour Dwarf' grows to 3 feet tall and wide, and is
a purplish color in the winter. 'Fire Power' grows to 18 inches and
has brilliant-red, non-twisting leaves. The groundcover 'San Gabriel'
grows to 8 inches. 'Gulf Stream' has fine, dense foliage. Common
nandinas grow to 7 feet—'Alba' has yellow fruits and 'Moyers Red'
has red fruits.

Firethorn

Firethorn, commonly called *Pyracantha*, is a handsome ever-green that is extremely practical. Maturing to a height of 6 to 15 feet, this woody ornamental shrub serves well as an impenetrable thorny hedge. In our age of rising crime and burglaries, sometimes a shrub that will discourage intruders is useful when designing a "security landscape." The narrow, dark-green leaves of this vigorous grower often hide the stiff 1- to 3-inch barbs that can make you dread a pruning job. In North Carolina, a favorite use of *Pyracantha* is as an espalier on stark, blank walls—despite the daunting task of training this determined grower. *Pyracantha* is a mainstay of the fall garden, and it is adored for its showy yellow, orange, or scarlet berries. Songbirds find this rangy ornamental a haven for nesting and feasting on the pea-sized fruit. I have even seen screech owls take up residence in the densely twigged firethorns where they have a sense of security. The attractive white flowers in spring are lightly scented and comparable in beauty to the delightful native hawthorns found in our woodlands.

WHEN TO PLANT

Because of its moderate sensitivity to cold, plant firethorn in the spring west of Raleigh. In eastern North Carolina, plant any time the ground can be prepared. The large container-grown trellised specimens bring a good price at the nursery. They are, in my opinion, the best ones to purchase if you are going to plant *Pyracantha* for an espalier.

WHERE TO PLANT

Pyracantha prefers full sun for berry production. Plant in well-drained soil or dry sites. Espaliered specimens flourish even in the heat of a south-facing brick wall. One gardening friend trained a pair of robust pyracanthas into a wonderful garden gate. For foundation plantings, use low-dense (*P. koidzumii*), a compact species that surrenders to routine shearing. Please don't butcher the other varieties!

How to Plant

Pyracantha transplants with some difficulty. Referring to a soil test, amend the soil with limestone to achieve a final pH of 6. Thoroughly loosen the roots of container-grown *Pyracantha*. For an individual plant, prepare a wide, shallow hole 3/4 as deep and 3 times as wide as the rootball. Mix 3 inches of bark soil conditioner into the backfill soil. Firm the backfill around the roots. Water to settle in the soil using 4 gallons of water from a bucket, or let water trickle from a garden hose for 30 minutes. Apply mulch to a 2-inch depth, beginning 3 inches away from the base of the plant. Avoid working in clay soils within several days of rain.

Care and Maintenance

Pyracantha is a member of the rose family, thus it is a continuous grower. When planted in close quarters it will need constant pruning—this is just another reason to use it as a hedge. When used this way, removal of wild shoots is all that is really needed. If you do want to shear it, do so liberally from early March to August. Fertilize using a slow-release product in March at a rate of 1/2 cup per 10 square feet, but only if the plant seems to need it. Lacebugs and aphids are perennial but rather benign pests. Spray with an appropriate insecticide or horticultural oil in May and again in August. Prune out twigs that are killed by fireblight disease.

Additional Information

Extension offices are constantly asked why a *Pyracantha* failed to fruit. The lack of berries is often due to improper pruning practices, overfertilization, or winter injury. It is best to prune this shrub after the flowers or berries are showing in the spring. Just prune around them, leaving what you can. And avoid hard fall pruning!

Additional Species, Cultivars, or Varieties

'Shawnee' is a hardy cultivar with bright-yellow berries. 'Mohave' is a pest-resistant hybrid bearing huge masses of orange-red fruit. Cold-hardy 'Kasan' has a low spreading habit. 'Victory' is a dwarf form sporting red berries. Low-dense *Pyracantha*, *P. koidzumii*, is a more compact species.

Forsythia

OTHER COMMON NAME: Yellow Bells

*F*ew shrubs herald the coming of spring like forsythia. By January, this hardy deciduous plant is raring to go. Bright-yellow starlike flowers erupt sporadically during warm spells. When the soil temperatures rise sufficiently in late winter, forsythias explode into bloom, and in a matter of days the leafless branches are aglow with 1-inch golden flower clusters. Many transplants from Yankee-land complain about the poor flowering of our forsythias in North Carolina. My response to them is that no one seems to count the blossoms in my garden. Any shrub that is as cold hardy and resilient as forsythia has earned a spot in the Tar Heel garden. It is fast-growing, reaching a height of 6 to 10 feet. There are many new forsythia cultivars being examined here in our state. Forsythia trials were placed around the state by Dick Bir, our Extension Horticulturist. Some of these cultivars, like 'Spring Glory' and 'Lynwood Gold,' are great for landscape borders and cut flowers. Many traditional gardens in the South feature this spring gem.

WHEN TO PLANT

Plant container-grown forsythias any time the soil can be worked. Even the smallest specimens will take off once the roots establish. Very few forsythia are grown and sold as balled-and-burlapped plants, but if this is the way you buy your shrubs, plant them from late fall to March while they are dormant.

WHERE TO PLANT

Forsythia appreciates full-sun locations with good drainage. It will tolerate dry sites if watered during the first growing season. This shrub has an erect to arching growth habit and is best planted in masses on the perimeter of your property and in borders. Don't make the mistake of using forsythia in a foundation planting, for it will need to be pruned mercilessly. Underplant this shrub with spring bulbs.

How to Plant

Forsythias are adaptable to a wide range of soil types and environments. The term "potbound" was undoubtedly coined for container-grown forsythias. These shrubs are no trouble to get established quickly, if you first unravel the roots once the pot is removed. Some root pruning is helpful. Space forsythias 6 to 8 feet apart to allow for arching stems. Dig a wide planting hole that is will accommodate the big root system, but plant no deeper than the depth of the container. Firm-in the roots with the backfill soil. Form an earthen saucer on the edge of the planting hole and water-in well. Mulch with 2 inches of hardwood or pine-straw mulch. Water every 3 days for the first 2 weeks.

Care and Maintenance

Forsythias can benefit from monthly fertilizing with a soluble fertilizer such as Peter's. Continue fertilizing thorough September. When planting in masses, consider using a pre-emergent herbicide to keep grassy weeds under control. Prune forsythias immediately after they flower, then fertilize them. I prefer to cut the entire plant back to 10 to 15 inches to force long, flowing, graceful branches to develop. Water your newly planted shrubs routinely the first season, but afterwards they can take droughts very well. Pests are only a minor concern.

Additional Information

Occasionally a forsythia will succumb to a bacterial disease known as crown gall. Golfball-sized galls may be noticed on the lower half of the shrub's branches. Prune these away by removing the affected branches, and spray the plant with a copper fungicide; then disinfect your pruning shears. When the galls occurs on the roots, the plant will die.

Additional Species, Cultivars, or Varieties

Without sufficient cold weather in winter, certain varieties fail to bloom well. From my observations at our forsythia trials in the Tanglewood Park Arboretum in Clemmons, all of the following cultivars thrived with very little care: 'Beatrix Farrand,' 'Karl Sax' (gold), 'Arnold Brilliant,' 'Spring Glory,' 'Spectabilis,' and 'Farrand Hybrid.' Some are fragrant!

Fothergillas

OTHER COMMON NAME: Dwarf Witch Alder

When azaleas are everywhere in sight during the month of April, witch alders offer a breath of fresh air. This native deciduous ornamental boasts showy 2-inch white "bottlebrush" flowers and dazzling fall colors from yellow to orange-red. What a terrific find it is when you locate a native plant nursery that offers the fothergillas. The name of the genus is credited to John Fothergill, an 18th-century physician and gardener who introduced the plant to the English. This shrub is a relative of the witch hazels and exhibits some of the same traits, particularly pest resistance, shade tolerance, and fall coloration. Dwarf witch alder is a low, mounded shrub that grows to a height of 4 feet and has a similar spread. Where the shrub gets at least a half-day of sun, the dense twigs will produce a profusion of oblong, airy blooms that are reminiscent of the fragrant, petite mimosa blooms. My first introduction to the plant was the cultivar 'Mt. Airy,' which has been a delightful addition to my perennial border. *F. major* is found in dry woods along ridges in our mountains. This plant is a good companion for rhododendrons in partial shade.

WHEN TO PLANT

Container-grown dwarf witch alders can be planted in fall, spring, or in late winter when the ground can be worked. Research in propagation of this shrub at the North Carolina Botanical Garden has not been encouraging. Propagation via cuttings and seeds has been tricky. This native must be preserved!

WHERE TO PLANT

Witch alders can grow relatively fast in moist, acidic soils. They will flourish in full sun to partial shade. Landscape designers use this shrub as specimen plantings, in small groups, and in shrub borders. Since they are deciduous, plant them in front of an evergreen background such as hollies or rhododendrons. This species is native to our Coastal Plains where it can be found growing by ponds or bogs.

HOW TO PLANT

Fothergillas require growing conditions similar to those of the azaleas: acid soils that are well drained. The addition of compost or sphagnum peat moss will improve the soil environment for these plants and keep the roots moist as well. Small container-grown plants are a little slow to take off until well established. Dig a planting hole as deep and 3 times as wide as the container. Carefully free up the roots and firm them in with the backfill soil mix. Water with a garden hose to settle the soil around the roots. Apply a 3-inch layer of pine-needle mulch after planting. Keep the soil moist throughout the first growing season. Don't keep the planting hole soggy, even though this plant sometimes survives "wet feet"!

CARE AND MAINTENANCE

This is a pest-free woody ornamental that's easy to care for. Find the right location and give it time to develop into the beauty it is destined to become. Once established, it will be as hardy as the azaleas and rhododendrons that share a space with it in the garden. During extended dry periods, drag out a soaker hose for daily watering. Apply a specialty slow-release fertilizer in spring around the fothergilla plantings. Do not apply the fertilizer to the root collar area at the base of the plant, but out at the dripline and beyond. Be sure you water the day before, as you should not fertilize on dry soil for fear of injuring the shrubs.

ADDITIONAL INFORMATION

Some selective thinning of branches may be needed in the early years to train the shrubs into a pleasing open form. Most of the pruning should be delayed until after the spring blooming period. Late summer pruning is a good practice for permanently removing sucker growth or rangy shoots. Replenish the mulch layer annually to keep the soil moist.

ADDITIONAL SPECIES, CULTIVARS, OR VARIETIES

'Blue Mist' has exceptional blue-green leathery foliage. 'Mt. Airy' is named not for the mountain town in North Carolina, but for the site in Ohio where it was collected (so I am told). The plant in my garden came from the North Carolina State University Arboretum; it has medium-green leaves and 2-inch white blooms. *F. major* is the larger-growing North Carolina mountain cousin.

Gardenia

OTHER COMMON NAME: Cape Jasmine

Throughout most of North Carolina, the choice of garden plants is defined by the limitations of a hot, wet climate. The farther east you go, the more problematic is the situation. Yet there is one precious advantage of our often maligned climate—gardenias will grow here! Gardenias are one of our most valued landscape ornamentals, especially in the eastern half of the state. They bloom in profusion, emitting a sweet fragrance that brings the ambience of the Old South to our gardens. This delightful evergreen has distinctive glossy foliage that is a dark-green color. The beautiful 2- to 3-inch-wide flowers are pure white with an appearance not unlike the waxy flowers of southern magnolia. The flowering period begins in late May and continues through early summer. This is a rounded shrub that reaches 4 to 6 feet in height. Gardenias make wonderful specimen plants near walks or patios or anywhere their fragrance can be appreciated. They are not well adapted to the higher elevations of our state, but they will grow reasonably well throughout most of the Piedmont and Coastal Plain. This native of China has found a place in the hearts of Southerners for more than a century.

WHEN TO PLANT

Because of their sensitivity to winter weather, gardenias should be planted in the spring and early summer. If planted later in the year, aim for early fall so this tender evergreen will have time to establish its roots before the soil freezes.

WHERE TO PLANT

Gardenias are found growing in a wide range of soils, but they seem best adapted to a moist, loamy, well-drained soil. Plant gardenias where they are protected from cold winter winds and from early morning sun which causes sunburned foliage. Sunlight is important for flowering, but modest blooming occurs in a half-day of direct sun. This is a good specimen plant and makes a good foundation shrub in the right location.

ZONE
7,8

HOW TO PLANT

Gardenias require a well-drained soil with a pH range of 5.0 to 6.0.
The addition of organic matter like compost or pine-bark soil conditioner is an aid to growth. The organic matter should be mixed in
the planting hole along with some superphosphate fertilizer. This
can be added as bonemeal, rock phosphate, or 0-20-0 fertilizer.
Gardenias are easily planted as container-grown shrubs. When setting the plant, be sure to disturb the rootball and cut roots that are
matted together. Place the gardenia in a wide planting hole that is
no deeper than the container it was growing in. Water the rootball
very well to settle the soil around the roots, and then mulch the
newly planted evergreen.

CARE AND MAINTENANCE

Fertilize your gardenias twice each year with a complete garden
fertilizer such as 10-10-10 at a rate of 2 tablespoons per foot of
height. One application is needed in early April and the second in
mid-June. To green up the foliage, an iron-rich fertilizer can be sub-
stituted for one of the above applications. (A soil-drench of Epsom
salts in warm water will green up chlorotic evergreens.) Prune off
cold-damaged twigs in March. Gardenias need only occasional trimming. Prune selectively with hand shears to maintain the natural
shape. The best time to complete pruning is immediately after flowering in June or July.

ADDITIONAL INFORMATION

This shrub prefers moist soil and would benefit from a drip irrigation system or at least a soaker hose. For tips on winter protection,
contact Extension agents. Unfortunately, whiteflies and wax scales
may be pests on your gardenias. If left untreated, the leaves will
turn black from sooty mold fungus. Use summer oil sprays to treat.

ADDITIONAL SPECIES, CULTIVARS, OR VARIETIES

'Chuck Hayes' is a new introduction with superior cold and
heat tolerance. Fall-blooming 'August Beauty' has small leaves.
'Fortuniana' has large leaves and 4-inch blooms. 'Mystery' is a large
plant with large flowers. 'Klein's Hardy' is touted for its cold hardiness. G. radicans is a groundcover species for gardens east and south
of Raleigh.

Glossy Abelia

With the concern these days about pesticide use in the home landscape, it is encouraging to find a plant that is virtually pest resistant. One such ornamental is the glossy abelia. Most gardeners are not particularly fond of abelia because it has been outclassed by many of the newer introductions of evergreens. But when you consider the fact that this semi-evergreen shrub is a pest-resistant "no spray" shrub, the picture changes. It may be exactly what busy homeowners are looking for in landscape plants these days! My interest in glossy abelia was heightened significantly when I was introduced to the stunning new variegated forms. Joe Marion, a Forsyth County nurseryman, gave me the new compact cultivar Abelia 'Confetti' for a display garden. This cultivar has white leaf margins with tinges of pink in the new twigs. Its counterpart, 'Francis Macon,' has gold foliage. Both are fabulous specimen plants. The standard glossy abelia matures at 3 to 5 feet and is a handsome plant with glossy green foliage in summer and burgundy leaves in winter. It flowers freely, a treat for foraging honeybees.

WHEN TO PLANT

Glossy abelia can be planted any time soil conditions permit. The shrub can be rooted easily from cuttings taken in July. Plant rooted cuttings in the spring from potted plants. Protect cuttings through the first winter in a cold frame, or nestle the pots against the east side of the house, possibly tucking them up under other shrubs.

WHERE TO PLANT

This evergreen shrub makes a nice informal hedge. The newer groundcover form 'Prostrata' would dress up a sunny bank or can be used as an edging plant. When used in a mass you get a better effect with glossy abelia. My favorite is the 'Confetti' abelia. Its exciting new variegation will liven up a humdrum front entrance bed. Planters can be filled with this shrub.

How to Plant

Thoroughly loosen the roots of plants grown in pots. Shake off most of the soil mix. Prepare a wide, shallow hole 3/4 as deep and twice as wide as the rootball. Pack soil firmly around the sides of the rootball. Form an earthen saucer at the perimeter of the planting hole using the backfill soil. This will direct water to the rootball when it rains. Water the soil well while backfilling, and again after mulching to settle the soil. Add a 2-inch layer of shredded hardwood mulch after planting, staying clear of the crown of the plant. Water regularly each week for the first month. Avoid planting when the soil is wet enough to form a mudball in your fist.

Care and Maintenance

Using an open-ended garden hose, water newly planted shrubs directly for 10 minutes every 3 days. Do this until the shrub's roots are established, generally in 3 to 4 weeks, or when new growth is evident. When in doubt, check soil wetness with a hand spade or trowel. Pruning is required only to remove dead wood and to maintain the desired size. Late winter is the best time for heavy pruning of overgrown evergreens and invigorating old hedges. In early fall, apply a slow-release fertilizer such as 12-6-6 (or equal) at a rate of 1/2 cup per 10 square feet; broadcast it under the canopy of the shrub.

Additional Information

You may find some leaf spot disease on abelia, but nothing serious is expected. After a hard freeze the older leaves will drop. A little cleaning up of the fallen leaves is in order, particularly if leaf spot was noticed. The spreading forms make a decent groundcover when planted closely in masses. These can be cut back severely in winter to keep dense.

Additional Species, Cultivars, or Varieties

'Edward Goucher' has lavender-pink flowers and dark-green foliage and grows to 4 feet. 'Prostrata' is a white-flowered groundcover. 'Sherwood' has a 2- to 3-foot trailing form; it is not as popular with landscapers. 'Confetti' is green with prominent white, variegated foliage. 'Francis Macon,' a colorful accent plant, has gold foliage.

Hinoki Cypress

OTHER COMMON NAME: False Cypress

*I*f you like dwarf conifers, you will love Hinoki cypress. The diversity in this group of false cypress is truly outstanding. *Chamaecyparis* is largely made up of Japanese natives which include Hinoki cypresses and numerous varieties of the species *C. pisifera*. These evergreens perform exceptionally well in North Carolina landscapes. The striking color and form they add to a winter garden is unsurpassed. These slow-growing shrubs have soft, compressed foliage that can be a rich-green to golden color. The better cultivars have a low, spreading habit that makes them useful in borders, rock gardens, and specimen plantings. Dwarf Hinoki, 'Nana Gracilis,' has tufted, dark-green foliage and a pyramidal shape. It can be used on a corner in a foundation planting to soften the lines of the house. It can also be planted in partial shade accompanied by the large foliage of hosta and other perennials. Another exciting variety is golden-thread, or mops. The fine-textured foliage of this cypress is a bright yellow in spring and winter. Its thread-like weeping branches add a special feature to any garden. The versatile Hinoki cypress is virtually pest-free.

WHEN TO PLANT

A Hinoki cypress can be planted from a container any time during the year as soil conditions permit. These shrubs are not difficult to transplant; move established plants in the fall or in early spring.

WHERE TO PLANT

Plant in full sun to partial shade. The plants are quite adaptable for a wide range of soil types. Most prefer moist, slightly acidic soil that drains well. Hinoki cypresses are excellent as accent or specimen plants. They are generally not used in mass plantings.

HOW TO PLANT

Prepare a wide, shallow planting hole 3/4 as deep and twice as wide as the rootball. Remove the plant from the container and disturb the roots by scoring with a knife or shovel. Except in the poorest soils, amendments are not needed. Spread the roots out in the planting

hole and firm the soil around the roots. Using a garden hose, water well to settle the soil. Form an earthen saucer on the edge of the planting hole to help funnel water to the rootball during irrigation. Apply a 2-inch layer of mulch over the rootball, then water again, applying several gallons to the planting area. Water twice a week for the first month after planting.

CARE AND MAINTENANCE

Hinoki cypresses are slow to establish and should not be subject to dry soils during the first growing season. Keep in mind that the false cypresses are native to bog areas and love moisture. There is no benefit to fertilizing the first year. Apply a slow-release nursery-grade fertilizer in September each year thereafter for the health of the plants. Any pruning should be done in late spring; these plants should not need any pruning that cannot be done with a pair of hand shears. Reapply mulch as often as necessary to enrich the soil and reduce the need for watering these shrubs.

ADDITIONAL INFORMATION

Members of the genus can be quite large, but in fifteen years most of the Hinoki cypresses reach 6 to 10 feet in height. It is very important with this diverse group of dwarf conifers that properly-labeled plants be purchased. Planting location and proper spacing is dependent upon the cultivar selected.

ADDITIONAL SPECIES, CULTIVARS, OR VARIETIES

Most nurseries carry the top 6 dwarf false cypresses. Dwarf Hinoki 'Nana Gracilis' grows to 6 feet. 'Filicoides' is also called fernspray cypress. 'Crippsii' is known as golden Hinoki. 'Tetragona Aurea' is known as gold Hinoki. 'Filifera Aurea Nana' is known as dwarf gold thread. 'Boulevard' is a blue cypress. New cultivars are 'Compacta,' 'Graciosa,' and 'Ivans Column.'

Hybrid Azaleas

OTHER COMMON NAMES: Kurumes, Gumpo

*A*dmired the world over, azaleas epitomize spring in the Old North State. April in the Piedmont is an awesome sight, with landscapes that are a riot of color from the various hybrid azaleas, dogwoods, and spring-flowering bulbs. Tar Heel gardeners are hooked on the dwarf evergreen azalea varieties that mature to 2 to 6 feet in height. These members of the heath and rhododendron family are the most popular and readily available at garden shops. The kurumes are the "dime-store" variety that include the pink 'Coral Bells' and the white cultivar 'Snow.' They are very floriferous and durable in spite of the poor planting sites they are frequently destined to endure. The newer Carla hybrids, developed at North Carolina State University by my former horticulture professor Dr. Fred Cochran, are more cold tolerant than others, allowing our Mountain neighbors to get in on the azalea craze. 'Sunglow' is a pink-red variety that has been widely planted since it was introduced in the late 1970s. Another group of hybrid azaleas that is increasing in popularity with landscape designers is the gumpo or Satsukis. These plants stay compact and have a spreading habit. They are a good choice for sunny locations.

WHEN TO PLANT

The hybrid azaleas can be planted any time from March through November. Most gardeners prefer to wait until they bloom to be sure of their true colors. I prefer to plant them a couple of weeks before the flowering or to wait until October when the weather has moderated. Winter planting can be hard on azaleas due to water loss.

WHERE TO PLANT

Hybrid azaleas do best when planted in dappled shade; protect them from the afternoon summer sun. The gumpos will do fine in full sun with mulched beds. Azaleas are species of rhododendrons and have similar cultural requirements such as excellent soil drainage and moist, rich soil. Azaleas offer a wide range of forms and colors. They can be used as specimen plant accents, but they are usually planted in masses.

How to Plant

Hybrid azaleas will thrive if they are "planted high" in a bed of loose organic soil. Prepare the planting area as you would for rhodies, by mixing in 4 inches of leaf compost or bark soil conditioner. (When planting single plants, a wide, shallow hole is acceptable, but be careful you do not overwater in clay soils.) Loosen and cut the rootball by cutting from the bottom about halfway. Butterfly the rootball, and place the plant in the prepared soil. No fertilizer is needed in the planting hole. Cover the roots partially and water to settle the soil. Finish filling in around the roots with the soil mix, and water again after mulching. The azalea's roots should be positioned higher than the surrounding ground.

Care and Maintenance

The biggest challenge is watering hybrid azaleas during the early years. Irrigate new plantings 3 times the first week, twice the second, and weekly as needed thereafter. Prune azaleas immediately after they flower; and shear as needed to keep rangy shoots removed. Use a specialty azalea fertilizer in spring. Contrary to popular belief, old established beds of azaleas may need a little limestone even though they are acid-loving shrubs. Have your soil tested before liming a bed of struggling azaleas, as the problem could be disease or soil compaction. Stunted azaleas may be terminally ill due to root knot nematodes or root rot fungus.

Additional Information

When hybrid azaleas are planted in hot locations, be prepared for an attack by lacebugs. You can find the translucent 1/4-inch bugs on the undersides of the leaves with their black flyspecks. Spray to prevent injury; 2 insecticide applications are needed, in April and August. Yellow foliage may indicate a need for nitrogen, magnesium, or iron.

Additional Species, Cultivars, or Varieties

Kurumes include 'Christmas Cheer' (red), 'Coral Bells' (pink/coral), 'Hershey Red' (red double flowers), 'Hinode-giri' (vivid red), 'Pink Pearl' (salmon), 'Snow' and 'Delaware Valley' (both white), and 'Appleblossom' (light pink). Late-blooming gumpos, which grow to 2 feet high and 4 feet wide, include the Robin Hill varieties (pink and white) and Carla hybrids, which grow to 5 feet: 'Sunglow,' 'Elaine,' and 'Wolf Pack Red.'

Indian Hawthorn

Gardeners on the Coast should not be without Indian hawthorn. This shrub is an answer to the Piedmont's kurume azaleas, as it flourishes in hot locations where azaleas would wither. There are even cultivars that will survive the harsh winters in the Winston-Salem vicinity. In general, this shrub is best suited to the more temperate regions of the Tar Heel State. These evergreen shrubs have round, dark-green, leathery leaves and dense clusters of fragrant pink or white flowers. The flowering period is later than that of azaleas, so Indian hawthorn is useful for extending the season of bloom in the garden. Its slow to medium growth rate makes it a good choice for low-mainte-nance landscapes. In Coastal plantings, Indian Hawthorns tolerate drought and salt spray. This broadleaf shrub forms a compact mound with a height to 4 feet and a spread that is equal or larger. It will flour-ish in full sun or partial shade if given well-drained, fertile soil. According to my cohort, David Barkley in the Wilmington Extension Center, the hybrid hawthorn *R. x delacourii* is a hardier variety for many gardens in the state.

WHEN TO PLANT

In Coastal regions, plant container-grown Indian hawthorns any time the ground is workable. In the Piedmont and westward, plant this evergreen in the early spring after most of the serious cold weather has passed.

WHERE TO PLANT

Plant Indian hawthorn in full sun or in partial-shade landscapes. It will grow its best in fertile, fast-draining soils. It is ideal for founda-tion plantings as a specimen or grouped in masses for a dense border. Use in raised planters where they will cascade gracefully over the sides, or as a low-growing buffer by the street. The dense flower clusters are beautiful and will complement any garden.

How to Plant

This shrub prefers a slightly alkaline soil, so add limestone if needed to bring the pH to the 7.0 to 7.5 range. Dig a shallow planting hole that is 3/4 as deep and twice as wide as the rootball. Spade in the lime (and bark soil conditioner in clay soils) before planting. After removing the plant from its container, score the rootball with a sharp tool to fray out circling roots. Firm-in the roots using the backfill or soil mix, and water thoroughly. Irrigate every 3 days after planting for 2 weeks. At that time, apply a soluble fertilizer with the irrigation water. Use a fertilizer with a 1-2-1 analysis or similar to get the Indian hawthorn off to a good start. Mulch well in sandy soils.

Care and Maintenance

Be sure to irrigate during dry periods in the first growing season. This is especially important in Coastal gardens. Drip irrigation and mulching will be necessary where the hawthorns are planted in open locations at the beach. In the Piedmont, we are destined to have a harsh winter every few years that will burn the foliage of Indian hawthorns and possibly kill a few plants. Prune only lightly in the winter to remove damaged foliage. This shrub flowers from buds formed the previous fall, so delay most of the shearing until the blooming period is over. Fertilize hawthorns in midsummer using a nursery-grade fertilizer or 10-10-10.

Additional Information

When growing Indian hawthorns in full shade, the plants will get leggy and need shaping periodically. The best blooms are found on plants in hot, sunny locations. Irrigate established plantings during periods of drought. Old plantings can be rejuvenated by pruning them back to 1 foot in late winter.

Additional Species, Cultivars, or Varieties

Dwarf early-blooming 'Enchantress' offers large flower clusters. 'Ballerina' grows to 2 feet high and has dark-pink flowers. Compact, spreading 'Snow White' has white flowers that bloom into summer. 'Fascination' has starlike rose flowers with white centers. Newer cultivars are 'Gulf Green,' 'Cameo,' and 'Pinkie.' *R. umbellata* 'Springtime' is a good choice for hedges.

Japanese Holly

The 15 or so shrubs that most building contractors select for a new home site are more than likely an assortment of Japanese hollies. This holly adapts well to a wide range of environmental conditions. There are scores of Japanese holly cultivars to choose from, and new ones like the 'Soft Touch' holly, a 'Helleri' holly improvement, appear every year. Mature Japanese hollies vary in height from 2 to 10 feet. Dark-green foliage and a moderate growth rate make these evergreens a choice shrub for home landscapes. The small leaves are less than 1 inch in length and 1/2 as wide. 'Compacta' is a viable substitute for boxwoods, and in most cases people won't know the difference without a second glance. The flowers of Japanese hollies are rather uninteresting, as are the black berries that follow later. The dwarf mounding forms such as 'Helleri' and Kingsville are the most popular with gardeners. They produce symmetrical new growth in spring that is a lighter shade of green, and they generally require very little attention. The main problem with Japanese hollies can be a soil-inhabiting fungus called black root rot. A holly planted in clay soil must be planted high to avoid this problem and extend the life of the plant.

WHEN TO PLANT

Japanese hollies purchased in containers can be planted any time the ground can be prepared. Their roots need to be established several weeks before a period of drought and before the ground freezes.

WHERE TO PLANT

Japanese hollies grow successfully in moist, well-drained soil in sunny to partial-shade locations. Use an upright form like 'Convexa' as a hedge, screen, or evergreen backdrop for other landscape plantings. The low-growing varieties should be grouped together in mass plantings or used in a border as a groundcover. The dwarf forms such as Kingsville can be planted as an edging in the flowerbed.

How to Plant

Thoroughly loosen the roots of plants grown in pots. Prepare a wide, shallow hole 3/4 as deep and 3 times as wide as the rootball. Make a mix of 1/2 soil and 1/2 organic humus or soil conditioner. Pack firmly around the sides of the rootball. Water slowly, applying 4 gallons to settle the plant. Add 1 to 3 inches of mulch, staying clear of the crown of the plant. Avoid planting when soil is frozen or when soil is wet enough to form a mudball in your fist.

Care and Maintenance

Japanese holly requires very little attention if planted properly. Always water the plants in dry periods, as they appreciate moisture. In hot, dry sites, a combination of landscape fabrics and mulches can help eliminate drought stress. (I have observed good-looking hollies in full-sun situations where homeowners had used a black plastic as a mulch, though this is not advisable.) Fertilize with low rates of a slow-release product in the fall or spring. Use fertilizer sparingly since Japanese hollies are injured by overfertilizing. Buy healthy, vigorous plants that are grown in large containers.

Additional Information

Black root rot fungus can kill Japanese holly as it approaches 10 years of age. The fungus that infects this plant is especially fond of heavy clay soils. Plant your hollies high as a means of preventing fungal attack. Nematodes can play havoc with Japanese hollies in Coastal regions where the soils are light.

Additional Species, Cultivars, or Varieties

Mound-shaped 'Helleri' grows to 4 feet. 'Green Luster' grows to 4 feet and has great lustrous foliage. Drought-tolerant 'Compacta' grows 3 to 5 feet. 'Soft Touch' grows to 3 feet and has small, serrated leaves and fine foliage. Vigorous 'Convexa' grows to 4 to 5 feet. Its leaves are convex above—it is good for a formal hedge. 'Golden Heller' is a gold variegated form not readily available in North Carolina.

Japanese Pittosporum

This shrub is hardy only in the warmer regions of the state, from Raleigh eastward. It is a plant that takes many forms and has a different look depending on the cultivar. Japanese pittosporum is distinguished by its lustrous, dark-green leaves and full, rounded appearance. Where winter temperatures drop below 15 degrees Fahrenheit, the plant must be placed in a sheltered location or grown as a container plant. When in a container, this beautiful ornamental can be enjoyed indoors during the winter months. Whitespot pittosporum makes a fine houseplant as well as an attractive landscape specimen. All the pittosporum shrubs are well behaved and have dense foliage that extends to the ground. The leaves are 3 inches long with wavy leaf margins. The foliage is arranged in tightly whorled clusters at the tips of the branches. If you are fortunate enough to grow pittosporums, you will enjoy the orange-blossom fragrance that comes from their diminutive flowers. Japanese pittosporum can be used as an evergreen screen or to soften the corner of a house. This shrub can reach a height of 12 feet with an equal spread. In Coastal counties, overgrown specimens can be "limbed up" to make small multitrunk trees.

WHEN TO PLANT

Plant this shrub successfully in late winter or spring. Except in southeastern North Carolina, fall plantings of Japanese pittosporum are subject to winter injury when placed in exposed locations. Cuttings can be rooted in the summer months but should not be planted in the landscape until the following spring.

WHERE TO PLANT

Plant Japanese pittosporum in well-drained soil. Either sun or partial shade is fine for this shrub. Allow plenty of growing room and you will not have to shear this lovely plant. Its best use is as an informal screen used on the property line or in a mixed shrub border. The shrub can be used as a specimen plant where it can draw attention to a landscape feature. The dwarf and variegated forms need a shady location.

How to Plant

Japanese pittosporum requires a well-drained soil with a pH range of 5.0 to 6.0. The addition of organic matter like compost or pine-bark soil conditioner is an aid to this shrub's growth. The organic matter should be mixed in the planting hole along with some superphosphate fertilizer. This can be added as bonemeal, rock phosphate, or 0-20-0 fertilizer. This plant is easily planted as a container-grown shrub. When setting the plant, be sure to disturb the rootball, and cut roots that are matted together. Place Japanese pittosporum in a wide planting hole that is no deeper than the container it was growing in. Water the rootball well to settle the soil around the roots, and then add 2 inches of mulch.

Care and Maintenance

In sandy soils, water pittosporums weekly during the first growing season. Once they are established, they are drought resistant. For a sheared hedge, begin pruning in spring while the plants are still young. On more mature plants, you can control the height by removing the new growth before the leaves mature. Fertilize these plants in March and July, using a 5-10-10 fertilizer at the rate of $1/2$ cup per plant, or 1 ounce per foot of height on mature shrubs. In Zone 8 plantings, where cold weather may harm pittosporums, withholding fertilizer and water in early fall will increase cold hardiness.

Additional Information

Pittosporums are very popular plants for Coastal landscapes. They are durable in dry sites, are pest-free, and they tolerate salt spray. In Piedmont gardens, plant them on a south-facing exposure where they are protected from winter winds. The dwarf varieties make out-standing specimens for containers and low borders.

Additional Species, Cultivars, or Varieties

'Variegata' (whitespot pittosporum) has attractive green leaves with white leaf tips and margins; it is less hardy than the species and smaller. Cold-sensitive 'Wheeler's Dwarf' has dark-green foliage and grows to 4 feet in height. 'Nana' is a compact spreading shrub that grows to 2 feet high; it is suitable for containers or in a mass as a low border. Plant sources include mail-order and Coastal nurseries.

Japanese Privet

OTHER COMMON NAME: Wax-Leaf Privet

This favorite Southern plant is found in gardens throughout the state of North Carolina. Its evergreen foliage is a shiny dark green, and the plant is fast-growing to 9 feet or more. Japanese privet is a good choice for the landscape since it can be used as a hedge or planted in a mass for privacy. Overgrown privets can be "limbed up" to create interesting multitrunked specimens. Nurserymen apparently approve of this practice, as is evidenced by the growing numbers of Japanese privets pruned in various topiary forms. There are several undesirable species of *Ligustrum*, incuding the Chinese privet. These small-leaved deciduous shrubs have escaped cultivation and have become weeds, giving the whole family a bad reputation. This is unfortunate, for these plants are quite affordable for screening purposes where large quantities are needed. Few evergreen shrubs tolerate such a wide range of planting conditions from full sun to shade, and from dry to moist soil types. The lustrous foliage of this shrub and its bluish black clusters of berries make it a handsome choice for the garden. When in bloom, the white-to-yellow flowers are fragrant and quite showy against the large deep-green leaves.

WHEN TO PLANT

Container-grown Japanese privets can be transplanted any time during the year as long as the ground is not frozen, though fall or spring are considered best for planting. Don't plant in early winter or the leaves will burn from wind and exposure. Cuttings of this shrub root easily when taken from new growth in July.

WHERE TO PLANT

The Japanese privet will perform well in sun or shade, and even in moist soils. It is very pH adaptable. In exposed locations in the western region and foothills, it is subject to sunburn and moderate defoliation in the winter, but it rebounds in the spring like a trooper. Ligustrums are popular plants because they take pruning well and are good for formal hedges and topiaries. You can use the curly-leaf privet in foundation plantings.

HOW TO PLANT

Dig a planting hole equal in depth to and twice as wide as the rootball. Locate the rootball on solid soil, not loose backfill, to prevent planting too deeply. The backfill should, in most cases, be the soil removed from the planting hole. "What comes out . . . goes back in." An exception can be made for poor soils where the addition of soil amendments will improve drainage. Firm-in around the rootball as you backfill around the roots. (Frill out the roots if potbound.) To aid in watering, form an earthen basin after planting to channel water back to the rootball. Apply a 2-inch layer of mulch.

CARE AND MAINTENANCE

Overlapping and crowded branches should be removed at planting time. Watering is essential during the first growing season. Water weekly for the first month after planting. Later, water only when the soil is dry to the touch. It is good to water deeply when irrigating. Pruning should be done to improve the shape of the shrub and to keep the plant in bounds. Japanese privets can tolerate heavy pruning in late winter. They can be sheared following growth flushes in the summer months. To hold the plant in check, do not overfertilize. Use a slow-release fertilizer in spring to improve the color of the shrub.

ADDITIONAL INFORMATION

There are no serious diseases or insects associated with the Japanese privet, although leaf spots may occur from cold weather injury. Once established, privets are quite drought-tolerant, among the most resilient of evergreen shrubs. Keep in mind that honeybees are attracted to the sweet-smelling blooms.

ADDITIONAL SPECIES, CULTIVARS, OR VARIETIES

L. japonicum 'Variegated' or 'Silver Star' has deep-green leaves with creamy white borders. This plant is a compact cultivar to 5 feet high. *L. ovalfolium* aureo-marginatum is a popular small-leaved shrub with semi-evergreen foliage and yellow leaf margins. *L.* 'Recurvifolium' is the handsome curly-leaf privet.

Koreanspice Viburnum

Among the fine flora you will discover as you tromp through the woodlands of North Carolina are the viburnums. Their berries are important to wildlife, and they are the perfect landscape plants, thriving on virtual neglect. If I had to choose one viburnum as my favorite ornamental, it would be a non-native, the Koreanspice viburnum. It has beautiful dark-green leaves and reaches 6 feet in height with a nearly equal spread. The 3-inch rounded flower clusters of pastel pink buds open into waxy white 1/3-inch blooms that have a mouth-watering spicy scent. The hybrid 'Mohawk' offers colorful fall foliage as well. If you need a flowering border, the hybrid 'Eskimo' is a wonderful choice.

WHEN TO PLANT

Container-grown viburnums can be planted any time the soil is not frozen, though late-summer plantings will need attention to watering. If available, young balled-and-burlapped specimens will establish best. Cuttings taken in midsummer will produce rooted plants for setting out in late spring the following year.

WHERE TO PLANT

The Koreanspice viburnum prefers full sun or a spot where there's a few hours of afternoon sun. These plants are not fussy about soil types, but a moist, well-drained soil will quickly produce mature shrubs in a few short years. Plant this gem in a fragrance garden or by a patio or deck wherever the fragrance can be enjoyed. It can be planted in masses in the border or for a privacy screen. It also makes a nice specimen shrub.

HOW TO PLANT

Koreanspice viburnum is content with our slightly acid soils. Most of these shrubs are grown in containers, so it is important to loosen the roots in the rootball before planting. Make several vertical slits in the rootball with a shovel; or shake the soil from the roots, which will help the plants get established more quickly. Make a planting hole that is twice the diameter of the rootball and 3/4 its depth. Firm-

in the roots with the backfill soil and slowly pour on 4 gallons of water to settle the soil. Form an earthen saucer on the perimeter of the planting hole to aid in watering. Mulch with 2 to 3 inches of shredded hardwood mulch or similar material. Water twice a week for the first month.

CARE AND MAINTENANCE

Korean viburnums grow fairly symmetrically without much pruning. Pruning of an occasional wild shoot, however, will keep the plant in a pleasing shape. Heavy pruning should be done immediately after spring bloom, or in late winter if you want to invigorate old specimens. In shady sites, or during summer rains, leaf spot disease may occur on this shrub. Raking up fallen leaves under the plant should help in disease control. The use of a fungicide can be a solution if the problem persists. Some irrigation during the first growing season is beneficial. After the first season, this plant will exhibit amazing drought tolerance.

ADDITIONAL INFORMATION

Some references indicate that viburnums are sensitive to sulfur spray as a disease control product. Horticultural oils are a good remedy for scale insect infestations. Apply the summer oils in June or November. If the color is not as green as you like, apply iron chelated fertilizer in late spring and Epsom salts in July.

ADDITIONAL SPECIES, CULTIVARS, OR VARIETIES

'Aurora' is a disease-resistant deciduous shrub with red flower buds that turn to white. It is a rapid grower. Other species cultivars are 'Cayuga,' a compact shrub that grows to 5 feet and has clove-scented flowers, and 'Anne Russell' and 'Mohawk,' both compact Burkwood cultivars that grow to 6 feet. Hedge forms include Judd and Prague viburnums and 'Conoy,' a 2- to 3-foot shrub form.

Lacecap Hydrangea

*C*arolina gardeners know the big-leaf French hydrangeas as the large blue-flowering shrubs found in old gardens or at farmhouses. But few residents are familiar with the new selections of lacecap hydrangeas that are appearing in area nurseries. Unlike the large blue ball types, lacecaps have a flattened flower structure with rings of large petal-like flowers surrounding a rather lacy, floral center. This deciduous shrub family offers both a touch of nostalgia and a contemporary classy look to the garden. Maturing to 5 to 6 feet in height and 4 feet in width, this group offers plenty of color from pink, blue, and red to pure white. The airy blossoms are produced from midsummer until early fall. Lacecaps are moderate- to fast-growing shrubs. Their large dark-green foliage offers great texture for a background or mass planting. You can plant the variegated kinds in a shade garden that needs a touch of light. 'Lemon Wave,' a yellow-and-white cultivar, or 'Tricolor' with its green-and-white variegated foliage can add a much-needed accent to a full-shade garden spot. The beauty of the lacecaps is that they have multiple bloom flushes that occur up until frost time.

WHEN TO PLANT

Plant lacecap hydrangeas spring through summer as soil conditions permit. Only the container-grown plants are available at nurseries. Cuttings taken in the summer are rooted easily in a mixture of equal parts sand and peat moss. Protect the rooted lacecaps during the winter in an unheated building or cold frame. Plant them out in spring.

WHERE TO PLANT

Most cultivars of lacecap hydrangea prefer protection from summer sun. A partial-shade location away from afternoon sun ensures good-quality foliage. The large leaves often wilt in hot weather. To avoid this, plant hydrangeas where the soil is moist and where irrigation is available. Plant lacecaps in groups of several shrubs for a border. Use them as specimens, or plant them for cut flowers.

ZONE
7,8

How to Plant

The standard French hydrangea flower color depends on the soil pH and, ultimately, the soil aluminum available to the plant. In acid soil (pH below 5.5), the color is blue. In well-limed soil (6.5 to 7), the flowers turn pink. Flower color appears to be more stable with lacecaps. Though they prefer moist soil, they need good water drainage. Where the soil is tight clay, incorporate 1/2 bushel of leaf compost or bark mulch. Plant in a wide, shallow hole after superphosphate has been added. Once the plant is set in the hole and the soil firmed in around the ball, the top inch or so of the roots will be visible. Cover these roots with 2 inches of loose mulch and water well.

Care and Maintenance

Prune lacecaps in early spring and again, lightly, immediately following the bloom period. This ensures more flowers and keeps viable young wood actively growing. Hard cold may kill the flower buds of hydrangeas formed the previous fall. With the onset of warm weather, when the new growth is several inches long, fertilize lacecaps with a general garden fertilizer or a special nursery product. Protect lacecaps from cold in late December with a deep mulch of leaves or pine needles. Remove this deep mulch layer as new growth resumes. Irrigation will be necessary during the summer months.

Additional Information

Though moist soil is recommended, use a pine-bark soil conditioner to aerate clay soils. In poorly drained conditions, plant above grade in a berm or well-prepared bed containing copious amounts of organic matter. French hydrangea needs a protected location when planted west of Winston-Salem. A deep winter mulch will give added protection.

Additional Species, Cultivars, or Varieties

'Snowball Hydrangea' (hortensia) cultivars include 'Nikko Blue,' 'Candied' (dark pink), and 'Glory Blue.' The lacecap hydrangea Teller series has larger blooms. 'Teller White' is the "whitest" pure-white cultivar available. Mop Heads, another variation, escapes late freezes by flowering on new wood; consider 'All Summer Beauty' when planting.

Mountain Laurel

OTHER COMMON NAME: Ivy

*T*his attractive shrub may be the most underrated broadleaf evergreen plant. Mountain laurel is a large, robust shrub that can range in height from 7 to 15 feet. Magnificent specimens are found along the roadside on the Blue Ridge Parkway in western North Carolina. In May, mountain laurel features beautiful 4-inch clusters of white to pink flowers that often mask the lustrous dark-green foliage. Modern improvements in propagation techniques have made new hybrids available to commercial growers. Today, mountain laurels can be found in pure-white, deep-pink, near-red, and maroon-banded flower colors. A miniature form of mountain laurel is also grown commercially. This ornamental is often found in large groupings in the wild and is terrific when planted in masses. As a young plant, it is symmetrical and densely branched. Older plants develop character with an open branch structure and gnarled trunks and limbs. Mountain laurel is an excellent plant for naturalizing and performs well on the woodland edge. The most important reason for planting it is its outstanding display of flower clusters in the spring. Its attractive evergreen foliage is delightful throughout the year.

WHEN TO PLANT

Transplant mountain laurel any time soil conditions allow. Spring is the ideal time to plant this shrub from balled-and-burlapped plants. Transplant established shrubs, if need be, in late October. Spring plantings and fall plantings of container-grown shrubs are also successful.

WHERE TO PLANT

This evergreen shrub will grow in sun or shade, depending on how warm your summer temperatures get. A partially shaded location would be ideal. Once established, mountain laurels are more drought tolerant than rhododendrons. Well-drained soil is critical to the survival of mountain laurel. Plant as a background shrub or as a specimen shrub.

ZONE
6,7,8

How to Plant

Mountain laurels may be found as balled-and-burlapped plants or container-grown plants. If they are balled and burlapped, be sure to remove any nylon strings from the rootball. The burlap can remain around the rootball as long as the burlap is not plastic. Container-grown plants should have their roots loosened before transplanting. In heavy clay soil, prepare a raised bed for drainage. Build up around the rootball (not on top) with "native soil" amended with organic matter. In sandy soil, mix organic matter in the entire plant bed as well. Use something like pine-bark soil conditioner or garden compost. Most soils in North Carolina need additional phosphate. Water thoroughly, then water every 3 days for 3 weeks.

Care and Maintenance

Mountain laurel does not show signs of water stress like its rhododendron and azalea relatives. These plants are shallow rooted and should not be allowed to dry out—but do not overwater! Frequent shallow watering may be needed during the summer months, when rainfall is sparse, but too much watering encourages root rot. Pruning is seldom needed on mountain laurel, though light trimming (12 inches or less) can be completed after bloom time if desired. In the Piedmont in North Carolina, February 15 is the ideal time to prune. Dormant pruning stimulates dense, well-branched plants. Early spring pruning reduces flowering in May.

Additional Information

These evergreen plants are light feeders. Mountain laurels that are kept well mulched should not need fertilizing in the early years. When fertilizing, use an organic product or a specialty azalea fertilizer. Leaf spot is the most alarming problem. It is not life-threatening, but it does affect the attractiveness of the foliage. Root rot is life-threatening in clay soils.

Additional Species, Cultivars, or Varieties

'Carousel' has flowers that have purple banding on white. 'Olympic Fire' has large deep-red buds that open to pink. 'Pink Charm' has deep red-pink buds that open to a uniform pink. 'Pristine' has pure-white flowers. 'Sarah' has red buds and reddish pink flowers. 'Elf ' is a dwarf plant with light-pink buds and white flowers. 'Minuet' is a dwarf plant that has a broad maroon band inside each flower.

Oak Leaf Hydrangea

O ak leaf hydrangea is one of the finest native shrubs in the Tar Heel State. Maturing to 6 feet in height and width, this bold-textured shrub has large 8-inch leaves that resemble those of red oak. To some it appears unattractive, even scraggly, but to the landscape designer it has a distinct beauty all its own. During June and July, oak leaf hydrangea displays large showy panicles of white flowers that later fade to a soft rose color. These blooms are long-lasting and can be cut for dried arrangements. The plant's coarse leaves are loosely arranged and can give the woodland garden a lush, almost tropical appeal. This deciduous shrub has outstanding cinnamon exfoliating bark on spindly, crooked stems. As oak leaf hydrangeas mature, their wide-spreading branches form an open canopy in light shade. They can be used to create walls and space in open forests. The new cultivars like 'Snow Queen' are superior to the species when it comes to profusion of flowers and development of exceptional fall color. The oak leaf hydrangea is a well-kept secret among horticulturists. Unfortunately, it is often confused with its old-fashioned country cousin, the blue-flowering hydrangea. Every gardener with enough space would do well to plant the native ornamental oak leaf in a shade garden.

WHEN TO PLANT

Plant oak leaf hydrangea year-round as soil conditions permit. All the varieties that are grown in containers are very durable when planted even by the novice gardener.

WHERE TO PLANT

Place this shrub in partial-shade areas with moist, fertile, well-drained soil. Due to its fibrous roots which tend to sucker and spread, oak leaf hydrangea is a candidate for mass bank plantings. Give it plenty of room to grow so it can develop wide, drooping branches that sweep the ground. Plant on the edge of a wood line or use for a screen. It can be overpowering, but it may be used as a focal point in a small garden.

HOW TO PLANT

Oak leaf hydrangea is more frequently purchased as container-grown stock than as a balled-and-burlapped plant. Position the rootball in a wide, shallow hole 3/4 as deep and 3 times as wide as the rootball. If the native soil is friable, no amendments are necessary at planting time. For balled-and-burlapped plants, cut the twine from around the trunk and top of the rootball, remove any nails, and fold burlap back to the sides of the rootball. Loosen the roots in container-grown plants before planting. For heavy soils, make a mix of 2/3 soil and 1/3 pine-bark soil conditioner. Pack the backfill soil firmly around the sides of the rootball. Water with 4 gallons of water. Add 2 to 3 inches of mulch on top to keep the roots cool.

CARE AND MAINTENANCE

Water routinely after planting by irrigating 3 times the first week, twice the second week, and then once a week until the shrub's roots are established. Oak leaf hydrangea likes moist soil but not soggy sites. Keep moisture available to the developing roots, especially during the first and second growing season. After that, they tolerate dryness very well. Pruning is rarely needed unless space is limited. Prune just after blooming is finished by cutting back the spent blooms. The oak leaf hydrangea is not fussy about fertilizing. In spring and fall, scatter a slow-release product (analysis 12-6-6 or equal) at the label rate.

ADDITIONAL INFORMATION

The oak leaf hydrangea is worry-free, making it quite appealing as a choice for the North Carolina gardener. The biggest problem may be the overall size of the species variety. It is certainly suitable for planting in parks or on large-scale grounds. Consider planting the compact cultivars if your garden space is limited.

ADDITIONAL SPECIES, CULTIVARS, OR VARIETIES

There are many new cultivars. 'Snow Queen' bears large, upright, cone-like flowerheads and has the best fall color. 'Alice' is a vigorous grower, good for big landscapes. 'Allison' has upright blooms. 'Snowflake' has large double flowers that contain both sterile and fertile florets. 'Harmony' has heavy blooms up to 12 inches long.

Ornamental Pomegranate

The ornamental pomegranate is a gorgeous but underused decid-uous shrub—it is seen commonly in the Coastal region but rarely elsewhere in North Carolina. It is hardy throughout Zone 7, where it can provide a tropical accent when used as a specimen plant in the landscape. With its lustrous dark-green leaves that turn yellow in fall and exotic 2-inch double orange flowers, it is more than just a conver-sation piece. It blooms heavily by midsummer, then sporadically until the autumn season. It is unusual for ornamental pomegranate to develop fruit outside of Zone 8 or 9. The dwarf form 'Nana' is most suited to mass plantings. One reason ornamental pomegranate is not used more often is its unavailability in most commercial nurseries. Consumers in the warmer regions seem to prefer the fruiting pome-granates like the cultivar 'Wonderful.'

WHEN TO PLANT

Plant container-grown pomegranate in spring or early summer. North of Zone 8, it may not become established and survive winter if planted late in the season.

WHERE TO PLANT

Plant this beauty in full sun or on a south-facing location in the landscape. The standard size can be used as a hedge or as a back-drop for perennials, or it can stand alone as an accent shrub. By all means, plant ornamental pomegranate where you can view it often or pass by the plant while it is in bloom.

HOW TO PLANT

Prepare a planting hole that is several times larger than the con-tainer and spade in plenty of pine-bark soil conditioner. Limestone is not needed, but a small handful of super phosphate is beneficial. Frill out the roots if the plant is rootbound. Fill in around the roots, firming occasionally, and water well when finished. Ornamental pomegranate isn't fussy about soil types—sandy loam or clay loam is fine. Once established, it is quite drought tolerant.

CARE AND MAINTENANCE

This showy ornamental will bloom freely if established in a sunny spot. A spring application of general garden fertilizer or just a couple of inches of compost will get it started for the next season. Very little pruning is needed except for height control; do this while the plant is dormant and before growth begins in April. Thinning and removal of small suckers from the base is recommended. Ornamental pomegranate will grow equally as well in slightly alkaline soil conditions. This interesting shrub has virtually no pests.

ADDITIONAL INFORMATION

In Zone 7, it is a good idea to protect the young plants for the first couple of winters. An application of a wilt-proofing spray and a wind screen constructed around the plant in mid-December will help it through the coldest weather.

ADDITIONAL SPECIES, CULTIVARS, OR VARIETIES

'Chico' is a large shrub that grows to 8 feet. 'Flore Pleno' is very vigorous, growing to 10 feet or more in warmer zones. 'Nana' is a dwarf that grows to 4 feet. 'Eight Ball' was selected by Tony Avent for its hardiness and large black fruit. 'State Fair' is another one of his selections—it has silver dollar-sized fruit and flowers throughout the summer months. It grows to 5 feet.

Persian Lilac

*E*very girl or boy growing up in the mountains or foothills of North Carolina knew of a shabby lilac bush somewhere on the homeplace. The common lilacs (*S. vulgaris*) of that era were marvelously fragrant but tall and ungainly. After the spring flower flush had faded and powdery mildew set in, they were "ugly as sin"! You might say they were the kind of shrub that only a grandmother could love. Well, there is good news for lilac-lovers in the warmer regions of the state— the Persian lilacs and the Manchurian lilac 'Miss Kim' will hold up better in our gardens. Like the common lilac, the Persian variety has a fragrance which has few rivals in the world of horticulture. The flowerheads are much smaller than those of the garden variety, and the shrub itself is more compact, making it an attractive landscape shrub. The 'Miss Kim' lilac, a 3- to 5-foot-tall deciduous shrub with a similar spread, has icy-blue flowers. You will find that lilacs are versatile ornamentals. The Japanese tree lilac can be used as a small tree. Small varieties like the bonsai-like littleleaf-lilac fit well in a border.

WHEN TO PLANT

Persian lilac is grown in 5-gallon or larger-sized containers and can be planted any time the ground is workable. I prefer to plant lilacs in the early spring. I have bought some bargain plants in September, however, and planted them promptly with no regrets.

WHERE TO PLANT

As you do with roses, give your Persian lilac full sun and good air circulation. Natural air flow will help stave off mildew diseases in Tar Heel gardens. Any decent garden soil is acceptable, but lime it before planting. This plant is wonderful for the garden and patio areas where its fragrance can be enjoyed. A row of lilacs will eventually provide a modest privacy screen, but they are most at home in a border planting.

HOW TO PLANT

Thoroughly loosen the roots of plants grown in pots. Prepare a wide, shallow hole 3/4 as deep and twice as wide as the rootball. Lilacs prefer neutral soil, so the addition of limestone before plant-

ing is often necessary to reach a pH of 6.5. When planting in groups of 3, rototill the entire area to create a planting bed. This is of particular importance when planting shrubs in clay soils, where individual holes frequently turn into aquariums. Firm the soil around the rootball. Add a 2-inch layer of mulch on top, staying clear of the crown of the plant. Water well. Avoid planting when soil is wet enough to form a mudball in your fist.

CARE AND MAINTENANCE

Using a slow trickle from the garden hose, water your newly planted lilac approximately 1 minute for each inch of diameter of the rootball. Repeat 3 times the first week, twice the second week, and then once a week until the shrub's roots are established. Prune to the desired height and shape after blooming in the summer. In the spring following planting, select a slow-release nursery fertilizer and apply it at a rate of 1/2 cup per 10 square feet. Spread it under the canopy of the shrub and a little beyond. Overgrown lilacs can be pruned back severely in late winter. This will remove the flower buds for the upcoming season.

ADDITIONAL INFORMATION

As is true of common lilacs, powdery mildew may present a problem for Persian lilacs, particularly in shaded areas. When buying new plants, select disease-resistant cultivars. Suckers arising any time from the root collar area should be removed. Lilac hornets are common pests that remove the plant's bark for their nests; an insecticide spray may be warranted.

ADDITIONAL SPECIES, CULTIVARS, OR VARIETIES

Persian lilac has graceful, arching branches and matures at 4 to 8 feet. Its bluish green foliage and pale lavender flowers are its best assets. Notable cultivars are: *S. vulgaris* 'Alba' (white) and 'Sensation' bicolor; *S. prestoniae* 'J. MacFarlane' (pink); *S. patula* 'Miss Kim' (lavendar); *S. meyeri* 'Pabilin' (pale pink); and *S. reticulata* 'Ivory Silk' (white, tree form).

Pink Loropetalum

ink loropetalum is a showy evergreen shrub with burgundy leaves. There is an interesting story behind the procurement of this woody ornamental. Apparently Dr. J.C. Raulston, late Director of the North Carolina State University Arboretum, discovered pink loropetalum while browsing through a book describing rare botanical species in Asia. With the help of a noted plant collector, a small plant was placed in the Arboretum for evaluation. This plant has thrived here in North Carolina, and since 1994 it has been for sale in most reputable nurseries, where it has received much praise. In late spring, its wide-spreading branches light up with hot-pink feathery flowers. Blooms occur sporadically during the summer as growth continues. This plant is a vigorous grower and will thrive in sun or partial shade. In full sun, its small leaves will turn a dark green, but as autumn arrives, shiny plum-colored foliage appears. In my garden, this shrub is magnificent and rich-looking just in time for Christmas. The standard white-flowering loropetalum has been in use for decades as a hedge or screening plant. In early spring, this Asian cousin bears blooms resembling the spider-like flowers of witch hazel. Its roundish green leaves are small and leathery. Both types are pest-free in my garden.

WHEN TO PLANT

Loropetalums can be planted any time they are available and when attention can be given to watering. For winter plantings, allow 1 month for root growth before the soil freezes. In western North Carolina, plant this shrub in the spring when apple trees begin blooming.

WHERE TO PLANT

Your pink loropetalum thrives in moist, well-drained soil, regardless of soil type. The plum-to-burgundy foliage will show up best when it is planted in a sunny location or in front of lighter, variegated foliage. This evergreen can be planted as a standard in the garden or used in small groups for an accent. I have not seen a mature specimen, but I would guess it can reach a height and spread of 6 feet.

HOW TO PLANT

When planting groups of loropetalum, prepare a bed by tilling an area and incorporating organic matter into the soil. For individual plantings, dig a hole that is as deep as the rootball and twice as wide. Remove the plant from its container and disturb the rootball to hasten establishment and prevent girdling roots. Firm-in the backfill soil around the rootball, then water thoroughly. When planting in the fall, a slow-release nursery fertilizer can be mixed with the soil in the beds before planting time. Wait to fertilize spring-planted ornamentals, however, until there has been sufficient root growth—possibly 3 to 6 months after planting.

CARE AND MAINTENANCE

When loropetalum is planted in late spring, pay close attention to watering. Water new plantings every 3 days for the first 2 weeks, then water weekly until dry weather arrives. This shrub would benefit from a 2- to 3-inch mulch layer. Loropetalum, especially the species plant, may need some pruning after the second season to keep it shaped and to control height. This is especially true of the species plant. Prune in late winter or after the spring bloom period. Fortunately, the small leaves on this ornamental never make a real mess. Fertilize this shrub after Labor Day with a nursery special fertilizer (3-1-2 analysis).

ADDITIONAL INFORMATION

Pink loropetalum is a versatile new ornamental that is destined to show up in gardens all over the state. Its hardiness west of Asheville is not well documented. I would plant this shrub in a warm location in the Mountain region. I feel certain it will survive, but it will likely be deciduous, not evergreen, in these colder climates. Enjoy its lovely foliage!

ADDITIONAL SPECIES, CULTIVARS, OR VARIETIES

There are 3 cultivars of pink loropetalum being offered in the larger wholesale nurseries: 'Burgundy,' 'Plum Delight,' and 'Zhuzho Fushia.' The standard hedge plant Chinese loropetalum has white blooms in spring. It can be used as a specimen, as a screen, or espaliered.

Pinkshell Azalea

*I*n his most recent book, *Showy Native Woody Plants*, Dick Bir extols the virtues of one of our finest natives, pinkshell azalea. Woodland gardens, particularly those in the Mountain region of North Carolina, are most hospitable when this fine ornamental is included. Pinkshell azaleas occur naturally in seven Mountain counties at elevations above 3000 feet. Unlike other deciduous azaleas, this one is unscented when in bloom. What it lacks in fragrance it compensates for with the clearest pure apple-blossom-pink petals. Some pinkshell plants offer a range of color from deep pink to white. This shrub matures at a height of 5 to 7 feet with a spread slightly less than that. Pinkshell azalea thrives in the cold, and has been grown in hardiness zones colder than its native Zone 6. This Southern plant is a good one to send back home to your cousins that live north of the Mason-Dixon Line. It is nonsense to say that an azalea must be evergreen to make a statement in the garden. There are many terrific deciduous azaleas available at garden centers. As you cross the state, you will find several other native azalea species. In the Piedmont are pinxterbloom azaleas that grow to a height of 8 feet and flower early to complement our serviceberry trees. They grow naturally in shady hardwood forests from Charlotte northward. Plum-leaf azalea bears red flowers in summer. The flame azalea with its brilliant-orange flower trusses is probably the biggest carstopper.

WHEN TO PLANT

Plant pinkshell azalea any time during the spring through the fall as soil conditions permit. Seedlings and small container-grown plants should be planted in the spring.

WHERE TO PLANT

Plant pinkshell azalea in the sun or shade and in well-drained, moist, acidic soil (pH should be 5.0 to 6.0). When pinkshell azalea is unavailable, Exbury azalea is a good alternative; it tolerates full sun and comes in a range in colors. Deciduous azaleas should be planted in front of evergreen borders to show them off a bit as they bloom before the foliage appears. Plant pinkshell alongside early-flowering ornamentals.

How to Plant

It is generally recommended that native azaleas be planted in raised beds that have been amended with compost. Elevating the beds ensures good internal water drainage. A hole dug in poorly drained soils will only fill with water and continue to hold excess moisture, regardless of the size of the hole. Thoroughly loosen the roots of plants grown in pots. If individual plants are planted, prepare a wide but shallow planting hole that is 3 times the width of the root-ball and 2/3 the depth. When preparing raised beds, mix equal parts soil, compost, and pine-bark soil conditioner. Firm-in the rootball with the soil mix, and water well. Complete the job by adding 2 to 3 inches of mulch. Avoid fertilizing at planting time. Plant well before the soil freezes in the fall.

Care and Maintenance

Water your pinkshell azalea every 3 days for the first 2 to 3 weeks. Then water weekly as needed until established. Pruning is rarely needed. If it is, prune after flowering (some time during the spring), trimming out branches to maintain a natural appearance. The plants may also be "headed-back" to keep a desired height. Feed azaleas immediately after blooming ceases, then again 6 to 8 weeks later.

Additional Information

Powdery mildew is not a problem with pinkshell zaleas. You may need 2 sprays for lacebugs in April and August. Do not dig native azaleas from the wild unless you have the permission of the property owner—there is a law against this! It is best to buy azaleas from nurseries that propagate them from seeds or cuttings. Plants dug from the wild frequently fail to survive in the garden.

Additional Species, Cultivars, or Varieties

Pinxterbloom *R. periclymenoides* is the common Piedmont variety. A short white-flowered azalea found in the Coastal region is the swamp azalea, *R. serrulatum*, which has sticky petals and a sugary scent. The fragrant white azalea with red stamens often found in the central Piedmont is *R. arborescens*, sweet or smooth azalea, which can grow to 20 feet. This "tree azalea" blooms in summer and can continue blooming until September.

Red Twig Dogwood

OTHER COMMON NAME: Redosier Dogwood

*T*his colorfully branched shrub will create winter interest with its blood-red stalks that rise from the ground. Unlike the flowering dogwood, the red twig dogwood is a deciduous multistemmed ornamental that matures at 7 to 9 feet. Each branch from the vase-shaped shrub has a minimum of lateral twigs, giving this plant a rather linear form. The colorful branches spreading upward from the base add contrast to the garden. Red twig dogwood is excellent when planted in a sunny location in a grouping such as a bed or informal hedge. It effectively prevents soil erosion on a sloping bank since it is stoloniferous and spreads freely by underground stems. Its foliage is medium- to dark-green in spring and summer, and purple to red in the fall. Clusters of white flowers appear in late spring, followed by bluish fruit. For a real thrill, try planting the yellow twig dogwood in a border. Its showy silhouette in front of an evergreen planting is breathtaking. Dr. Michael Dirr, noted plantsman from the University of Georgia, offers some sage advice on using the yellow twig dogwood. His suggestion is to use it "with taste, for a small planting goes a long way on any residential landscape."

WHEN TO PLANT

Plant any time the soil is workable during the fall, winter, or spring. These dogwoods are generally sold in large-sized containers at nurseries. These are rather fast-growing plants, so small specimens are not a bad purchase; they do adapt more easily than the larger specimens when planted.

WHERE TO PLANT

Plant red twig dogwoods in the sun in mass groupings, or in sets of 3 for accent during the winter. They are adaptable to most soil conditions, and will do quite well in wet soils such as on a stream bank or by a water garden. Be creative as you plan for color coordination: this plant will stand out if placed with variegated foliage. Underplant these shrubs with dwarf ornamentals or groundcovers.

ZONE
6,7,8

How to Plant

Thoroughly loosen the roots of plants grown in pots. Prepare a wide planting hole as deep and twice as wide as the rootball. Cover the roots with the soil excavated from the hole and use your foot to firm the soil. Form an earthen basin at the edge of the planting hole to help collect water. Water well with a garden hose. Add a 2- to 3-inch layer of shredded hardwood mulch around the dogwood, staying a few inches away from the crown of the plant. Water routinely until the red twig dogwood is established.

Care and Maintenance

To water, use a garden hose set for a slow trickle at the base of the plant. Water about 1 minute for each inch of diameter of the root-ball. Repeat 3 times the first week, twice the second week, and then once a week until the shrub's roots are established. Remove older canes down to the ground during late winter or early spring to keep vigorous growth as the dogwood matures. In spring, apply a slow-release fertilizer (with an analysis of 12-6-6 or equivalent) at a rate of 1/2 cup per 10 square feet, broadcasting it at the dripline and a little beyond. "Limb up" this shrub if you want to create a small tree.

Additional Information

Red twig dogwood is a low-maintenance shrub. Watch for twig canker, which is not usually severe. Pruning off blighted twigs will solve this problem. Keep unwanted basal suckers removed. Find a wet location for this plant and it will grow vigorously.

Additional Species, Cultivars, or Varieties

'Cheyenne' is a good selection for blood-red stem color, and it does not grow as tall as the variety. 'Flaviramea,' the yellow-stemmed form (yellow twig dogwood), is great for flower arrangements. 'Isanti' is a compact cultivar with brilliant red stems. *C. amomum* grows to 10 feet and has purplish branches in winter.

Rhododendron

*T*he rhododendron has been called the "Crown Jewel of the Garden." Many gardeners unfairly rate other flowering shrubs by using this woody ornamental as the standard. Rhododendrons are members of the Ericaceae family which includes other fine plants such as mountain laurel, *Pieris*, and heathers. One does not have to travel to distant estate gardens to see marvelous specimens. The Tar Heel State boasts many fine collections in the Mountain regions and throughout the Piedmont. Great numbers of tourists flock to our state annually to see the lavender-pink blooms of our native *R. catawbiense* in the Smokies. Since the mid-1800s when the Ironclad hybrids were introduced from England, gardeners have diligently searched for the hardiest cultivars for gardens in the hot, humid Sunbelt. According to my friend Dr. Robert Means, President of the Piedmont Rhododendron Society, many tough hybrids have come from the parent species *R. yakushimanum*. This evergreen shrub combines handsome leathery foliage with an endless variety of flower colors. A love affair with this evergreen shrub can be a bittersweet addiction. Without proper planting and variety selection, many rhododendrons are destined for a short life.

WHEN TO PLANT

Plant container-grown rhododendrons any time of the year except during periods of intense heat and drought. This shrub is still sold from cutbacks grown in mountain nursery fields. Field-grown rhododendrons should be planted from December though April. Unless the plants are handled properly and planted promptly, planting them is a risky business.

WHERE TO PLANT

It is true that it has always been difficult to grow rhododendrons in the lower Piedmont and Coastal Plains. The secret to success in any area in North Carolina is to create a niche that is comparable to the plant's native habitat. This means planting this evergreen in partial shade where there is well-drained, moist, acidic soil. An east- or north-facing exposure in a woodland garden or foundation planting is ideal. Use as a background hedge for finer-textured ornamentals.

HOW TO PLANT

Rhododendrons do well in our native soils which are generally acidic. Do not add lime to the planting hole unless a soil test report reveals a pH below 4.5. Alkaline soils (above pH 7) can be acidified with the addition of 1 pound of sulfur per 100 square feet. Test the soil for drainage by digging a hole 1 foot deep with a post hole digger and filling the hole twice with water. Check the next day to see if it has drained out. If it has, you can safely plant in that site. Otherwise, plant in a raised bed. Thoroughly cut the rootball. Starting from the bottom, cut upward halfway with a knife or shovel. The roots can be "butterflied" and set into soil amended with 50 percent pine-bark soil conditioner or leaf compost.

CARE AND MAINTENANCE

Rhododendrons are not heavy feeders and can extract most of their nutrients from natural mulches. Always keep 2 to 3 inches of mulch over the roots of this shrub. Shredded leaves, compost, and pine needles are perfect mulching materials. Rhododendrons planted in raised beds will need constant watering from a drip irrigation system. Irrigate all new plantings of rhododendron every third day for the first 3 to 4 weeks. Water weekly or when the soil feels dry to the touch during the first 2 growing seasons. Once established, the plants are fairly drought tolerant and durable. Do not overwater—root rot is the primary killer of rhodies.

ADDITIONAL INFORMATION

Rhododendrons do not like shearing. Hard pruning in late winter will help control their height. After bloom, remove the old wilted flower trusses by twisting them off the stems (be careful not to damage the buds at the bases of the flowerheads). A sudden wilting of a branch in summer may indicate borers or stem dieback fungus. Promptly prune out this branch. A fungicide used as a soil drench will help prevent root rot.

ADDITIONAL SPECIES, CULTIVARS, OR VARIETIES

There are numerous cultivars that thrive in our gardens. Dr. Means has over 100 named varieties in his lovely landscape in Winston-Salem. My preference is for compact shrubs with lustrous foliage; all the flowers are great. Favorites include 'Anna Rose Whitney,' 'English Roseum,' 'Scintillation,' 'Chionoides,' 'Nestucca,' 'Janet Blair,' and 'Colonel Coen.'

Sasanquas

amellias have been grown by the Chinese as far back as the ninth century, but Americans didn't catch the camellia fever until the 1920s. Today, Camellia Society shows are held all over the South. Much of the excitement is caused by *C. japonica*, which is a spectacular flower when "gibbed" and displayed at a flower show. From my experience with camellias, however, I believe *C. sasanqua* is the most durable in the landscape. It is vigorous, flowering consistently without the cold devastation problems suffered by *C. japonica* in the Piedmont of North Carolina and westward. Sasanquas adorn the North Carolina State University campus, where they form massive hedges to 10 feet high in sun or shade. Though the leaves and flowers are nearly 1/2 the size of *C. japonica*, their versatility is unmatched. Raleigh residents frequently use this evergreen as an espalier on a wall, or they "limb up" an overgrown specimen to create a small tree in an overplanted foundation. Delightful single and double blossoms can be enjoyed from late October into the winter months, when sasanquas such as 'Yuletide' or 'Jean May' are chosen for the home garden.

When to Plant

Sasanquas should be planted from March through October. It is best to get the roots established during warm weather.

Where to Plant

Sasanquas are more tolerant of the sun than are japonicas. Expect some sunscald on their leaves, however, as they emerge from a winter season on a sunny windswept site. This versatile evergreen can be planted as a specimen to soften the corner of a house or planted in trios for screening. It is appropriate for hedges along the property line, or for training on a trellis. Use the dwarf cultivars when planting in close quarters.

How to Plant

Using a knife or spade, loosen the roots of a plants grown in a containers by scoring the rootball. Prepare a wide but shallow planting hole, 1/2 as deep as the rootball and 3 times as wide. Make a mix of 2/3 soil and 1/3 bark soil conditioner. Pack this backfill soil mix firmly

around the sides of the rootball. Water slowly, applying 4 gallons of water to settle the plant. A sasanqua that is larger than 3 feet should be staked with a single stake on the windward side. This is of particular importance in a windy location. Add a 2- to 3-inch layer of mulch to protect the roots from exposure. Avoid planting when soil is frozen or when soil is wet enough to form a mudball in your fist. Water weekly as needed.

CARE AND MAINTENANCE
The worst thing that can happen to a sasanqua is that it be "butchered" when it is time to prune. Don't shear it unless it is used as a formal hedge. This shrub needs plenty of head room and should be allowed to grow open and full. The best time to prune is immediately after flowering; use hand shears to take off wild shoots. Some gardeners despise the accumulation of flower petals that collect under sasanquas. William Lanier Hunt's response? "The petal-covered ground underneath these beauties is one of their charms." Water sasanquas regularly the first summer and fall. Keep an eye out for scale insects and spray any with horticultural oil.

ADDITIONAL INFORMATION
Sasanqua camellias are shallow-rooted shrubs. The dense root mass of established shrubs makes it impossible to plant perennials under them. Fertilize this camellia with a specialty camellia fertilizer in spring. Apply compost, aged manure, or cottonseed meal for fall fertilization during early September. Prune out blighted shoots!

ADDITIONAL SPECIES, CULTIVARS, OR VARIETIES
White cultivars include 'Setsuggeka' (double with prominent yellow stamens and hardy to 0 degrees Fahrenheit), 'White Dove,' 'Mine No Yuki,' and 'Dawn.' Red cultivars include 'Yuletide' (has prominent yellow stamens), 'Kanjiro,' and 'Bonanza.' Pink cultivars include 'Pink Snow,' the double shell-pink 'Jean May,' 'Hana-Jiman,' 'Daydream,' and 'Maiden Blush.' *C. sinensis* (tea camellia) is fragrant.

Southern Indian Azalea

For many North Carolina residents, the annual Azalea Festival in Wilmington affords the best opportunity to see the huge southern Indian azaleas that grow throughout the southeast region. These enormous azaleas can reach 8 feet in height and 10 or more feet in width in the deep sandy loam soils of the Coastal counties. Most of these azaleas have large 3-inch purple-to-white flowers. Very few of these massive plants can be found west of Durham. From the Piedmont westward they are tender shrubs, and they may be injured by our cold winters. In most cases, the plants survive but the flower buds are killed by the cold. I have had success in growing both the 'George Tabor' and 'Mrs. G. G. Gerbing' varieties in the Piedmont. The latter is hardy to Winston-Salem and possibly into the foothills. 'George Tabor' and 'Formosa' will bloom more reliably from Raleigh eastward. In the colder climates, the Glenn Dale azaleas are a better choice. Grow beautiful southern Indian azaleas for use as a flowering evergreen screen or border. One of its advantages is its general resistance to pests and drought.

WHEN TO PLANT

Plant the southern Indian azalea in spring throughout the Piedmont. In Coastal counties and the Lower Piedmont, fall is an acceptable time to plant.

WHERE TO PLANT

Southern Indian azaleas are quite tolerant of direct sun. As you travel west, they will need to be planted in a protected area such as the northeast side of a house. They adapt quite well to planting in a mass in the filtered shade of pine trees. Give this shrub plenty of room to grow, because it is a vigorous grower once established. Use it for a background shrub, for a border, or to flank the corner of your home.

HOW TO PLANT

Try to purchase this azalea in the largest pots available. It gets root-bound quickly in small containers. When it is time to plant, use a knife or handtool to split the rootball. Beginning from the bottom,

cut upward halfway so the rootball can be opened. Prepare a planting hole by mixing in a generous amount of organic matter such as compost or bark soil conditioner. The roots can be opened in a butterfly fashion so the plant can be set in the planting hole. Shallow placement is important when planting azaleas, since the fine roots grow on the surface of the ground. In most cases, it's best to mound the soil up 4 to 6 inches higher than grade to allow for settling. Water thoroughly.

CARE AND MAINTENANCE

All azaleas are shallow-rooted plants. It is important to keep the soil moist during the first 2 summers, but if overwatered during the first season, these members of the rhododendron family may suffer from irreversible damage from root rot diseases. If they are planted properly, they can later be watered regularly without fear of such diseases. Southern Indian azaleas can be pruned immediately after flowering as well as during the summer to remove wild twigs. Always prune out dying branches promptly, as this is a sign of twig dieback or borers. Well-mulched azaleas need very little fertilizing.

ADDITIONAL INFORMATION

Fertilize azaleas after they have finished blooming. Use a specialty slow-release fertilizer or an organic product. Overfertilizing is one of the biggest mistakes gardeners make when growing these plants. Don't fertilize when the soil is dry! Control lacebugs by spraying your azaleas in April and again in September.

ADDITIONAL SPECIES, CULTIVARS, OR VARIETIES

Tender 'Formosa' has single deep-purple flowers, each with a darker blotch. 'George L. Tabor' has 3$\frac{1}{2}$-inch single blooms, each white with a dark-pink hue. 'Mrs. G.G. Gerbing,' a mid-sized shrub that is a little more cold hardy than the others, has 3-inch single white flowers. Glen Dale hybrids include white 'Glacier' and lavender 'Martha Hitchcock.'

Sweet Pepperbush

OTHER COMMON NAME: Summersweet Clethra

*T*here are many plants that contribute to the sensuality of summer's landscape, and among the most delightful of these are the species and cultivars of the genus *Clethra*. Clethras are large shrubs to small trees with dark-green, very beautiful foliage. They have the attraction of flowering in summer when few other shrubs are in bloom. Some have exquisite bark character and all are excellent garden plants that are relatively trouble-free. Clethra offers the passerby a delicious reward in exchange for a moment of time. Perhaps the best known of the clethras is *Clethra alnifolia*, sweet pepperbush. I got my first whiff of sweet pepperbush during a lazy summer stroll near the Mordecai House in Raleigh. The intense fragrance of this old-fashioned shrub permeated the air that day in late June. "Sweet pepperbush is a well-named native deciduous shrub whose small fruits are reminiscent of the dried black peppercorns that stock peppermills," says Dr. Kim E. Tripp. This species is the most cold hardy of the clethras. It is a low- to medium-sized rounded shrub that reaches 3 to 8 feet in height. The cultivar 'Hummingbird' is my favorite with its lustrous dark-green foliage and compact form. It makes a great specimen shrub.

WHEN TO PLANT

Plant sweet pepperbush any time of the year that soil conditions permit. After the leaves fall in November, divide the shrub by removing sucker growth for transplanting into borders. Seed propagation of clethra is not recommended for homeowners. The seeds are tiny and hard to handle.

WHERE TO PLANT

Sweet pepperbush is very adaptable and thrives in shade or full sun. This is a shrub that doesn't mind "wet feet"—it will grow in wet sites. There are almost no pest or disease problems with this plant as long as there is adequate moisture. It is completely hardy throughout the Southeast, from the Coast to the Mountains. *C. alnifolia* is surprisingly salt tolerant, making it an excellent plant for Coastal gardens.

SHRUBS

How to Plant

Loosen the roots of a plant grown in a pot. Prepare a wide, shallow hole 3/4 as deep and twice as wide as the rootball. Make a mix of 1/2 soil and 1/2 compost, soil conditioner, or commercial planting mix. Commercial cow manure is an acceptable amendment for moisture-loving shrubs like these. Pack the amended soil firmly around the sides of the rootball. Add a 2- to 3-inch layer of mulch around the planting area and water well. Remember to avoid planting when the soil is beginning to freeze. Sometimes in early spring the soil is too wet for planting. If you can form a mudball in your fist, wait 5 days before trying to work the soil.

Care and Maintenance

Use a handheld open-ended hose to water newly planted shrubs directly for 10 to 15 minutes a day for the first week. Then water twice a week until the shrub's roots are established, generally for one growing season. Water deeply and less frequently during the summer months. Prune sweet pepperbush in late fall or early spring to train the shrub and encourage the next season's growth. Apply a slow-release fertilizer with an analysis of 12-6-6 (or equal) at a rate of 1/2 cup per 10 square feet. Broadcast it under the canopy of the shrub and a little beyond.

Additional Information

I have grown clethras in full sun and on the edge of our woods. They will sucker out freely if the soil is rich and moist, but in drier locations I have had no problem with the "maintenance nightmare" caused by too many suckers. In their natural setting, clethras form small groves from underground sucker shoots.

Additional Species, Cultivars, or Varieties

Prolifically flowering 'Hummingbird' is compact, reaching 3 feet. Spectacular 'Creel's Calico' displays large splashes of creamy white on its foliage. Vigorous 'Paniculata' has large flower spikes. 'Pink Spires' has soft-pink buds that lighten to pale pink as the flowers open. 'Rosea' has pink flower buds that open into pinkish-white blooms.

Yaupon Holly

When you see as many sick plants as I do around an Extension office, you pay attention when a particular landscape plant species never comes through the doors. In fact, I don't recall ever having a client bring in a yaupon holly for a postmortem. With all the excitement these days about using native plants and "xeriscaping", yaupon hollies should be selling like hotcakes. This evergreen species offers great versatility, from the 15-foot weeping yaupon trees to the ground-hugging 'Schellings Dwarf.' All of these lovely hollies have shiny, dark-green, narrow leaves that are nearly an inch long. Along the clear gray stems of the species are small, bright-red berries. Legend has it that Native Americans used the leaves to make a black tea to induce vomiting (hence "vomitoria") and thereby cleanse the body. I have learned first-hand that some rural North Carolinians in the Coastal counties also grew up drinking this local tea substitute. If I have my choice of holly for a foundation planting, it is unequivocally dwarf yaupon. Unlike the Japanese hollies they resemble, yaupons tolerate drought and salts from fertilizers or the sea and, what is even better, they don't succumb to root rot and nematodes!

WHEN TO PLANT

Yaupon hollies may be planted year-round as soil conditions permit. Yaupon trees and large field-grown balled-and-burlapped nursery stock should be planted in the winter or spring season soon after they are dug. Balled-and-burlapped plants must be conditioned for out-of-season planting. Plant potted hollies early in fall to allow root establishment.

WHERE TO PLANT

This holly is probably the most adaptable evergreen in the Tar Heel garden. Yaupons are found thriving in dry sites as well as extremely wet locations. Planting location will depend on the form and variety you choose. Trees and large native shrubs can be used as specimens, hedges, barriers, and informal screens. They can be "limbed up" to make trees or espaliered on a wall. The dwarfs are terrific foundation shrubs.

How to Plant

A yaupon holly is a strong grower and will fill its container with roots. Thoroughly loosen the roots after removing the plant from the pot. Spade up a planting hole that is twice the diameter of the root-ball and equal to its depth. Except where drainage is poor, there is no advantage to amending the soil. Where drainage is poor, plant high in berms or rototill a large bed. Work the soil in around the roots, firming them in with the native backfill. Water well with 4 gallons of water; repeat this twice a week for a month. An irrigation system will help get these plants through the first year or two when planted in Coastal sands. If you buy your container plants well before you begin your landscaping project, water the pots often.

Care and Maintenance

These evergreen shrubs are tolerant of extremes in planting sites, though they do prefer hot locations. In western North Carolina, wet clay soils and winter weather can injure fall plantings if they are put in too late. Mulch yaupons in the warmer months for the health of the plants. These shrubs are tolerant of severe pruning done from late winter until fall. Shape the large shrub forms into small trees, topiaries, or formal "green meatballs." The dwarf yaupons need nothing more than an occasional light shearing. Fertilize in spring with a complete garden fertilizer, and water during drought.

Additional Information

Yaupon hollies appear to have a greater ability to survive in our Carolina climate than do the Japanese hollies. On occasion, a male dog will spray a branch, which will eventually brown out. Prune these out as noticed. Insect and disease pests are not a problem on yaupon hollies. Waterlogged soils may kill young, poorly established plantings.

Additional Species, Cultivars, or Varieties

Dwarf yaupons are 'Nana,' 'Schellings Dwarf,' and 'Strokes.' Weeping trees are 'Pendula,' which grows to 18 feet, 'Folsom's Weeping,' and 'Grey's.' Berried shrub forms are 'Shadows Female,' 'Jewel,' and 'Yellow Fruit.' Many of the berried shrubs are attractive, free-form, upright plants that have heavy fruit production. The berries add winter interest and attract birds.

CHAPTER ELEVEN

Vines

$\mathcal{T}$HE POPULARITY OF VINES CONTINUES TO GROW AS RAPIDLY as the plants themselves. Gardeners are always looking for a quick fix when they need instant shade or want to hide an unsightly area. Vines fit the bill in both cases. There are beautiful vines, like the climbing hydrangea, that provide a burst of color in the off season when little else is in bloom. Others, like the spring-flowering clematis, are the pride of many seasoned gardeners.

Vines offer diverse visual qualities and are valued for the rich texture of their foliage. Some, like the wisterias, perfume the evening air with delightful fragrances. Others, such as moonvine, evoke intrigue and wonder as they open spontaneously. Many attract hummingbirds and provide nesting sites for songbirds.

Vines can soften the architecture of a home and cool a harsh sitting area by a patio. A vine is a must on a decorative arbor or trellis where it adds distinction and interest. Many lampposts and mailboxes serve as supports for a host of showy vines. Recently, many gardeners have gotten hooked on vines by planting the tropical mandevilla vine. Unfortunately, it is not hardy in most of North Carolina, but those who can grow it love it.

A vine has a mind of its own. One will refuse to climb a trellis in spite of much coaxing, while another will gallop up a tree trunk unaided. Every vine has a unique mechanism for clinging; many have specialty plant tissues for this physical attachment. Clematis cling by way of leafy stems that twine around posts and arbors. Climbing hydrangeas and English ivy form "roots" on their

Introduction

branches that act like tiny suction cups, giving them an advantage on a brick or stone wall. A wisteria's rampant stem growth ensures a tight hold on anything that crosses its path. Whether twining in a clockwise or counterclockwise direction, a vine has "a plan" to reach its destination and make its presence known.

Get to know a vine's requirements before planting one in the garden. Who wants more work to do? Don't be shy about pruning them—they need some handholding. They're a lot like toddlers . . . give them an inch and they will take a mile. A trellis constructed for a vine can add an important vertical element to a rather uninteresting garden design.

If the commonplace ornamental vines do not excite you, consider a tender annual vine for the landscape. Annual vines grow quickly and can add marvelous color while inviting bees and butterflies to the garden. Good choices include cypressvine, hyacinth bean, and passion flower. If you want edible plants, kiwis and muscadine grapes will be right at home on an arbor in your garden.

Whether flowering or evergreen, vines are versatile ornamental plants that have yet to come into their own in the Old North State. They can be planted in so many wonderful locations. A vine may just be the piece that your garden is yearning for.

Carolina Jessamine

*T*his native evergreen vine with its bright-yellow spring flowers is a great choice for a sunny spot in the garden. Though the flowers of Carolina jessamine are small, they appear in clusters, making a great show against the glossy foliage. The dark-green leaves are lance-shaped and arranged opposite each other on rich brown stems. As you head into eastern North Carolina, Carolina jessamine is found growing as a groundcover in woodlands where it can make its way up under-story trees. This vine matures to 20 feet and requires a trellis for support, without which it will make a 3-foot mound of twining vegetation. It behaves itself on an arbor, but it does require some training since it does not have tendrils for clinging. Carolina jessamine is not overly invasive. It has a distinct fragrance and often flowers sporadically in the fall. A real novelty is the double-flowered variety. This plant has thrived for many years in my garden after I received it from my friend Ed Steffek, a curator at Duke Gardens. I've propagated the plant a number of times and shared it with friends and relatives. Its blossoms are small and resemble those of the Lady Banks rose. Carolina jessamine has many uses in the landscape; plant it on fences, arbors, or even mailboxes.

When to Plant

Carolina jessamine can be planted any time from March through November. If planting in fall, allow time for this vine to establish in order to avoid winter injury and burned foliage. Small transplants should be set in spring or early summer.

Where to Plant

Plant Carolina jessamine in sun or shade locations. This vine prefers moist, rich soil. Plant it where you can enjoy its spring color and smell its wonderful fragrance. Carolina jessamine cascading over a wall or fence is very effective, and it makes a good screen. In large gardens, it makes a good groundcover if properly maintained. It blooms profusely over a long period.

 ZONE 6,7,8

 VINES

How to Plant

Carolina jessamine is container-grown and simple to plant. Loosen the roots of the plant, especially if it is a potbound specimen. Shake at least 1/2 the soil off the roots and prune back the longest roots. Some root pruning is not harmful and can encourage faster establishment. Dig a planting hole that is as deep as the depth of the rootball and 3 times as wide. Add a couple of tablespoons of slow-release flower fertilizer to the planting hole, or use a phosphorus-rich organic fertilizer if the former is unavailable. Firm-in the roots with the backfill soil, and water thoroughly. Put down a 2-inch layer of compost or mulch to enrich the soil. Water twice a week for the first month.

Care and Maintenance

This vine is a vigorous grower but has no tendrils for clinging. The biggest challenge will be to carefully, patiently train it to a support or wall. Eventually it will manage to hang on to its place. Carolina jessamine flowers in spring on new growth, so summer is the appropriate time to prune this workhorse. Fertilize your vine in September using a high-phosphorus fertilizer such as 15-30-15, or a specialty flower fertilizer. I see nothing wrong with using soluble fertilizers for monthly "feedings" if you desire more rapid growth.

Additional Information

Prune your vine to remove weak or dying twigs any time you notice them. As the plant matures, the lower branches will be shaded out and may die off. This is normal for vigorous vines on trellises. Overgrown specimens can be pruned severely in early March to control their size and invigorate the wood. Water deeply during dry summers. *A word of caution:* All parts of the plant are poisonous to livestock.

Additional Species, Cultivars, or Varieties

'Pride of Augusta' is the double-flowering cultivar.

Chinese Trumpetvine

*E*very year the North Carolina Association of Nurserymen (NCAN) used to work with Dr. J.C. Raulston at the North Carolina State University Arboretum to select special plants to introduce to the nursery trade. The selection process is an arduous task. Those that make the cut have outstanding landscape attributes and can be propagated successfully by our talented nurserymen. Chinese trumpetvine was the first vine ever selected for the NCAN Plant Introduction Program. It bears large, stunning, apricot-colored flowers. It is a strong grower and it is recommended that it be grown as a standard in tree form. It does not cling by aerial roots as does its weedy cousin, the American trumpetvine. Chinese trumpetvine needs a substantial support to grow on; it is excellent on a garden arbor or similar structure. When exposed to direct sunlight, this vine blooms throughout the summer. Removal of old blossoms will revitalize the vine and encourage even more flowering. This showy vine with its petunia-shaped blossoms and its large compound leaves is appealing to gardeners and to hummingbirds!

WHEN TO PLANT

Chinese trumpetvine grown in containers should be planted in early spring or fall. In the Mountain region, plant your new vine after the last hard frost in spring. Rooted cuttings can be planted in early fall in the other regions of North Carolina, but only in protected locations.

WHERE TO PLANT

Sunny locations with well-drained soil are ideal for growing Chinese trumpetvine. An arbor or west-facing wall is preferred for this warm-natured woody ornamental. On a masonry wall, the vine will need tying. Use masonry nails and clothesline wire or a similar sturdy wire. Plant this deciduous vine as a summer screen or backdrop for a perennial border. Its main use is as an accent on a pergola or trellis.

How to Plant

Chinese trumpetvines are grown in containers and quite simple to plant. Loosen the roots of the plant, especially if it is a potbound specimen. Shake at least ½ the soil off the roots and prune back the longest roots. Root-pruning vigorous plants like this vine encourages quicker establishment and development of feeder roots. Dig a planting hole that is as deep as the depth of the rootball and 3 times as wide. Add ¼ cup of slow-release flower fertilizer to the planting hole, or use 5-10-10 if the other product is not available. Firm-in the roots with the unamended backfill soil and water thoroughly. Put down a 2-inch layer of compost to enrich the soil. Water well if the soil dries.

Care and Maintenance

This vine is a vigorous grower but has no tendrils for clinging. The biggest challenge will be to carefully, patiently train it to a support or wall. Eventually it will manage to hang on to its place. Chinese trumpetvine flowers in the summer on new growth, so early spring or late winter is the appropriate time to prune this workhorse. Fertilize your vine in late March and again in June, using a high-phosphorus fertilizer such as 15-30-15 or a specialty flower fertilizer. I see nothing wrong with using a soluble fertilizer for monthly feedings if you so desire.

Additional Information

Prune your vine to remove weak or dying twigs any time you notice them. As the plant matures, the lower branches will be shaded out and may die off. This is normal for vigorous vines on trellises. Overgrown specimens can be pruned severely in early March to control their size and invigorate the wood. Water deeply during dry summers.

Additional Species, Cultivars, or Varieties

'Grandiflora' is the only cultivar of this species. It has large apricot blooms with pink centers. Three other species are *C. radicans* 'Flava,' a yellow-blooming American trumpetvine; *C. radicans* 'Minnesota Red,' which is orange-red; and salmon-colored *C.* 'Madame Galen.'

Clematis

*T*he brilliant starlike flowers of this deciduous vine are showstoppers. Select from types that have cloudbursts of small fragrant flowers or from those that have huge, "in-your-face," 6-inch-diameter blooms. Popular flower colors run the gamut from pure-white and pink to rich red, mauve, and purple. The evergreen deciduous clematis plants need support to be appreciated. Some species climb better than others, by means of leafy stems that wind around a trellis. The uncommon *C. armandii* has long, leathery leaves that make a marvelous evergreen vine for the arbor or a wall espalier. Its deep-green leaves and 2-inch white flowers in spring put on quite a show. Probably the most commonly grown clematis is jackman, known for its pinwheel-shaped flowers. Jackman clematis and 'Lord Nevill' bloom profusely from May until July; if pruned properly, they may have a second round of flowers in the fall. Another favorite found along the roadsides is sweet autumn clematis. It has naturalized throughout the state, perfuming the air with its sprays of sweet-smelling, lacy white flowers in late summer. There is a clematis for every garden.

WHEN TO PLANT

Container-grown plants are normally available from garden centers, more in the spring than in the fall. Both fall and spring plantings will work fine. Clematis can be started from seeds as well, but seeds are harder to come by. Some gardeners collect their own seeds and sow them in the summer.

WHERE TO PLANT

Clematis vines like their roots in the cool shade and their foliage in warm sunlight. They like well-drained soil that is very fertile. They will thrive in moist soil and will grow for decades in a good location. Clematis is easily trained to a wall or a fence. Many homeowners use the posts on their decks as a trellis; other possible structures include wooden lattice, arbors, chain-link fences, mailboxes, and lampposts.

How to Plant

Dig a hole 12 to 15 inches deep and wide. Amend the excavated soil with compost or aged manure before refilling. Add limestone or wood ashes to neutralize acidic soils. Knock the rootball out of the pot and thoroughly loosen the roots. Tamp the soil in around the roots, planting the clematis at the same level it was growing in the pot. Clematis likes mulch, so apply a 2-inch-thick layer of mulch in a 15-inch radius around the plant. Keep the soil moist around your clematis at all times. In tight clay soils where waterlogged conditions may occur, plant the clematis with at least 1/3 of the rootball above grade. Mulch these plantings much deeper.

Care and Maintenance

There is no need to prune clematis. Prune only to clean up the tangle of vines or to confine growth. If you do prune, do so immediately after flowering for spring-flowering types since their buds are formed the previous fall. The late-summer bloomers can be pruned in early spring. Always cut shoots back to 2 leaf buds after flowering is finished. Pruning is important to increase the profusion of flowers. Don't overfertilize clematis; add organic fertilizer or 2 inches of manure to the mulch ring in spring. Withhold fertilizer from October to February. Water your clematis in dry periods that coincide with bloom time.

Additional Information

Use bamboo stakes and "twist'ems" to get young plants trained to a trellis. On a brick or rock wall, the use of masonry nails and wire is practical. The worst disease of clematis is a stem rot fungus that occurs in wet soils. Don't replant in the same spot, but move to higher ground. These vines like periodic liming. Control aphids with horticultural spray oil.

Additional Species, Cultivars, or Varieties

There are 8 species of clematis and over 100 varieties that will grow in our state. The common cultivars include 'Henryii' (white), 'Nelly Moser' (pink with dark bars), 'Duchess of Edinburgh' (double-white), and C. × jackmanii (purple). I will never forget the pink C. montana on the stucco homes in the Cotswolds in England.

Climbing Hydrangea

Climbing hydrangea is a "rare jewel" with four-season interest. There is no better clinging vine for use on our brick walls when shade is desired. This vine is a slow grower in the early years, but once established, climbing hydrangea can grow 2 feet every year, producing glossy dark-green foliage that can eventually climb to 60 feet. As summer approaches, magnificent white flower clusters appear. These flowers are similar to the lacecap hydrangeas except for the 6- to 10-inch-diameter showy white bracts that are mildly fragrant. When in bloom, the airy floral display of climbing hydrangea can give a cooling effect to the garden. In addition to the flower clusters, the woody stems of this delightful ornamental are a bonus feature in the years to come—as fall arrives, the leaves drop and the handsome exfoliating bark becomes visible. The bark is a pleasing bronze-cinnamon color with a show that improves with age. There are few serious pests of climbing hydrangea, making it a formidable survivor of harsh environments. Climbing hydrangea is one of the few truly great vines for shade.

WHEN TO PLANT

Plant climbing hydrangea in the spring and up until the middle of June in North Carolina gardens. Large container-grown plants can be planted again later in the year, following the dry season beginning in late September.

WHERE TO PLANT

Climbing hydrangea thrives in sun or shade; flowering is more consistent, however, when the vine receives a few hours of direct sunlight daily. This beauty makes a respectable groundcover in moist locations in the cooler regions of North Carolina. It is used most frequently in rustic settings as a vine, cascading over a garden wall. An eastern or northern exposure is ideal for climbing hydrangea.

ZONE
6,7

VINES

How to Plant

Amend gravelly soils with aged compost or peat moss. Spade up
an area 3 times the diameter of the rootball. Free up the roots using
a hand cultivator or pocketknife. Carefully work the backfill soil
around the roots in the planting hole. The climbing hydrangea
should be set 2 inches above grade to allow for settling. Use some
of the soil to form an earthen saucer. This will help facilitate watering later. Water thoroughly and again every 3 days for 2 weeks if
there has not been a significant rainfall. Climbing hydrangea can
be a little slow to become established. A hot, dry site will frustrate
this vine—not to mention the impatient gardener!

Care and Maintenance

Especially when planted in a sunny location, this magnificent vine
needs attention to watering for several seasons or until it has established well. Both drought and hot planting sites predispose the plant
to spider mite infestations which will require remedial treatments.
Syringe with a forceful stream of water using the garden hose, or
apply either horticultural oil or a miticide. For general care, irrigate
your vine every 10 days, applying the equivalent of 1 inch of water
(5 to 7 gallons of water). Maintain a layer of mulch to conserve
moisture and enrich the soil. Prune immediately after bloom.

Additional Information

Construct a sturdy trellis for a free-standing climbing hydrangea.
According to some horticulturists, the vine can be invasive, though I
have not seen this. Hard-pruning in late winter will certainly keep it
in bounds. A little hand-training may be needed at first to get it
started up onto a wall. Apply slow-release fertilizer in spring or fall.

Additional Species, Cultivars, or Varieties

There are no named cultivars available. The species was formerly
named *H. petiolaris*.

Japanese Wisteria

*P*lanting wisteria can be a bittersweet experience. This deciduous vine is a rampant grower all across the Tar Heel State. Some rural folk would put wisteria and kudzu in the same category. Some landscapers even mumble a few expletives under their breath when the name comes up. But under strict management, Japanese wisteria can be a gem in the spring garden. It is best trained in tree form. It features attractive gray bark and abundant grape-like hanging panicles of lilac flowers. Since the flowers appear before the large compound leaves, the display is spectacular. When planted with spring-flowering bulbs and other showy ornamentals, the garden can be stunning. The Japanese wisteria has a longer flowering period than its Chinese counterpart *W. sinesis*. There are numerous colorful varieties ranging from white to reddish violet, including 'Rosea,' a fragrant pink cultivar. *W. frutescens* 'Alba' is a later-blooming Asian cultivar that is less susceptible to our late spring frosts. A permanent display has been designed and planted at the J.C. Raulston Arboretum at North Carolina State University for educating the public on the use of wisterias. You will fall in love with these vines if you are lucky enough to catch the wisteria arbor in bloom at Duke Gardens.

WHEN TO PLANT

Wisterias are somewhat difficult to transplant during their active growth period. To achieve success, plant them in late winter or during late summer and fall. Suckers from the roots of old established plants can be dug up in the fall and moved to a permanent location.

WHERE TO PLANT

For the best flowering effect, plant Japanese wisteria in a sunny site. The plant will grow well in filtered shade, but it will need careful supervision and pruning. Wisterias are wonderful when planted on pergolas, arbors, and gazebos. My preference is the tree form, as it requires less maintenance. I have seen some great wisterias trellised on posts and espaliered on walls or fences.

HOW TO PLANT

First construct the trellis for this fast-growing vine. A cedar post circled with a welded-wire cage is a cost-effective but durable support.

Tack the cage to one side of the post using stout, galvanized fencing staples. If you already have an arbor or fence, you're ready to plant the wisteria. Thoroughly loosen the roots of container-grown plants; don't be apprehensive about doing a little root pruning if it seems necessary. Prepare a wide planting hole by spading up an area the diameter of a bushel basket and 1 foot deep. If the soil is not well drained, plant high and mulch deeply. Wisterias are not fussy about the soil type—just provide them with light.

CARE AND MAINTENANCE

Japanese wisteria plants should be watered twice a week for the first 2 weeks, then every 10 days for a month thereafter. Irrigate the established plants during dry periods when there is active growth. These vines are very drought tolerant. Use an organic fertilizer or slow-release product to supply nutrients immediately following the bloom period in late spring. Don't overfertilize them or you will end up with rangy growth and few flowers. It is important to keep the basal suckers removed from the tree forms; do this in summer and fall to prevent regrowth. Do any severe pruning soon after the flowers fade.

ADDITIONAL INFORMATION

It never hurts to keep a pair of hand shears in your pocket when you go out into the garden during the summer and fall. You will never go wrong when you set out to do a little training or thinning of the wisteria. After the late spring growth surge has slowed, prune back the twigs to 8-inch stubs. Continue with this practice throughout the year. After the first of September, preserve the flower buds by avoiding pruning or fertilizing.

ADDITIONAL SPECIES, CULTIVARS, OR VARIETIES

W. floribunda cultivars include 'Alba' and 'Snow Showers,' both of which have dense white blooms; 'Rosea,' pink and fragrant; 'Issai,' violet; 'Violacea Plena,' double violet; and 'Macrobotrys,' which has 2- to 3-foot clusters of fragrant violet flowers. *W. sinensis* (Chinese wisteria) cultivars include 'Amethyst,' a rosy purple; 'Black Dragon,' with double purple flowers; 'Jako,' intensely fragrant; and 'Blue Sapphire.'

Moonvine

OTHER COMMON NAME: Moonflower

Almost everyone is familiar with the morning-glory vine, particularly the gorgeous variety 'Heavenly Blue.' The striking blue flowers, which open with the first rays of the sun, stay in bloom all morning and, on cloudy days, all day. A lesser known member of the family, moonvine, is just as intriguing. The major difference is that the moonvine reserves its beautiful fragrant white blooms for evening. This vine has the ability to grow 20 feet or more in one season, so it requires a trellis or fence for support. Moonvine has saucer-sized white blooms that open each night. You can plan a "Moon Party" in this plant's honor, with the unfurling of its pure-white flowers as the grand finale. In a matter of a few minutes, the huge blossoms open from twisted buds. My friends at Sedge Garden Nursery tell me that you can't set your watch by the blooms, but you can expect the nightly spectacle to occur some time between 9 p.m. and midnight. The summer foliage is a medium-green color with 6- to 8-inch heart-shaped leaves. Plant this annual vine near a patio where you can appreciate its large flowers.

WHEN TO PLANT

Plant moonvine seeds after all frost danger has passed. The seeds of this tender vine are larger than a pea, making them easy to handle by amateurs. Moonvine can be started in individual pots indoors in late winter so it will have a longer period of bloom when planted outdoors in May. A few full-service garden centers offer moonvine in containers.

WHERE TO PLANT

Plant anywhere you want a quick cover such as on a chain-link fence, on a wire trellis, cascading on a deck railing, or around mailboxes. The moonvine is especially nice placed where it can be enjoyed in the evenings. With some masonry nails and wire, it can be trained onto a brick wall. Moonvine will grow best with at least a half-day of direct sun.

How to Plant

When starting moonvine from seed indoors, you will get better germination by nicking the seed with a file or sandpaper (this is called "scarifying"). Some gardeners soak the large seeds overnight in water before planting 3 seeds per 6-inch pot. Container-grown plants establish easily when planted after the soil warms up in late spring. To plant a potted moonvine, dig a hole as deep and twice as wide as the container. If potbound, use a pencil to unravel the roots, and do disturb the rootball. Firm the soil around the root and water well. This vine does not transplant well, so it should be started where the plant is to grow for the season. Seeds can be planted directly in the garden.

Care and Maintenance

No major care is needed other than to provide support and training for this fast-growing beauty. Apply a liquid plant fertilizer to the plant every 2 weeks. Be sure you use an analysis for flowering plants, such as a 15-30-15 analysis. In very poor soils, maintain a 3-inch layer of leaf compost around the base of the vine in a 2-foot circle. Keep your newly transplanted container-grown plant well watered during the first few weeks and in very dry periods. A late autumn frost will kill the moonvine. When that occurs, cut it back to the ground and dig out the roots. Compost the debris.

Additional Information

Moonvine will be a perennial in our most southeastern zone, Zone 9 below Fort Fisher. In that region, the vine can be pruned heavily in late winter to shape and clean out sun-scorched twigs. Moonvine is a plant that comes with its own entertainment. You may see a few mosquito-catching bats nearby!

Additional Species, Cultivars, or Varieties

There are no known cultivars of moonvine. The most common variety of its morning-glory relative is *I. purpurea* 'Heavenly Blue,' which has 4-inch true sky-blue flowers. There are numerous other morning-glory cultivars in colors from white to rose, but 'Heavenly Blue' stays open longer during the day. *I. quamoclit*, cypress vine, has scarlet blooms and ferny foliage.

Porcelain Ampelopsis Vine

*M*ost homeowners who seek out a vine for a landscape accent want fast growth. Kudzu or kiwi may not be exactly what they're looking for, but porcelain ampelopsis vine may be the answer. It is a member of the grape family, so it has a vigorous growth habit. It clings by tendrils as it winds its way around a trellis. The leaves of porcelain vine are 4 to 5 inches long and look like those of bunch grapes. Though it is capable of quickly covering a trellis, it is not without ornamental value in the garden. Porcelain vine's gift to the gardener is its compact clusters of 1/3-inch berries that sparkle in the sunlight, resembling tiny lilac pearls. The berries begin as a yellowish color and gradually turn amethyst-blue in autumn before fading away. I had never seen this hardy vine, or probably not paid any attention to it, until I walked through the entrance to Sedge Garden Nursery in Kernersville and saw the stunning 'Elegans' cultivar. Its pink-and-white variegated leaves and the ease with which it is transplanted make this beautiful vine a treasure for a Carolina garden.

WHEN TO PLANT

Container-grown plants of porcelain vine can be planted out any time plants are available and the soil is not frozen. Seeds can be sown directly into the garden after they have fully ripened in the fall. If rodents do not feast on the berries, the seedlings should emerge in May. *A.* 'Elegans' should be propagated by rooted cuttings rather than seeds.

WHERE TO PLANT

Porcelain vine is perfect for a trellis or an arbor. It is a vigorous vine and can make a dense screen when supported by a sturdy fence. Since this vine is so good at attracting birds, plant it near a birdfeeding station or a window for the best view of your feathered friends. Plant it in sun for an abundance of berries.

HOW TO PLANT

Break the soil with a shovel or tiller in an area 3 feet square. Dig a planting hole that is 6 inches wider than the rootball. Loosen the rootball with a handtool and firm the soil around the roots. Plant the

rootball even with grade. Water your porcelain vine well at planting time and water deeply once a week for the first 6 weeks. Your permanent trellis should be in place at planting time, or use a bamboo stake and cotton string to provide some temporary support. Mulch with 2 to 3 inches of leaf compost or bark. Once established, this vine will tolerate dry weather with little attention.

CARE AND MAINTENANCE
Porcelain vine can grow with virtual neglect, but a little 5-10-10 fertilizer each spring is suggested. Prune as much as you like after the flowers appear in order to train the vine or to keep it shaped to your liking. Dormant pruning of twiggy growth will keep your vine in better health and better contained. As the vine gets older, you can keep it in check by root pruning in September. Root prune by pushing a spade in the ground in 4 places near the dripline of the plant. Use the directions of the compass for siting the placement of the spade (insert it on the east, north, south, and west sides). Water during prolonged dry periods.

ADDITIONAL INFORMATION
In order to optimize berry production, this vine should be planted where root growth can be restricted. The 'Elegans' porcelain vine grows more slowly than the species, making it your best choice for general maintenance. Please do not apply too much fertilizer around this ornamental, since it can grow 15 feet in one season.

ADDITIONAL SPECIES, CULTIVARS, OR VARIETIES
'Elegans,' the showiest of the genus, has flowers that are variegated white with a pinkish tinge. It is not overly aggressive. Var. *Maximowiczii* has deeply lobed leaves and a rampant growth habit. *A. aconitifolia* (monk's hood vine) has small leaves and looks delicate. *A. arborea* is considered a pest in the South, says Dr. M. A. Dirr, University of Georgia.

Trumpet Honeysuckle

OTHER COMMON NAME: Coral Honeysuckle

*L*ooking for a vine that is hardy and will also attract humming-birds? Trumpet honeysuckle is such a vine. Most Southerners are a hard sell for this ornamental since the evergreen vine Japanese honeysuckle has naturalized and taken the countryside by storm. But unlike this weedy cousin that was promulgated to abate erosion, trumpet honeysuckle behaves itself. It is a semi-evergreen vine that features trumpets, or tubular clusters of flowers, and matures to 20 to 40 feet. The flowers range in color from creamy white, yellow, gold, and orange to pink or red. Most gardeners will select the one with scarlet blooms and yellow throats. The fragrance is unmistakable. Some vines produce 1/4-inch bright-red berries in early autumn. In eastern North Carolina, this honeysuckle may be evergreen. Trumpet honeysuckle is great for the gardener who has a large area to devote to a vine. The new foliage is purplish-tinged and changes to a bluish green as it matures. This plant is desirable for its long blooming period and ease of culture. With a little age, the bark peels and is held in loose strands. These twining vines can be cut and twisted into wreaths and other decorative pieces.

WHEN TO PLANT

Trumpet honeysuckle can be planted spring through fall as soil conditions permit. Divisions and cuttings should be set in the landscape in early spring.

WHERE TO PLANT

Plant honeysuckle in sun or a slightly shaded area in a well-drained soil. This plant is a rapid grower, so think big. Honeysuckle can certainly take over an area, so keep this in mind when selecting a place to plant. It is best to plant trumpet honeysuckle on a sturdy trellis, and it can also be used as an espalier on a wall. Be sure to plant it where you can watch the hummingbirds work the scarlet flowers.

How to Plant

Loosen the roots of plants grown in containers. Prepare a wide hole that is twice as wide but just as deep as the rootball. There is no need to amend the soil if it has decent drainage. (For heaven's sake, this is a relative of the wild species that farmers are trying to eradicate! Isn't it wonderful to find a plant you can approach with combat boots?) Firm the backfill soil around the sides of the rootball with your foot. Form an earthen basin at the edge of the planting hole. Water thoroughly; then add 2 inches of mulch on top to complete the planting project. Honeysuckle naturalizes very well.

Care and Maintenance

Use an open-ended garden hose to water your new vine. Deep irrigation is needed twice a week. (Light frequent watering would be a waste of your time.) Do this until the plant's roots are established, generally in 3 to 4 weeks, or when new growth begins. Prune to train the trumpet honeysuckle for a training period during the first season or two. Prune to control the size of honeysuckle after the summer blooming period. Avoid severe winter pruning or the next year's flower buds may be removed. Select a slow-release formulation with a 1-2-2 or similar analysis, and fertilize in May if needed.

Additional Information

There are no serious insect problems. On occasion, powdery mildew may be observed where honeysuckle vines are planted in shade gardens. If you suspect a problem, contact your local garden center or County Extension Center for proper advice. Don't overfertilize or you will have too few blooms and overabundant growth.

Additional Species, Cultivars, or Varieties

Vigorous 'Dropmore Scarlet' has scarlet blooms. Late-blooming 'Magnifica' has bright-red flowers. 'Sulfurea' has clear yellow blooms that repeat until frost. 'Superba' has broad leaves and orange-scarlet flowers. *L. japonica* 'Halliana' is a very fragrant vine with white blooms that change to yellow. *L. × heckrottii* 'Pink Lemonade' is a twining vine with blooms in carmine and yellow. The newest is Park's 'Alabama Crimson,' a carefree and colorful reblooming vine.

RESOURCES

Public Gardens

Asheboro	North Carolina Zoological Park
Asheville	The North Carolina Arboretum UNC-Asheville Botanical Garden The Biltmore Estate Gardens
Boone	Daniel Boone Native Gardens Martha Franck Fragrance Garden, Blowing Rock, NC
Chapel Hill	The North Carolina Botanical Garden
Charlotte	Daniel B. Stowe Botanical Gardens Wing Haven Gardens and Bird Sanctuary University of North Carolina-Charlotte Gardens Charlotte Biblical Garden
Clemmons	Tanglewood Park, Arboretum, and Rose Garden
Clyde	Haywood Community College Campus Arboretum
Davidson	Davidson College Arboretum
Durham	Sarah P. Duke Gardens
Greensboro	The Greensboro Arboretum Bicentennial Garden
Manteo	The Elizabethan Gardens
New Bern	Tryon Palace Gardens
Pinehurst	Sandhills Community College Horticultural Gardens
Raleigh	The J.C. Raulston Arboretum at North Carolina State University NCSU Horticultural Field Laboratory Raleigh Rose Garden WRAL-TV Azalea Gardens Mordecai House and Gardens
Reidsville	Chinqua-Penn Plantation
Wilmington	New Hanover County Extension Arboretum Arlie Gardens Greenfield Park
Winnabow	Orton Plantation and Gardens
Winston-Salem	Reynolda Gardens of Wake Forest University Old Salem and Gardens Bethabara Herb Garden

Gardening Definitions

With tongue in cheek, I offer these "unofficial definitions."

Annual: any plant that dies before blooming.

Bed: where most prized flowers are located when rabbits visit.

Fertilizer: plant food applied by one or more of five methods— Too Much, Too Little, Too Late, Too Early, and Wrong Kind.

Garden: an outdoor restaurant operated by charity-minded amateurs to provide balanced meals for birds and pests and other wildlife.

Green Thumb: a condition suffered by Master Gardeners in which the skin on the thumb develops a greenish hue from handing large amounts of money to garden centers.

Mulch: organic material placed at the base of plants to provide subsidized housing for voles and slugs.

Perennial: any plant which, had it lived, would have bloomed wonderfully year after year.

Rose: the National Flower, a favorite of Japanese beetles and fungi.

Seed: highly nutritious bird food sold at outrageous prices in decorative packets in the spring.

Weed: an unwanted garden plant that will sprout again after being sprayed with lethal poisons and chopped into pieces.

RESOURCES

Bibliography

Armitage, Allan M. 1989. *Herbaceous Perennial Plants*. Varsity Press. Athens, Georgia.

Bender, Steve and Felder Rushing. 1993. *Passalong Plants*. University of North Carolina Press. Chapel Hill, North Carolina.

Bir, Richard E. 1992. *Growing and Propagating Showy Native Woody Plants*. University of North Carolina. Chapel Hill, North Carolina.

Clausen, Ruth Rogers and Nicolas H. Ekstrom. 1989. *Perennials for American Gardens*. Random House. New York.

Cox, Jeff and Marilyn. 1985. *The Perennial Garden*. Rodale Press. Emmaus, Pennsylvania.

Dirr, Michael A. 1990. *Manual of Woody Landscape Plants*. Stripes Publishing Company, Champaign, Illinois.

Floyd, John Alex. 1980. *Southern Living Gardening Trees and Shrubs*. Oxmoor House, Birmingham, Alabama.

Glenn, Walter and Lark Foster. 1996. *The Tennessee Gardener's Guide*. Cool Springs Press. Franklin, Tennessee.

Halfacre, Gordon R. And Anne R. Shawcroft. 1992. Fifth Edition. *Landscape Plants of the Southeast*. Sparks Press. Raleigh, North Carolina.

Harper, Pamela and Frederick McGourty. 1985. *Perennials*. HP Books. Los Angeles, California.

Heriteau, Jacqueline. 1992. *The American Horticultural Society Flower Finder*. Simon and Schuster. New York, New York.

Heriteau, Jacqueline with Dr. Marc Cathey. 1990. *The National Arboretum Book of Outstanding Plants*. Simon and Schuster. New York, New York.

Hunt, William L. *Southern Gardens, Southern Gardening*. Duke University Press. Durham, North Carolina.

Ladendorf, Sandra F. 1989. *Successful Southern Gardening*. University of North Carolina Press. Chapel Hill, North Carolina.

Lathrop, Norma Jean. 1981. *Herbs*. HP Books. Los Angeles, California.

Meredith Corporation. 1993. *Successful Rose Gardening*. Des Moines, Iowa.

Raulston, J. C. 1987. *Friends of the NCSU Arboretum Newsletter*. Department of Horticultural Science, North Carolina State University. Raleigh, North Carolina.

Tripp, Kim E. And J. C. Raulston. 1995. *The Year in Trees*. Timber Press. Portland, Oregon.

MAGAZINE/ TRADE ASSOCIATIONS

American Nurseryman Publishing Co. *American Nurseryman* (semimonthly publication). Chicago, Illinois.

Covington, Howard E. *Carolina Gardener*. Greensboro, North Carolina.

North Carolina Association of Nurserymen, Inc. *Plants for Enjoyable Living*. Knightdale, North Carolina.

INDEX

Abelia, Glossy 334
Abelia × grandiflora 334
Acer palmatum 96
Acer rubrum 102
Acer saccharum 108
Achillea spp. 236
A. chinensis 144
Actinidia arguta 144
A. deliciosa 144
Aesculus pavia 100
Ajuga 160
Ajuga reptans 160
Alder, Dwarf Witch 330
Allium schoenoprasum 194
Alumroot 230
Amaryllis 48
Ampelopsis brevipedunculata 390
Andromeda 302
Anemone, Japanese 246
Anemone × hybrida 246
Apple 138
Aquilegia 226
Artemisia 220
Artemisia dracunculus 198
Artemisia spp. 220
Asimina triloba 150
Aster, New England 254
Aster novae-angliae 254
Aucuba 304
Aucuba japonica 304
Azalea, Pinkshell 362
Azalea, Southern Indian 370
Azaleas, Hybrid 338
Barberry 'Crimson Pygmy' 320
Begonia semperflorens 44
Begonia, Wax Leaf 44
Berberis thunbergii 320
Bermudagrass 270
Betula nigra 'Heritage' 92
Birch, Heritage River 92
Blackberry, Thornless 156
Blanket Flower 222
Blue Oat Grass 180
Bluebeard 306
Blueberries 140
Boxwood, American 300
Buckeye, Red 100
Buddleia davidii 310
Bugleflower 160
Busy Lizzy 30
Butterfly Bush 310

Buxus sempervirens 300
Caladium 54
Caladium bicolor 54
Camellia sasanqua 368
Campsis grandiflora 380
Canna 56
Canna × generalis 56
Carya illinoensis 152
Caryopteris incana 306
Cedar, Deodar 120
Cedar, Japanese 122
Cedrus deodara 120
Centaurea montana 252
Centipede Grass 272
Cercis canadensis 84
Chamaecyparis obtusa 336
Cherry, Japanese Flowering 94
Chives 194
Chrysanthemum nipponicum 256
Chrysanthemum × morifolium 238
Cilantro 196
Cladrastis kentukea 112
Clematis 382
Clematis spp. 382
Clethra alnifolia 372
Colchicum byzantinum 50
Columbine 226
Coneflower 228
Coneflower, Purple 228
Coralbells 230
Coreopsis lanceolata 266
Coriander 196
Coriandrum sativum 196
Cornflower, Perennial 252
Cornus florida 82
Cornus sericea 364
Cortaderia selloana 188
Cosmos 24
Cosmos bipinnatus 24
Cottage Pinks 232
Crab Apple, Flowering 86
Crape Myrtle 80
Crinum 58
Crinum bulbispermum 58
Crocus, Autumn 50
Cryptomeria japonica 122
Cyclamen 234
Cyclamen 234
Cynodon dactylon 270
Cypress, False 336
Cypress, Hinoki 336

Index

Cypress, Leyland 124
Daffodil 60
Dahlia 62
Dahlia variabilis 62
Daisy, Nippon 256
Daylily, 'Stella de Oro' 264
Delosperma cooperi 166
Dianthus plumarius 232
Diospyros kaki 148
Dogwood .82
Dogwood, Red Twig 364
Dogwood, Redosier 364
Dwarf Burning Bush 322
Echinacea purpurea 228
Eremochloa ophiuroides 272
Euonymus alatus 'Compacta' 322
Euonymus, Winged 322
Fern, Christmas 224
Fescue, Blue Clump 178
Fescue, Sheep's 178
Fescue, Tall 278
Festuca .278
Festuca ovina var. *glauca* 178
Ficus carica 142
Fig 142
Firethorn 326
Forsythia 328
Forsythia × *intermedia* 328
Fothergilla gardenii 330
Fothergillas 330
Fountain Grass 182
Gaillardia × *grandiflora* 202
Gardenia 332
Gardenia jasminoides 332
Gelsemium sempervirens 378
Geranium 26
Ginkgo 90
Ginkgo biloba 90
Gladiolus 64
Gladiolus 64
Glads 64
Globe Amaranth 28
Gomphrena globosa 28
Grapes, Muscadine 146
Gumpo .338
Halesia tetraptera 78
Hamamelis virginiana 316
Hawthorn, Indian 340
Hedera helix 164
Helianthus annuus 42
Helictotrichon sempervirens 180

Hellebore 242
Helleborus 242
Hemerocallis 264
Heuchera sanguinea 230
Hippeastrum spp. 48
Holly, 'Carissa' 312
Holly, 'Nellie R. Stevens' 128
Holly, 'Shamrock' 318
Holly, American 116
Holly, Compact Inkberry 318
Holly, Japanese 342
Holly, Yaupon 374
Honeysuckle, Coral 392
Honeysuckle, Trumpet 392
Hosta 244
Hosta spp. 244
Hydrangea anomala subsp.
    petiolaris 384
Hydrangea, Climbing 384
Hydrangea, Lacecap 350
Hydrangea macrophylla 350
Hydrangea, Oak Leaf 354
Hydrangea quercifolia 354
Iceplant, Hardy 166
Ilex 'Nellie R. Stevens' 128
Ilex cornuta 'Carissa' 312
Ilex crenata 342
Ilex glabra 'Shamrock' 318
Ilex opaca 116
Ilex vomitoria 374
Impatiens 30
Impatiens wallerana 30
Imperata cylindrica 'Red Baron' . . .184
Ipomoea alba 388
Iris, Bearded 52
Iris, German 52
Iris germanica 52
Iris, Japanese 248
Iris kaempferi 248
Ivy 352
Ivy, English 164
Japanese Blood Grass 184
Jasmine, Cape 332
Jessamine, Carolina 378
Juniper, Blue Rug 162
Juniperus horizontalis 'Wiltoni' . . .162
Kalmia latifolia 352
Kentucky Bluegrass 274
Kiwi 144
Kurumes 338
Lagerstroemia indica 80

I n d e x

Lamb's-Ear 200
Laurel, Cherry 314
Laurel, Mountain 352
Lavandula angustifolia 202
Lavender 202
Lavender Cotton 170
Lemon Balm 204
Ligustrum japonicum 346
Lilac, Persian 358
Lilac, Summer 310
Lilies, Sword 64
Lilium spp. 68
Lily, Magic 66
Lily, Oriental 68
Lily, Plantain 244
Liquidambar styraciflua
   'Rotundiloba' 88
Liriope 172
Liriope muscari 172
Lonicera sempervirens 392
Loropetalum chinensis var. *rubrum* .360
Loropetalum, Pink 360
Lungwort 250
Lycoris squamigera 66
Magnolia grandiflora 132
Magnolia, Saucer 106
Magnolia, Southern 132
Magnolia × soulangiana 106
Maiden Grass 186
Maidenhair Tree 90
Malus 86
Malus pumila 138
Maple, Japanese 96
Maple, Red 102
Maple, Sugar 108
Marigold .32
Marjoram 206
Melampodium 34
Melampodium paludosum 34
Melissa officinalis 204
Mentha 208
Mint 208
Miscanthus sinensis
   'Gracillimus' 186
Miscanthus sinensis 'Zebrina' 190
Monkey Grass 172
Moonflower 388
Moonvine 388
Mountain Bluets 252
Mums, Garden 238
Nandina domestica 324

Nandina, Dwarf 324
Narcissus .60
Oak, Red 104
Oak, Willow 110
Obedience 258
Obedient Plant 258
Ocimum basilicum 216
Oregano .206
Origanum 206
Ornamental Pomegrante 356
Pachysandra 174
Pachysandra terminalis 174
Paeonia 260
Palmetto .130
Pampas Grass 188
Pansy 36
Parsley 210
Pawpaw .150
Pear, Bradford 76
Pecan 152
Pelargonium × hortorum 26
Pennisetum alopecuroides 182
Pentunia 38
Peony 260
Periwinkle 176
Persimmon, Oriental 148
Petroselinum crispum 210
Petunia × hybrida 38
Phlox, Garden 240
Phlox paniculata 240
Physostegia virginiana 258
Picea pungens 118
Pieris japonica 302
Pine, Longleaf 126
Pine, White 134
Pinus palustris 126
Pinus strobus 134
Pittosporum, Japanese 344
Pittosporum tobira 344
Poa pratensis 274
Polianthes tuberosa 70
Polystichum acrostichoides 224
Porcelain Ampelopsis Vine 390
Privet, Japanese 346
Prunus laurocerasus 314
Prunus spp. 94
Pulmonaria saccharata 250
Punica granatum 356
Pyracantha coccinea 326
Pyrus calleryana 'Bradford' 76
Quercus phellos 110

Index

Quercus rubra 104
Raspberry 154
Redbud, Eastern 84
Rhaphiolepis indica 340
Rhododendron 366
Rhododendron indica 370
Rhododendron spp. 338, 366
Rhododendron vaseyi 362
Rosa 284, 286, 288, 290, 292,
    294, 296
Rose, Floribunda 286
Rose, Lenton 242
Rosemary 212
Roses, Climbing 284
Roses, Groundcover 288
Roses, Hedge 296
Roses, Miniature 292
Roses, Old Garden 294
Roses, Shrub 296
Rosmarinus officinalis 232
Rubus 156
Rubus spp. 154
Sabal palmetto 130
Sage 214
Sage, Blue 22
Sage, Mealy-cup 22
Salvia farinacea 22
Salvia officinalis 214
Santolina chamaecyparissus 170
Sasanquas 368
Sedum 'Autumn Joy' 262
Sedum spectabile 262
Silverbell, Carolina 78
Spiraea × bumalda 308
Spirea, Blue Mist 306
Spirea, Bumald 308
Spirea, Dwarf 308
Spruce, Colorado Blue 118
Spurge, Japanese 174
St. Augustinegrass 276
Stachys byzantina 200
Stenotaphrum secundatum 276

Sunflower 42
Sweet Basil 216
Sweet Gum, Fruitless 88
Sweet Pepperbush 372
Syringa × persica 358
Tagetes erecta 32
Tarragon, French 198
Teas, Hybrid 290
Thyme 218
Thymus vulgaris 218
Tickseed .266
Trumpetvine, Chinese 380
Tuberose .70
Tulip 72
Tulipa 72
Vaccinium 140
Verbena, 'Homestead Purple' . . .168
Verbena 'Homestead Purple' 168
Viburnum carlesii 348
Viburnum, Koreanspice 348
Vinca 176
Vinca minor 176
Viola × wittrockiana 36
Vitis rotundifolia 146
Wisteria floribunda 386
Wisteria, Japanese 386
Witch Hazel, Common 316
Woolly Betony 200
Wormwood 220
× Cupressocyparis leylandii 124
Yarrow, Fern-Leaf 236
Yellow Bells 328
Yellowwood 112
Zebra Grass 190
Zebra Maiden Grass 190
Zelkova, Japanese 98
Zelkova serrata 98
Zinnia angustifolia 40
Zinnia, Narrow-Leaf 40
Zinnia, Spreading 40
Zoysia 280
Zoysia japonica 280

ABOUT THE AUTHOR

Toby Bost

TOBY BOST is a Forsyth County Extension Agent living in
Winston-Salem, North Carolina. Born and raised in Piedmont,
North Carolina, the author has worked as an Extension Agent for
twenty-one years, and was awarded a Distinguished Service Award
in 1995. He is a regular guest on television and radio programs in
the Piedmont Triad area, where he serves as an advisor to the
Piedmont Triad Association of Landscape Professionals, as well
as coordinating the Master Gardener Volunteer Program in
Forsyth County.

It may be hard to imagine, but in his leisure time, Toby gardens.

GARDENING TITLES
FROM COOL SPRINGS PRESS

The What, Where, When, How & Why
of Gardening in Your State

Alabama Gardener's Guide	ISBN 1-888608-28-5
Arizona Gardener's Guide	ISBN 1-888608-42-0
California Gardener's Guide	ISBN 1-888608-43-9
Colorado Gardener's Guide	ISBN 1-888608-48-X
Florida Gardener's Guide	ISBN 1-888608-31-5
The Garden Book for Wisconsin	ISBN 1-888608-53-6
Georgia Gardener's Guide	ISBN 1-888608-08-0
Illinois Gardener's Guide	ISBN 1-888608-41-2
Indiana Gardener's Guide	ISBN 1-888608-40-4
Kentucky Gardener's Guide	ISBN 1-888608-17-X
Louisiana Gardener's Guide	ISBN 1-888608-33-1
Michigan Gardener's Guide	ISBN 1-888608-29-3
Mississippi Gardener's Guide	ISBN 1-888608-44-7
Missouri Gardener's Guide	ISBN 1-888608-50-1
New Jersey Gardener's Guide	ISBN 1-888608-47-1
New Mexico Gardener's Guide	ISBN 1-888608-55-2
New York Gardener's Guide	ISBN 1-888608-45-5
North Carolina Gardener's Guide	ISBN 1-888608-09-9
Ohio Gardener's Guide	ISBN 1-888608-39-0
Oklahoma Gardener's Guide	ISBN 1-888608-56-0
Philadelphia Gardener's Guide	ISBN 1-888608-46-3
South Carolina Gardener's Guide	ISBN 1-888608-10-2
Tennessee Gardener's Guide	ISBN 1-888608-38-2
Texas Gardener's Guide	ISBN 1-888608-30-7
Virginia Gardener's Guide	ISBN 1-888608-11-0